COLLECTIBLE MAGAZINES

IDENTIFICATION & PRICE GUIDE

COLLECTIBLE MAGAZINES

IDENTIFICATION & PRICE GUIDE

FIRST EDITION

DAVID K. HENKEL

The CONFIDENT COLLECTOR™

AVON BOOKS ◆ NEW YORK

Important Notice: All of the information, including valuations, in this book has been compiled from the most reliable sources, and every effort has been made to eliminate errors and questionable data. Nevertheless, the possibility of error always exists in a work of such scope. The publisher and the author will not be held responsible for losses which may occur in the purchase, sale, or other transaction of property because of information contained herein. Readers who feel they have discovered errors are invited to *write* the author in care of Avon Books so that the errors may be corrected in subsequent editions.

THE CONFIDENT COLLECTOR: COLLECTIBLE MAGAZINES (1st edition) is an original publication of Avon Books. This edition has never before appeared in book form.

AVON BOOKS
A division of
The Hearst Corporation
1350 Avenue of the Americas
New York, New York 10019

Copyright © 1993 by David K. Henkel
Cover photo by Brian Edwards
The Confident Collector and its logo are trademarked properties of Avon Books.
Interior design by Robin Arzt
Published by arrangement with the author
Library of Congress Catalog Card Number: 93-13639
ISBN: 0-380-76926-3

Library of Congress Cataloging in Publication Data:
Henkel, David K.
  Collectible magazines identification and price guide / David K. Henkel.
    p. cm.
  1. American periodicals—Collectors and collecting—Handbooks,
manuals, etc. 2. American periodicals—Prices. I. Title.
PN4877.H38 1993   93-13639
051'.029'4—dc20   CIP

First Avon Books Trade Printing: August 1993

AVON TRADEMARK REG. U.S. PAT. OFF. AND IN OTHER COUNTRIES, MARCA REGISTRADA, HECHO EN U.S.A.

Printed in the U.S.A.

OPM 10 9 8 7 6 5 4 3 2 1

This book is dedicated to . . .
my father, my family, and my sister-in-law, Nancy Henkel,
who let me keep all those extra magazines in her attic and basement.

Special thanks to my brother Robert Henkel,
for convincing Nancy to allow me to store
all those extra magazines in her house;
and to Darryl Henkel, my nephew,
who has always been there
to help run things for the past twenty years.

And thanks also to Gladys Bugeler.

Acknowledgments

Back Issue, 24 Orchard Street, Ridgefield Park, New Jersey 07660 (Back Issue Magazines).

James Dee Photography, Weehawken, New Jersey, (201) 392-9494.

Dennis C. Jackson and ''The Illustrator Collector's News,'' P.O. Box 1958, Sequim, Washington 98382.

Passaic Book Center, 594–96 Main Avenue, Passaic, New Jersey 07055.

Buddy Scalera, Scarlet Street Magazine, 271 Tarrant Terrace, Teaneck, New Jersey 07666.

Don Smith, 3930 Rankin Street, Louisville, Kentucky 40214.

TV Guide Specialists, Box 20, Macomb, Illinois 61455.

Contents

Introduction

In each succeeding decade, magazine collecting has continued to grow tremendously. Areas of magazine collecting that just a few years ago were the realm of a limited group of collectors have now developed into a nationwide—worldwide—interest. Today, an entire collectors' convention will be held based on one specific theme. There is such tremendous interest in magazine collecting that quite often this theme can be based on a single magazine title, such as *Famous Monsters of Filmland*. At such a convention, collectors of horror magazines will travel from across the nation to purchase the issues needed to complete their collections. Publishers, editors, writers, photographers, horror film celebrities, and other related persons often attend conventions as special guests, lending to the overall theme atmosphere. Conventions and paper memorabilia shows are going on somewhere in the United States and abroad every week of the year on themes such as movie stars, TV personalities, magazine illustrators and illustrations, pinups, sport stars, and countless other topics. A bonus to the magazine collector and investor is that the hobby is growing not only among the collecting world but also among the general reading public, who quite often find themselves purchasing a magazine that catches their eye. Drawn by a complete spectrum of magazine covers and features that span the grotesque to the sublime, Americans find it hard not to pick up and purchase a magazine of interest, be it the most recent newsstand copy or an issue published sixty years ago. Today, readers purchase an estimated one billion magazine issues per year in the United States alone.

Using the Guide

As there have been literally tens of thousands of magazine titles and millions of different issues published within the last hundred years, it would be impossible to list and individually value them all. Furthermore, the vast majority of magazines published within the past century hold very little, if any, value. In this guide we have focused on those magazine types that are currently most in demand.

Throughout this guide, after certain values there will appear the symbol (+)—this informs the reader that this particular issue is presently in greater demand than are the other issues listed, and its listed value is soon expected to rise.

All magazines in this guide are listed according to specific collecting themes—they are then listed alphabetically by title. Each title is then listed by year and issue date or issue number. When applicable, both issue date and number are listed. Within certain magazine sections the cover subject may be listed, followed by a detailed description of that issue's contents. Occasionally, information from the Year, Issue/Number, or Description columns may be missing—this absence of information indicates material that was either *not applicable* or *not available* at press time. Prices listed in this guide represent a retail price range based on actual dealer and auction sales throughout the United States, Canada, and Europe. Prices apply to magazines in very good to mint condition.

MAGAZINE GRADES

Poor: Any magazine that has been clipped and/or has pages or cover missing. Any magazine that has been more than moderately water damaged, has its cover and/or pages written on, or in any way is marked or defaced. Issues in this condition are worthless. The only exceptions are

2

magazines that contain, in at least good condition, collectible illustrations, pinups, ads, photos, or rare articles. When these exceptions are found, they should be carefully removed from the magazine and placed in protective plastic with an acid-free cardboard backing. They can then be added to your collection or offered for sale.

Good: A good-condition magazine is a copy that has been well read and handled often, and shows the wear. Color from the cover may be fading. There may be some light water staining, minor tears, spine fraying, cover separating from spine, and chipping from its cover and pages. Pages will be showing signs of yellowing.

Fine: Magazines in fine condition will show sharp covers with no fading of color photos and no stains, marks, tears, or chipping. Cover will be firmly attached to spine. Some very light wear may exist. A subscription label may be on cover but does not affect cover subject. Pages will be white and will fit tightly within the magazine.

Mint: Mint copies are issues that are nearly flawless and are as first printed and received by newsstands. A subscription copy can be mint if it is received in a mailing envelope and does not have a subscription label attached to its cover.

On our value charts we have occasionally included a column marked *Cameo.* A cameo is an article that is less than one full page in length.

PROTECTING MAGAZINES

The best way to preserve the condition of your magazines is to place them individually in specially designed plastic magazine bags backed by acid-free cardboard inserts, and then store them collectively in acid-free boxes. Magazine bags, cardboard inserts, and boxes come in a wide variety of sizes to accommodate the many different sizes of magazines. They can be purchased through the mail, at comic book shops, and at back-issue magazine stores. Mail-order dealers selling these necessary supplies regularly advertise in comic books, magazines, and trade publications. Consider well where you will store your magazines—a basement may be too humid, and an attic quite often is too dry. If your basement is damp or if your attic is hot and dry during the summer months, do not store your magazines in these places. Humidity and excessive dryness will quickly destroy your magazines.

The Average Magazine

An average magazine is any magazine that can be found in most households and that does not fall into a specific collecting category. Such titles as *Reader's Digest, Woman's Day, Collier's, Saturday Evening Post, The New Yorker,* and countless others that do not contain collectible illustrations, photos, or stories have a minimal value. This type of magazine is purchased for casual reading and the purchaser usually pays a modest price for an issue.

The best way to price these average issues is by their age. Most issues from 1960 to the present will have a value of .25 to .50; 1940–1959, .50 to $1; and 1939 and earlier $1 to $2.

We have listed *special* values for two of the most popular "average" magazines. Both *Life Magazine* and *National Geographic Magazine* have maintained throughout the years a very strong following of dedicated collectors, causing their values to steadily rise.

COLLECTING LIFE MAGAZINE

LIFE MAGAZINE SPECIAL VALUES

YEAR	ISSUE	COVER SUBJECT	VALUE
1936	November 23	Fort Peck Dam	$25–50
	November 30	West Point	15–30
	December 7	Skiing	10–25
	December 14	Archbishop of Canterbury	10–20
	December 21	Granddaughter of Lord Beaverbrook	7–15
	December 28	Metropolitan Opera Ballet	7–15

YEAR	ISSUE	COVER SUBJECT	VALUE
1937	January 4	Franklin D. Roosevelt	$ 5–10
	January 11	Japanese Soldiers	6–12
	January 18	Henry and Edsel Ford	4–8
	January 25	English Lion	3–7
	February 1	Vassar Tennis	3–7
	February 8	Wyoming Winter	5–10
	February 15	Japan's General Senjuro Hayashi	10–20
	February 22	St. Louis Fountain Triton	3–6
	March 1	Laboratory Mice	5–10
	March 8	Sun Valley Ski Lift	5–10
	March 15	The British Coronation Throne	5–10
	March 22	Parachute Test	5–10
	March 29	Easter Singers	5–10
	April 5	Dog	4–8
	April 12	English Centenarian	4–8
	April 19	S.S. Queen Mary	5–10
	April 26	Rooster	4–8
	May 3	Jean Harlow	25–50+
	May 10	Boy with Marbles	5–10
	May 17	Dionne Quintuplets	10–20+
	May 24	Spring Lambs	5–10
	May 31	The Golden Gate Bridge	10–20
	June 7	Saddle Shoes	5–10
	June 14	Senator James Lewis	4–8
	June 21	Reno Divorcée	4–8
	June 28	The Beach	4–8
	July 5	July Corn	5–10
	July 12	Mannequin	5–10
	July 19	Harlem Street Shower	6–15
	July 26	Polo Pony	5–10
	August 8	Nun	5–10
	August 9	Watermelon Wagon	5–10
	August 16	Camper on a Boat	5–10
	August 23	Transoceanic Airplane	5–12
	August 30	Frog Hunt	5–10
	September 6	Harpo Marx	15–30
	September 13	Steel Master	5–10

YEAR	ISSUE	COVER SUBJECT	VALUE
1937	September 20	The Hands of Yehudi Menuhin	$ 4–8
	September 27	Nelson Eddy	10–20
	October 4	Legionnaire's Living Room	5–10
	October 11	USC Football Captain Chuck Williams	5–10
	October 18	Veils in Fashion	3–6
	October 25	Hunting Dog	5–10
	November 1	Alfred Lunt and Richard Whorf	3–5
	November 8	Greta Garbo	15–30+
	November 15	Lightship Engineer	5–10
	November 22	Life's Birthday Baby	7–15
	November 29	The United States Capitol	3–6
	December 6	Japanese Soldier	5–10
	December 13	Locomotive Repair	5–10
	December 20	Chorus Girl	5–10
	December 27	Comtesse d'Haussonville	5–10
1938	January 3	Swedish Skater	5–10
	January 10	Koalas	5–10
	January 17	Oil Tankers	4–8
	January 24	Alpine Skiers	5–10
	January 31	Student Nurses	5–10
	February 7	Gary Cooper	5–10
	February 14	Egypt's Queen	5–10
	February 21	Carl Sandburg	5–10
	February 28	Monte Carlo Fireworks	5–10
	March 7	High School Girls	5–10
	March 14	Jane Froman	3–7
	March 21	Marriage Clinic Couple	3–6
	March 28	German Bugler	5–10
	April 4	Anthony Eden	3–6
	April 11	Fashion	3–5
	April 18	Paulette Goddard	10–20
	April 25	Tom Winsett/Brooklyn Dodger	5–10
	May 2	John N. Garner	3–6
	May 9	Fashions of Summer	3–6
	May 16	Chinese Soldier	5–10
	May 23	Errol Flynn	10–20
	May 30	Czech General Jan Sirvoy	4–8

February 7, 1938

July 11, 1938

February 13, 1939

July 24, 1939

December 9, 1940

August 25, 1941

March 20, 1942

July 12, 1943

December 11, 1944

YEAR	ISSUE	COVER SUBJECT	VALUE
1938	June 6	Youth Problems	$ 3–5
	June 13	Gertrude Lawrence	5–10
	June 20	Rudolph Valentino	15–30
	June 27	Franklin D. Roosevelt	5–10
	July 4	West Point Wedding	5–10
	July 11	Shirley Temple	20–35+
	July 18	Camisoles in Fashion	5–10
	July 25	Queen Elizabeth	5–10
	August 1	Garment Workers at Play	4–8
	August 8	Divers	4–8
	August 15	Sumerian High Priest	4–8
	August 22	Fred Astaire and Ginger Rogers	15–30
	August 29	Goodbye to Summer	5–10
	September 5	Fall Fashions	3–6
	September 12	Hungarian Police	3–6
	September 19	James A. Farley	3–6
	September 26	Country Fair Barker	5–10
	October 3	Czech Soldier	5–10
	October 10	Legion Drum Majorettes	5–10
	October 17	Carole Lombard	15–30
	October 24	Columbia College's Sid Luckman	5–10
	October 31	Raymond Massey	10–20
	November 7	California Gubernatorial Candidate Culbert Olsen	3–6
	November 14	Brenda Duff Frazier	3–6
	November 21	Japanese Boy	5–10
	November 28	LIFE Birthday Baby	6–12
	December 5	Ballerina Yvette Chauviré	5–10
	December 12	Champion Labrador Retriever	5–10
	December 19	Mary Martin	10–20
	December 26	Lutist Mrs. Otto Baldauf	3–6
1939	January 2	Wimples in Fashion	3–7
	January 9	Romanian Boy	3–7
	January 16	Lucius Beebe	3–6
	January 23	Bette Davis	20–35
	January 30	Air Cadet	3–6
	February 6	Peruke Hairstyle	3–6

YEAR	ISSUE	COVER SUBJECT	VALUE
1939	February 13	Norma Shearer	$10–20
	February 20	France's Chief of Staff	5–10
	February 27	On a Nassau Beach	2–7
	March 6	Tallulah Bankhead	10–20
	March 13	World's Fair Sculpture	10–20
	March 20	Rep. Joseph Martin	3–6
	March 27	Spring Shower	3–7
	April 3	Realistic Dolls	3–7
	April 10	Texas Ranger	4–8
	April 17	Hildegarde	5–10
	April 24	Neville Chamberlain	5–12
	May 1	Joe DiMaggio	20–35
	May 8	Cottons in Fashion	2–6
	May 15	Anne Morrow Lindbergh	5–10
	May 22	World's Fair Guide	15–30
	May 29	Eleanor Roosevelt	5–10
	June 5	Statue of Liberty	5–10
	June 12	June Week at Annapolis	3–6
	June 19	USC Sprinter Payton Jordon	3–6
	June 26	Fads in Fashion	3–7
	July 3	Swimsuits in Fashion	4–8
	July 10	Japanese Home Guard	5–10
	July 17	Lord Halifax	3–7
	July 24	Ann Sheridan	5–15
	July 31	Diana Barrymore	10–25
	August 7	U.S. Official Paul McNutt	3–6
	August 14	Actress Sandra Lee Henville	3–8
	August 21	Boy Meets Girl	3–7
	August 28	Alice Marble	3–6
	September 4	Rosalind Russell	5–10
	September 11	Benito Mussolini	10–20
	September 18	British Soldier	4–8
	September 25	Britain's General Edmund Ironside	4–8
	October 2	Cordell Hull	3–6
	October 9	Kids' Football	3–6
	October 16	German U-boat	5–10
	October 23	War and Fashion	4–8

YEAR	ISSUE	COVER SUBJECT	VALUE
1939	October 30	Veloz and Yolanda	$ 3–6
	November 6	Planes over England	6–12
	November 13	Claudette Colbert	10–20
	November 20	German Warship	5–10
	November 27	Arturo Toscanini	3–7
	December 4	UCLA Coed and Date	3–7
	December 11	Betty Grable	10–25
	December 18	Canadian General Andrew McNaughton	4–8
	December 25	Merry Christmas	3–7
1940	January 1	Queen Elizabeth	5–10
	January 8	Bowdoin House Party	3–7
	January 15	USC's Basketball Star Ralph Vaughn	3–7
	January 22	Dutch East Indians	3–7
	January 29	Starlet Lana Turner	10–20
	February 5	Swedish Aviators	3–7
	February 12	Valentine's Day Hat	3–7
	February 19	Romania's King Carol and Son Mihai	3–6
	February 26	Carhop	3–6
	March 4	Springtime Hats	3–6
	March 11	French Soldier	4–8
	March 18	Chorus Girl	4–8
	March 25	Sir Neville Henderson	3–6
	April 1	N.Y. Giants Baseball Rookie John Rucker	4–7
	April 8	Actress Anna Neagle	3–7
	April 15	Government and Youth	3–6
	April 22	Dude Outfit	3–5
	April 29	Winston Churchill	5–10
	May 6	British Aerial Gunner	5–10
	May 13	Silk Shawls in Fashion	3–7
	May 20	French General Maxime Weygand	3–7
	May 27	German Soldier	4–8
	June 3	Statue of Liberty	5–10
	June 10	Emperor Hirohito	5–10

YEAR	ISSUE	COVER SUBJECT	VALUE
1940	June 17	General Motors' William Knudson	$ 3–6
	June 24	Italy's Marshal Rodolfo Graziani	3–7
	July 1	Red Cross Girl	4–7
	July 8	Admiral Harold Stark	3–7
	July 15	Rita Hayworth	10–20
	July 22	Tank Commander	4–8
	July 29	Girl Lifeguard	4–8
	August 5	U.S. Vacations	3–6
	August 12	Republican Vice President Nominee Charles McNary	3–5
	August 19	Parachute Trainee	3–7
	August 26	Couple at Jasper National Park	3–7
	September 2	Dionne Quintuplets	10–20
	September 9	Singer Carol Bruce	3–6
	September 16	Flight across America	3–6
	September 23	Air Raid Victim	3–7
	September 30	Wendell Willkie	4–8
	October 7	Gary Cooper	5–10
	October 14	Jinx Falkenburg	3–6
	October 21	Sweaters in Fashion	3–7
	October 28	U.S. Sailor	3–7
	November 4	San Diego Campaign Rally	2–5
	November 11	Michigan's Tom Harmon	2–5
	November 18	Franklin D. Roosevelt	4–8
	November 25	Fur Coats in Fashion	3–5
	December 2	Balloonists	5–10
	December 9	Ginger Rogers	15–30
	December 16	Greek Soldier	3–6
	December 23	Couple Dressed for a Party	3–5
	December 30	Britain's Desert Fighters	5–10
1941	January 6	Katharine Hepburn	10–25
	January 13	Bathing Suits in Fashion	4–8
	January 20	U.S. Ski Trooper	3–6
	January 27	Winston Churchill II and His Mother, Pamela	5–10
	February 3	Joseph Goebbels and Hermann Göring	7–15

YEAR	ISSUE	COVER SUBJECT	VALUE
1941	February 10	Lord Halifax	$ 3–7
	February 17	Actress Cobina Wright Jr.	3–5
	February 24	New Zealanders	3–7
	March 3	Fashion	3–7
	March 10	Washington Worker	2–5
	March 17	Panama Canal Defense	4–8
	March 24	Veils in Fashion	2–5
	March 31	U.S. Navy's New Dive-bomber	4–8
	April 7	Spring Showers	3–5
	April 14	New York Harbor	3–7
	April 21	U.S. Cavalryman	2–4
	April 28	Red in Fashion	2–4
	May 5	John Harvard	2–4
	May 12	Army Parachutist	3–6
	May 19	Floppy Hats in Fashion	2–4
	May 26	Army Nurse	3–6
	June 2	Sunday School	2–4
	June 9	The Duke and Duchess of Windsor	5–10
	June 16	British Soldier with His First U.S. Soda	3–7
	June 23	Lazy Fishing	3–6
	June 30	Mme. Chiang Kai-shek	3–7
	July 7	General George Patton	5–10
	July 14	Sand Sailing	3–7
	July 21	British Air Chief Marshal Sir Robert Brooke	3–7
	July 28	Circus Family	2–5
	August 4	British Women Auxiliary	3–5
	August 11	Rita Hayworth	10–20
	August 18	U.S. Marine	3–7
	August 25	Fred Astaire and Son	10–20
	September 1	Ted Williams	5–10
	September 8	Smith College Girl	3–5
	September 15	British Captain Lord Louis Mountbatten	5–10
	September 22	Brazilian Dancer Eros Volusia	2–4
	September 29	Radio's Quiz Kid Gerald Darrow	3–5

YEAR	ISSUE	COVER SUBJECT	VALUE
1941	October 6	Farmer's Daughter	$ 3–6
	October 13	Lana Turner and Clark Gable	15–30
	October 20	Pan American Clipper	3–7
	October 27	Air Raid Spotter	3–6
	November 3	West Point Cadet	3–5
	November 10	Gene Tierney	10–15
	November 17	Texas Football	2–4
	November 24	How to Knit	2–4
	December 1	B-17 Bomber	5–10
	December 8	General Douglas MacArthur	5–10
	December 15	Junior Miss	3–7
	December 22	American Flag	2–4
	December 29	U.S. Aerial Gunner	2–4
1942	January 5	Wanted . . . 50,000 Nurses	2–4
	January 12	Pacific Coast Defense	3–6
	January 19	North Atlantic Patrol	3–6
	January 26	Air Force Women's Auxiliary	3–6
	February 2	Thunderbolt Fighter	5–10
	February 9	Versailles Nightclub Chorus in New York	2–4
	February 16	Singer and Soldier	2–4
	February 23	Guns for Merchantmen	4–8
	March 2	Ginger Rogers	15–30
	March 9	Barrage Balloon	5–10
	March 16	Infantryman	3–6
	March 23	Making Plane Models	2–4
	March 30	Shirley Temple	20–40
	April 6	Tail Gunner	5–10
	April 13	General Brehon Somervell	2–4
	April 20	Slacks in Fashion	2–4
	April 27	Nelson Rockefeller	2–4
	May 4	Chinese Air Cadet	3–6
	May 11	Ruffles in Fashion	2–4
	May 18	Cadet Bomber	4–8
	May 25	Spring Planting	2–4
	June 1	Hedy Lamarr	10–25
	June 8	Nurse's Aide	2–4
	June 15	General Joseph Stilwell	2–5

YEAR	ISSUE	COVER SUBJECT	VALUE
1942	June 22	War Bride	$ 2–4
	June 29	USO Belle	3–5
	July 6	American Flag	3–5
	July 13	Air Corps Gunnery School	4–8
	July 20	Short Coat in Fashion	2–4
	July 27	Atlantic Convoy	3–6
	August 3	General MacArthur's Son	2–5
	August 10	General Claire Chennault	3–5
	August 17	Guerrilla Warfare Expert	3–7
	August 24	Johnny Jeep	3–5
	August 31	Torpedo Boat Ensign	5–10
	September 7	Cargo Glider	2–4
	September 14	U.S. Official Leon Henderson	2–4
	September 21	Iran's Queen Fawzia	2–4
	September 28	Admiral William Leahy	2–4
	October 5	Hats in Fashion	2–4
	October 12	California Assembly	2–4
	October 19	Sandbagged Sphinx	3–7
	October 26	Actress Joan Leslie	2–4
	November 2	Praise the Lord and Pass the Ammunition Phrasemaker Captain William Maguire	3–7
	November 9	Infantry Mountain Trooper	3–7
	November 16	Vests in Fashion	2–4
	November 23	New England Church	2–4
	November 30	Eighteen-year-old Awaiting Draft	3–5
	December 7	Marine Ace Major John L. Smith	3–6
	December 14	Coast Guard Skipper	2–5
	December 21	Lonely Wife	2–4
	December 28	Madonna	2–4
1943	January 4	Assistant to the President Jimmy Bymes	2–4
	January 11	Kids' Uniforms	2–4
	January 18	Rita Hayworth	10–20
	January 25	Eddie Rickenbacker	10–20
	February 1	Dating in Casablanca	2–5

YEAR	ISSUE	COVER SUBJECT	VALUE
1943	February 8	Plane Spotter	$ 3–5
	February 15	Princess Elizabeth	5–10
	February 22	Army Air Observer	3–5
	March 1	Bow Ties in Fashion	2–4
	March 8	General Brehon Somervell	2–4
	March 15	WAVES	3–6
	March 22	General George Kenney	3–5
	March 29	Joseph Stalin	5–10
	April 5	Montgomery Berets in Fashion	2–4
	April 12	Jefferson Memorial	2–4
	April 19	Soldier's Farewell	3–7
	April 26	Junior Army-Navy Organization	2–4
	May 3	Matching Dress and Parasol in Fashion	2–4
	May 10	PT Boat Skippers	4–7
	May 17	Boy Welder	2–4
	May 24	Actress Peggy Lloyd	2–4
	May 31	Saudi Arabian King Ibn Saud	2–4
	June 7	Captain Joe Foss	2–4
	June 14	High School Graduation	2–5
	June 21	Igor Sikorsky with Helicopter	3–6
	June 28	War Souvenir	3–6
	July 5	America's Combat Dead	5–10
	July 12	Roy Rogers and Trigger	15–30
	July 19	Air Force Auxiliary Pilot	3–6
	July 26	8th Air Force B-24	5–10
	August 2	British Admiral Sir Max Kennedy	2–5
	August 9	Steelworker	2–5
	August 16	Japanese Soldiers	4–8
	August 23	Lindy Hoppers	2–4
	August 30	Anthony Eden with His Dog Nipper	2–4
	September 6	American Soldiers Hunting Japanese	5–10
	September 13	Leotards in Fashion	2–4
	September 20	Cambridge Don Charles Seltman	2–4

YEAR	ISSUE	COVER SUBJECT	VALUE
1943	September 27	Harvester	$ 2–4
	October 4	U.S. Ambassador to Governments-in-exile Anthony Biddle	2–4
	October 11	Half Hats in Fashion	2–4
	October 18	Wartime Romances	2–4
	October 25	Mary Martin	10–15
	November 1	Thunderbolt Fighter	5–10
	November 8	British Field Marshal Jan Smuts	2–4
	November 15	Fur-lined Coats in Fashion	2–4
	November 22	Foot Soldiers	3–6
	November 29	General Ira Eaker	2–5
	December 6	Earmuffs in Fashion	2–4
	December 13	Chinese Muslim	2–3
	December 20	U.S. Pilot's Wife	3–5
	December 27	Wounded Soldier with Nurse	3–5
1944	January 3	Alaska Holiday	2–5
	January 10	Bob Hope	10–15
	January 17	Historian Charles Beard	2–4
	January 24	Margaret Sullavan	5–10
	January 31	British Air Chief Marshal Sir Arthur Tedder	3–6
	February 7	George Bernard Shaw	3–6
	February 14	Wall of Fame Facade of Earl Carroll Theater	2–4
	February 21	Patrice Munsel	2–4
	February 28	Actress Ella Raines	2–4
	March 6	Admiral Chester Nimitz	5–10
	March 13	Junior School Dance	2–4
	March 20	Ballerina Nana Gollner	2–4
	March 27	Landing Craft	2–5
	April 3	Pooch	2–5
	April 10	British Air Marshal Arthur T. Harris	2–5
	April 17	Esther Williams	6–12
	April 24	Princess Elizabeth	5–10
	May 1	Homecoming	3–6
	May 8	Hattie Carnegie Suit in Fashion	2–4

YEAR	ISSUE	COVER SUBJECT	VALUE
1944	May 15	British General Sir Bernard Montgomery	$ 4–8
	May 22	Model Mother and Son	3–5
	May 29	General Carl Spaatz	2–4
	June 5	U.S. Infantrymen	3–6
	June 12	Bombs Falling on Italy	4–7
	June 19	General Dwight D. Eisenhower	4–8
	June 26	Statue of Liberty	4–8
	July 3	Back from the Front	3–7
	July 10	Admiral Chester Nimitz	3–7
	July 17	Peasant Clothes in Fashion	2–4
	July 24	Jennifer Jones	5–10
	July 31	Soviet Marshal Georgi Zhukov	3–8
	August 7	Geraldine Fitzgerald	2–5
	August 14	Airborne Infantry Officer	4–7
	August 21	Amphibious Tractors	4–6
	August 28	Pedal Pushers in Fashion	2–5
	September 4	Cordell Hull	2–5
	September 11	Nazi Prisoners	5–10
	September 18	Thomas E. Dewey	3–5
	September 25	A Letter to GIs	3–5
	October 2	General Lucian Truscott	3–5
	October 9	Helena Rubenstein's Dali Room	3–5
	October 16	Lauren Bacall	10–25
	October 23	Soviet Scientist Alexei Kryov	2–4
	October 30	U.S.S. Iowa	5–10
	November 6	Celeste Holm	5–10
	November 13	General Charles de Gaulle	5–10
	November 20	Thanksgiving	5–10
	November 27	Gertrude Lawrence	2–4
	December 4	B-29s over Formosa	5–10
	December 11	Judy Garland	15–30
	December 18	Fredric March	5–10
	December 25	Madonna and Child	2–5
1945	January 1	Soldier Cleaning Gun	4–8
	January 8	Scarves in Fashion	2–4
	January 15	General George Patton	5–12
	January 22	St. John's University Basketball	2–4

YEAR	ISSUE	COVER SUBJECT	VALUE
1945	January 29	Wounded Soldier	$ 3–6
	February 5	Florida Fashion	2–4
	February 12	Soviet Soldier	2–5
	February 19	Ski Clothes in Fashion	3–5
	February 26	Winter Soldiers	5–10
	March 5	Flying over San Francisco's Presidio	3–7
	March 12	General William Simpson	3–5
	March 19	Dutch Girl	3–6
	March 26	Carol Lynn	3–5
	April 2	Subdeb Clubs	3–4
	April 9	Iwo Jima	10–15
	April 16	General Dwight D. Eisenhower	3–6
	April 23	Harry S Truman	3–6
	April 30	War Artists	3–6
	May 7	The German People	3–5
	May 14	Victorious Yank	3–6
	May 21	Winston Churchill	3–6
	May 28	Starlet Barbara Bates	3–5
	June 4	War Loan Drive	2–4
	June 11	Teenage Boys	2–3
	June 18	Girl Scouts in Washington	3–5
	June 25	Kindergarten Graduation	3–5
	July 2	Pacific Fleet Destroyers	3–6
	July 9	Bathing Suits in Fashion	3–5
	July 16	Audie Murphy	10–20
	July 23	Actress Peggy Ann Garner	10–15
	July 30	Playing on the Beach	3–5
	August 6	Junior Sailors	2–4
	August 13	Jet Plane	2–4
	August 20	General Carl Spaatz	2–3
	August 27	Ballet Swimmer	2–3
	September 3	House Party	2–3
	September 10	Autoworker	2–3
	September 17	General Douglas MacArthur	4–8
	September 24	Colonel Jimmy Stewart	8–15
	October 1	June Allyson	5–8
	October 8	General Robert Eichelberger	2–3

April 5, 1945

May 21, 1945

May 27, 1946

June 3, 1946

June 14, 1946

July 22, 1946

July 29, 1946

August 12, 1946

September 30, 1946

YEAR	ISSUE	COVER SUBJECT	VALUE
1945	October 15	Fall Jewelry in Fashion	$ 2–3
	October 22	Ohio State's Paul Sarringhaus	2–3
	October 29	Autumn	2–4
	November 5	Fleet's In	3–5
	November 12	Ingrid Bergman	5–10
	November 19	Big Belts in Fashion	2–4
	November 26	Champion Afghan	2–4
	December 3	Spencer Tracy	5–10
	December 10	Party Dresses in Fashion	2–3
	December 17	Paulette Goddard	6–12
	December 24	Procession to Bethlehem	2–4
	December 31	Mountain Climbing	2–4
1946	January 7	Winston Churchill's Paintings	3–5
	January 14	Southern Resort Fashion	2–3
	January 21	Cardinal Spellman	2–3
	January 28	Actress Jan Clayton	2–3
	February 4	Bob Hope and Bing Crosby	10–15
	February 11	Lincoln Memorial	2–3
	February 18	Dorothy McGuire	4–8
	February 25	Pointer	2–4
	March 4	Figure Skater	2–4
	March 11	Senator Arthur Vandenberg	2–3
	March 18	Eiffel Tower	2–3
	March 25	Actress Lucille Bremer	2–3
	April 1	St. Louis Cardinals' Red Barrett	3–6
	April 8	Clown Lou Jacobs	2–3
	April 15	Spring Fashions	2–3
	April 22	Denver High School	2–3
	April 29	Marble Pagoda in Peiping	2–3
	May 6	Margaret Leighton	2–3
	May 13	Northwest Vacation	2–4
	May 20	Ice Capades	2–4
	May 27	Ozark Farmer	2–4
	June 3	Children in Church	2–4
	June 10	Donna Reed	10–20
	June 17	Play Dresses	2–4
	June 24	Chief Justice Fred Vinson	2–3
	July 1	Sailing Season	2–4

YEAR	ISSUE	COVER SUBJECT	VALUE
1946	July 8	Basque Shirts in Fashion	$ 2–3
	July 15	Water Gadgets	2–3
	July 22	Mrs. Cornelius Vanderbilt Whitney with Coachman	2–3
	July 29	Vivien Leigh	10–20
	August 5	Radio's Juvenile Jury Participant	2–3
	August 12	Loretta Young	7–15
	August 19	Old Faithful	2–4
	August 26	College Fashions	2–3
	September 2	Vacation's End	2–3
	September 9	Jane Powell	4–8
	September 16	West Point's Glen Davis and Felix Blanchard	2–3
	September 23	Dachshund	2–4
	September 30	Jeanne Crain	5–12
	October 7	Bing Crosby and Joan Caulfield	5–10
	October 14	Fall Fashions	2–3
	October 21	Gloria Grahame	2–3
	October 28	One-room School	2–4
	November 4	Arab Policeman with Camel in Palestine	2–4
	November 11	High School Model Shirley Arnow	2–3
	November 18	Party Raincoats in Fashion	2–3
	November 25	LIFE's 10th Anniversary Issue	3–6
	December 2	Ingrid Bergman	5–10
	December 9	Jet Pilot	2–4
	December 16	Teresa Wright	2–4
	December 23	The Flight into Eygpt	2–4
	December 30	Dorothy Kristen	2–3
1947	January 6	Annapolis ''Drag''	2–3
	January 13	Resort Fashions	2–3
	January 20	Homesteading Veteran	2–3
	January 27	Nantucket Lighthouse	3–5
	February 3	Actress Susan Douglas	2–3
	February 10	Occupation of Germany	2–4
	February 17	Water Skier	2–3

YEAR	ISSUE	COVER SUBJECT	VALUE
1947	February 24	Texas Coed	$ 2–3
	March 3	Renaissance Man in Armor	2–3
	March 10	Father's Day Bath	2–5
	March 17	Youth Center Director	2–3
	March 24	Eskimo Baby	2–4
	March 31	Spring Hats in Fashion	2–3
	April 7	Sunday School Pupils	2–4
	April 14	Pretty Girls and Flowering Dogwood	2–4
	April 21	Student Veteran	2–3
	April 28	Actress Bambi Linn	2–3
	May 5	Riding Clothes in Fashion	2–3
	May 12	Bulgarian Prime Minister Georgi Dimitrov	2–3
	May 19	Teenager's Sundae	2–3
	May 26	Medieval Castle	2–4
	June 2	Jane Greer	2–4
	June 9	Ballerina Ricky Soma	2–3
	June 16	Cape Hatteras Bay	2–4
	June 23	Bathing Suits in Fashion	2–4
	June 30	Ancient and Modern Mayan Sculpture	5–10
	July 7	Little Girl on a Merry-go-round	3–6
	July 14	Elizabeth Taylor	15–30
	July 21	Americans in Heidelberg	2–4
	July 28	Princess Elizabeth	4–8
	August 4	Portrait of a Man in a Red Cap	3–5
	August 11	Actress Ella Raines	2–3
	August 18	Lord Louis Mountbatten	3–7
	August 25	Model Gail Sullivan	2–3
	September 1	Auto Racer John Cobb	3–4
	September 8	Lady Sarah Fitzalan-Howard	2–3
	September 15	Madame Du Barry	2–4
	September 22	Fall Fashions	2–4
	September 29	Notre Dame's Johnny Lujack	2–5
	October 6	Franklin D. Roosevelt at 13	3–5
	October 13	Katrina von Oss in Allegro Opening on Broadway	2–4

November 25, 1946

April 28, 1947

September 8, 1947

October 20, 1947

January 26, 1948

June 7, 1948

July 18, 1949

April 1, 1951

June 25, 1951

YEAR	ISSUE	COVER SUBJECT	VALUE
1947	October 20	Child Listening to Folk Songs	$ 3–6
	October 27	Admiral Lewis Douglas	2–3
	November 3	Ballerinas Ruth Koesun and Melissa Hayden	2–4
	November 10	Rita Hayworth	5–10
	November 17	Boxers	3–5
	November 24	Subdeb Pamela Helene Dudley Curran	2–3
	December 1	Gregory Peck	5–10
	December 8	Boyhood Portrait of the Duke of Windsor	3–6
	December 15	Nightclub Girls	3–5
	December 22	Christmas Carols	2–4
	December 29	Pretty Girl in Miami	2–4
1948	January 5	Pakistan's Muhammed Ali Jinnah	2–3
	January 12	Midwinter Accessories in Fashion	2–3
	January 19	Violinist Marcia Van Dyke	2–3
	January 26	Resort Fashions	2–3
	February 2	Maine Schoolboy	2–4
	February 9	Robert A. Taft	2–3
	February 16	Actress Joan Tetzel	2–3
	February 23	Skiing	2–4
	March 1	Harold E. Stassen	2–3
	March 8	Model Gaby Bouche	2–3
	March 15	Sir Laurence Olivier	5–10
	March 22	Thomas E. Dewey	3–6
	March 29	Basket Handbags in Fashion	2–3
	April 5	Baseball Rookies	3–7
	April 12	Barbara Bel Geddes	4–7
	April 19	Winston Churchill	4–8
	April 26	Collegians in Bermuda	2–3
	May 3	Career Girl	2–3
	May 10	Governor Earl Warren	2–3
	May 17	Mrs. David Niven	3–4
	May 24	Senator Arthur Vandenberg	2–3
	May 31	Television Ingenue Kyle MacDonnell	3–6

YEAR	ISSUE	COVER SUBJECT	VALUE
1948	June 7	Hooded T-shirts in Fashion	$ 3–5
	June 14	Actress Phyllis Calvert	2–3
	June 21	Cape Cod Weekend	2–4
	June 28	Member of Kent School Crew	2–3
	July 5	F-84 Thunderjets	3–7
	July 12	Small-Town Girl	2–4
	July 19	Fun on the Beach	2–4
	July 26	Children's Ballet School	2–4
	August 2	Olympic Sprinter Mel Patton	3–5
	August 9	Marlene Dietrich	10–20
	August 16	Little Fisherman	2–4
	August 23	Young Hunter with Pet Deer	3–5
	August 30	Actress Colleen Townsend	2–3
	September 6	The Good Life in Madison, Wisconsin	2–4
	September 13	Marshal Tito	2–4
	September 20	Actress Joan Diener	2–3
	September 27	SMU's Doak Walker	2–3
	October 4	Big Industry in America	2–3
	October 11	Actress Rita Cotton	2–3
	October 18	Fur Jackets in Fashion	2–3
	October 25	University of California Football Fans	2–3
	November 1	General Lauris Norstadt	2–3
	November 8	Actress Helena Carter	2–3
	November 15	Ingrid Bergman	4–8
	November 22	Harry S Truman	3–6
	November 29	Dinner Hats in Fashion	2–3
	December 6	Montgomery Clift	5–10
	December 13	Dwight D. Eisenhower	5–8
	December 20	Teenage Fun	3–5
	December 27	The Story of Christ	3–6
1949	January 3	Famous Baby Dwight D. Eisenhower II	2–4
	January 10	Debutante Joanne Connelley	2–4
	January 17	Resort Fashions	3–4
	January 24	Skier Emile Allais	3–4
	January 31	Champion Cocker Spaniel	3–4

YEAR	ISSUE	COVER SUBJECT	VALUE
1949	February 7	Winston Churchill's Memoirs	$ 3–7
	February 14	Viveca Lindfors	2–4
	February 21	Dean Acheson	2–3
	February 28	Children's Costume Clothes	3–4
	March 7	Marge and Gower Champion	2–3
	March 14	Dorothy McGuire's Baby	3–6
	March 21	Fashion Wardrobe	2–4
	March 28	Actress Joy Lansing	2–4
	April 4	U.S. Official Paul Hoffman	2–3
	April 11	Boy on Fence during Spring along the Mississippi	3–6
	April 18	Mary Martin	4–8
	April 25	Paris Fashion	2–4
	May 2	West Point's Arnold Galiffa	2–3
	May 9	Missouri Coed Jane Stone	2–4
	May 16	Little Boxer	3–5
	May 23	Sarah Churchill	3–6
	May 30	Baby Franklin D. Roosevelt	3–6
	June 6	Summer Play Clothes in Fashion	2–4
	June 13	Actress Marta Toren	2–3
	June 20	High School Graduate	2–4
	June 27	Inland Sailing	2–4
	July 4	Beach Holiday	2–4
	July 11	Olympian Bob Mathias	2–3
	July 18	Hollywood Child Sharon Harmon	3–6
	July 25	Girl in Plastic Beach Boat	3–5
	August 1	Joe DiMaggio	10–25
	August 8	Straw Hats in Fashion	2–3
	August 15	Actress Brynn Noring	2–3
	August 22	Cowboy	2–4
	August 29	College Fashions	2–5
	September 5	Ben Turpin	2–3
	September 12	Marshal Tito	2–5
	September 19	Arlene Dahl	4–8
	September 26	Fashion Secret	2–4
	October 3	North Carolina's Charlie Justice	2–3

YEAR	ISSUE	COVER SUBJECT	VALUE
1949	October 10	J. Robert Oppenheimer	$ 2–4
	October 17	Actress Jeanne Craine	5–10
	October 24	Sweden's Ideal Pretty Girl	2–5
	October 31	Princess Margaret	2–4
	November 7	Alfred Lunt and Lynn Fontanne	3–7
	November 14	Pearls in Fashion	2–3
	November 21	Actor Ricardo Montalban	4–7
	November 28	Dancer Nita Bieber	2–3
	December 5	General Hoyt Vandenberg	2–3
	December 12	Beauty on Fifth Avenue	2–5
	December 19	Little Girl Clothes in Fashion	2–5
	December 26	God the Creator from the Sistine Chapel	2–5
1950	January 2	Gibson Girl Look	3–6
	January 9	Actress Norma de Landa	2–3
	January 16	Young Skater	2–3
	January 23	Man-tailored Shirts in Fashion	2–3
	January 30	Childbirth without Fear	2–4
	February 6	Eva Gabor	4–8
	February 13	Indonesian Woman	3–5
	February 20	Gregory Peck	5–10
	February 27	Atomic Explosion	4–8
	March 6	Actress Marsha Hunt	3–4
	March 13	Spring Fashions	2–3
	March 20	Artist Edward John Stevens Jr.	2–3
	March 27	Model Anne Bromley	2–4
	April 3	Iris Mann and David Cole on Broadway	2–4
	April 10	Young Horsewoman	2–4
	April 17	Dwight D. Eisenhower	3–6
	April 24	Inexpensive Blouses in Fashion	2–4
	May 1	Actress Ruth Roman	3–5
	May 8	Jackie Robinson	15–30+
	May 15	Beach Fashions	3–5
	May 22	The Duke and Duchess of Windsor	5–10
	May 29	Mrs. William O'Dwyer	2–3
	June 5	Actress Stasia Kos	2–3

YEAR	ISSUE	COVER SUBJECT	VALUE
1950	June 12	Hopalong Cassidy (William Boyd)	$10–20
	June 19	Children's Beach Fashions	3–4
	June 26	Actress Cecile Aubry	2–3
	July 3	Washington at Trenton	3–6
	July 10	Actress Miroslava Stern	2–3
	July 17	Jet Pilot	2–4
	July 24	Boy Scout	3–5
	July 31	24th Division Soldiers	3–5
	August 7	Actress Peggy Dow	2–3
	August 14	Admiral John Hoskins	2–3
	August 21	Broadway Chorines	2–3
	August 28	General Douglas MacArthur	4–8
	September 4	Two Marines on Reconnaissance	3–6
	September 11	American Elegance in Fashion	2–3
	September 18	Ezio Pinza	2–4
	September 25	Swedish Red Cross Girl	2–4
	October 2	U.S. Official Stuart Symington	2–3
	October 9	Jean Simmons	5–10
	October 16	Winnetka High School Girl	2–4
	October 23	Ed Wynn	3–6
	October 30	Faye Emerson	2–4
	November 6	Horse Show Rider	2–3
	November 13	SMU's Kyle Rote	2–4
	November 20	Girl of Shilluk Tribe	2–4
	November 27	UCLA Homecoming Queen	2–4
	December 4	Berlin Girl	2–4
	December 11	Lilli Palmer and Rex Harrison	4–8
	December 18	General George Marshall	2–3
	December 25	Girls Painting	3–5
1951	January 1	U.S. Official Charles E. Wilson	2–3
	January 8	Starlet Janice Rule	2–3
	January 15	Rose Parade Grand Marshal	2–3
	January 22	Air Warning Supervisor	2–3
	January 29	Actress Betsy von Furstenberg	2–4
	February 5	N.Y.C. Police Commissioner Thomas F. Murphy	2–3

YEAR	ISSUE	COVER SUBJECT	VALUE
1951	February 12	Veiled Hats in Fashion	$ 2–3
	February 19	Adoption of Linda Joy	2–4
	February 26	Debbie Reynolds	6–12
	March 5	Dior Fashions	2–4
	March 12	Actor Paul Douglas	2–4
	March 19	Navy Couple	2–4
	March 26	Child Choir Singers	2–4
	April 2	Jet-setter Mercedes Spradling	2–3
	April 9	General Omar Bradley	3–6
	April 16	Esther Williams	4–8
	April 23	Dalai Lama	2–4
	April 30	General Matthew Ridgway	2–3
	May 7	Actress Phyllis Kirk	2–3
	May 14	Michigan's Senator Blair Moody and Sons	2–3
	May 21	Beach Fashions	2–4
	May 28	Paratroopers	3–5
	June 4	Model Ursula Theiss	2–3
	June 11	Actress Vivian Blaine	2–4
	June 18	Iran's Royal Crown	2–3
	June 25	Actress Janet Leigh	7–15
	July 2	Sergeant John Pittman	2–4
	July 9	Summer Party in Charlotte, North Carolina	2–3
	July 16	TV Actress Dagmar	2–4
	July 23	Swimmer Mary Freeman	2–4
	July 30	Singer Gary Crosby	2–3
	August 6	Vacationing High School Girl	2–4
	August 13	Dean Martin and Jerry Lewis	7–15
	August 20	Swimmer Barbara Hobelmann	2–3
	August 27	Model Rosemary Coover	2–4
	September 3	Gina Lollobrigida	5–10
	September 10	Japanese Prime Minister	2–3
	September 17	Chorus Girl	2–4
	September 24	Gene Tierney	5–10
	October 1	Princess Elizabeth	3–7
	October 8	Baby Malayan Snow Loris	2–4
	October 15	Zsa Zsa Gabor	3–7

YEAR	ISSUE	COVER SUBJECT	VALUE
1951	October 22	Bronc Rider Casey Tibbs	$ 2–4
	October 29	TV Prop Girl	2–3
	November 5	Ginger Rogers	10–20
	November 12	Anthony Eden	2–3
	November 19	Lynn Fontanne, Katharine Cornell, and Helen Hayes	4–8
	November 26	Photography Contest Winner Regina Fisher	2–4
	December 3	Christmas Lingerie in Fashion	2–4
	December 10	Harry S Truman	3–6
	December 17	Vivien Leigh and Laurence Olivier	5–10
	December 24	Nativity	2–4
1952	January 7	Hairstyles	2–3
	January 14	Augustus John	2–3
	January 21	Dwight D. Eisenhower	3–6
	January 28	Model, Pianist, and Painter Phyllis Newell	2–3
	February 4	Skater Barbara Ann Scott	2–4
	February 11	Olympic Skier Henri Oreiller	2–3
	February 18	Queen Elizabeth II	5–10
	February 25	Gloves in Fashion	2–3
	March 3	Patrice Munsel	2–3
	March 10	Actor Brandon de Wilde	2–5
	March 17	Broadway Chorus Girl	2–4
	March 24	Democratic Presidential Candidates	2–4
	March 31	Li'l Abner Characters	2–5
	April 7	Marilyn Monroe	15–30+
	April 14	Italian Fashions	2–3
	April 21	Marshal Tito	2–4
	April 28	Ike and Mamie Eisenhower's Wedding Photo	3–5
	May 5	Actress Diana Lynn	2–3
	May 12	General Matthew Ridgway	2–3
	May 19	Actress Miriam Charriere	2–3
	May 26	Stewart Granger	3–6
	June 2	Children's Party Outfits	2–3

April 7, 1952

April 20, 1952

June 16, 1952

July 25, 1955

March 11, 1966

YEAR	ISSUE	COVER SUBJECT	VALUE
1952	June 9	Bridal Model Martha Boss	$ 2–4
	June 16	Dwight D. Eisenhower	3–6
	June 23	Mail-Order Fashions	2–3
	June 30	Nancy Kefauver	2–3
	July 7	Arlene Dahl	4–8
	July 14	Hangover Victim	2–3
	July 21	Dwight D. Eisenhower	2–5
	July 28	British Starlets Joan Elan, Dorothy Bromiley, and Audrey Dalton	2–4
	August 4	Adlai Stevenson	2–4
	August 11	Actress Joan Rice	2–3
	August 18	Marlene Dietrich and Daughter, Maria Riva	7–15
	August 25	College Fashions	2–4
	September 1	Ernest Hemingway	5–10
	September 8	Fall Fashions	2–4
	September 15	Rita Gam	2–3
	September 22	LST at Polar Base	2–4
	September 29	Jackie Gleason TV Chorus Girls	4–8
	October 6	Mrs. Peter Thieriot at San Francisco Opera Opening	2–3
	October 13	Mamie Eisenhower	3–5
	October 20	Actress Lucia Bose	2–3
	October 27	Jon Linbergh	2–4
	November 3	New UN Assembly Building	2–3
	November 10	Duck Hunter Jean Huston	2–4
	November 17	Dwight D. Eisenhower and Mamie Eisenhower	3–6
	November 24	Jewelry in Fashion	2–4
	December 1	Actress Suzanne Cloutier	2–3
	December 8	The Earth Is Born	3–6
	December 15	Refugee Homecoming Queen	2–4
	December 22	Midget Horse	2–3
	December 29	Salzburg Marionettes	2–4
1953	January 5	$15,000 Houses	2–4
	January 12	Resort Fashions in Majorca	2–3

YEAR	ISSUE	COVER SUBJECT	VALUE
1953	January 19	U.S. Officials Charles E. Wilson and George M. Humphrey	$ 2–4
	January 26	Fashion Stylist Sigrid Soelter	2–3
	February 2	Dwight D. Eisenhower's Inauguration	3–7
	February 9	Miracles of the Sea	3–6
	February 16	Coldstream Guard	2–4
	February 23	Prettiest Teacher	2–4
	March 2	Formosan Soldiers	2–4
	March 9	Stoles in Fashion	2–3
	March 16	Joseph Stalin and Georgy Malenkov	3–5
	March 23	Starlet Elaine Stewart	2–3
	March 30	Coronation Fashion	2–3
	April 6	Lucille Ball, Desi Arnaz, and Children	10–20+
	April 13	Delicate Arch in Utah	2–4
	April 20	Marlon Brando	5–10
	April 27	Queen Elizabeth II	5–10
	May 4	Masai Warrior	2–4
	May 11	Denim in Fashion	2–4
	May 18	Indiana Coed	2–4
	May 25	Marilyn Monroe and Jane Russell	15–30+
	June 1	Brooke Hayward	2–3
	June 8	Roy Campanella	5–10
	June 15	Coronation of Elizabeth II	5–10
	June 22	Miss College Graduate	2–4
	June 29	Cyd Charisse	5–10
	July 6	Actress Terry Moore	10–20
	July 13	Sir Edmund Hillary and Tenzing Norgay	4–8
	July 20	Senator John F. Kennedy	5–10
	July 27	Can-Can Lingerie in Fashion	2–4
	August 3	Actress Nicole Naurey	2–3
	August 10	Irish Fashions	2–4
	August 17	Actresses Barbara, Madelyn, and Alice Whittlinger	2–3

YEAR	ISSUE	COVER SUBJECT	VALUE
1953	August 24	Mormon Ballerinas on Connecticut Beach	$ 2–4
	August 31	Donna Reed	5–10
	September 7	Stegosaurus and Brontosaurus	3–5
	September 14	Casey Stengel	3–6
	September 21	Photographer's Daughter	2–4
	September 28	De Cuevas Ball	2–3
	October 5	New Citizens	2–3
	October 12	Bare Backs in Fashion	2–4
	October 19	Prehistoric Mammals	3–6
	October 26	Actress Vikki Dougan	2–3
	November 2	Sir Winston Churchill	3–6
	November 9	Singer Jill Corey	2–4
	November 16	Greece's Queen Frederica	2–3
	November 23	College Art Student	2–3
	November 30	Queen Triggerfish	2–3
	December 7	Audrey Hepburn	5–10
	December 14	Richard M. Nixon	3–6
	December 21	Pajamas in Fashion	2–4
	December 28	Madonna and Child in St. Mark's	2–4
1954	January 4	Regulus Missile	2–3
	January 11	Debutante Wardrobe	2–3
	January 18	U.S. Officials Leverett Saltonstall, William Knowland, and Richard M. Nixon	2–4
	January 25	Dancer Diane Sinclair	2–4
	February 1	Tropical Wardrobe	2–4
	February 8	Sea Turtle	2–4
	February 15	Italian Hairdo	2–3
	February 22	Disney Moviemaking	3–6
	March 1	Actress Rita Moreno	4–8
	March 8	Winston Churchill's Granddaughter	3–5
	March 15	Mrs. Winthrop Rockefeller	2–3
	March 22	Emperor Penguin	2–4
	March 29	Actress Pat Crowley	1–2
	April 5	The Desert	2–4

YEAR	ISSUE	COVER SUBJECT	VALUE
1954	April 12	Subteen Fashions	$ 1–2
	April 19	H-Bomb Test	2–4
	April 26	Grace Kelly	10–20
	May 3	Rarest Stamps	2–3
	May 10	Bavaria's Neuschwanstein Castle	2–4
	May 17	Starlet Dawn Addams	2–4
	May 24	Actress Kaye Ballard	2–4
	May 31	William Holden	3–5
	June 7	Arctic Tundra	2–4
	June 14	California Fashions	2–4
	June 21	Las Vegas Chorus Girl	2–3
	June 28	Bathing Suits in Fashion	2–3
	July 5	Fourth of July	2–3
	July 12	Actress Pier Angeli	5–10
	July 19	Eva Marie Saint	5–10
	July 26	Army Counsel Joseph Welch	1–2
	August 2	Arabian Nights at Jones Beach Theater	2–3
	August 9	Boy Cowpuncher with His Father	2–3
	August 16	Africa's Spirited Children	2–3
	August 23	Philip, Duke of Edinburgh	2–4
	August 30	Singer Anna Maria Alberghetti	2–4
	September 6	Dior Fashions	1–2
	September 13	Judy Garland	10–20
	September 20	Tropical Rain Forest	2–4
	September 27	Hydrofoil	1–2
	October 4	Wesley Girl and UN Guide	1–2
	October 11	Mountain Climber	2–4
	October 18	Tacoma Congressional Campaigner	1–2
	October 25	The Big Ten Look of Coeds	2–4
	November 1	Actress Dorothy Dandridge	1–2
	November 8	New Jersey Deer	1–2
	November 15	Gina Lollobrigida	4–7
	November 22	Actress Judy Holliday	3–7
	November 29	Broadway Twins Tani and Dran Seitz	2–3

YEAR	ISSUE	COVER SUBJECT	VALUE
1954	December 6	Jet Age man	$ 2–3
	December 13	Pope Pius XII	1–2
	December 20	Measureless Space	2–5
	December 27	Joseph and Mary	2–4
1955	January 3	Food Shopping	1–2
	January 10	Greta Garbo	5–10
	January 17	Soviet Soldiers Eye the Girls	2–3
	January 24	Tahitian Girl Bathing	2–4
	January 31	Spencer Tracy	3–5
	February 7	Vigil of Indian Girl in Hindu Festival	1–2
	February 14	Photographer's Family	1–2
	February 21	Princess Margaret	1–2
	February 28	Actress Shelley Winters	3–6
	March 7	Golden Buddha	2–3
	March 14	Convoy Shepherd	1–2
	March 21	Actress Sheree North	5–10
	March 28	Kilauea Volcano	2–4
	April 4	Confucianism Festival Boats	1–2
	April 11	Grace Kelly	6–12
	April 18	Frigate Figurehead	2–4
	April 25	Sir Anthony Eden and Lady Clarissa	2–3
	May 2	Oklahoma Dancers	2–4
	May 9	Pakistani Muslim Girl	2–3
	May 16	Happi Coats in Fashion	1–2
	May 23	Actress Leslie Caron	5–10
	May 30	Rare Playing Cards	2–3
	June 6	Henry Fonda	4–8
	June 13	Scranton Mother and Sabbath Candles	1–2
	June 20	Las Vegas Dancers	2–3
	June 27	The Constitution and Its Crew	2–4
	July 4	The Fourth of July	2–4
	July 11	Susan Strasberg	3–6
	July 18	Audrey Hepburn	3–6
	July 25	Cathy Crosby	2–4

YEAR	ISSUE	COVER SUBJECT	VALUE
1955	August 1	Nikolay Bulganin, Dwight D. Eisenhower, Edgar Faure, and Anthony Eden	$ 1–2
	August 8	Golfer Ben Hogan	1–2
	August 15	General Douglas MacArthur	2–4
	August 22	Sophia Loren	5–10
	August 29	Grandson with Grandfather	2–4
	September 5	Dior Fashions	1–2
	September 12	Joan Collins	5–10
	September 19	Guys and Dolls	3–5
	September 26	Harry and Bess Truman	3–6
	October 3	Rock Hudson	3–6
	October 10	Princess Margaret	1–2
	October 17	Princess Ira Furstenberg and Gondolier	1–2
	October 24	Cecil B. DeMille	2–4
	October 31	Partygoer Mrs. Averall Clark Jr.	2–4
	November 7	Europe's First True Human: Swanscombe Man	1–2
	November 14	Dwight D. Eisenhower	2–4
	November 21	Actress Judy Tyler	1–2
	November 28	Carol Channing	4–8
	December 5	Man-made Mink in Fashion	1–2
	December 12	Neanderthal Bear Cult	2–3
	December 19	Suits of Armor for Children	2–3
	December 26	Christianity Special Issue	2–4
1956	January 9	Riviera Fashions	1–2
	January 16	Anita Ekberg	5–10
	January 23	Harry S Truman	3–5
	January 30	Henry Ford III	2–3
	February 6	Shirley Jones	5–10
	February 13	Harry S Truman and General Douglas MacArthur	5–10
	February 20	Claire Bloom	3–6
	February 27	Eskimo Family	2–4
	March 5	Kim Novak	5–10
	March 12	Dwight D. Eisenhower	3–5

YEAR	ISSUE	COVER SUBJECT	VALUE
1956	March 19	Sir Winston Churchill	$ 3–5
	March 26	Julie Andrews	3–6
	April 2	Teenage Telephone Tie-up	1–2
	April 9	Grace Kelly	5–10
	April 16	Berber Girls	1–2
	April 23	Jayne Mansfield	15–30
	April 30	Margaret Truman and Husband	2–3
	May 7	Lazy Susan Sunbathers	2–3
	May 14	Gainsborough Look in Fashion	1–2
	May 21	Beach Towels	1–2
	May 28	Deborah Kerr and Yul Brynner	4–8
	June 4	Primping in Ancient Sumer	1–3
	June 11	Carroll Baker	4–8
	June 18	Air Age Special Issue	2–4
	June 25	Mickey Mantle	5–10
	July 2	Actress Stephanie Griffin	1–2
	July 9	Debutante Beatrice Lodge	1–2
	July 16	Gary Cooper and Tony Perkins	3–6
	July 23	The Battle of Buena Vista	1–3
	July 30	Pier Angeli	3–6
	August 6	Stricken S.S. Andrea Doria	5–10
	August 13	Dirndls in Fashion	1–2
	August 20	Audrey Hepburn	3–5
	August 27	Adlai Stevenson and Eleanor Roosevelt	2–3
	September 3	Slave Auction	2–4
	September 10	Actress Siobhan McKenna	1–2
	September 17	S.S. Andrea Doria salvage	5–10
	September 24	Actress Janet Blair	1–2
	October 1	Egyptian Artist	1–2
	October 8	Masonic Grand Masters	2–4
	October 15	Elizabeth Taylor	6–12
	October 22	Bather of Valpincon	1–3
	October 29	Plane Crash Rescue	2–4
	November 5	Dwight D. Eisenhower	2–4
	November 12	Rosalind Russell	2–4
	November 19	Wounded Egyptian Soldier	2–3
	November 26	Ingrid Bergman	3–6

YEAR	ISSUE	COVER SUBJECT	VALUE
1956	December 3	Flag on Sunken U.S.S. Arizona	$ 3–7
	December 10	Olympic Sprinter Bobby Morrow	1–2
	December 17	Baptism	1–2
	December 24	American Women Special Issue	1–3
1957	January 7	Richard M. Nixon and Hungarian Refugee Children	1–2
	January 14	Li'l Abner Chorus	1–3
	January 21	Harold Macmillan	1–2
	January 28	B-52	2–4
	February 4	Audrey Hepburn	2–4
	February 11	Vacationing Swimmer	1–2
	February 18	Julie London	2–4
	February 25	Masked Dancer	1–2
	March 4	Queen Elizabeth II and the Duke of Edinburgh	2–5
	March 11	John F. Kennedy	2–4
	March 18	Beatrice Lillie and Ziegfeld Follies Chorus	1–2
	March 25	Princess Caroline of Monaco	2–5
	April 1	Model Marie-Helene Arnaud	1–2
	April 8	Flying Blue Brothers	1–2
	April 15	Ernie Kovacs	5–10
	April 22	Carol Lynley	4–8
	April 29	Drag Race	1–2
	May 6	Sophia Loren	5–8
	May 13	Bert Lahr	3–6
	May 20	Air Force Vertijet	1–2
	May 27	Knights of Columbus	1–2
	June 3	Making of a Satellite	1–2
	June 10	Helicopter Safari	1–2
	June 17	Mayflower II Voyage	1–2
	June 24	Prince Juan Carlos of Spain	1–2
	July 1	Billy Graham	2–3
	July 8	King Ranch Roundup	1–2
	July 15	Maria Schell	2–4
	July 22	Dr. Hannes Lindemann in a Transatlantic Canoe	1–2

YEAR	ISSUE	COVER SUBJECT	VALUE
1957	July 29	Babysitter	$ 2–3
	August 5	Debutante Julia Williamson	2–3
	August 12	Mai Britt	3–5
	August 19	Four DuPonts	1–2
	August 26	San Simeon's Pool	1–2
	September 2	Balloonist	2–4
	September 9	New York Street Gang	2–3
	September 16	Cincinnati Police Chief	2–3
	September 23	Suzy Parker	1–2
	September 30	Kay Kendall and Husband, Rex Harrison	2–4
	October 7	U.S. Troops in Little Rock	1–2
	October 14	Milwaukee Parade for Braves and Manager Fred Honey	2–4
	October 21	U.S. Scientists Plot Sputnik Orbit	2–3
	October 28	Queen Elizabeth II Opens Canada's Parliament	2–4
	November 4	Elizabeth Taylor and Daughter	5–10
	November 11	Air-Supported Dome for Swimming	1–2
	November 18	Rocket Designer Wernher von Braun	2–4
	November 25	Elsa Martinelli	2–4
	December 2	Nikita Khrushchev	2–3
	December 9	Richard M. Nixon	2–4
	December 16	Mary and Jesus	2–4
1958	January 6	Space Pilot Scott Crossfield	2–4
	January 13	Revolution in Petrograd	2–4
	January 20	Texas Senator Lyndon B. Johnson	2–3
	January 27	Ski Fashions	1–2
	February 3	Shirley Temple and Her 3-year-old Daughter	10–20
	February 10	Ralph Bellamy	2–4
	February 17	Tracking a U.S. Satellite	2–3
	February 24	Fishing in Germany	1–2
	March 3	Sally Ann Howes	2–4

YEAR	ISSUE	COVER SUBJECT	VALUE
1958	March 10	Yul Brynner	$ 3–6
	March 17	The McGuire Sisters	5–8
	March 24	Soviet and U.S. High Schoolers	2–3
	March 31	Science Teachers	1–2
	April 7	Sugar Ray Robinson and Carmen Basilio	5–8
	April 14	Actress Gwen Verdon	1–2
	April 21	Jacqueline, Caroline, and John F. Kennedy	1–2
	April 28	Willie Mays in San Francisco	5–8
	May 5	Cancer Patient and Radiation Machine	1–2
	May 12	Former Iranian Queen Soraya	1–2
	May 19	Margaret O'Brien	2–4
	May 26	Venezuelan Rioters Attack Richard M. Nixon's Car	1–2
	June 2	Charles de Gaulle	1–2
	June 9	French Veteran	1–2
	June 16	Children in Swings	2–3
	June 23	Seniors with Yearbooks	1–2
	June 30	Sherman Adams and Dwight D. Eisenhower	1–2
	July 7	Lebanese Rebels	1–2
	July 14	Oklahoma Wheat	2–3
	July 21	Roy Campanella	5–10
	July 28	Marines in Lebanon	2–3
	August 4	General James M. Gavin	1–2
	August 11	Couple Sailing	1–3
	August 18	Anne Frank	3–5
	August 25	Two Airline Stewardesses	1–2
	September 1	Commander William Anderson of the Submarine Nautilus	2–4
	September 8	Galápagos Tortoise and Flycatcher	1–2
	September 15	Bing Crosby's Four Sons	2–4
	September 22	George Burns and Gracie Allen	5–10
	September 29	Gun Draw	2–4
	October 6	Actress France Nuyen	1–2

YEAR	ISSUE	COVER SUBJECT	VALUE
1958	October 13	British Field Marshal Montgomery	$ 2–4
	October 20	Mamie Eisenhower	1–2
	October 27	College of Cardinals	1–2
	November 3	Aga Khan	1–2
	November 10	Pope John XXIII	1–2
	November 17	Nelson and Happy Rockefeller	1–2
	November 24	Kim Novak	3–8
	December 1	Ricky Nelson	10–20+
	December 8	New York Society Women	1–2
	December 15	Prehistoric Explosion	1–3
	December 22	U.S. Entertainment Special Issue	2–4
1959	January 5	New Generation in Shanghai	1–2
	January 12	Senator Hubert Humphrey	1–3
	January 19	Fidel Castro	2–4
	January 26	Saber-toothed Cat	1–3
	February 2	Pat Boone	3–7
	February 9	Shirley MacLaine with Daughter	2–4
	February 16	Miami Chorus Girls	2–4
	February 23	Gwen Verdon	1–2
	March 2	Princess Luciana Pignatelli	1–2
	March 9	Jack Parr	2–4
	March 16	Brazilian Jaguar	2–3
	March 23	ID Cards of a Soviet Agent	1–2
	March 30	Debbie Reynolds in Spain	3–7
	April 6	Wagons on the Oregon Trail	3–6
	April 13	Weightless in Space Test	1–3
	April 20	Marilyn Monroe	10–20+
	April 27	Early California Bear Hunt	2–4
	May 4	Dalai Lama	1–2
	May 11	Old West Silver Queen Baby Doe Tabor	1–2
	May 18	Jimmy Hoffa	1–3
	May 25	Mr. and Mrs. Sherman Adams	1–2
	June 1	Boating in Kansas	1–3
	June 8	Audrey Hepburn	2–4

YEAR	ISSUE	COVER SUBJECT	VALUE
1959	June 15	Space Monkeys Able and Baker	$ 2–3
	June 22	First Air Force Academy Graduates	2–3
	June 29	Zsa Zsa Gabor and Her Ghostwriter	2–4
	July 6	Gardner McKay	1–2
	July 13	Old Age	1–2
	July 20	Ingemar Johansson and Fiancée	1–3
	July 27	Peace Ships	2–3
	August 3	Kingston Trio	3–6
	August 10	Wives of Mikoyan, Nixon, Khrushchev, and Kozlov	2–3
	August 17	Mai Britt	2–4
	August 24	Senator and Mrs. John F. Kennedy	2–4
	August 31	Rip Van Winkle	2–4
	September 7	Bill Lundigan and Gene Barry	2–3
	September 14	Astronauts	2–4
	September 21	Astronauts' Wives	2–4
	September 28	Migrating Ducks	2–4
	October 5	Nikita Khrushchev with Iowa Farmer	2–4
	October 12	Family Doctor	2–3
	October 19	Mums and Missiles in Peking	2–4
	October 26	Quiz Star Charles van Doren	1–2
	November 2	Jackie Gleason	4–8
	November 9	Marilyn Monroe	10–15
	November 16	Jewelry in Fashion	1–2
	November 23	Mary Martin	2–3
	November 30	Pretty Postage Stamps	1–2
	December 7	Shah's Fiancée Farah Diba	1–3
	December 14	Hawaiian Volcano Erupts	2–5
	December 21	Dwight D. Eisenhower in Pakistan	2–4
	December 28	The Good Life Special Issue	2–4
1960	January 11	Actress Dina Merrill	1–2
	January 18	Ghanaian Speaker of the House	1–2

YEAR	ISSUE	COVER SUBJECT	VALUE
1960	January 25	Father Marquette Conquers Manitou	$ 2–3
	February 1	Dinah Shore	2–4
	February 8	U.S. Olympic Skiers	1–2
	February 15	Navy Bathyscaphe	1–2
	February 22	Henry and Jane Fonda	4–8
	February 29	Olympic Ski Jumper	1–2
	March 7	Hypnosis	1–2
	March 14	Princess Margaret and Anthony Armstrong	2–3
	March 21	Billy Graham in Africa	2–4
	March 28	Hubert Humphrey and John F. Kennedy	2–3
	April 4	Marlon Brando	3–7
	April 11	Silvana Mangano	1–2
	April 18	Elopers Gamble Benedict and Andrei Porumbeau	1–2
	April 25	Tourists on Lover's Leap	2–3
	May 2	Trampoliners	2–3
	May 9	Yvette Mimieux	3–7
	May 16	Princess Margaret	2–4
	May 23	Minuteman Statue	1–2
	May 30	Nikita Khrushchev	1–3
	June 6	Lee Remick	3–5
	June 13	Hayley Mills	10–20
	June 20	L.A. Freeway	1–2
	June 27	Alaskan Walrus	2–4
	July 4	U.S. Politics Special Issue	1–2
	July 11	Nelson Rockefeller and His Grandchildren	1–2
	July 18	Ina Balin	1–2
	July 25	Kennedy Demonstration	1–2
	August 1	Giraffes and Children in New-Style Amusement Park	2–3
	August 8	Richard and Patricia Nixon	2–3
	August 15	Marilyn Monroe and Yves Montand	10–20
	August 22	U.S. Olympic Swimmers	1–3

YEAR	ISSUE	COVER SUBJECT	VALUE
1960	August 29	Record Free-fall	$ 1–3
	September 5	Ernest Hemingway	2–4
	September 12	U.S. Olympic Gymnasts	1–2
	September 19	Grandma Moses	2–4
	September 26	Norell Fashions	1–2
	October 3	President Dwight D. Eisenhower	1–2
	October 10	Doris Day	3–7
	October 17	Henry Cabot Lodge and Wife	1–2
	October 24	Nancy Kwan	2–5
	October 31	Halloween	2–5
	November 7	The Earth in the Magnetic Field	2–4
	November 14	Sophia Loren	2–5
	November 21	Victorious John F. Kennedy	2–4
	November 28	Carroll Baker	2–4
	December 5	Baltimore Colts Kickoff	2–4
	December 12	Jill Haworth and Sal Mineo	3–6
	December 19	President Kennedy and Wife	2–4
	December 26	25th Anniversary Special	2–4
1961	January 6	Civil War Cavalry Charge	3–5
	January 13	Clark Gable	4–8
	January 20	Cancer Surgeon	1–2
	January 27	Kennedys	2–3
	February 3	Queen Elizabeth II in India	2–4
	February 10	Astrochimp Ham	1–2
	February 17	Shirley MacLaine	2–4
	February 24	UN's Dag Hammarskjold	1–2
	March 3	John Glenn	3–5
	March 10	Maurice Chevalier and Bing Crosby	3–5
	March 17	Model Sheila Finn	1–2
	March 24	Puppets of Pack Parr and Ed Sullivan	2–4
	March 31	Cherub	2–3
	April 7	Ocean Fishing	1–2
	April 14	Mrs. Clark Gable and Son John	2–4
	April 21	Cosmonaut Yury Gagarin	2–4
	April 28	Elizabeth Taylor	5–10

YEAR	ISSUE	COVER SUBJECT	VALUE
1961	May 5	Anna Maria Alberghetti with Puppets	$ 2–4
	May 12	Alan Shepard Picked Up at Sea	2–4
	May 19	Alan Shepard	2–4
	May 26	Jackie Kennedy in Canada	2–3
	June 2	Fidel Castro	2–4
	June 9	John F. Kennedy with Charles de Gaulle	2–3
	June 16	Princess Hohenioche	1–2
	June 23	Princess Grace	4–8
	June 30	Leslie Caron	3–5
	July 7	Dwight D. Eisenhower	2–3
	July 14	Ernest Hemingway	2–4
	July 21	Rio Slum Child	2–3
	July 28	Brigitte Bardot	5–10
	August 4	John F. Kennedy	2–3
	August 11	Sophia Loren	3–6
	August 18	Mickey Mantle and Roger Maris	6–12
	August 25	West Berliners	1–2
	September 1	Jacqueline Kennedy	1–2
	September 8	U.S. Tank Soldier	2–3
	September 15	Civilian Fallout Suits	2–3
	September 22	Hurricane Carla	2–4
	September 29	Dag Hammarskjold's Coffin	1–2
	October 6	Elizabeth Taylor	5–10
	October 13	African Warrior	2–4
	October 20	Communist Leaders	2–3
	October 27	GI in Training	2–3
	November 3	A Daughter's Goodbye to National Guardsman	2–4
	November 10	Nikita Khrushchev	1–2
	November 17	Minnesota Vikings	2–3
	November 24	One-year-old John F. Kennedy	1–3
	December 1	Italian Fashions	1–2
	December 8	Plum Pudding Flambé	1–2
	December 15	Chartres Cathedral	1–2
	December 22	Splendid Outdoors Special Issue	1–2

YEAR	ISSUE	COVER SUBJECT	VALUE
1962	January 5	Lucille Ball	$5–10
	January 12	Community Fallout Shelter	2–4
	January 19	Iceboating	1–3
	January 26	Robert Kennedy	1–3
	February 2	John Glenn	2–4
	February 9	Seattle World's Fair	2–4
	February 16	Rock Hudson	2–4
	February 23	Shirley MacLaine	2–4
	March 2	John Glenn Back from Space	2–5
	March 9	Motorcade for John Glenn	2–4
	March 16	Richard M. Nixon	2–3
	March 23	Desert Housing Development	2–3
	March 30	Robert Frost	2–3
	April 6	Stretching the Dollar	1–2
	April 13	Elizabeth Taylor and Richard Burton	4–8
	April 20	Audrey Hepburn	2–4
	April 27	Moonsuit Test	2–3
	May 4	Seattle World's Fair Monorail	2–5
	May 11	Bob Hope	2–4
	May 18	Scott Carpenter and Wife	2–3
	May 25	Prince Juan Carlos Weds His Princess	2–3
	June 1	Rene Carpenter Watching Scott Take Off	1–2
	June 8	Ticker Tape Parade Special	1–2
	June 15	Natalie Wood	5–10
	June 22	Marilyn Monroe	8–15
	June 29	Massachusetts Senatorial Candidates	2–4
	July 6	Balloon	2–4
	July 13	John F. Kennedy in Mexico	2–3
	July 20	H-bomb Fireball	2–4
	July 27	Elsa Martinelli	1–2
	August 3	Astronaut Bob White with His Son	1–3
	August 10	Janet Leigh	4–8
	August 17	Marilyn Monroe	8–15

YEAR	ISSUE	COVER SUBJECT	VALUE
1962	August 24	Soviet Space Capsules	$ 2–3
	August 31	Reenactment of the Great Mail Robbery	2–4
	September 7	Caroline Kennedy	1–2
	September 14	The Takeover Generation Special Issue	1–3
	September 21	Iran Earthquake Victims	2–4
	September 28	Don Drysdale	1–2
	October 5	Jackie Gleason with Sue Ane Langdon	5–10
	October 12	Pope John XXIII	1–2
	October 19	Special California Issue	2–4
	October 26	The Human Body	2–3
	November 2	U.S. Navy off Cuba	2–4
	November 9	U Thant and British Ambassador	1–2
	November 16	Indian Soldier	1–2
	November 23	Bounty of Food Special Issue	1–2
	November 30	Sid Caesar	5–7
	December 7	The Human Body	2–4
	December 14	Marlon Brando	2–5
	December 21	The Sea Special Issue	2–4
1963	January 4	Greek Statue	2–3
	January 11	Ann-Margret	5–8
	January 18	The Trojan Horse	3–5
	January 25	Vietcong Prisoners	3–6
	February 1	Alfred Hitchcock	3–5
	February 8	Greek Statue	2–4
	February 15	Moving Lincoln's Body	3–6
	February 22	Alice and Ellen Kessler	1–2
	March 1	Snakes	2–4
	March 8	Jean Seberg	3–6
	March 15	Fidel Castro	3–6
	March 22	Polaris Sub Commander John L. From Jr.	2–5
	March 29	Costa Ricans	2–4
	April 5	Spartans Stand at Thermopylae	3–6
	April 12	Helen Klaben Lost in the Yukon	3–6

YEAR	ISSUE	COVER SUBJECT	VALUE
1963	April 19	Elizabeth Taylor and Richard Burton	$5–10
	April 26	Young Jackie Kennedy	2–4
	May 3	Alexander the Great	4–8
	May 10	Bay of Pigs	4–8
	May 17	Nelson and Happy Rockefeller	2–3
	May 24	Gordon Cooper	1–2
	May 31	Gordon and Trudy Cooper	1–2
	June 7	Pope John XXIII	1–2
	June 14	St. Peter's	1–2
	June 21	Shirley MacLaine	2–4
	June 28	Medgar Evers's Widow	2–3
	July 5	Pope Paul VI	1–2
	July 12	Steve McQueen	5–8
	July 19	Greek Sculpture	3–4
	July 26	Tuesday Weld	5–10
	August 2	Sandy Koufax	3–5
	August 9	Averell Harriman and Nikita Khrushchev	1–2
	August 16	Hospital Vigil over President Kennedy	4–7
	August 23	Frank Sinatra and Frank Jr.	4–8
	August 30	Paris Fashions	1–3
	September 6	Washington March Leaders	1–2
	September 13	Special Russia Issue	2–3
	September 20	U.S. Team on Mt. Everest	2–4
	September 27	Astronauts Frank Borman, Thomas Stafford, and James Lovell	2–4
	October 4	DNA Molecule	2–3
	October 11	Vietnam's Madame Nhu	2–4
	October 18	Grand Duchess Anastasia and Family	2–4
	October 25	Yvette Mimieux	3–6
	November 1	Senator Barry Goldwater	2–3
	November 8	President Johnson's Former Aide Bobby Baker	1–2
	November 15	South Vietnam Soldiers	3–6

YEAR	ISSUE	COVER SUBJECT	VALUE
1963	November 22	Elizabeth Ashley	$2–3
	November 29	John F. Kennedy	2–3
	December 6	John F. Kennedy's Family Waiting to Join Funeral Procession	2–4
	December 13	Lyndon B. Johnson	1–2
	December 20	The Movies Special Issue	4–7
1964	January 3	S.S. Lakonia's Fire at Sea	2–4
	January 10	General Douglas MacArthur	2–4
	January 17	Pope Paul VI	2–3
	January 24	Canal Zone Rioters	2–3
	January 31	Geraldine Chaplin	2–4
	February 7	British Commando with Tanganyikan Mutineers	2–4
	February 14	Olympic Ski Jumper	1–2
	February 21	Lee Harvey Oswald	2–4
	February 28	Armed Turks on Cyprus	2–3
	March 6	Cassius Clay	2–4
	March 13	World War I British Wounded	2–5
	March 20	Ambassador Henry Cabot Lodge in Saigon	2–3
	March 27	Charles de Gaulle with President Lopez Mateos of Mexico	1–2
	April 3	Carol Channing	2–4
	April 10	Alaskan Earthquake	5–8
	April 17	General Douglas MacArthur's Hat	2–4
	April 24	Richard Burton	2–5
	May 1	The N.Y. World's Fair Opens	4–8
	May 8	Campaign Buttons	1–2
	May 15	Luci Baines Johnson	1–2
	May 22	Barbra Streisand	3–6
	May 29	Jacqueline Kennedy	2–3
	June 5	Cremation of Nehru	2–3
	June 12	U.S. Officer on Patrol in Vietnam	3–5
	June 19	LBJ's Beagles	2–4

YEAR	ISSUE	COVER SUBJECT	VALUE
1964	June 26	Pennsylvania Governor William Scranton	$ 1–2
	July 3	Robert Kennedy with Kennedy Family Children	2–3
	July 10	Lee Harvey Oswald with His Wife, Marina	3–6
	July 17	Carroll Baker with Masai Warriors	2–5
	July 24	Senator Barry Goldwater with His Wife	2–3
	July 31	Olympic Diver	1–2
	August 7	Marilyn Monroe	5–10
	August 14	LBJ	1–2
	August 21	South Vietnam's General Khanh	2–4
	August 28	The Beatles	10–20
	September 4	LBJ and Daughter	1–2
	September 11	Japan Special Issue	2–4
	September 18	Sophia Loren	2–4
	September 25	Saturn V Rocket	2–4
	October 2	John F. Kennedy's Assassination	3–5
	October 9	Olympic Swimmer	1–2
	October 16	Berlin Escape	2–4
	October 23	Leonid Brezhnev	1–2
	October 30	Olympic Gold Medalist Don Schollander	1–2
	November 6	Shirley Eaton	1–2
	November 13	LBJ and Hubert Humphrey	1–2
	November 20	Soviet Marshal Rodion Malinovsky and General A. P. Beloborodov	1–2
	November 27	Vietnam GIs	4–8
	December 4	Congo Missionary Dr. Paul Carlson	1–2
	December 11	The Rockettes	2–3
	December 18	Elizabeth Taylor	3–7
	December 25	The Bible Special Issue	2–5

YEAR	ISSUE	COVER SUBJECT	VALUE
1965	January 8	California Foods	$1–2
	January 15	Ted Kennedy	1–2
	January 22	Peter O'Toole	2–4
	January 29	LBJ's Inauguration	1–2
	February 5	Winston Churchill's Casket Carried by Grenadier Guard	2–4
	February 12	Mercenaries Mop Up in the Congo	2–4
	February 19	Albert Schweitzer	2–4
	February 26	North Vietnam Postage Stamp	2–4
	March 5	Aftermath of Malcolm X's Death	2–4
	March 12	Julie Andrews	3–5
	March 19	Civil Rights in Selma	2–4
	March 26	Martin Luther King, Jr.	2–3
	April 2	Gemini's Splashdown	2–4
	April 9	Robert Kennedy on Mountain Summit	2–3
	April 16	Aboard the U.S. Copter Yankee	2–5
	April 23	Frank Sinatra	2–4
	April 30	Fetus	2–4
	May 7	John Wayne	3–6
	May 14	Skateboarding	1–2
	May 21	Ku Klux Klan Defense Lawyer	1–2
	May 28	New York Congressman John Lindsay	1–2
	June 4	German Measles Blood Test	1–2
	June 11	Waterloo	3–5
	June 18	Astronaut Ed White in Space Walk	2–4
	June 25	Indian Tiger	2–4
	July 2	Wounded Marine Evacuated in Vietnam	3–6
	July 9	Yachting on the Riviera	1–2
	July 16	John F. Kennedy	1–2
	July 23	Adlai Stevenson	1–2
	July 30	Mickey Mantle	3–6
	August 6	U.S.S. Oklahoma City Shelling Vietcong	3–5

YEAR	ISSUE	COVER SUBJECT	VALUE
1965	August 13	Lady Bird Johnson	$ 1–2
	August 20	Draft Inductees	1–2
	August 27	Riots in Watts	2–4
	September 3	Astronaut Charles Conrad Lifting Off	2–4
	September 10	Expectant Mother	1–2
	September 17	Indian Soldier	1–2
	September 24	Baja California as Seen from Spaceship	2–4
	October 1	Eskimo Game	2–3
	October 8	Hawaiian Beauty Elizabeth Logue	1–2
	October 15	Pope Paul VI in Yankee Stadium	1–3
	October 22	Mary Martin in Vietnam	2–4
	October 29	The Temples of Abu Simbel	2–4
	November 5	John F. Kennedy	2–3
	November 12	New York City Mayor-elect John Lindsay	1–2
	November 19	Manhattan Power Blackout	2–5
	November 26	Vietcong Prisoner	3–6
	December 3	LBJ with Princess Margaret	1–2
	December 10	Texas Linebacker Tommy Nobis	1–2
	December 17	Vatican	1–2
	December 24	The City Special Issue	1–2
1966	January 7	Sean Connery	5–10
	January 14	North Vietnam's Ho Chi Minh and Prime Minister Pham Van Dong	2–4
	January 21	Indian Prime Minister Shastri Lies in State	1–2
	January 28	Actress Catherine Spaak	1–2
	February 4	Sammy Davis, Jr., Harry Belafonte, and Sidney Poitier	2–4
	February 11	Wounded GIs in Vietnam	3–6
	February 18	Model of the Flu Germ	1–2
	February 25	Sunrise Mission over South Vietnam	3–7

YEAR	ISSUE	COVER SUBJECT	VALUE
1966	March 4	Bust of Roman Citizen	$ 2–4
	March 11	Batman	10–20
	March 18	Barbra Streisand	3–6
	March 25	LSD Capsule	1–2
	April 1	Charlie Chaplin and Sophia Loren	2–4
	April 8	Captain Pete Dawkins	2–4
	April 15	Louis Armstrong	2–4
	April 22	Injured Monk in Vietnam	2–4
	April 29	Julie Christie	2–4
	May 6	Jacqueline Kennedy	1–2
	May 13	Mod Male Fashions	2–4
	May 20	Bugging Device	1–2
	May 27	Discotheque	1–3
	June 3	Bust of Marcus Aurelius	2–4
	June 10	Elizabeth Taylor	3–6
	June 17	Angela Lansbury	2–3
	June 24	Prescription Pills	1–2
	July 1	Moonscape	2–4
	July 8	Claudia Cardinale	3–5
	July 15	Young Black Militants	1–2
	July 22	Birth	2–4
	July 29	Murderer's Fingerprints	1–3
	August 5	Gemini 10 Docking with Agena 10	2–4
	August 12	Texas Store Window Shattered by Sniper	2–4
	August 19	Luci Johnson and Pat Nixon	1–2
	August 26	Strike Fever	1–2
	September 2	Paris Fashion	1–2
	September 9	Psychedelic Artist	2–4
	September 16	Sophia Loren	2–4
	September 23	Chinese Imperial Magistrate and Guards	1–2
	September 30	Rex Harrison	1–2
	October 7	Ian Fleming	2–4
	October 14	Pro Football Mayhem	1–2
	October 21	Zebra	1–2

YEAR	ISSUE	COVER SUBJECT	VALUE
1966	October 28	Wounded Marine	$3–6
	November 4	LBJ in Vietnam	1–3
	November 11	Jean-Paul Belmondo	1–2
	November 18	Robert Kennedy	1–2
	November 25	Frame 230 of John F. Kennedy Assassination Film Footage	2–3
	December 2	Actress Melina Mercouri	1–2
	December 9	Draftees	2–4
	December 16	Restoring The Last Supper	2–4
	December 23	Photography Special Issue	2–4
1967	January 6	Black Leopard	2–3
	January 13	Navy Patrol over Mekong River	4–8
	January 20	China's Red Guard	1–2
	January 27	Bathing Suits in Fashion	1–2
	February 3	Astronauts Roger Chaffee, Ed White, and Gus Grissom	2–4
	February 10	Gus Grissom's Caisson at Arlington Cemetery	2–4
	February 17	Underground Culture Leader	1–2
	February 24	Elizabeth Taylor	2–5
	March 3	Leonardo da Vinci Sketch	2–3
	March 10	U.S. Paratroopers over Vietnam	3–6
	March 17	Charlie Brown and Snoopy	3–5
	March 24	Easter in Jerusalem	3–5
	March 31	Infant	1–3
	April 7	Hanoi Air Raid Alert	3–6
	April 14	Sharon Percy Weds John D. Rockefeller IV	1–2
	April 21	The Individual	1–2
	April 28	U.S. Pavilion at Expo '67	1–2
	May 5	Mia Farrow	1–3
	May 12	Truman Capote, Scott Wilson, and Robert Blake	1–3
	May 19	Astronaut Wally Schirra	1–3
	May 26	General Lew Walt	1–2
	June 2	China's Cultural Red Guards	1–3
	June 9	Sir Francis Chichester	1–2

YEAR	ISSUE	COVER SUBJECT	VALUE
1967	June 16	Israeli Troops Take Prisoners in Gaza	$2–3
	June 23	Israeli Soldier Cools Off in the Suez Canal	2–3
	June 30	Aleksey Kosygin and LBJ	1–2
	July 7	LBJ	1–2
	July 14	Princess Lee Radziwill	1–2
	July 21	Kidnapped U.S. Official in Vietnam	2–4
	July 28	Newark Riot Victim	2–4
	August 4	Troops Patrol Detroit	2–3
	August 11	U.S.S. Forrestal Disaster	2–4
	August 18	Veruschka	2–4
	August 25	Marine and Young Vietnamese Friend	3–6
	September 1	Posters	1–2
	September 8	Carl Yastrzemski	3–5
	September 15	Svetlana Alliluyeva	1–2
	September 22	Svetlana Alliluyeva	1–2
	September 29	Antiballistic Missile Test	1–2
	October 6	S.S. Queen Mary	2–3
	October 13	Ingrid Bergman	2–3
	October 20	U.S. POW in Vietnam	3–6
	October 27	GI at Con Thien	3–6
	November 3	Runaway Kids	1–2
	November 10	Leningrad Music Hall Girls	2–3
	November 17	Jacqueline Kennedy in Cambodia	1–2
	November 24	Governor Connally, Kennedys in San Antonio	1–2
	December 1	The American Indian	2–4
	December 8	Pearl Bailey	2–3
	December 15	Human Heart Recipient Louis Washansky	1–2
	December 22	The Wild World Special Issue	2–3
1968	January 5	Katharine Hepburn	2–4
	January 12	Faye Dunaway	2–4
	January 19	Human Heart and Surgeon	1–2

YEAR	ISSUE	COVER SUBJECT	VALUE
1968	January 26	Diet Pills	$ 1–2
	February 2	Aleksey Kosygin	1–2
	February 9	Captured Vietcong Guerrilla	2–4
	February 16	North Vietnamese Soldiers	3–6
	February 23	Olympic Gold Medalist Figure Skater Peggy Fleming	1–3
	March 1	Georgia O'Keeffe	1–2
	March 8	Black Child	1–2
	March 15	Boris Karloff	10–20+
	March 22	Ho Chi Minh	2–4
	March 29	Jane Fonda	5–10
	April 5	King Tut	2–4
	April 12	Martin Luther King, Jr.	1–2
	April 19	Mrs. Martin Luther King, Jr.	1–2
	April 26	Phillipe Thyraud de Vosjoli	1–2
	May 3	James Earl Ray	1–3
	May 10	Paul Newman	1–3
	May 17	The Generation Gap	1–3
	May 24	John Lindsay	1–2
	May 31	Egyptian Goddess Serket	2–4
	June 7	Eugene McCarthy	1–2
	June 14	Robert F. Kennedy	1–2
	June 21	James Earl Ray and Sirhan Sirhan	1–2
	June 28	Jefferson Airplane	10–20
	July 5	Presidency Special Issue	1–2
	July 12	Starving Children of Biafra	1–2
	July 19	Young American Nomads on Crete	1–2
	July 26	American and Soviet Flight Attendants	1–2
	August 2	George Wallace, Nixon, Reagan	1–2
	August 9	Air Traffic Jams	1–2
	August 16	Richard Nixon and Wife	1–2
	August 23	Security Chiefs at Chicago Convention	1–2
	August 30	Czech Freedom Fighters	1–2
	September 6	Hubert Humphrey and Edmund Muskie	1–2

YEAR	ISSUE	COVER SUBJECT	VALUE
1968	September 13	The Beatles	$10–20
	September 20	Arthur Ashe	1–2
	September 27	Swedish Fashions	1–2
	October 4	Probing the Sea	2–3
	October 11	Pope John XXIII	1–2
	October 18	Paul Newman and Joanne Woodward	1–2
	October 25	Apollo 7	2–4
	November 1	Jacqueline Kennedy and Aristotle Onassis	1–2
	November 8	Vietnam War Victim	2–4
	November 15	Nixon	1–2
	November 22	Frederick Douglass	2–4
	November 29	Egyptian Soldier Tests Soviet Tank	2–3
	December 6	Police Violence at the Chicago Convention	1–2
	December 13	Baltimore Colts	2–4
	December 20	Mark Twain	2–4
	December 27	Picasso Special Issue	2–4
1969	January 10	The Incredible Year Special Issue	2–3
	January 17	Sirhan Sirhan	1–2
	January 24	Catherine Deneuve	1–2
	January 31	Aerial View of the Washington Monument	1–2
	February 7	Lloyd Bucher of the U.S.S. Pueblo	2–4
	February 14	Barbra Streisand	3–5
	February 21	Nixon	1–2
	February 28	Herons	1–2
	March 7	Nixon	1–2
	March 14	Lunar Module on Apollo 9	3–5
	March 21	Woody Allen	1–2
	March 28	Orangutan	1–3
	April 4	Sensuality in the Arts	1–3
	April 11	Dwight D. Eisenhower's Bier	2–4

YEAR	ISSUE	COVER SUBJECT	VALUE
1969	April 18	Mae West	$ 2–4
	April 25	Harvard Professor	1–2
	May 2	Judy Collins	3–6
	May 9	Peter Falk	2–4
	May 16	High School	1–2
	May 23	Rowan and Martin	3–5
	May 30	Ambulance	1–2
	June 6	The Moon's Surface	2–5
	June 13	Human Embryo and Mother and Infant	2–3
	June 20	Joe Namath	2–3
	June 27	American Dead in Vietnam	3–6
	July 4	Neil Armstrong	3–5
	July 11	Dustin Hoffman	2–3
	July 18	Youth Communes	1–2
	July 25	Neil Armstrong	2–4
	August 1	Ted Kennedy	1
	August 8	American Flag on the Moon	3–6
	August 15	Dollar Squeeze	1
	August 22	New York Fashions	1
	August 29	Norman Mailer	1
	September 5	Peter Max	5–10
	September 12	Coretta Scott King	1
	September 19	Children	1–2
	September 26	New York Mets	2–4
	October 3	Ballet Dancer	1–2
	October 10	Revolution	1–2
	October 17	Naomi Sims	1
	October 24	Dissent	1–2
	October 31	Marijuana	1–2
	November 7	Paul McCartney and Family	4–8
	November 14	Green Beret	2–4
	November 21	Johnny Cash	2–4
	November 28	The U.S. Mail Mess	1
	December 5	African Antelope	1–2
	December 12	Apollo 12 Moon Walk	2–4
	December 19	Charles Manson	2–4
	December 26	60s Special Issue	2–4

YEAR	ISSUE	COVER SUBJECT	VALUE
1970	January 9	Into the 70s Special Issue	$2–4
	January 23	Johnny Carson	2–4
	January 30	Snow Monkey	1–2
	February 6	Robert Redford	1–2
	February 13	The Dollar Bill	1
	February 20	Architect Turned Clown	1
	February 27	The Spirit of Cinema America	2–3
	March 6	Gold Medalist Skier Billy Kidd	1–2
	March 13	Hemlines in Fashion	1–2
	March 20	Former Nun	1
	March 27	Credit Cards	1
	April 3	Lauren Bacall	2–3
	April 10	Denton Cooley and Michael DeBakey	1–2
	April 17	Zero Population Growth Campaign Button	1
	April 24	Jim Lovell	1–2
	May 1	Chapel Hill Coed	1–2
	May 8	Spiro Agnew	1
	May 15	Wounded Kent State Student	1–2
	May 22	Our Forgotten Wounded	1–2
	May 29	Brenda Vaccaro	1–2
	June 5	A Bear Market	1
	June 12	Palestinian Training Camp for Kids	2–3
	June 19	Dennis Hopper	1–2
	June 26	Americans in a Spanish Prison	1–2
	July 3	Iowa Boy Scouts	2–3
	July 10	California Girls at the Beach	2–4
	July 17	Rose Kennedy with Ted and Joan	1
	July 24	Candice Bergen	2–4
	July 31	Bebe Rebozo	1
	August 7	LBJ, Robert Kennedy, and JFK	1
	August 14	Summer Nomads	1–2
	August 21	Midiskirts in Fashion	1–2
	August 28	Pornography	2–3
	September 4	Liberty Congratulates Woman Voter	2–3

YEAR	ISSUE	COVER SUBJECT	VALUE
1970	September 11	Angela Davis	$2–3
	September 18	Engelbert Humperdinck	3–5
	September 25	Male Plumage in Fashion	1
	October 2	Martha Mitchell	1
	October 9	Egypt's Abdel Nasser	2–4
	October 16	Spiro Agnew	1
	October 23	Muhammad Ali	1–2
	October 30	Dick Cavett	1
	November 6	Nixon at 14	2–3
	November 13	Nixon	1
	November 20	Oberlin Students in Coed Dorm	1–2
	November 27	Khrushchev	1
	December 4	Khrushchev	1
	December 11	Health Food	1
	December 18	Buckley and Families	1
	December 25	Prizewinning Pictures Special Issue	1
1971	January 8	The New Shape of America Special Issue	2–3
	January 22	Tricia Nixon	1–2
	January 29	Bob Hope	2–3
	February 5	The New Army	2–3
	February 12	Jacqueline Onassis	1
	February 19	Rita Hayworth	2–4
	February 26	Snowmobiles	1–2
	March 5	Joe Frazier and Muhammad Ali	1–2
	March 12	Explosion among South Vietnamese Soldiers	2–4
	March 19	Frazier Beating Ali	2–3
	March 26	Walter Cronkite	1
	April 2	Pregnant High Schooler	1–2
	April 9	J. Edgar Hoover	2–3
	April 16	Paul and Linda McCartney	4–8
	April 23	Jane Fonda	3–6
	April 30	Chinese Children Marching	1–2
	May 7	Germaine Greer	1
	May 14	Carol Burnett	2–4
	May 21	LBJ with Grandson	1–2

YEAR	ISSUE	COVER SUBJECT	VALUE
1971	May 28	Chris Brown	$ 1
	June 4	Christina Ford	1
	June 11	Ted and Joan Kennedy	1
	June 18	Tricia Nixon	1
	June 25	Frank Sinatra	2–4
	July 2	American Indians	2–4
	July 9	Photography Contest Winner	1–2
	July 16	Bess Myerson	1
	July 23	Clint Eastwood	2–4
	July 30	Chou En-lai	1–2
	August 6	Ann-Margret	2–4
	August 13	The Woman Problem	1
	August 20	Princess Anne	1–2
	August 27	Game Plan for the Dollar	1–2
	September 3	Americans Outdoors Special Issue	2–4
	September 10	TV's 25th Anniversary Special	2–4
	September 17	Heart Transplant Patient	1–2
	September 24	The Jackson Five with Their Parents	10–20
	October 1	The Human Brain	1–3
	October 8	Americans Shop for New Cars	1–2
	October 15	The Opening of Disney World	3–5
	October 22	The Brain	2–4
	October 29	David Cassidy	10–20
	November 5	Edmund Muskie	1–2
	November 12	Bobby Fischer	1–2
	November 19	Barred Window to Keep Crime Out	1–2
	November 26	Chemistry of Madness	1–2
	December 3	Los Angeles Rams and the Baltimore Colts	2–3
	December 10	Cybill Shepherd	2–4
	December 17	Children Special Issue	1–3
	December 31	The Year in Pictures	1–3
1972	January 14	Dallas Cowboys Roger Staubach and Tom Landry	2–4
	January 21	Single U.S. Vietnam Casualty in a Week	2–5

YEAR	ISSUE	COVER SUBJECT	VALUE
1972	January 28	John Wayne	$ 3–5
	February 4	Howard Hughes	1–2
	February 11	Nina van Pallandt	1
	February 18	Japanese Olympic Ski Jumper	1–2
	February 25	Elizabeth Taylor	2–4
	March 3	Mao Tse-tung	1–2
	March 10	Marlon Brando	2–4
	March 17	Dropout Wife	1–2
	March 24	Wilt Chamberlain and Kareem Abdul-Jabbar	1–2
	March 31	Jacqueline Onassis	1
	April 7	The Oscars	2–4
	April 14	Broiling Steak	1
	April 21	Charlie Chaplin and Wife	1–2
	April 28	The Marriage Experiment	1–2
	May 5	Olympic Gymnast Cathy Rigby	2–4
	May 12	Vietnam Soldier Carrying Wounded Buddy	4–7
	May 19	The Population Riddle	1–2
	May 26	Cornelia Wallace with George	1–2
	June 2	Raquel Welch	4–8
	June 9	Bella Abzug	1
	June 16	Girl with Hula Hoop	1–2
	June 23	Aleksandr Solzhenitsyn	1
	June 30	Young Crusaders for Jesus	1–2
	July 7	Senator George McGovern	1
	July 14	Mick Jagger	10–20
	July 21	McGovern	1
	July 28	The Bare Look in Fashion	2–4
	August 4	Flip Wilson	1
	August 11	Skyjackers Escape Hatch	1–2
	August 18	Mark Spitz	2–3
	August 25	Pat Nixon	2–3
	September 1	Autoworker	1
	September 8	Marilyn Monroe	3–6
	September 15	Israeli Olympic Team	2–4
	September 22	Frank Shorter	1
	September 29	POW Wife	1–3

YEAR	ISSUE	COVER SUBJECT	VALUE
1972	October 6	Dallas Cowboys Tackle Bob Lilly	$ 2–3
	October 13	S.S. Lusitania	3–7
	October 20	Youngster	1–2
	October 27	Dr. Edward Land	1
	November 3	Joe Namath	1
	November 10	U.S. Navy POW	3–5
	November 17	Nixon	1
	November 24	Governor George Wallace	1
	December 1	Harry S Truman	1–2
	December 8	Diana Ross	10–20
	December 15	Christmas Special Issue	2–3
	December 29	The Year 1972 in Pictures	2–3

Note: Between 1973 and 1977 *Life Magazine* did not issue a weekly magazine; instead they issued the following special issues.

SPECIAL ISSUE	VALUE
Spirit of Israel	$2–4
The Year in Pictures (1973)	2–4
One Day in the Life of America	3–6
The Year in Pictures (1974)	2–4
The 100 Events That Shaped America	3–6
The Year in Pictures (1975)	2–4
Remarkable American Women	2–4
The Year in Pictures (1976)	2–4
The New Youth	2–4
The Year in Pictures (1977)	3–6

Note: 1978 *Life Magazine* goes monthly.

YEAR	ISSUE	COVER SUBJECT	VALUE
1978	October	Balloon	$2–4
	November	Mickey Mouse	1–2
	December	Prince Charles	1–2
1979	January	Shar-Pei Dog	1–2
	February	Lingerie Fashions	2–3

YEAR	ISSUE	COVER SUBJECT	VALUE
1979	March	Lesley-Anne Down	$2–4
	April	Eclipse	2–3
	May	Three-Mile Island	1–2
	June	Marlon Brando	2–3
	July	Whale	2–3
	August	Microsurgeon	1
	September	Pope John Paul II	1–2
	October	Dolly Parton	3–5
	November	Ted Kennedy	1
	December	The Decade in Pictures Special	2–4
1980	January	Ayatollah Khomeini	1–2
	February	Mary Astor	1–3
	March	Mickey Rooney	1–3
	April	Hare Krishna Children	1
	May	Man-made Gene	1–2
	June	Sunday Cat	1–3
	July	Cape Hatteras Lighthouse	1–3
	August	Miss Piggy	1–3
	September	Summer Sun	1–2
	October	Chinese Child	1–2
	November	Walter Cronkite	1
	December	Child Cancer Patient	1–2
1981	January	The Year in Pictures	1–2
	February	Swimsuit Fashions	2–4
	March	Jimmy Lopez	1
	April	Meryl Streep	1–2
	May	Ronald Reagan	1–2
	June	Planets	1–3
	July	Dying Lake	1–2
	August	Girl under Waterfall	2–3
	September	Artificial Heart	1–2
	October	Marilyn Monroe	3–5
	November	Fetus	1–2
	December	Brooke Shields	3–5
1982	January	The Year in Pictures	1–2
	February	Christie Brinkley	2–4
	March	Elizabeth Taylor	2–3
	April	Handgun	1–2

YEAR	ISSUE	COVER SUBJECT	VALUE
1982	May	Laser Surgeon	$1–2
	June	Polar Bear	1–2
	July	Raquel Welch	3–5
	August	Marilyn Monroe	3–5
	September	Liver Transplant	1
	October	Arnold Schwarzenegger	1–2
	November	Test-tube Baby	1–2
	December	Princess Diana	1–2
1983	January	The Year in Pictures	2–3
	February	Brooke Shields	2–4
	March	Prince Rainier and Children	1–2
	April	Embryo Hand	1–3
	May	Debra Winger	2–4
	June	Star Wars	4–8
	July	Glacier National Park	2–4
	August	Willie Nelson	2–3
	September	The Best and Worst Cars Ever	2–3
	October	Nancy Reagan	2–3
	November	John F. Kennedy	1–2
	December	Barbra Streisand	2–4
1984	January	The Year in Pictures	2–3
	February	The Beatles	2–4
	March	Daryl Hannah in Bathing Suits	2–5
	April	Penguins	1–2
	May	History of Cocaine	1–2
	June	Harrison Ford and Kate Capshaw	3–5
	July	Dan Pisner and Quintuplets	1
	August	Grizzly Bear	2–3
	September	Michael Jackson	2–4
	October	Doonesbury Wedding	1–2
	November	John Jr. and Caroline Kennedy	1
	December	Princess Diana and Prince Andrew	1–2
1985–Present	All issues		1–4

COLLECTING
NATIONAL GEOGRAPHIC MAGAZINE

If you have ever read a *National Geographic Magazine,* you have discovered a means of knowledge, through travel, adventure, and exploration; showcasing scientific achievements not only from this Earth, but from the doorstep of the infinitesimal up the stairway to the universe, this magazine can open the door. You may be a student, a lawyer, a doctor, or perhaps a person who likes to read or collect things, no matter; it is important to know that this magazine has been popular in this world of knowledge for nearly a century. *National Geographic Magazine,* with its comprehensive stories and excellent illustrations, will continue to be published as long as the ideals of those honorable gentlemen who started the National Geographic Society are continued, as long as there are frontiers to explore, expeditions to sponsor, and dreams to fulfill.

The National Geographic Society, in Washington, D.C., has sold and circulated *National Geographic Magazine* every month since January, 1896 (except for the years 1897 and 1917, when one magazine was issued to cover a two-month period). There were nine publications of this magazine issued between 1888 and 1891, before the first monthly in 1896. Also, in 1891 and running through the year 1895 there were twenty-seven brochures produced, making a total of thirty-six early publications. In those early years the magazine was "red brick" in color, and some of these issues are still around. Altogether, there are six different cover designs up to the present.

If you have been thinking of collecting magazines, it would be best to give these magazines some serious thought. A complete set consisting of everything published by the National Geographic Society (all being originals) has a value of $25,000 to $75,000. Few hobbies give people as much satisfaction as collecting old *National Geographics.* The recent growth in the number of *National Geographic* collectors is astonishing and getting bigger every day. Currently, the circulation of the magazine is above twenty million. With circulation this high, there are more and more people demanding the earlier numbers. It is entirely up to you the type of collection you wish to arrange. Some collectors try to acquire all of the issues, while others add the maps and pictorial supplements. There are collectors who are not satisfied until they add the book publications also.

For the past twenty-five years the most reliable source for buying and selling *National Geographic Magazine* has been the mail-order dealer Don Smith, located at 3930 Rankin Street in Louisville, Kentucky 40214. Mr. Smith has continuously offered many of the early issues and is regarded as "the source" for acquiring copies of *National Geographic Magazine* and all other National Geographic Society publications. A copy of his reference guide, "National Geographic Magazine for Collectors 1888–1992," can be purchased by sending $12 to his Louisville, Kentucky, address. More common issues, 1920 to the present, can still, on occasion, be found in old book and magazine stores. The Salvation Army, the Goodwill, and other nonprofit secondhand stores are also excellent sources for the more common issues. These secondhand stores will generally sell common issues for as low as .25 to $1 per copy.

Within our listing of *National Geographic Magazines,* we have given the contents for the one hundred most popular issues. These one hundred issues are not among the most valuable or scarce issues, but are rather the issues that are sought after and purchased by collectors more often than other issues. To date there is no reference book that lists in chronological order the contents for all issues of *National Geographic.* An excellent source listing contents *by subject* is "The Quick Reference Guide to National Geographic 1955–1990," by Jack Hobart; it can be purchased by sending $8 (U.S.) to Geoimages Publishing Company, P.O. Box 45677, Los Angeles, California 90045.

Note: In 1964 the National Geographic Society published reprint issues of the original magazine from 1888 through 1907. These reprints are clearly marked "reprint" on the front covers.

NATIONAL GEOGRAPHIC MAGAZINE SPECIAL VALUES

YEAR	ISSUE/COVER SUBJECT	VALUE
1888	Volume 1, #1	$5,000–13,000
1888–1889	Volume 1, #2	3,000–5,000
	Volume 1, #3	3,000–5,000
	Volume 1, #4	3,000–4,500
1890	Volume 2, #1–5	200–500
1891–1892	Volume 3, #1–5	200–400
1892–1893	Volume 4, #1–5	250–500
	Volume 4, #6, #7	200–400

Vol. I.

No. 1.

THE

NATIONAL GEOGRAPHIC

MAGAZINE.

PUBLISHED BY THE

NATIONAL GEOGRAPHIC SOCIETY.

WASHINGTON, D. C.

Price 50 Cents.

Volume I, #1
Cover Format #1
(6″ by 9¾″)
Red-brick in color for Volume I, #2 through Volume IV, being of a little brighter shade.

YEAR	ISSUE/COVER SUBJECT	VALUE
1893–1894	Volume 5, #1–6	$150–350
1894–1895	Volume 6, #1–5	200–350
	Volume 6, #6–9	200–300
1896	January–March	100–250
	April–December	100–200
1897	January, February, April–December	100–200
	March	225–400
1898	January, February, April–December	100–200
	March	200–400
1899	January, February	100–175
	March, April, May	300–400
	June, July	175–250
	August–December	100–200
1900	January–December	100–200
1901	All months	90–180
1902	August	150–225
	All other months	100–180
1903	All months	100–150
1904	January, March, May, November	100–200
	All other months	75–125
1905	January, February, March	125–200
	April, May	50–100
	June–December	40–75
1906	All months	25–50
1907	All months	20–40
1908	All months	20–40
1909	October—Discovery of the Pole	35–50
	All other months	20–40
1910	All months	20–40
1911	April, May, June	10–20
	July—Reptiles of All Lands	20–40
	All other months	20–40
1912	January, February, March	20–40
	September—Headhunters of North Luzon	10–20

Vol. VIII   SEPTEMBER, 1897   No. 9

The
National Geographic
Magazine

AN ILLUSTRATED MONTHLY

Editor: JOHN HYDE

Associate Editors

A. W. GREELY   W J McGEE   HENRY GANNETT
C. HART MERRIAM   ELIZA RUHAMAH SCIDMORE

CONTENTS

WASHINGTON
PUBLISHED BY THE NATIONAL GEOGRAPHIC SOCIETY

AGENTS IN THE UNITED STATES AND CANADA
THE AMERICAN NEWS COMPANY, 39 AND 41 CHAMBERS STREET, NEW YORK
PARIS: BRENTANOS, 37 AVENUE DE L'OPERA

Price 25 Cents   **$2.50 a Year**

Entered at the Post-office in Washington, D. C., as Second-class Mail Matter.

Cover Format #2
(6" by 9¾")
*Ivory colored with table of contents on front cover in red ink. This format ran from
1896 through 1899.*

YEAR	ISSUE/COVER SUBJECT	VALUE
1912	October—China	$10–20
	All other months	10–20
1913	April—In the Wonderland of Peru	25–40
	September—Ancient Egypt	10–20
	November—The Philippines	10–20
	All other months	10–20
1914	January—Northern Africa	20–30
	May—Birds of Town and Country	10–20
	August—The Grand Canyon	10–20
	November—Young Russia	10–15
	All other months	10–15
1915	May—American Wildflowers	8–15
	August—American Game Birds	8–15
	All other months	5–10
1916	February—Flowers and Berries	8–15
	May—The Land of the Incas	8–15
	June—Common American Wildflowers	8–12
	November—Large North American Mammals	8–15
	All other months	5–10
1917	October—Our Flag Number	15–20
	All other months	4–8
1918	May—Smaller North American Mammals	8–15
	All other months	4–8
1919	February—Flowers and Berries	5–10
	March—Dogs	10–20
	December—Military Insignia	8–15
	All other months	4–8
1920	May—Common Mushrooms of the United States	6–12
	December—Falconry	6–12
	All other months	4–8
1921	March—America in the Air	5–10
	June—Grass and Their Flowers	5–10
	All other months	4–8
1922	July—Cathedrals of the Old and New Worlds, Flowers	6–12
	All other months	4–8

Vol. XI   MAY, 1900   No. 5

THE

NATIONAL GEOGRAPHIC

MAGAZINE

CONTENTS

WASHINGTON
PUBLISHED BY THE NATIONAL GEOGRAPHIC SOCIETY
FOR SALE AT BRENTANO'S:
31 UNION SQUARE, NEW YORK; 1015 PENNSYLVANIA AVENUE, WASHINGTON;
218 WABASH AVENUE, CHICAGO; 37 AVENUE DE L'OPERA, PARIS

Price 25 Cents $2.50 a Year /

Cover Format #3
(7" by 10")
Very close to the creamy tint of format #2 with the table of contents on the front
cover being in black ink. However, age has resulted in faded copies that resemble a
near yellowish brown. This design was used for only one year, 1900.

YEAR	ISSUE/COVER SUBJECT	VALUE
1923	May—The Tomb of Tutankhamen	$8–15
	October—The Auto Industry	5–10
	November—The Story of the Horse	8–15
	All other months	4–8
1924	June—Flowers and Berries	5–10
	October—Goldfish	5–10
	All other months	4–8
1925	May—Ferns As a Hobby	5–10
	July—Flowers and Berries	5–10
	December—Cattle of the World	6–12
	All other months	4–8
1926	January—Pigeons	5–10
	April—Slime Molds	5–10
	August—Jellyfish	5–10
	All other months	4–8
1927	April—Fowl	6–12
	May—Wildflowers of the West	5–10
	July—Moths and Butterflies	5–10
	All other months	4–8
1928	January—Seeing America with Charles Lindbergh	6–12
	May—To Bogota and Back by Air with Charles Lindbergh	6–12
	All other months	4–8
1929	July—Insects	5–10
	All other months	4–8
1930	March—Fowl	5–10
	June—First World Airship Flight	5–10
	August—Air Conquest of Antarctica	5–10
	All other months	4–8
1931	March—Tropical Fish	6–9
	All other months	3–7
1932	All months	3–7
1933	July—Eagles, Hawks, and Vultures	5–10
	All other months	3–7

THE
NATIONAL
GEOGRAPHIC
MAGAZINE

Vol. XIII   APRIL, 1902   No. 4

CONTENTS

Published for the National Geographic Society
By McClure, Phillips & Co., of New York

$2.50 a Year   25 Cents a Number

Entered at the Post-office in Washington, D. C., as Second-class Mail Matter.

Cover Format #4
(7″ by 10″)
Table of contents on the front cover of red paper in black ink was used from 1901 through 1903. Copies will probably be a bit faded.

<u>YEAR</u>	<u>ISSUE/COVER SUBJECT</u>	<u>VALUE</u>
1934	May—Common Birds of North America	$5–10
	September—Flags of the World	5–10
	October—Exploration of the	
	Stratosphere, Wild Geese, Ducks and Swans	5–10
	All other months	3–7
1935	February—Birds of the Night	4–8
	All other months	3–7
1936	February—Man's Oldest Ally . . . the Dog	5–10
	November—Trains	5–10
	All other months	3–7
1937	January—Field Dogs	5–10
	April—Colonial Williamsburg	6–12
	May—Butterfly Migrants	6–12
	October—Hounds	6–12
	All other months	4–8
1938	May—Monkeys	5–8
	November—Cats	6–12
	December—Canaries and Other Cage Birds	4–8
	All other months	3–7
1939	August—Flowers and Berries	4–8
	December—Cathedrals of England	4–8
	All other months	3–7
1940	January—Whales, Porpoises, and Dolphins	4–8
	February—Rubber	4–8
	March—Classic Lands	4–8
	July—The National Gallery of Art	4–8
	All other months	3–7
1941	October—Ancient Egypt	8–14
	December—Working Dogs	6–12
	All other months	3–7
1942	February—Dinosaurs	5–10
	April—California Wildflowers	5–10
	All other months	3–7
1943	February—Lions, Tigers, and Leopards	5–10
	June—Insignia of the United States	
	Armed Forces	8–15

YEAR	ISSUE/COVER SUBJECT	VALUE
1943	October—Decorative Medals and Service Ribbons	$6–12
	November—Non-Sporting Dogs	6–12
	December—War Insignia	5–10
1944	March—The Greek Way	6–9
	July—Indians of the Western Plains	6–9
	All other months	4–6
1945	January—Indians of the North Pacific Coast	6–9
	October—Wrens of Australia	5–8
	All other months	4–6
1946	November—The Roman Way	4–8
	All other months	4–6
1947	July—The World of Your Garden	5–7
	September—Bird Dogs	5–8
	October—Antarctica	5–7
	November—The Northern Lights	5–7
	All other months	4–6
1948	February—Indians of the Far West	4–8
	March—The Circus	5–10
	September—American Painting of the National Gallery	6–9
	December—Prehistoric Paintings of Lascaux	5–8
	All other months	4–6
1949	April—The British Way	4–8
	May—Flags of the Americas	4–8
	July—Shells	8–12
	August—Vegetables	6–8
	All other months	4–6
1950	June—The Vienna Treasures	5–7
	October—Peru and Bolivia	5–8
	December—Gems	5–10
	All other months	4–6
1951	January—Ancient Mesopotamia	5–7
	February—American Paintings	5–8
	September—Fruit	5–7
	November—Minerals	5–7
	All other months	4–6

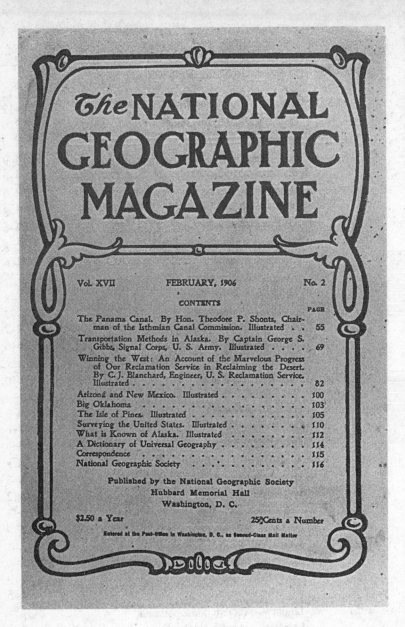

The NATIONAL GEOGRAPHIC MAGAZINE

Vol. XVII   FEBRUARY, 1906   No. 2

CONTENTS

Published by the National Geographic Society
Hubbard Memorial Hall
Washington, D. C.

$2.50 a Year   25 Cents a Number

Entered at the Post-Office in Washington, D. C., as Second-Class Mail Matter

Cover Format #5
(7″ by 10″)

Table of contents on a bright yellow cover in brown ink. Copies of this design were produced from 1904 through January 1910.

YEAR	ISSUE/COVER SUBJECT	VALUE
1952	January—The National Gallery of Art	$5–10
	All other months	4–6
1953	September—The Coronation of Queen Elizabeth II	5–8
	All other months	4–6
1954	July—Conquest of Mt. Everest	5–8
	October—Uranium	5–8
	All other months	4–6
1955	May—The Grand Canyon	5–8
	July—Lhasa and Tibet	5–8
	September—Literary England	5–8
	November—Egyptian Archaeology	5–8
	All other months	4–6
1956	January—Monkeys, Dodo Birds	5–7
	June—Alaska	5–7
	All other months	2–5
1957	April—Modern Rome	3–6
	December—Old Testament Times	3–7
	All other months	2–5
1958	May—The National Parks	2–7
	August—Dogs Who Work for Man	2–7
	December—Dead Sea Scrolls	2–7
	All other months	2–4
1959	June—Modern Germany	3–6
	September—The Soviet Union	3–6
	All other months	2–5
1960	February—The Drowned City of Port Royal	3–6
	September—Africa	3–6
	December—Japan	3–6
	All other months	2–5
1961	January—The White House	3–6
	March—Ireland	3–6
	April—The Civil War	3–6
	All other months	2–5
1962	March—Journey to Outer Mongolia	2–5
	June—John Glenn's Orbits	2–6

YEAR	ISSUE/COVER SUBJECT	VALUE
1962	September—Brazil	$2–6
	All other months	2–5
1963	May—India	2–6
	August—Disneyland	2–5
	September—Australia	2–5
	October—75th Anniversary Special	2–5
	All other months	2–4
1964	January—The National Capitol	2–5
	March—The Last Full Measure:	
	President Kennedy Funeral	2–5
	November—Profiles of the President Part I	2–5
	All other months	2–4
1965	January—Profiles of the President Part II	2–5
	May—Profiles of the President Part III	2–5
	August—Sir Winston Churchill	2–4
	October—Profiles of the President Part IV	2–5
	All other months	2–4
1966	January—Profiles of the President Part V	3–6
	March—Moscow, the U.S.S.R.	3–6
	July—Our National Parks	3–6
	August—Bayeux Tapestry	3–6
	All other months	1–4
1967	March—The National Gallery of Art	2–5
	December—Where Jesus Walked	2–4
	All other months	1–4
1968	All months	1–4
1969	March—Seashells	1–4
	December—Apollo 11	1–4
	All other months	1–3
1970	March—Japan	1–4
	June—Rome	1–4
	August—Planets	1–4
	December—Pollution	1–4
	All other months	1–3
1971	All months	1–3

YEAR	ISSUE/COVER SUBJECT	VALUE
1972	October—The Amazon	$2–4
	All other months	1–3
1973	January—Search for the Oldest People	2–4
	October—Chile	2–4
	All other months	1–3
1974	January—Gold	1–4
	May—The Universe	1–4
	All other months	1–4
1975	June—Alaska	2–5
	July—Food	2–4
	December—The Maya: Children of Time	2–6
	All other months	1–3
1976	January—In the Steps of Moses	2–5
	July—This Land of Ours	1–4
	August—Venezuela	1–4
	September—Exploring the New Biology	1–4
	December—Whales	1–4
	All other months	1–3
1977	February—Egypt	2–4
	September—Leonardo da Vinci	2–4
	All other months	1–3
1978	August—Dinosaurs	2–4
	December—First Atlantic Balloon Crossing	2–4
	All other months	1–3
1979	July—Our National Parks	2–4
	All other months	1–3
1980	June—The Mystery of the Shroud	2–4
	All other months	1–3
1981	January—Mt. Saint Helens	1–3
	February—Special Report on Energy	1–3
	July—Saturn: The Riddle of the Rings	1–3
	All other months	1–2
1982	February—Napoleon	1–3
	September—Our National Forest, the Bahamas	1–3
	All other months	1–2

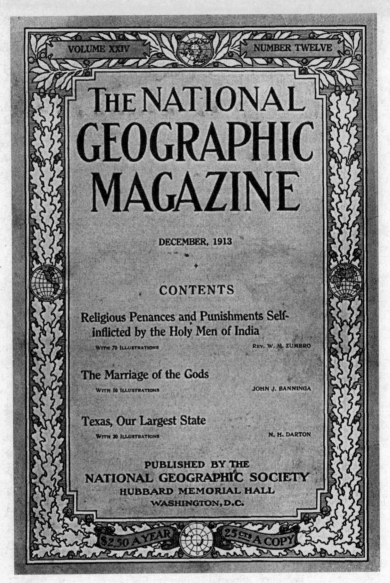

VOLUME XXIV   NUMBER TWELVE

The NATIONAL GEOGRAPHIC MAGAZINE

DECEMBER, 1913

CONTENTS

PUBLISHED BY THE
NATIONAL GEOGRAPHIC SOCIETY
HUBBARD MEMORIAL HALL
WASHINGTON, D.C.

$2.50 A YEAR   25 cts. A COPY

Cover Format #6
(7" by 10")
Cover of yellow paper with a white background. Early copies have a light yellow background with the table of contents on the front cover in black ink. This format was used from February 1910 to the present, with the acorn border design being only slightly modified from early copies. Illustrations on this format started in 1959.

YEAR	ISSUE/COVER SUBJECT	VALUE
1983	June—The Universe	$1–3
	All other months	1–2
1984	March—The Laser, Eagle Holograph Cover	2–5
	All other months	1–2
1985	January—The Planets	1–3
	November—Early Man Holograph Cover and Feature	1–3
	All other months	1–2
1986	December—The Titanic	2–4
	All other months	1–2
1987	December—The Oldest Known Shipwreck	2–4
	All other months	1–2
1988	January—100 Years of the National Geographic Society	1–2
	February—Australia	1–2
	September—100 Years of the National Geographic Society	1–2
	October—The Peopling of the Earth	1–2
	November—Exploring the Earth	1–2
	December—McDonald's Holographic Back Cover Ad	2–4
	All other months	1–2
1989	All months	1–2
1990	All months	1–2
1991	All months	1–2
1992–Present	All months	1–2

CONSECUTIVE RUN VALUES

1888–Present	$25,000–75,000
1896–Present	15,000–30,000
1900–Present	15,000–25,000
1908–Present	3,000–5,500

Adult Magazines

Any magazine that features nudity (male and/or female) and articles of a sexual nature is classified as an adult magazine. These magazines are for collectors eighteen or older. When collected they should at all times be kept well out of reach and sight of minors.

Adult magazines, at present, are a very large segment of the magazine-collecting world. The reasons they are collected are many, but primarily it is for the photos, artwork, and stories. Many well-known female celebrities posed nude early in their careers, and issues containing these nude photos are very much in demand. Artists such as Bode had their work published in such adult magazines as *Gallery*. *Playboy* and other adult magazines published stories by renowned authors of both fiction and nonfiction. They also offered exclusive interviews of such legends as Lenny Bruce and Jim Morrison. Many of these stories and interviews are accessible to the fan or researcher only in the pages of specific back-issue adult magazines.

BUYING ADULT MAGAZINES

The best source for buying adult magazines is mail order. Many dealers will advertise in trade papers and will offer their catalog for a small fee. Mail-order catalogs usually list the titles, issues, and contents of the specific magazines the dealer is currently offering. If a customer is ordering for the first time, the mail-order dealer will require from the buyer proof of age (eighteen or older only). This proof is generally supplied by a photocopy of the buyer's driver's license or birth certificate. Back-issue magazine stores are also a good source. However, the best places to find adult magazines at the very lowest prices are flea markets and garage sales. Quite often valuable issues can be scoffed up for as low as .25 to $1. When flea marketing or garage saling, keep a sharp eye out for adult magazines. Most people, although wishing to sell their old issues of *Playboy* and other adult magazines, will be very conservative in displaying them.

SELLING ADULT MAGAZINES

The easiest ways to sell adult magazines are to take out an inexpensive ad in a local paper, hold a garage sale, or drive your back issues down to a flea market. Selling through these outlets, you cannot expect low or top value for your magazines. The average garage saler and flea marketer is used to finding, and will expect to purchase, these issues at a fraction of their retail value. Generally issues will sell at .25 to $1. There are exceptions—rarer *Playboys* can sell for up to the low value given in this guide. It is also important that while planning on selling at a flea market, the seller check with the market's management for the rules on selling adult magazines. Generally, the rule is to keep all adult magazines out of reach and sight of minors. Displaying them from behind your table, in a manner in which only the title of the magazine can be seen, is the best way. The experienced collector will spot them.

Selling adult magazines to back-issue magazine stores will generally lead to a quick sale. The selling price should be roughly 10 percent of their retail value for common issues and up to 60 percent for rarer issues. Many back-issue magazine shops will offer the seller a combination of cash and trade value. These offers are generally beneficial to a collector who wishes to unload unwanted and/or duplicate issues and at the same time pick up issues that are needed for his or her collection. Dealers will, at most times, offer a much higher trade value than cash value.

Selling to a mail-order dealer will take more time. The seller must first compile a list of titles, issues, and conditions of each magazine being offered. When sending this list to the mail-order dealer, the seller may state his asking price outright or ask the dealer to make an offer. The seller may also wish to sell issues directly to collectors via the mails. After compiling your list, offer it through a classified ad in a trade paper. It may be wise to ask a small fee for this list to eliminate browsers. When selling adult magazines through the mail the seller must insist on proof of age by the purchaser (eighteen or older only). A photocopy of the buyer's birth certificate or driver's license will do.

August 1959

Volume 4, #7, 1960

Volume 4, #9, 1960

January 1957

#7, November 1955

May 1957

#4, January 1957

#5, March 1957

October 1941

May 1957

#7, 1960

December 1986

January 1957

January 1977

#1

Volume 10, 1959

February 1940

February 1966

September 1987   *October 1990*   *May 1984*

February 1978   *June 1964*   *June 1985*

Autumn 1955   *#6, August 1957*   *December 1957*

Autumn 1955

July 1965

February 1956

August 1956

April 1957

May 1957

January 1958

February 1958

March 1960

COLLECTING ADULT MAGAZINES

Most commonly it is the specific female or females that appear in an issue of an adult magazine that dictate its value. Early issues of *High Society's Celebrity Skin* and issues of *Celebrity Sleuth* can sell for as high as $50 each. This is due to the fact that these issues contain many, many nude photos of prominent female TV and movie stars and that the demand greatly outweighs the supply. A newer issue of *Playboy* will have a higher value than an issue twenty years its senior because it features nude photos of a star who is currently very popular. We have listed basic values for adult magazines for common issues for each decade. Common issues are issues that do not feature the current most collectible female models or stars. Values for these more collectible females will follow.

COMMON ADULT MAGAZINE VALUES

ISSUES	VALUE
1930–1939	$5–10
1940–1949	5–10
1950–1955	4–8
1956–1959	3–7
1960–1965	3–6
1966–1969	3–5
1970–1977	2–4
1978–1985	2–3
1986–1989	2–4
1990–Present	2–3

CURRENT MOST-COLLECTIBLE FEMALES
IN ADULT MAGAZINES

SUBJECT	VALUE	
	COVER AND PICTORIAL	COVER ONLY
Lee Aaron	$10–20	$ 3–5
Linda Blair	15–30	5–10
Samantha Fox (pre-1988)	15–30	8–15
Samantha Fox (1989–Present)	5–10	3–5
Shauna Grant	5–10	4–8
Debbie Harry	15–30	10–20
Traci Lords (pre-1988)	15–30	10–20
Traci Lords (1989–Present)	5–10	3–5
Betty Page (pre-1960)	25–50+	15–30+
Betty Page (pre-1970)	12–25	10–20
Betty Page (1971–Present)	10–20	10–15
Cassandra Petersen (Elvira) (pre-1980)	25–50	15–30
Cassandra Petersen (Elvira) (1981–1988)	15–30	10–20
Cassandra Petersen (Elvira) (1989–Present)	10–20	5–10
Sports Illustrated's models	5–10	3–6
TV or movie star(s)	5–10	3–6
Diane Weber	10–20	6–12

Note: For values for issues containing Marilyn Monroe, Jayne Mansfield, and other specific female stars, refer to our Movie Magazine section.

Important: To help collectors be absolutely sure of the value of their issues, this guide offers *The Official Collector's Hotline,* 201-641-7212. Call between normal business hours only please (EST).

PENTHOUSE VALUES

YEAR	ISSUE	DESCRIPTION	VALUE
1969	September	#1	$20–40
	October	#2	10–20
	November	#3	10–20
	December	#4	10–15
1976	March	Priscilla Barnes cover and Pet of the Month centerfold and pictorial	10–20
1977	August	The Nude Women of James Bond	5–10
1980	February	Debbie Harry cover and feature	5–10
1982	October	Morgan Fairchild cover and feature	4–8
1984	September	Vanessa Williams and Traci Lords	25–50
	November	More Vanessa Williams	10–25
1985	September	Madonna cover and nude photos	20–40
1986	January	Madonna poster	10–20
1987	June	Samantha Fox cover and feature	20–40
	September	Madonna cover and feature	10–20
All other issues			2–4

PLAYBOY VALUES

Note: 1. *Playboy* issues are listed by Playmate of the month first, followed by cover subject and or pictorial(s) and major feature(s).

2. Most issues of *Playboy* from 1961 on up will have not only a value range but also a price in parentheses ( ); this is the collector's price *Playboy* currently sells that issue for. If there is no price in parentheses ( ), *Playboy*'s back-issue department does not have that issue in stock.

3. Even though issues of *Playboy* can be acquired for much less, it is important to be aware of the prices that are being asked for and being received by the publisher of *Playboy*.

YEAR	ISSUE	DESCRIPTION	VALUE
1953	December	#1 Marilyn Monroe: Playmate and cover, an open letter from California pictorial	$1,000–2,000+
1954	January	#2 Margie Harrison, at home with Dienes, Playboy goes to Art Bell	1,000–2,000+
	February	#3 Margaret Scott, Yvonne Menard, Frankie and Johnny, Paris hot spots featuring Yvonne Menard	500–1,000
	March	#4 Dolores del Monte, Joanne Arnold cover and pictorial: sex sells a shirt	250–500
	April	#5 Marilyn Waltz, Playboy's eyeful	200–400
	May	#6 Joanne Arnold, nudes by Weegee	200–400
	June	#7 Margie Harrison, outside with Dienes	175–350
	July	#8 Neva Gilbert, Simone Silva, the evolution of the bathing suit	175–350
	August	#9 Arline Hunter, a bump, a grind and a gimmick: Yvette Dare, Lilly St. Cyr, and Evelyn West	100–200
	September	#10 Jackie Rainbow, Gina Lollobrigida pictorial	100–200
	October	#11 Madeline Castle, nudity in the foreign film	75–150
	November	#12 Diane Hunter, Paris round the world, the motoring Playboy	75–150

YEAR	ISSUE	DESCRIPTION	VALUE
1954	December	#13 Terry Ryan, photographing a Playmate pictorial featuring Terry Ryan, Marlene Dietrich, and Terry Moore, the Las Vegas skin game	$75–150
1955	January	Bette Page, Santa baby: Eartha Kitt, Babylon U.S.A.	50–100
	February	Jayne Mansfield, Leigh Lewin and Arlene Kieta, Nejla Ates: Broadway's Turkish delight, Voluptua	75–150
	March	No issue published	
	April	Marilyn Waltz, Leigh Lewin, nude advertising	25–50
	May	Marguerite Empey, Bunny Yeager, Terry Shaw and Bettie Page pictorial	25–50
	June	Eve Myer, Donna Kime, Eve pictorial	25–50
	July	Janet Pilgram Playmate and cover, tempest in a C-cup: Tempest Storm	25–50
	August	Pat Lawler, Gowland's cool pool: Joanne Arnold	25–50
	September	Anne Fleming, Marilyn Monroe pictorial	50–100
	October	Jean Moorehead, Marilyn McClintock, a stripper goes to college, two Playmates for the price of one: Jean Moorehead and Johnnie Nicely, Anita Ekberg	25–50
	November	Barbara Cameron Playmate and cover, West Coast strippers, Gina Lollobrigida	25–50
	December	Janet Pilgram Playmate and cover, burlesque in Tokyo	30–60

June 1961   June 1959   September 1973

September 1978   February 1979   January 1980

January 1981   March 1983   February 1991

YEAR	ISSUE	DESCRIPTION	VALUE
1956	January	Lynn Tutner, the first two dozen Playmates	$25–50
	February	Marguerite Empey, Chuckles with your cocktails, Jayne Mansfield pictorial	25–50
	March	Marian Stafford Playmate and cover, Eve Meyer	20–40
	April	Rusty Fisher, DD in 3-D: Diana Dors pictorial	20–40
	May	Marion Scott, Dolores Taylor, the lynx with the lusty larynx: Meg Myles	15–30
	June	Gloria Walker, champagne flight to Texas: Sally Todd	15–30
	July	Alice Denham, peekaboo pants: Marla English	15–30
	August	Johnnie Nicely, the Ekberg bronze: Anita Ekberg	15–30
	September	Elsa Sorensen, Diane Harmsen, filming the Folies-Bergere	15–30
	October	Janet Pilgram, how to bathe a poodle: Joan Bradshaw, Janet's date at Dartmouth: Janet Pilgram pictorial	15–30
	November	Betty Blue	15–30
	December	Lisa Winters Playmate and cover, Tallulah's follies	15–30
1957	January	June Blair, Playmate review	25–50
	February	Sally Todd, Jayne Mansfield cover and pictorial	25–50
	March	Sandra Edwards, Zsa Zsa in Las Vegas	15–30
	April	Gloria Windsor, Elaine Conte	15–30
	May	Dawn Richard, Li'l Abner's gals: Julie Newmar, Tina Louise, Carmen Alvarez, and Edith Adams	17–35

February 1971

March 1976

September 1984

June 1987

Summer 1956

August 1979

#2, October 1937

December 1957

May 1957

YEAR	ISSUE	DESCRIPTION	VALUE
1957	June	Carrie Radison, most popular Playmate 1956: Lisa Winters, the back: Vikki Dougan	$15–30
	July	Jean Jani, Playboy's yacht party	15–30
	August	Dolores Donlon Playmate and cover, view from a penthouse	15–30
	September	Jacquelyn Prescott, westerns are better than ever: Jana Davi	15–30
	October	Colleen Farrington, Latin Quarter lovelies	15–30
	November	Marlene Callahan, Sophia Loren and Jayne Mansfield pictorial	20–40
	December	Linda Vargas, alone with Lisa: Lisa Winters	15–30
1958	January	Elizabeth Ann Roberts, Playmate review	20–40
	February	Cheryl Kubert, the nude Jayne Mansfield	15–30
	March	Zahra Norbo, Michiko Hamamura, Brigitte Bardot	15–30
	April	Felicia Atkins, Minsky in Vegas	15–30
	May	Lari Laine, Playboy's little acre: Tina Louise, Elga Anderson	15–30
	June	Judy Lee Tomerlin Playmate and cover, photographing your own Playmate	15–30
	July	Linne Nanette Ahlstrand, Joyce Nizzari, Agnes Laurent	15–30
	August	Myrna Weber	15–30
	September	Teri Hope, the bosom: June Wilkinson	15–30

April 1971

#2, April 1957

May 1959

September 1973

July 1958

January 27, 1975

February 1938

April 1938

May 1965

YEAR	ISSUE	DESCRIPTION	VALUE
1958	October	Mara Corday and Pat Sheehan, les girls: girls of Las Vegas	$15–30
	November	Joan Staley, peekaboo Brigitte: Brigitte Bardot	15–30
	December	Joyce Nizzari, Playboy's most popular Playmates: Barbara Cameron, Jayne Mansfield, Elizabeth Ann Roberts, Janet Pilgram, and Lisa Winters, Playboy's 5th anniversary scrapbook	20–40
1959	January	Virginia Gordon, Playmate review	20–40
	February	Eleanor Bradley, girls in their lairs	15–30
	March	Audrey Daston, the classic figure: June Blair	15–30
	April	Nancy Crawford, Tina Louise, Marguerite Empey	15–30
	May	Cindy Fuller, Playboy's house party: Cindy Fuller, Bonnie Harrington, Fran Stacy, Dottie Sykes, and Mary Jane Ralston	15–30
	June	Marilyn Hanold, Oriental sex pictorial	15–30
	July	Yvette Vickers, making a splash: Tania Velia	15–30
	August	Clayre Peters, the bosom in Hollywood: June Wilkinson	15–30
	September	Marianne Gaba, Bunny's honeys: Lisa Winters, Bunny Yeager, Bonnie Harrington, Myrna Weber, Mary Jane Ralston, Cindy Fuller, and Joyce Nizzari	15–30

#7, June 1958   #14, September 1959   #6, July 1959

May 1979   July 1980   July 1981

December 1990   March 1991   Volume 3, 1986

YEAR	ISSUE	DESCRIPTION	VALUE
1959	October	Elaine Reynolds, sultry Miss Stewart: Elaine Stewart, Kim Novak pictorial	$15–30
	November	Donna Lynn, Hollywood goes European: Linda Cristal	15–30
	December	Ellen Stratton, building a better Brigitte (Bardot)	20–40
1960	January	Stella Stevens, Playmate review	15–30
	February	Susie Scott, Jayne Mansfield pictorial	20–40
	March	Sally Sarell	10–20
	April	Linda Gamble, Isabel Sarlis pictorial	10–20
	May	Ginger Young	10–20
	June	Delores Welles, Playmate of the year: Ellen Stratton	10–20
	July	Teddi Smith, Marie Renfro: the nude look	10–20
	August	Elaine Paul, Sophia Loren pictorial, Playboy Club Bunnies: Marie Renfro, Annette Prescott, June Wilkinson, Joyce Nizzari, and Cynthia Maddox	10–20
	September	Anne Davis, Marie Renfro	10–20
	October	Kathy Douglas, the girls of Hollywood: Tuesday Weld, June Wilkinson, Tina Louise, Abby Dalton, and Yvette Mimieux	10–20
	November	Joni Mathis, June Wilkinson pictorial	10–20
	December	Carol Eden, Teddi Smith, Marilyn Monroe pictorial, Janet Pilgram, Lisa Williams, Linda Vargas, Joyce Nizzari, Ellen Stratton	20–40

YEAR	ISSUE	DESCRIPTION	VALUE
1961	January	Connie Cooper	$10–20
	February	Barbara Ann Lawford, the girls of New York	($100) 15–30
	March	Tonya Crews, the nude wave in Hollywood	($150) 15–30
	April	Nancy Nielsen, Playmate of the year: Linda Gamble	15–30
	May	Susan Kelly, the girls of Sweden	($175) 15–30
	June	Heidi Becker, Ann Richards pictorial	15–30
	July	Sheralee Connors, le Crazy Horse pictorial	15–30
	August	Karen Thompson, the girls of Hawaii	15–30
	September	Christa Speck, the Miami Playboy Club	15–30
	October	Jean Connors, anthology of pros pictorial	10–20
	November	Dianne Danford, Anita Ekberg pictorial	15–30
	December	Lynn Larrol, Playboy's Playmate holiday house party	15–30
1962	January	Merle Pertile, Playmate review	15–30
	February	Kari Knudsen, Cynthia Maddox covergirl, the girls of Rome pictorial	($125) 15–30
	March	Pamela Anne Gordon, New Orleans Playboy Club	($125) 15–30
	April	Roberta Lane, Playmate of the year: Christa Speck	($125) 15–30
	May	Marya Carter, the villain still pursues her: a pictorial, Cynthia Maddox	15–30
	June	Merissa Mathes, toast to bikinis and scuba gear and scuba gear pictorials	($125) 15–30

YEAR	ISSUE	DESCRIPTION	VALUE
1962	July	Unne Terjesen, Janet Pilgram pictorial	($75) 15–30
	August	Jan Roberts, return to Rome: Gesa Meiken	($75) 15–30
	September	Mickey Winters	15–30
	October	Laura Young, Bonnie Jo Halpin cover, girls of London pictorial	($150) 20–40
	November	Avis Kimble, Playmates of history	15–30
	December	June Cochran, Sheralee Connors cover, Arlene Dahl pictorial, Playboy's other girlfriends: Tina Louise, Anita Ekberg, Jill St. John, Sophia Loren, Ann Richards, Elga Anderson, Abby Dalton, Kim Novak, Elaine Stewart, Tania Velia, and June Wilkinson	($100) 15–30
1963	January	Judi Monterey, Elizabeth Taylor/Cleopatra pictorial	20–40
	February	Toni Ann Thomas, Cheryl Lamphey cover, the chicks of Cleopatra, the Playmate pillow fight: Teddi Smith, Christa Speck, Delores Wells, and Carrie Radison	15–30
	March	Adrienne Moreau, Cynthia Maddox cover, Playmate of the year run-off: June Cochran, Avis Kimble, and Laura Young	($200) 15–30
	April	Sandra Settani, Kelly Collins cover, the girls of Africa, the New York Playboy Club	($125) 15–30
	May	Sharon Cintron, Playmate of the year: June Cochran, the femlin comes to life	15–30

YEAR	ISSUE	DESCRIPTION	VALUE
1963	June	Connie Mason, Jayne Mansfield cover and pictorial	($200) 25–50
	July	Carrie Enwright, Judy Newton cover, the Bunnies pictorial, Christa Speck, Pam Gordon, Linda Gamble, Carrie Radison, Joyce Nizzari, and June Cochran	($125) 15–30
	August	Phyllis Sherwood, Nancy Perry cover, African queen: Gillian Tanner pictorial	($75) 15–30
	September	Victoria Valentino, Joey Thorpe cover, Europe's new sex sirens: Elke Sommer, Sylvia Koscina, Shirley Ann Field, Dany Saval, Sarah Miles, June Ritchie, Claudia Cardinale, Catherine Deneuve, and others	($125) 15–30
	October	Christine Williams, Teddi Smith cover, Playboy clubs: Disneyland for adults, Elsa Martinelli pictorial	($125) 15–30
	November	Terre Tucker, Sharon Rogers cover, the girls of Canada, Cleopatra, Italian style: Pacale Petit	($100) 15–30
	December	Donna Michele, Susan Strasberg, and Kim Novak pictorial, the editors' choice: Lisa Winters, Janet Pilgram, Heidi Becker, Ellen Stratton, Joyce Nizzari, Christa Speck, Avis Kimble, Connie Mason, Donna Michelle, Christine Williams	($200) 20–40

YEAR	ISSUE	DESCRIPTION	VALUE
1964	January	Sharon Rogers, Marilyn Monroe pictorial	$25–50
	February	Nancy Jo Hopper, Cynthia Maddox cover, in bed with Beckett: Mamie Van Doren and Veronique Vendell, 1954 Playmates revisited	10–20
	March	Nancy Scott, Olga Schoberova cover, the girls of Russia, 1955 Playmates revisited	10–20
	April	Ashlyn Martin, Karen Lynn and Peter Sellers cover, Peter Sellers mimes the movie Lovers, 1956 Playmates revisited	10–20
	May	Donna Michelle Playmate and cover, 1957 Playmates revisited	10–20
	June	Lori Winston, Mamie Van Doren cover and pictorial: the nudest Mamie Van Doren, Susannah York pictorial, 1958 Playmates revisited	10–20
	July	Melba Ogle, Cynthia Maddox cover, the sex kitten grows up: Brigitte Bardot, 1959 Playmates revisited	12–25
	August	China Lee, Barbara Reeves cover, the Bunnies of Chicago, 1960 Playmates revisited	10–20
	September	Astrid Schulz, Heather Hewitt cover, Playboy in Jamaica, Elke Sommer pictorial, 1961 Playmates revisited	12–25

YEAR	ISSUE	DESCRIPTION	VALUE
1964	October	Rosemary Hillcrest, Judy Newton cover, 1962 Playmates revisited, Marco Polo's spices pictorial	$10–20
	November	Kai Brendinger, Maria Hoff cover, the girls of Germany, 1963 Playmates revisited	($100) 10–20
	December	Jo Collins, Ian Fleming interview, Carroll Baker pictorial, the readers' choice top ten Playmates: Connie Mason, Laura Young, June Cochran, Christa Speck, Janet Pilgram, Toni Ann Thomas, Joyce Nizzari, Lisa Winters, Heidi Becker, and Donna Michelle	10–20
1965	January	Sally Duberson, Ustinov's harems pictorial	10–20
	February	Jessica St. George, Teddi Smith cover, the Beatles interview, Donna Michelle and Kim Novak pictorials	($200) 20–40
	March	Jennifer Jackson, Carol Lynley pictorial, the unsinkable Fanny Hill picture essay	($175) 20–40
	April	Sue Williams, Lannie Balcom cover, the Playboy bed, the Playboy playoff: Jo Collins, China Lee, and Astrid Schulz	10–20
	May	Maria McBane, the kiss: Barbara Bouchet, Stella Stevens pictorial	12–25
	June	Hedy Scott, Turid Lundberg cover, the big bunny hop picture essay, Ursula Andress pictorial	10–20

YEAR	ISSUE	DESCRIPTION	VALUE
1965	July	Gay Collier, Joey Thorpe cover, the girls of the Riviera	($125) 10–20
	August	Lannie Balcom, Jo Collins cover and Playmate of the year pictorial, Ursula Andress	10–20
	September	Patti Reynolds, Teddi Smith cover, Saturday night with Genghis Khan pictorial, Jeanne Moreau	($75) 10–20
	October	Allison Parks, Penny James cover, Catherine Deneuve pictorial, the Bunnies of Miami	10–20
	November	Pat Russo, Beth Hyatt cover, James Bond's girls pictorial, the nude look	($125) 15–30
	December	Dinah Willis, Allison Parks cover, the Playboy portfolio of sex stars: Brigitte Bardot, Ursula Andress, Arlene Dahl, Carroll Baker, Sophia Loren, Tina Louise, Elizabeth Taylor, Jayne Mansfield, Elsa Martinelli, Kim Novak, Mamie Van Doren, and Carol Lynley	($125) 15–30
1966	January	Judy Tyler, the Playboy mansion pictorial, Princess Grace (Kelly) interview	12–25
	February	Melinda Windsor, the girls of Rio	($80) 10–20
	March	Priscilla Wright, trio con brio: Rossana Podesta, Christiana Schmidtmer, Shirley Anne Field, Bob Dylan interview	($80) 10–20

YEAR	ISSUE	DESCRIPTION	VALUE
1966	April	Karia Conway, Cynthia Maddox cover, the Playboy story, history of sex in the cinema featuring the Jean Harlow nudes, Mae West, Greta Garbo, Marlene Dietrich, and Hedy Lamarr	($75) 10–20
	May	Dolly Read, Allison Parks cover and Playmate of the year pictorial, Jo Collins in Vietnam pictorial	($80) 10–20
	June	Kelly Burke, Mary Warren cover, the girls of Texas	($55) 10–20
	July	Tish Howard, Patti Reynolds, Penny James, Joann Russell, Barbara Shaw and Joey Thorpe cover, Sean Connery strikes again: Sue Ane Langdon and Jean Seberg, Ursula Andress	($80) 10–20
	August	Susan Denberg, Jane Fonda pictorial, the Bunnies of Dixie	($70) 10–20
	September	Dianne Chandler Playmate and cover, topless pictorial, Jocelyn Lane	($100) 10–20
	October	Linda Moon, Penny James cover, Ann-Margret as art nude pictorial	($100) 12–25
	November	Lisa Baker, Sue Bachelor cover, see-through and micro female fashions, Ingrid Weber, Francisca Gedzek and Uta Levika	($55) 9–18
	December	Sue Bernard, Nancy Gould cover, the girls of Tahiti, London: Playboy on the town	($55) 10–20

YEAR	ISSUE	DESCRIPTION	VALUE
1967	January	Surrey Marshe, the Playmates of the fine art, sex in the cinema: sex stars of the fifties	($70) 10–20
	February	Kim Faber, Helen Kirk cover, the girls of Casino Royale pictorial with Woody Allen and Joanne Pettet	($70) 10–20
	March	Fran Gerard, Nancy Chamberlain cover, the Tate Gallery: Sharon Tate pictorial, the Bunnies of Missouri	($50) 7–15
	April	Gwen Wong, Cheryl Shrobe cover, Playmate playoff pictorial: Lisa Baker, Susan Denberg, and Tish Howard	($50) 7–15
	May	Anne Randall, Beth Hyatt, Sylvia Koscina pictorial, Woody Allen interview	($50) 6–12
	June	Joey Gibson, Sharon Kristie cover, You Only Live Twice: 007's Oriental eyefuls pictorial	($50) 10–20
	July	Heather Ryan, Venita Wolf cover, the girls of Paris pictorial, Michael Caine interview	($50) 6–12
	August	Dede Lind, Lisa Baker cover, Sherry Jackson pictorial, Playmate of the year Lisa Baker	($75) 10–20
	September	Angela Dorian, Bo Bussmann cover, the trip: Mara Sykes pictorial	($50) 7–15
	October	Reagan Wilson, the fox: Anne Heywood and Sandy Dennis pictorials	($50) 6–12

YEAR	ISSUE	DESCRIPTION	VALUE
1967	November	Kaya Christian, Beth Hyatt cover, Playboy's charter yacht party	($50) 6–12
	December	Lynn Winchell Playmate and cover, Elke Sommer pictorial, the Bunnies of Hollywood	($50) 10–20
1968	January	Connie Kreski, Stella Stevens pictorial	($150) 15–30
	February	Nancy Harwood, Paulette Lindberg cover, the lady in blue: Joanna Pettet, the Miss Nude Universe contest	($55) 6–12
	March	Michelle Hamilton, Sharon Kristie cover, the bizzarre beauties of Barbarella: Jane Fonda and others, brush-on fashions pictorial	($55) 10–20
	April	Gaye Rennie, Dolly Read cover and pictorial	($55) 6–12
	May	Elizabeth Jordon, Angela Dorian cover and Playmate of the year pictorial, Julie Newmar	($55) 10–20
	June	Britt Fredriksen, Jeannie Wallace cover, the girls of Scandinavia pictorial	($55) 6–12
	July	Melodye Prentiss, Lynn Hahn cover, Leicia pictorial, sex in the cinema	($40) 5–10
	August	Gale Olson, Aino Korva cover, Carroll Baker pictorial	($40) 5–10
	September	Dru Hart, Erika Toth cover, student body pictorial featuring Vicky Drake, the girls of Funny Girl	($55) 5–10
	October	Majiken Haugedal, Dale Fahey cover, Barbara McNair	($55) 5–10

YEAR	ISSUE	DESCRIPTION	VALUE
1968	November	Paige Young, Theater of the Nude	($40) 5–10
	December	Cynthia Myers Playmate and cover, the girls of the Orient, erotica	10–20
1969	January	Leslie Bianchini, fifteenth anniversary issue, sex stars of the 'sixties: Natalie Wood, Stella Stevens, Sharon Tate, Carol Lynley	($120) 15–30
	February	Lorrie Menconi, Nancy Chamberlain cover, Pamela Tiffin pictorial	($55) 5–10
	March	Kathy MacDonald, Penny James cover, Connie Kreski, Joan Collins, Marie Lijedahl	($55) 6–12
	April	Lorna Hopper, Sharon Krisstie cover, the language of legs pictorial, Brigitte Bardot, Vanessa Redgrave	($55) 5–10
	May	Sally Sheffield, Paulette Lindberg cover, Camille 2000 pictorial with Danielle Gaubert, Lake Geneva Playboy Club, auto erotica	($55) 5–10
	June	Helena Antonaccio, Connie Kreski cover and Playmate of the year pictorial, De Sade	($75) 7–15
	July	Nancy McNeil, Barbara Klein cover: Barbi Benton before name change, Tina Aumont pictorical	($55) 10–20
	August	Debbie Hooper, Penny James cover, the Bunnies of Detroit, Paula Kelly pictorial	($40) 5–10
	September	Shay Knuth Playmate and cover, Julie Newmar pictorial, the girls of Australia	($75) 10–20

YEAR	ISSUE	DESCRIPTION	VALUE
1969	October	Jean Bell, Paulette Lindberg cover, Oh Calcutta movie pictorial, war games pictorial	($55) 5–10
	November	Claudia Jennings	($55) 5–10
	December	Gloria Root, Jorja Beck cover, the girls of Hair pictorial, homage to Toulouse-Lautrec	($55) 5–10
1970	January	Jill Taylor, The Beauty Trap featuring Jeanne Rejaunier, Vargas Revisited, Raquel Welch interview	($125) 12–25
	February	Linda Forsythe, Norma Bauer cover, Bibi Andersson and Barbara Parkins pictorial	($75) 5–10
	March	Chris Koren, Barbi Benton cover and pictorial, Bunny of the year: Gina Byrams, the girls of Julius Caesar	($75) 10–20
	April	Barbara Hillary, Pamela Nystul cover, Bunny Myra: Myra Van Heck pictorial, the girls of Israel	($55) 5–10
	May	Jennifer Liano, Phyllis Babila cover, bedsprings eternal pictorial, Susanne Benton	($55) 5–10
	June	Elaine Morton, Claudia Jennings cover and Playmate of the year pictorial, Tiny Tim interview	($55) 5–10
	July	Carol Willis, Janet Wolf covers, the dolls of Beyond the Valley of the Dolls pictorial featuring Dolly Read and Cynthia Myers, shaping up for Oh Calcutta	($55) 5–10

YEAR	ISSUE	DESCRIPTION	VALUE
1970	August	Sharon Clark, Linda Donnelly cover, Raquel Welch and Mae West in Myra Goes Hollywood pictorial, the Bunnies of 1970	($40) 6–12
	September	Debbie Ellison, Jackie Ray cover, the no-bra look, Elke Sommer, posterotica	($40) 6–12
	October	Mary and Madeleine Collinson Playmates and cover, Paula Prentiss, Laine Kazan, pornography and the unmelancholy Danes	($40) 5–10
	November	Avis Miller, Crystal Smith cover, Gallo's girls, Jane Birkin pictorial	($40) 5–10
	December	Carol Imhof, Shay Knuth cover, Paula Pritchett, the classic woman	($100) 5–10
1971	January	Liv Lindeland, stalking the wild Veruschka pictorial, Playmate review, the act of love, Mae West interview	($100) 10–20
	February	Willy Rey, Fran Jeffries pictorial, the bejeweled body, the statue	($55) 5–10
	March	Cynthia Hall, Peggy Smith cover, the girls of Holland, Alex in Wonderland: Cherie Latimer	($40) 5–10
	April	Chris Cranston, Simone Hammerst, Lana Wood pictorial, pretty maids	($40) 5–10
	May	Janice Pennington, Diane Davies cover, the Bunnies of New York, Sarah Kennedy	($40) 5–10

YEAR	ISSUE	DESCRIPTION	VALUE
1971	June	Lieko English, Sharon Clark cover, the Nude Theater, premier Playmates revisited: 1960–1970, Playmate of the year pictorial: Sharon Clark	($40) 5–10
	July	Heather Van Every, Kay Sutton York cover, blooming beauty: Linda Evans pictorial	($40) 6–12
	August	Cathy Rowland, Christy Miller cover, the age of awakening, the Bunnies of 1971	($40) 5–10
	September	Crystal Smith Playmate and cover, McCabe and Mrs. Miller pictorial featuring Julie Christie, girls of the golden West, surreal ladies	($40) 5–10
	October	Clare Rambbeau, Darine Stern cover, the porno girls picture essay, Marisa Berenson pictorial	($40) 5–10
	November	Danielle de Vabre, Debbie Hanlon cover, the life and times of Henry Miller, retiring personalities pictorial, sex in the cinema	($40) 5–10
	December	Karen Christy, Diamonds Are Forever: Vegas comes up 007, personal views of the erotic	($40) 5–10
1972	January	Marilyn Cole, A Clockwork Orange	($50) 5–10
	February	P. J. Lansing, Barbara Carrera cover, the making of Macbeth picture essay, Angel Tomkins pictorial, signs of love	($40) 5–10

YEAR	ISSUE	DESCRIPTION	VALUE
1972	March	Ellen Michaels, Savages pictorial, the shirt off her back, Dominique Sandra pictorial	($40) 5–10
	April	Vicki Peters, Pop's girls, Tiffany Bolling pictorial	($40) 4–8
	May	Deanna Baker, Barbi Benton cover, Monday's child, Valerie Perrine pictorial	($40) 5–10
	June	Debbie Davis, Liv Lindeland cover and Playmate of the year pictorial, those sexy French literary ladies, Sissy Spacek	($40) 5–10
	July	Carol O'Neal, Paula Pritchett and Paula Kelly pictorial	($40) 4–8
	August	Linda Summers, Carole Vitale cover, Box Car Bertha featuring Barbara Hershey, the girls of Munich	($40) 5–10
	September	Susan Miller, Sandra Jozefski cover, student bodies, M.A.S.H.'s Karen Phillip pictorial, skinetic art	($40) 5–10
	October	Sharon Johansen, Lynn Myers cover, black and white: Brenda Sykes and Stella Stevens, the Bunnies of 1972, body work	($40) 4–8
	November	Lenna Sjooblom, Pamela Rawlings cover, Gwen Welles pictorial	($40) 4–8
	December	Mercy Rooney, women eternal, Nancy Robinson, sex stars of 1972: Victoria Principal, Barbara Hershey, Ali McGraw, and others	($40) 6–12

YEAR	ISSUE	DESCRIPTION	VALUE
1973	January	Miki Garcia, Peter Turner's turn-ons, Playmate review	($50) 6–12
	February	Cyndi Wood, Jeanette Larson cover, the Ziegfeld girls featuring Susan Clark, Last Tango in Paris star Maria Schneider pictorial, In Search of Love's sure thing	($40) 4–8
	March	Bonnie Large, Mercy Rooney cover, Edy Williams pictorial, A Name for Evil featuring Samantha Eggar and Sheila Sullivan, legends in their own time	($40) 4–8
	April	Julie Woodson, Lenna Sjooblom cover, Linda Lovelace, women with a twist, ballerina Dayle Haddon pictorial	($40) 4–8
	May	Anulka Dziubinska, Bernie Becker cover, Barbara Leigh pictorial as The Indian, sex and the automobile	($40) 4–8
	June	Ruthy Ross, Marilyn Cole cover and Playmate of the year pictorial, women's work	($40) 4–8
	July	Martha Smith, Karen Christy cover, Tisa Farrow pictorial, the sainted Bond: Jane Seymour and Gloria Hendry, Summer of '72	($40) 5–10
	August	Phyllis Coleman, Cyndi Wood cover, The Tender Trap featuring Heather Menzies, porno chic	($40) 4–8
	September	Geri Glass, A Star Is Made featuring Lee Meredith, The Naked Ape star Victoria Principal pictorial	($75) 15–30

YEAR	ISSUE	DESCRIPTION	VALUE
1973	October	Valerie Lane, Sheila Ryan cover, the Bunnies of 1973, Sacheen Littlefeather pictorial	($40) 4–8
	November	Monica Tidwell, Anne Randall cover, Ursula Andress pictorial	($40) 4–8
	December	Christine Maddox, Bonita Lou Rossi cover, Barbi Benton pictorial, pinups, sex stars of 1973	($40) 9–18
1974	January	Nancy Cameron, Cyndi Wood cover, twentieth anniversary special, twenty years of Playboy, Painted Lady featuring Veruschka	($150) 12–25
	February	Francine Parks, Karen Christy cover, Butterfly Girl featuring Ratna Assan, Alexandra Hay, the girls of skiing, Candice Bergen	($50) 4–8
	March	Pamela Zinszar, Debbie Shelton cover, The Don's Daughter-in-law featuring Simonetta Stefanelli, Sean Connery in Zardoz movie photos, the loving touch	4–8
	April	Marlene Marrow, Carron June Sliger cover, Donna Michele pictorial, sex, soap and success: Marilyn Chambers foreplay	($50) 4–8
	May	Marilyn Lange, Marsha Kay cover, the devil and the flesh, sheer delights	($50) 4–8
	June	Sandy Johnson, Cyndi Wood cover and Playmate of the year pictorial, hindsight	($50) 4–8

YEAR	ISSUE	DESCRIPTION	VALUE
1974	July	Carole Vitale, Christine Maddox, Let My People Come, Isela Vega, ladies in hats pictorial	($40) 4–8
	August	Jean Manson, Lynnda Kimball cover, Brown Sugar featuring Claudia Lennear, Here Comes the Bride	($40) 4–8
	September	Kristine Hanson, model Zoya cover, Jane Lubeck: sis, boom, ah!	($40) 4–8
	October	Ester Cordet, Suzann Shery cover, Lepke's Lady featuring Mary Wilcox, the Bunnies of 1974	($40) 4–8
	November	Bebe Buel, Claudia Jennings cover, sex in the cinema, spec-tacular	($40) 4–8
	December	Janice Raymond, Robyn Douglas cover, the erotic world of Salvador Dali, Claudia Jennings pictorial, sex stars of 1974: Candice Bergen, Raquel Welch, and others	($125) 12–25
1975	January	Lynnda Kimball, Brigitte Bardot pictorial, Playboy mansion west featuring Barbi Benton, Playmate review	($75) 10–20
	February	Laura Misch Playmate and cover, Linda Lovelace pictorial, the French maid	($75) 6–12
	March	Ingeborg Sorensen, Eva Maria, Margot Kidder pictorial, shaping up, ripped off	5–10

YEAR	ISSUE	DESCRIPTION	VALUE
1975	April	Victoria Cunningham, Cyndi Wood cover, bed and board, Valerie Perrine pictorial, Donyale Luna	($40) 4–8
	May	Bridgitte Rollins, Carol Christie cover, the splendor of Gwen: Gwen Welles pictorial, T-shirts	($40) 4–8
	June	Azizi Johari, Marilyn Lange cover and Playmate of the year pictorial	($75) 5–10
	July	Lynn Schiller Playmate and cover, super surfer: Laura Blears Ching, a long look at legs	($50) 4–8
	August	Lillian Muller Playmate and cover, the department store, the girl from Playboy: Kim Komar pictorial	($50) 4–8
	September	Mesina Miller, Amy Arnold cover, put it on pictorial	($50) 4–8
	October	Jill de Vries, Agneta Eckemyr and Zoe Z. Cover, Sappho, Lisztomania, Fiona Lewis pictorial, Cher	($40) 4–8
	November	Janet Lupo, Patricia McClain cover, the Bunnies of 1975	($50) 4–8
	December	Nancie Li Brandi, Lillian Muller cover, The Story of O: Corine Clery, peep show pictorial, Susan Sarandon and Margot Kidder	($50) 4–8
1976	January	Daina House, Playmates of 1975 cover, Fegley pictorial, woman, Elton John interview, Playmate review	6–12

YEAR	ISSUE	DESCRIPTION	VALUE
1976	February	Laura Lyons, Jill de Vries cover, Krbrick's countess: Marisa Berenson, funderwear pictorial	($40) 4–8
	March	Ann Pennington, Vicki Cunningham cover and pictorial: fire belle, Sylvia Kristel: encore Emmanuelle	($75) 4–8
	April	Denise Michele, Kristine del Bell cover, Ursula Andress pictorial, Nanci Li Brandi	($75) 4–8
	May	Patricia McClain, Nancy Cameron cover, Barbara Parkins pictorial, Suze Randall	($55) 4–8
	June	Debra Peterson, Lillian Muller cover and Playmate of the year pictorial, women at work	($55) 4–8
	July	Deborah Borkman, Cyndi Wood cover, Jayne Mansfield's daughter pictorial: Jayne Marie Mansfield, Sarah Miles	($75) 4–8
	August	Linda Beatty, sex in the great outdoors, Kristine de Bell	($40) 4–8
	September	Whitney Kine, the girls of Washington, D.C., Newton's physiques	($55) 4–8
	October	Hope Olson, Karen Hafter cover, Melanie Griffith collector's item pictorial, the Bunnies of 1976	($55) 10–20
	November	Patti McGuire Playmate and cover, Misty Rowe pictorial	($50) 4–8

YEAR	ISSUE	DESCRIPTION	VALUE
1976	December	Karen Hafter, Deborah Borkman cover, Pompeo Posar portfolio featuring over a dozen women, Fellini's Casanova, Karen Black, Sarah Miles, David Bowie	($40) 4–8
1977	January	Susan Lynn Kiger, Barbara Leigh pictorial, Spermula, Playmate review	($75) 4–8
	February	Star Stowe, Lena Kansbod cover, the year in sex, Playmate preview, love feast pictorial	($40) 4–8
	March	Nicki Thomas, Susan Kiger cover, Comeback for Casanova pictorial featuring Lillian Muller	($40) 4–8
	April	Lisa Sohn Playmate and cover, the girls of the new South, Jennifer Edi	($40) 4–8
	May	Sheila Mullen, Lillian Muller cover, bewitched by older women, Patti D'Arbanville, Kellie Everts	($75) 4–8
	June	Virve Reed, Patti McGuire cover and Playmate of the year pictorial, Barbara Bach bondage pictorial	($75) 6–12
	July	Sondra Theodore, Pamela Serpe cover, Barbara Carrera pictorial, the new girls of porn	($100) 7–15
	August	Julia Lyndon, Karen Christy, Playboy's Playmate photo contest, riverboat gamblers pictorial featuring Patti McGuire, Hope Olson, and Cindy Russell, Madame Claude	($40) 4–8

YEAR	ISSUE	DESCRIPTION	VALUE
1977	September	Debra Jo Fondren, Denise Michele, Hope Olson and Lisa Sohm cover, girls of the Big Ten, Jean Manson	($100) 4–8
	October	Kristine Winder, Barbara Streisand cover and interview, Nureyev's Valentino featuring Michelle Phillips, a masked ball	($75) 4–8
	November	Rita Lee, Susan Kiger cover, the Bunnies of 1977, sex in the cinema 1977	($50) 4–8
	December	Ashley Cox, Sondra Theodore cover, Playboy's Playmate house party, swingers' scrapbrook, Melanie Griffith nude, kiss in Japan, John Denver interview, Barbara Bach	6–12
1978	January	Debra Jenssen, Rita Lee cover, the year in sex: Farrah Fawcett, Cheryl Ladd, and others, 15-page Playmate review, erotic fantasies pictorial	($40) 10–20
	February	Janis Schmitt, Hope Olson cover, close encounters of the fourth kind, Playmates international: foreign edition pictorial	($75) 4–8
	March	Christina Smith, Debra Jensen cover, Pretty Baby featuring Brooke Shields, sex on wheels, Bob Dylan interview	($75) 6–12
	April	Pamela Jean Bryant, Susan and Patty Kiger cover, sisters pictorial, the girls of Crazy Horse	($40) 4–8

YEAR	ISSUE	DESCRIPTION	VALUE
1978	May	Kathryn Morrison, Debra Peterson cover, Chameleon featuring Anita Russell pictorial	($40) 4–8
	June	Gail Stanton, Debra Jo Fondren cover and Playmate of the year pictorial, moons in June: Debra Jo Fondren, Rita Lee, Bebe Buel, Cyndi Wood, and others	($75) 6–12
	July	Karen Morton, Pamela Sue Martin cover and pictorial, Call of the Wild pictorial featuring Susan Jensen	($40) 10–20
	August	Vicki Witt, Nicki Thomas cover, Eyes of Laura Mars featuring Faye Dunaway, the girls in the office/secretaries	($40) 4–8
	September	Rosanne Katon, Sue Paul cover, the girls of the PAC 10, Simone Boisseree/stunt girl pictorial	($40) 4–8
	October	Marcy Hanson, Dolly Parton cover and interview, Girl on a Dolphin pictorial featuring Denice Creedon, girls of the PAC 10: part II, Older Women featuring Karen Black, Alexandra Stewart and Helen Shaver, Cheryl Tiegs	($40) 5–10
	November	Monique St. Pierre Playmate and cover, the Bunnies of 1978, sex in the cinema	($40) 4–8
	December	Janet Quist, Farrah Fawcett cover, interview, and pictorial, cheerleaders pictorial, viva Vargas	10–20

YEAR	ISSUE	DESCRIPTION	VALUE
1979	January	Candy Loving, the great Playmate hunt, grin and bare it, Playboy's 25 beautiful years: Marilyn Monroe, Jayne Mansfield, and others, special 25th anniversary issue	($125) 10–20
	February	Lee Ann Michelle, Candy Collins cover, the girls of Las Vegas, Lexi Vogel: Father knows best, the year in sex	($40) 4–8
	March	Denise McConnell, Debra Jensen cover, naked cheerleaders, Denise Crosby pictorial	($75) 7–15
	April	Missy Cleveland, Rita Lee cover, Debra Jo Fondren pictorial, Grace Jones, disco queens, 25 years of rock and roll featuring Elvis Presley and others	($50) 5–10
	May	Michele Drake, Cheryle Larsen, foreign sex stars, the secret life of Marilyn Monroe . . . with rare photos, Ken Marcus photo pictorial featuring Janet Quist, Hope Olson, Martha Smith, Lillian Muller, and others	($75) 4–8
	June	Louann Fernald, Monique St. Pierre cover and Playmate of the year pictorial, Playboy's past playmates of the year: featuring all 19, dance hall demoiselles	($40) 4–8
	July	Dorothy Mays, Denise Gauthier cover, the girls of Moonraker pictorial, Patti McGuire pictorial	($40) 6–12

YEAR	ISSUE	DESCRIPTION	VALUE
1979	August	Dorothy Stratten, Candy Loving cover and pictorial, Nastassja Kinski, Monique St. Pierre, Marilyn Cole, Bunny Anika Pavel and Gail Stanton	($100) 15–30
	September	Vicki McCay Playmate and cover, Claudia Jennings pictorial, Ivy League coeds	($75) 4–8
	October	Ursula Buchfellner, Gig Gangel cover, the Bunnies of 1979, Bunny costumes, Linda Beatty Carpenter and Cyndi Wood pictures from Apocalypse Now	($100) 4–8
	November	Sylvie Garant, Phyllis McCreary cover, Colleen Donovan pictorial, carnival knowledge, sex in the cinema	($40) 4–8
	December	Candy Collins, Raquel Welch cover and pictorial, Playmates forever featuring: Connie Kreski, Lisa Baker, Jo Collins, Sharon Johansen, Liv Lindeland, Nancy Scott, Jean Bell, Heidi Becker, Dede Lind, and others, sex stars	($50) 10–20
1980	January	Gig Gangel, Amy Miller and Michele Drake with Steve Martin, NFL cheerleaders pictorial, Playboy pajama party, Star Trek's enterprising return	($100) 5–10
	February	Sandy Cagle, Candice Collins cover, the year in sex, Suzanne Somers Playmate test pictorial	($100) 7–15

YEAR	ISSUE	DESCRIPTION	VALUE
1980	March	Henriette Allais, Bo Derek cover and pictorial, All Fosse, Melonie Haller	($100) 5–10
	April	Liz Glazowski, Shari Shattuck cover, women of the armed services, Playboy's Playmate reunion featuring 136 Playmates, Linda Ronstadt interview	($100) 5–10
	May	Martha Thomsen, Teri Welles cover, flight attendants pictorial, Silvana Suarez: the real Miss World	($100) 5–10
	June	Ola Ray, Dorothy Stratten cover and Playmate of the year pictorial, Fellini's feminist fantasy	($150) 15–30
	July	Teri Peterson, Sandra Dumas cover, ten ways to find the perfect 10 pictorial	($125) 5–10
	August	Victoria Cooke, Bo Derek cover and pictorial, the girls of Hawaii	($125) 6–12
	September	Lisa Welch, Rita Lee cover, girls of the Southwest Conference, new girl on campus pictorial, Evelyn Guerrero	($100) 6–12
	October	Mardi Jacquet, S. J. Fellowes cover, the girls of Canada, Lisa Lyon: body beautiful	($150) 6–12
	November	Jeana Tomasino, Mardi Jacquet cover, the women of the U.S government, sex in the cinema: Brooke Shields, Bo Derek, and others	($125) 6–12

YEAR	ISSUE	DESCRIPTION	VALUE
1980	December	Terri Welles, an erotic portfolio, the twenty-year pictorial, sex stars of 1980: Lesley Anne Down, Misty Rowe, Dorothy Stratten, Linda Kerridge pictorial	($150) 10–20
1981	January	Karen Price, Barbara Bach cover and pictorial, honky-tonk angels, John and Yoko	($150) 9–18
	February	Vicki Lasseter, Candy Loving, Sandra Theodore and Terri Welles cover and Playmate roommates pictorial, the year in sex, the girl next door	($125) 5–10
	March	Kimberly Herrin, Cybil and Tricia Barnstable cover and featured in twins pictorial, Jo Penny	($125) 5–10
	April	Lorraine Michaels, Liz Wickersham cover, the girls of Kokomo, Indiana, Rita Jenrette	($75) 4–8
	May	Gina Goldberg, Gabriella Brum cover and pictorial, girls of the Adriatic Coast, the Dorothy Stratten story	($125) 5–10
	June	Cathy Larmouth, Terri Welles cover and Playmate of the year pictorial, the ladies of You Only Live Twice	($125) 5–10
	July	Heidi Sorenson, Jayne Kennedy cover and pictorial, tender cousins	($125) 6–12
	August	Debbie Boostrom, Valerie Perrine cover and pictorial	5–10

YEAR	ISSUE	DESCRIPTION	VALUE
1981	September	Susan Smith, Bo Derek cover and pictorial, girls of the Southeastern Conference	($50) 4–8
	October	Kelly Ann Tough, Cathy St. George cover, Maud Adams pictorial, Terri Garr interview, girls of the Southeastern Conference part II	($50) 5–10
	November	Shannon Tweed, Teri Petersen cover, Vikki LaMotta pictorial, Jamie Lee Curtis interview	5–10
	December	Patricia Farinelli, Bernadette Peters cover and pictorial, captured women, Cheryl Tiegs, and the Playmates sing	($50) 4–8
1982	January	Kimberly McArthur, Natalie Levy Bencheton cover, John Derek's wives pictorial featuring Ursula Andress, Linda Evans, and Bo Derek, soap stars pictorial	5–10
	February	Anne-Marie Fox, Kimberly McArthur cover, the year in sex, Sylvia Kristel, Susan Smith	($50) 5–10
	March	Karen Witter, Barbara Carrera cover and pictorial, Pia Zadora, Melani Martin	($40) 5–10
	April	Linda Rhys Vaughn, Mariel Hemingway cover and pictorial, Henriette Alais	($40) 6–12
	May	Kym Main, Vickie Reigle, beauty and the badge: Barbara Schantz pictorial, Rae Dawn Chong	($40) 4–8

YEAR	ISSUE	DESCRIPTION	VALUE
1982	June	Lourdes Ann Kananimanu Estores, Shannon Tweed cover and Playmate of the year pictorial	($40) 5–10
	July	Lynda Wesmeier Playmate and cover, the girls of Ma Bell, dreams pictorial featuring Debra Jo Fondren, Lillian Muller and Rita Lee	($50) 5–10
	August	Cathy St. George, Vicki McCarty, Marilyn Michaels pictorial, summer sex '82, California girls	($40) 4–8
	September	Connie Brighton, Kym Herrin cover, the girls of the Big Eight, Fran Jeffries pictorial	($40) 4–8
	October	Marianne Gravatte, Tanya Roberts cover and pictorial, the girls of Japan	($40) 10–20+
	November	Marlene Janssen, Lorraine Michaels, the women of Braniff	($50) 4–8
	December	Charlotte Kemp, Marcy Hanson cover, Sydne Rome pictorial, the women of Playboy, Brooke Shields	($40) 5–10
1983	January	Lonny Chin, Audrey and Judy Landers cover and pictorial, Playboy's Playmate review, provocative period pieces	($40) 5–10
	February	Melinda Myers, Kim Basinger cover and pictorial, the women of Aspen	($50) 10–20+
	March	Alana Soares, Kim McArthur, Kelly Tough and Karen Witter, Marina Verola: taking stock of Marina, the first Playmate playoffs	($35) 4–8

YEAR	ISSUE	DESCRIPTION	VALUE
1983	April	Christina Ferguson, Carry Lee cover, ladies of Spain, Pamela Bellwood pictorial: going ape	($35) 4–8
	May	Susy Scott, Nastassja Kinski cover and pictorial, Meet the Mrs. featuring Marilyn Griffin and Marilyn Parver	($50) 4–8
	June	Jolanda Egger, Marianne Gravatte cover and Playmate of the year pictorial, Morganna, Debra Winger interview	($35) 4–8
	July	Ruth Guerri Playmate and cover, James Bond girls nude featuring Kim Basinger and others, erogenous parts	($50) 4–8
	August	Carina Persson, Sybil Danning cover and pictorial, permanent vacation	($75) 4–8
	September	Barbra Edwards, Kym Herrin cover, the girls of the Atlantic Conference	($40) 4–8
	October	Tracy Vaccaro, Charlotte Kemp cover, redheads pictorial, Loretta Martin: brunette ambition	($75) 4–8
	November	Veronica Gamba, Donna Ann cover, women in white: nurse pictorial, Jamie Lee Curtis, Sybil Danning	($35) 5–10
	December	Tery Nihen, Joan Collins cover and pictorial, flashdancers	($40) 4–8
1984	January	Sherry Arnett, Melanie Griffith and Don Johnson pictorial	($35) 4–8

YEAR	ISSUE	DESCRIPTION	VALUE
1984	February	Julie McCullough, Michael Douglas	($75) 4–8
	March	Kim Morris, Sally Field	($50) 4–8
	April	Terri Weigel, Victoria Sellers pictorial	($75) 4–8
	May	Christine Ricjters, Kathleen Turner cover, interview, and poster	($40) 3–6
	June	Rebecca Ferratti, Linda Evans pictorial, Kathy Shower	($75) 4–8
	July	Lynne Austin, Carrie Leigh pictorial, Tom Cruise	($50) 3–6
	August	Carina Persson, Terry More cover and nude pictorial	($75) 3–6
	September	Rebekka Armstrong, Maral Collins, the Chicago Club	($100) 4–8
	October	Katherine Hushaw, the girls of the Ivy League, Wendy O. Williams	($50) 4–8
	November	Donna Edmondson, Dolph Lundgren pictorial	($100) 4–8
	December	Karen Valez, Suzanne Somers cover and special 8-page nude pictorial	($40) 5–10
1985	January	Joan Bennett, Goldie Hawn cover and feature	($35) 3–6
	February	Cheri Witter, Sybil Danning, Girls of Texas	($35) 3–6
	March	Donna Smith, Women in Lingerie pictorial	($35) 3–6
	April	Cindy Brooks, Playmate sisters pictorial	($35) 3–6
	May	Kathy Shower, Vanity pictorial	($35) 3–6
	June	Devon de Vasquez, Roxanne Pulitzer pictorial	($40) 3–6

YEAR	ISSUE	DESCRIPTION	VALUE
1985	July	Hope Marie Carlton, Grace Jones, Jamie Lee Curtis	($35) 3–6
	August	Cher Butler, Judy Norton	($35) 3–6
	September	Venice Kong, Madonna cover and 14-page pictorial, Brigitte Nielsen	($35) 10–20
	October	Cynthia Brimhall, Jerry Hall pictorial	3–6
	November	Pamella Sanders, Women of Mensa	($50) 3–6
	December	Carol Fiscatier, Barbi Benton 12-page pictorial, Vanity, Bruce Springsteen, Don Johnson	($35) 5–10
1986	January	Sherry Arnett, Melanie Griffith and Don Johnson pictorial	($35) 3–6
	February	Julie McCullough, Michael Douglas	($75) 3–6
	March	Kim Morris, Sally Field	($50) 3–6
	April	Terri Weigel, Victoria Sellers pictorial	($75) 3–6
	May	Christine Richters, Kathleen Turner cover, story and poster	($40) 3–6
	June	Rebecca Ferratti, Kathy Showers and Linda Evans pictorials	($75) 3–6
	July	Lynne Austin, Carrie Leigh pictorial, Tom Cruise	($50) 3–6
	August	Ava Fabian, Brigitte Nielsen pictorial, Sigourney Weaver	3–6
	September	Rebekka Armstrong	($100) 3–6
	October	Sachiko, Women of the Ivy League, Wendy O. Williams	($50) 3–6
	November	Donna Edmondson, Dolph Lungren pictorial	($100) 3–6
	December	Laurie Carr, Brooke Shields cover and feature, Women of the 7/11	3–7

YEAR	ISSUE	DESCRIPTION	VALUE
1987	January	Luann Lee, Marilyn Monroe 10-page pictorial	($75) 4–8
	February	Julie Peterson, Stephanie Bachman 10-page pictorial	($40) 3–6
	March	Marina Baker	($40) 3–6
	April	Anna Clark	($30) 3–6
	May	Kymberly Paige, Vanna White pictorial, Barbara Hershey	($35) 4–8
	June	Sandy Greenberg, Donna Edmondson cover and Playmate of the year pictorial	($50) 4–8
	July	Carmen Berg, beach party special featuring 20 pages of sun, surf, and sex	($35) 4–8
	August	Sharry Konopski, Paulina Porizkova cover and pictorial, women of Florida	($50) 4–8
	September	Gwen Hajek, girls of James Bond: a historical pictorial of all the 007 movies and women . . . a 16-page special	($35) 4–8
	October	Brandi Brandt, Donna Mills cover and pictorial	($50) 4–8
	November	Pam Stein, Jessica Hahn cover and 8-page pictorial, Cher, Kelly McGillis	($35) 4–8
	December	India Allen, Brigitte Nielsen pictorial, Jessica Hahn	($25) 4–8
1988	January	Kimberly Conrad, Kim Basinger 8-page nude pictorial	($25) 3–5
	February	Kari Kennell, the nude girls of Britain	($10) 3–5
	March	Susie Owens, 10-page lingerie pictorial	($10) 3–5

YEAR	ISSUE	DESCRIPTION	VALUE
1988	April	Eloise Broady, Vanity cover and nude pictorial	($10) 3–6
	May	Diana Lee, Denise Crosby nude pictorial, Cathy Shower pictorial	($10) 3–6
	June	Emily Arth, Theresa Russell pictorial	($10) 3–5
	July	Terri Lynn Doss, Cindy Crawford cover and nude pictorial	($20) 4–8
	August	Helle Michaelsen, Kimberly Conrad nude pictorial	($10) 3–5
	September	Laura Richmond, Jessica Hahn cover and special nude pictorial	($20) 4–7
	October	Shannon Long, nude college girl pictorial	($10) 3–5
	November	Pia Reyes, nude women of Washington	($10) 3–5
	December	Kata Karkkainen, Samantha Fox, Cher, Vanessa Williams, Vanity, Jessica Hahn	($10) 3–6
1989	January	Fawna MacLaren, 35th anniversay special	($20) 3–6
	February	Simone Eden, Brazilian sex stars	($10) 3–5
	March	Laurie Wood, LaToya Jackson cover and nude pictorial	($25) 4–8
	June	Tawni Cable, Kimberly Conrad cover and Playmate of the year, Dana Plato (Different Strokes) nude pictorial	($10) 5–10
	July	Erika Eleniak, broadcast nudes . . . Shelly Jamison	($10) 3–5
All other issues			3–5

Best from Playboy (and Playboy Annual)
(1954–1957 are hardcovers; 1964 up are softcovers)

YEAR	ISSUE	VALUE
1954		$50–100
1955		40–80
1956		35–70
1957		50–100
1964	#1	15–30
1964	#1 (deluxe edition)	20–40
1968	#2	12–25
1969	#3	12–25
1970	#4	12–25
1971	#5	10–20
1972	#6	10–20
1973	#7	10–20
1975	#8	10–20
1978	#8	4–8
1982 up		4–8

Playboy Presents 50 Beautiful Women (a Special Collection)

YEAR	DESCRIPTION	VALUE
1989	Maud Adams, Ursula Andress, Carroll Baker, Penny Baker, Brigitte Bardot, Sonia Braga, Barbara Carrera, Kimberly Conrad, Farrah Fawcett, Linda Evans, Jessica Hahn, Elke Somers, Jayne Kennedy, Jayne Mansfield, Donna Mills, Victoria Principal, Marilyn Monroe, June Pointer, Dorothy Stratten, Vanna White, Vanity, and others	$10–20

Playboy Specials

Playboy special editions are currently very popular with collectors. These issues in general are valued at $5 to $10 each, and acquire a collector's value after just a few short months of their being published. Issues that feature one or more photos of such noted females as Madonna,

Vanity, Jessica Hahn, Vanna White, Patti McGuire, Dorothy Stratten, Jayne Mansfield, Marilyn Monroe, Janet or LaToya Jackson, Kimberly Conrad, Barbara Carrera, Tanya Roberts, and any other star who is currently popular, are valued at $7 to $15. Following are but a few of the many, many titles that are *Playboy* specials.

Playboy's Holiday Girls	*Bathing Beauties*
The Year in Sex	*Playmates in the Spotlight*
Vanna White	*Kimberly Conrad*
Playboy's Book of Lingerie	*Playmate Review*
Playboy Photography	*Sex and Other Late Night Laughs*
Playboy's Great Playmate Hunt	*College Girls*
Playboy's Nudes	*Blondes, Brunettes, and Redheads*
Women on the Move	*Wet & Wild Women*
Girls of Winter	*Working Women*
Girls of Summer	*Entertaining Women*

SWIMSUIT MAGAZINES AND SPECIALS VALUES

Swimsuit magazines, such as *Swimwear Illustrated, Swimwear U.S.A,* and *Swimsuit International,* as well as swimsuit special editions of *Sports Illustrated, Sports and Inside Sports,* are extremely popular and their value is based on the models shown in a particular issue. Swimsuit magazines from the 'seventies, 'eighties, and 'nineties generally have a value of $1 to $3. Issues containing photographs of current popular female actresses, female athletes, and models such as Kathy Ireland, Christie Brinkley, Paulina Porizkova, Elle MacPherson, Stephanie Seymour, Cheryl Tiegs, and others have a value of $5 to $10, depending on number of photos and if there is a cover photo. *Sports Illustrated's* swimsuit issues are currently the only titles that hold a higher value to the collector; this is mostly due to the high quality of photography and the quantity of photographs modeled by extremely popular models.

Sports Illustrated/Swimsuit Issues

YEAR	ISSUE	DESCRIPTION	VALUE
1964	January 20	Babette cover	$15–30
1965	January 18	Sue Peterson cover	10–20
1966	January 17	Sunny Bippus cover	10–20

January 19, 1976   *February 4, 1980*   *February 9, 1981*

February 8, 1982   *February 13, 1984*   *February 10, 1986*

February 11, 1991   *February 1987*   *February 1990*

YEAR	ISSUE	DESCRIPTION	VALUE
1967	January 18	Marilyn Tindall cover	$10–20
1968	January 15	Turia Mau cover	7–15
1969	January 13	Jamie Becker cover	7–15
1970	January 12	First Cheryl Tiegs cover	12–25
1971	February 1	Tannia Rubiano cover	6–12
1972	January 17	Sheila Roscoe cover	6–12
1973	January 29	Dayle Haddon cover	7–15
1974	January 28	Ann Simonton cover	6–12
1975	January 27	Cheryl Tiegs cover	12–25
1976	January 19	Yvette and Yvonne Sylvander cover	7–15
1977	January 24	Lena Kansbod cover	6–12
1978	January 16	Maria Joao cover	5–10
1979	February 5	First Christie Brinkley cover	15–30
1980	February 4	Christie Brinkley cover	10–20
1981	February 9	Christie Brinkley cover	10–20
1982	February 8	Carol Alt cover	5–10
1983	February 14	Cheryl Tiegs cover	7–15
1984	February 13	First Paulina Porizkova cover	6–12
1985	February 11	Paulina Porizkova cover	5–10
1986	February 10	First Elle MacPherson cover	7–15
1987	February 9	Elle MacPherson cover	6–12
1988	February 15	Elle MacPherson cover	5–10
1989	February 17	25th Anniversary swimsuit issue, Kathy Ireland cover, issue shows every swimsuit cover and feature on the cover models today	7–15
1990	February 12	Rachel Hunter, Kathy Ireland, and others	5–10
1991	February 11	Ashley Montana, Stephanie Seymour, and others	5–10

Detective, Romance, and True Story Magazines

There are basically two types of buyers of this type of magazine. The first is the collector who is intrigued by the cover artwork and/or cover photography. This collector is mainly interested in magazines that were issued prior to 1950. The second type of buyer is mainly interested in reading the stories—generally issues from 1960 to the present. Values for this second category are constant. However, values for issues from 1950 and earlier, which are collected for the cover art, will vary. Higher prices are paid for issues with covers that feature highly seductive women, women in bondage, or women in extremely threatening situations. The more intriguing and/or revealing the female cover subject is, the higher the issue's value will be.

DETECTIVE, ROMANCE, AND TRUE STORY MAGAZINE VALUES

YEAR	VALUE
Pre-1930	$10–20
1931–1940	5–20
1941–1950	4–15
1951–1960	3–8
1961–1965	3–5
1966–1970	2–3
1971–Present	1–2

December 1945

June 1945

July 1945

May 1943

June 1938

January 1938

February 23, 1939

December 1944

February 19, 1938

December 3, 1938

May 27, 1939

November 25, 1939

March 4, 1944

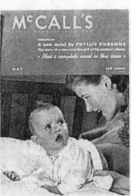

March 1940

May 1940

August 1961

March 4, 1965

July 1941

October 11, 1947

October 25, 1947

July 1936

January 1949

January 1938

March 8, 1938

October 4, 1938

July 25, 1939

May 1940

December 1937

March 1939

July 1944

August 1944

December 1944

November 1945

December 1945

#18, December 13, 1954

#2, 1941

June 1941   February 1951   January 1959

March 1964   July 1950   November 1963

November 1961   March 1965   October 1960

August 1966

June 1967

September 1965

November 1960

Spring 1967

July 1965

October 1959

#16, 1967

May 1940

July 1940

September 1940

February 1946

January 1946

December 1940

May 1943

February 1938

May 1938

March 1940

February 1941   April 1941   October 1944

April 1940   October 1940   November 1940

April 1950   October 1940   May 1943

March 1940

February 1938

April 1940

May 1940

May 1941

September 1941

April 1940

October 1951

February 1940

Entertainment Magazines: Movie/TV Magazines

WHAT ARE MOVIE/TV MAGAZINES?

A movie/TV magazine is any magazine that features stories, interviews, gossip, and photos on the cinema and television. They have been in existence since the time of the silent picture. For the past eighty years they have continued to be extremely popular with movie/TV fans and the population in general. TV magazines first appeared in the early 'fifties, often including features about movie stars and cinema highlights. Magazines such as *Woman's Day, Cosmopolitan, Ladies' Home Journal* and other similar magazines are considered related movie/TV magazines when they feature a movie or TV celebrity on the cover and include a story within on that celebrity. Likewise, any magazine, be it on home improvements, health, beauty, fashion, or any other subject, that highlights a star on its cover becomes a movie/TV-related magazine and will be valued by the collector. Thus, a very common, uncollected magazine title, when featuring a star, quickly enters into the realm of collectibles.

WHAT MAKES A MOVIE/TV MAGAZINE VALUABLE?

What does make a movie/TV magazine valuable? Quite simply, its cover and contents. Movie and TV magazines are collected basically by people and fans interested in particular stars, movies, and television shows. For example, Marilyn Monroe has remained a strong collectible figure to the magazine market. Any magazine, be it from the early 1950s right up to the present, that features her is in high demand. If an issue has an exceptional cover—say, a photo with Marilyn Monroe looking even more alluring than usual, or one of Shirley Temple looking sweeter

March 1977

June 1977

November 1977

March 1978

November 1982

June 1984

#5, April 1977

#17, 1975

#27, 1976

#59, 1979

April 1957

#57, 1970

#1, October 1955

#2, 1972

May 1981

#3, September 1972

December 1982

March 1938

than ever—that issue can sell for up to double the value listed in our value section. Throughout this section we have listed the values for average issues, as well as the magazines that feature the current most popular collectible celebrities.

BUYING MOVIE/TV MAGAZINES

Buying movie/TV magazines can in itself be an adventure. There is no telling where an ambitious collector can turn up a stack of common-to-rare issues. In my thirty years of gathering and collecting, I have come to the conclusion that your own imagination and instincts are the greatest aids in finding possible sources. The most reliable sources, of course, are mail-order dealers, magazine stores, and trade publications such as "Paper Collectors' Marketplace" (470 Main Street, P.O. Box 127, Scandinavia, Wisconsin 54977) and "Film Collectors World" (700 East Main Street, Iola, Wisconsin 54990). Other reliable sources are comic book shops, old book stores, garage sales, flea markets, auctions, house sales, local want ads, memorabilia conventions, and paper collectible shows. Many major malls throughout the nation hold annual collectible shows. It is advisable to call the malls in your area and learn of any upcoming events. One collectible show that has been around for many years is Gallagher's Paper Collectibles and Movie Memorabilia Show, located at St. Francis Xavier, 30 West Sixteenth Street (near Sixth Avenue), in New York City. This show is held once a month on a Saturday, and features many dealers who each month bring in new hordes of thrilling collector memorabilia. Not only will the collector find vintage movie and TV magazines, but sheet music, photos, postcards, advertising, movie posters, and character-related dolls and toys as well. At this show, it is not unusual, while perusing a stack of dusty magazines, to find yourself brushing elbows with a noted TV, movie, or radio personality. For more information regarding this particular favorite show of mine, call Gallagher at 1-718-497-6575 or write to: Gallagher, 72–39 Sixty-sixth Place, Glendale, New York 11385. Other paper collectible shows are held all across the United States and Canada. To find out if there is a show in your area check your local newspaper or get a copy of "Film Collectors World" (1-715-445-2214), which lists a calendar for upcoming events. Many shows will advertise locally via newspapers and/or radio.

September 1938

April 1941

January 1992

1954

July 1992

Summer 1992

September 1989

August 1930

December 1930

October 1944   November 1944   February 1945

October 1945   March 1948   May 1952

August 1954   September 1954   January 1955

On the unusual side of acquiring movie magazines, I have stumbled upon hundreds of issues thrown in Dumpsters, which were probably thrown there by work crews. There is no rhyme or reason as to where or how you may find collectible movie magazines. Some collectors have found collectible magazines placed in stacks for the garbage man on trash night in their community. One such collector, while placing a neatly tied stack of old *Photoplay*s in his trunk, was stopped by the owner of the house and invited to the garage to remove four more stacks. These unorthodox sources are very rare, but I continue to hear of them more and more. A collector should pursue any possible source, no matter how unusual.

SELLING MOVIE/TV MAGAZINES

Many collectors and dealers of movie and TV magazines, when selling, should first put together a detailed listing or catalog of all issues listing the titles, dates, and contents. This listing can then be made available to collectors throughout the collecting world via an inexpensive classified ad in a trade paper such as "Film Collectors World," "PCM," "The Comic Buyers Guide," and others. Ads can also be placed in many local want ad publications. Often you pay only a small percentage of the sale price for these local want ads, and only if their ad sells your collection. You may consider a mall show or convention, or even driving your inventory to the local flea market. At most flea markets, you will be pleasantly surprised to see just how many people are interested in movie and TV magazines. Highest prices will be achieved by selling your magazines to hard-core collectors, who are generally found through the trade papers and paper shows. Lower prices are expected by the buyer at flea markets, so when selling there price your issues competitively.

MOST-COLLECTIBLE FEMALE STARS OF THE 'THIRTIES

| | VALUE | | | |
SUBJECT	COVER & FEATURE	COVER ONLY	FEATURE ONLY	CAMEO
Joan Crawford	$15–30	$10–25	$10–20	$5–15
Bette Davis	15–30	10–25	10–20	7–15
Olivia de Haviland	10–20	10–20	5–15	5–10

February 1955

April 1955

June 1955

August 1957

December 1957

#6, 1963

January 1938

April 1938

June 1939

| SUBJECT | VALUE | | | |
	COVER & FEATURE	COVER ONLY	FEATURE ONLY	CAMEO
Olivia de Haviland/ Gone with the Wind	$25–50	$25–50	$10–25	$ 6–12
Marlene Dietrich	10–20	10–20	10–20	5–10
Alice Faye	7–15	7–15	5–10	5–10
Greta Garbo	15–30	15–30	10–20	5–10
Judy Garland	25–50	15–30	10–20	5–10
Judy Garland/ The Wizard of Oz	50–150	50–100	25–50	10–20
Jean Harlow	20–40	20–40	10–20	5–15
Katharine Hepburn	10–25	10–25	10–20	5–15
Vivien Leigh	15–20	10–25	5–10	5–10
Vivien Leigh/ Gone with the Wind	50–100	25–50	15–30	5–10
Carole Lombard	10–20	10–20	5–10	5–10
Ginger Rogers	10–20	10–20	10–15	5–10
Rogers & Astaire	15–35	15–30	10–20	6–12
Elizabeth Taylor	25–50	25–50	10–20	10–20
Shirley Temple	20–40	20–40	15–30	10–20
Mae West	15–30	15–30	7–15	5–10

MOST-COLLECTIBLE MALE STARS OF THE 'THIRTIES

| SUBJECT | VALUE | | | |
	COVER & FEATURE	COVER ONLY	FEATURE ONLY	CAMEO
Fred Astaire	$15–30	$15–30	$10–20	$6–10
Astaire & Rogers	15–35	15–30	10–20	6–12
Gene Autry and Western Stars	10–20	10–20	5–15	5–10
Humphrey Bogart	15–30	15–30	5–15	5–10
James Cagney	15–30	10–25	5–12	5–10

March 1940

August 1940

October 1944

November 1951

February 1952

May 1971

January 1972

July 1947

October 1990

SUBJECT	VALUE			
	COVER & FEATURE	COVER ONLY	FEATURE ONLY	CAMEO
Gary Cooper	$10–20	$10–20	$ 5–10	$ 5–10
Jackie Cooper	10–25	10–25	6–12	5–10
Bing Crosby	10–20	10–20	5–12	5–10
Disney Themes	30–75	25–60	20–30	10–20
W. C. Fields	10–25	10–25	5–15	5–15
Errol Flynn	15–30	15–25	5–10	5–10
Clark Gable	10–20	10–20	10–20	5–10
Clark Gable/ Gone with the Wind	25–50	25–50	15–25	10–20
Laurel and Hardy	25–75	20–50	10–30	10–20
Boris Karloff	25–50	25–50	10–25	10–20
Peter Lorre	15–30	15–30	7–15	5–10
Bela Lugosi	20–50	20–50	10–20	10–20
Marx Brothers	15–30	15–25	10–20	5–10
Basil Rathbone	15–35	15–30	10–20	5–10
Edward G. Robinson	10–20	10–20	5–12	5–10
Mickey Rooney	10–20	10–20	5–15	5–10
Three Stooges	50–100	50–100	40–75	20–40

MOST-COLLECTIBLE FEMALE STARS OF THE 'FORTIES

SUBJECT	VALUE			
	COVER & FEATURE	COVER ONLY	FEATURE ONLY	CAMEO
Lauren Bacall	$10–20	$10–20	$ 5–12	$5–10
Joan Crawford	10–20	10–20	10–20	5–10
Bette Davis	10–25	10–25	10–20	5–10
Judy Garland	10–25	10–20	10–20	5–10
Betty Grable	10–20	10–20	5–12	5–10
Katharine Hepburn	10–20	10–20	5–15	5–10

November 1990

December 1990

October 1991

March 1992

June 1992

July 1992

1971

#3, November 1931

December 1932

SUBJECT	VALUE			
	COVER & FEATURE	COVER ONLY	FEATURE ONLY	CAMEO
Dorothy Lamour	$10–20	$10–20	$ 5–10	$5–10
Vivien Leigh	10–20	10–20	10–20	5–12
Carole Lombard	10–20	10–20	5–10	5–10
Ginger Rogers	10–20	10–20	5–12	5–10
Rogers & Astaire	10–20	10–20	5–15	5–10
Elizabeth Taylor	15–35	15–35	5–10	5–10
Shirley Temple	10–25	10–25	5–15	5–10

MOST-COLLECTIBLE MALE STARS OF THE 'FORTIES

SUBJECT	VALUE			
	COVER & FEATURE	COVER ONLY	FEATURE ONLY	CAMEO
Abbott & Costello	$15–30	$10–25	$10–20	$ 5–10
Fred Astaire	10–20	10–20	5–10	5–10
Astaire & Rogers	10–20	10–20	5–15	5–10
Humphrey Bogart	10–20	10–15	5–10	5–10
James Cagney	10–20	10–15	5–10	5–10
Bing Crosby	10–15	10–15	5–10	5–10
Disney Themes	20–40	20–40	15–30	5–10
Errol Flynn	10–20	10–20	5–10	5–10
Clark Gable	10–20	10–15	5–10	5–10
Roy Rogers and Western Stars	10–20	10–20	6–12	5–10
Three Stooges	30–80	30–75	20–40	10–20
John Wayne	15–30	15–30	10–20	6–12

October 1934

January 1935

June 1960

August 1937

June 1939

May 1951

November 1954

January 1938

August 1951

MOST-COLLECTIBLE FEMALE STARS OF THE 'FIFTIES

SUBJECT	COVER & FEATURE	COVER ONLY	FEATURE ONLY	CAMEO
Joan Crawford	$ 5–15	$ 5–10	$ 4–8	$ 4–8
Bette Davis	5–15	5–15	5–10	4–8
Annette Funicello	10–25	10–20	10–20	4–8
Judy Garland	10–20	10–20	5–15	5–10
Grace Kelly	5–10	5–10	5–10	4–8
Jayne Mansfield	10–25	10–25	10–25	8–15
Marilyn Monroe	15–30	15–30	10–25	8–20
Betty Page	25–50+	25–50+	20–40+	4–8
Elizabeth Taylor	10–20	10–20	10–15	4–8
Shirley Temple	10–20	10–20	10–20	5–10
Natalie Wood	10–20	10–20	10–20	5–10

MOST-COLLECTIBLE MALE STARS OF THE 'FIFTIES

SUBJECT	COVER & FEATURE	COVER ONLY	FEATURE ONLY	CAMEO
Abbott & Costello	$ 5–15	$ 6–12	$ 6–12	$ 4–8
Humphrey Bogart	6–12	6–12	5–10	4–8
James Dean	20–40	20–40	20–30	5–10
Disney Themes	10–20	10–20	10–15	5–10
Rock Hudson	5–10	5–10	5–10	4–8
Elvis Presley	20–40	20–40	15–30	6–12
Three Stooges	20–30	15–30	10–20	5–10
John Wayne	10–20	10–20	10–15	4–8

February 1952

September 1957

August 1947

December 1954

February 1942

February 1938

February 1939

May 1943

September 1943

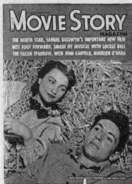

October 1943

#4, 1946

February 1968

#1, March 1970

May 1953

June 10, 1977

August 15, 1942

April 1941

June 1941

September 1943

June 1945

July 1945

March 1954

January 1955

April 1955

June 1956

March 25, 1939

February 1938

March 22, 1938

October 1934

May 1936

#6, May 1935

#6, 1971

#7, 1972

June 1937

October 1937

October 1938

February 1940

January 1966

1937

January 1992

December 1979

September 1990

Summer 1937

1937

#47, 1949

August 10, 1957   January 1969   March 1937

1951   March 1938   June 1938

July 1938   November 1951   May 1947

MOST-COLLECTIBLE FEMALE STARS OF THE 'SIXTIES

SUBJECT	COVER & FEATURE	COVER ONLY	FEATURE ONLY	CAMEO
Jane Fonda	$ 6–15	$ 6–12	$ 5–10	$3–6
Jane Fonda/Barbarella	10–20	10–20	10–15	3–6
Brigette Bardot	10–20	10–20	5–10	3–6
Barbara Eden	10–20	10–20	6–12	4–8
Annette Funicello	10–20	10–15	8–15	3–6
Judy Garland	10–20	10–15	5–10	3–6
Jayne Mansfield	10–15	10–15	10–15	3–6
Marilyn Monroe	10–20	10–20	8–15	4–8
Betty Page	10–20	10–20	10–20	4–8
Elizabeth Taylor	5–10	4–8	4–8	3–6
Shirley Temple	6–12	6–12	6–12	4–8
Raquel Welch	5–10	5–10	4–8	3–6
Natalie Wood	5–10	5–10	4–8	3–6

MOST-COLLECTIBLE MALE STARS OF THE 'SIXTIES

SUBJECT	COVER & FEATURE	COVER ONLY	FEATURE ONLY	CAMEO
Beatles	$15–30	$10–20	$10–20	$3–6
Elvis Presley	5–15	5–10	5–10	3–6
Three Stooges	5–15	5–10	5–10	4–8

February 1951

February 1952

December 1953

February 1956

June 1956

June 1966

March 1988

June 1989

August 20, 1970

May 1943   #14, Spring 1972   June 1932

March 1933   October 1940   November 1952

January 1953   November 1942   July 1959

December 1960

March 1972

August 1954

February 1964

December 1964

March 1954

July 1960

July 1979

October 1991

Most-Collectible Female Stars of the 'Seventies

SUBJECT	VALUE			
	COVER & FEATURE	COVER ONLY	FEATURE ONLY	CAMEO
Lynda Carter	$5–10	$5–10	$ 4–7	$2–4
Linda Blair	5–10	5–10	5–10	3–6
Cher	5–10	5–10	4–8	2–4
Farrah Fawcett	5–10	5–10	3–6	2–4
Jane Fonda	4–8	3–6	3–6	2–4
Cheryl Ladd	4–8	3–6	3–6	2–4
Marilyn Monroe	4–8	4–8	4–8	2–4
Marie Osmond	5–10	5–10	5–10	2–4
Victoria Principal	4–8	3–6	3–6	2–4
Jaclyn Smith	4–8	3–6	3–6	2–4
Suzanne Somers	3–6	3–6	3–6	2–4
Lindsay Wagner	3–6	3–6	3–6	2–4
Sigourney Weaver	3–7	3–6	3–6	3–5
Raquel Welch	4–8	4–8	3–6	2–4

Most-Collectible Male Stars of the 'Seventies, 'Eighties and 'Nineties

Note: There are no outstanding collectible male stars of this period; most issues featuring male movie and/or TV star covers from the 'seventies, 'eighties, and 'nineties sell for $2 to $4 each.

MOST-COLLECTIBLE FEMALE STARS OF THE
'EIGHTIES AND 'NINETIES

| | VALUE | | | |
| | COVER & | COVER | FEATURE | |
SUBJECT	FEATURE	ONLY	ONLY	CAMEO
Cher	$ 4–8	$ 3–6	$ 3–5	$2–4
Kim Basinger	3–6	3–6	2–5	2–4
Christie Brinkley	4–8	4–8	3–5	3–5
Megan Follows	5–10	5–10	5–10	3–5
Kathy Ireland	3–6	3–6	3–6	3–6
Madonna	4–8	3–6	3–5	2–4
Demi Moore	3–6	3–5	2–5	2–4
Sharon Stone	4–7	3–6	3–5	2–4

PEOPLE VALUES

People (Weekly)

YEAR	ISSUE	DESCRIPTION	VALUE
1974	March 4	Mia Farrow: The Great Gatsby, Jim Croce, Alice Cooper	$15–30
	March 11	Martha Mitchell	5–10
	March 18	J. Paul Getty	5–10
	March 25	Raquel Welch	7–15
	April 1	Gerry Ford, Alice Cooper: The Jekyll and Hyde of Glitter Rock, Pat Nixon, Minnie Pearl, Chris Evert	5–10
	April 8	Ted Kennedy and Ted Jr., Stevie Wonder	2–4
	April 15	Lorne Greene	5–10
	April 22	Tatum O'Neal	5–10

YEAR	ISSUE	DESCRIPTION	VALUE
1974	April 29	Joan Baez: New Life, New Songs, New Causes, Bruce Dern, Marilyn Monroe, Cheech & Chong, Sally Struthers	$2–4
	May 6	George and Cornelia Wallace	2–4
	May 13	Bogdanovich and Shepherd	2–4
	May 20	E. Howard Hunt	2–4
	May 27	Pat Nixon	2–4
	June 3	Cicely Tyson	2–4
	June 10	The Kissingers	2–4
	June 17	Jack Lemmon	2–4
	June 24	Joan Kennedy: Her Nervous Breakdown, James Earl Jones, Jimmy the Greek, Maria Muldaur: Classic Blues	2–4
	July 1	Telly Savalas	2–4
	July 8	Suzy and Mark Spitz, Gene Kelly, Linda Lovelace	2–4
	July 15	Carol Burnett, Rock Hudson	2–4
	July 22	Larry Csonka	2–4
	July 29	Faye Dunaway	4–8
	August 5	Eagleton	1–2
	August 12	Barbara Walters and Jim Hartz, the Duchess of Windsor at Home, Mia Farrow	1–2
	August 19	Charles Bronson	2–4
	August 26	President Ford	1–2
	September 2	Catherine Deneuve	1–2
	September 9	John and Mo Dean in California, Paul Anka Is on Top Again, Valerie Harper, The Private World of Happy Rockefeller	2–4
	September 16	Joe Namath	1–2
	September 23	Gloria Steinem: Fighting Sexism with New Tactics, Three Sinatras on One Stage, Lauren Bacall	2–4

April 15, 1974   June 30, 1975   July 26, 1976

August 23, 1976   August 30, 1976   June 13, 1977

July 18, 1977   August 1, 1977   September 26, 1977

YEAR	ISSUE	DESCRIPTION	VALUE
1974	September 30	Mary Tyler Moore	$ 3–6
	October 7	Paul Newman	2–4
	October 14	Jackie Onassis	2–4
	October 21	Susan Ford	1–2
	October 28	Burt Reynolds and Dinah Shore	2–4
	November 4	Richard Burton	2–4
	November 11	Prince Charles	2–4
	November 18	Katharine Hepburn, John Wayne	3–6
	November 25	Johnny Carson and Wife	2–4
	December 9	Cloris Leachman, Hedy Lamarr, Yul Brynner	2–4
	December 16	Kathy and Bing Crosby	2–4
	December 23	Dustin Hoffman	2–4
	December 30	Double Issue Special	2–4
1975	January 6	25 Most Intriguing People Issue . . . Faye Dunaway, Karen Black, Cher, Linda Ronstadt, Bad Company	2–4
	January 13	Elvis Presley Is 40, Friends of Jack Benny Say Goodbye, Lynn Redgrave: The Happy Hooker	3–6
	January 20	Judge Sirica, Richard Burton, Britt Ekland, Tony Perkins	2–4
	January 27	Liv Ullmann, Tammy Wynette, The Wiz	2–4
	February 3	Chris Evert and Billy Jean King	2–4
	February 10	Cher	5–10
	February 17	Happy Rockefeller, Patricia Neal, Archie Bunker, Susan Blakely	2–4
	February 24	Olivia Newton-John	5–10
	March 3	Onassis	2–4
	March 10	James Caan and Barbra Streisand	2–4

YEAR	ISSUE	DESCRIPTION	VALUE
1975	March 17	Alan Alda	$ 2–4
	March 24	Ann-Margret	4–8
	March 31	Jackie Onassis	2–4
	April 7	The Fondas	3–5
	April 14	Warren Beatty	2–4
	April 21	Paul and Linda McCartney	3–6
	April 28	Ellen Burstyn, Robert Blake	2–4
	May 5	Jimmy Connors	2–4
	May 12	Lauren Hutton	2–4
	May 19	Elizabeth Taylor	3–6
	May 26	Nancy Walker	2–4
	June 2	Clint Eastwood: A Box-Office Killing, Jimmie Walker	3–6
	June 9	Mick Jagger: His Stones Hit the U.S. While Bianca Conquers the Continent, Pat Nixon Reappears, Joe Namath Nixes $5 Million, Ann-Margret at Cannes	5–10
	June 16	Betty in Europe, The Endless Summer of the Beach Boys, Arnold Schwarzenegger, Britt Ekland	2–4
	June 23	Jane Fonda	2–4
	June 30	Bette Midler	2–4
	July 7	Ali	2–4
	July 14	Carroll O'Connor	2–4
	July 21	Paul Newman and Joanne Woodward	2–4
	August 8	Peter Sellers	2–4
	August 11	Sonny Bono	2–4
	August 18	Elton John: His New Look . . . Everything's Slimmer but His Wallet, Diane Keaton: Woody Allen's Spacy Star, Tatum O'Neal	3–6
	August 25	Jaws's Roy Scheider, Paul Newman	1–2

YEAR	ISSUE	DESCRIPTION	VALUE
1975	September 1	Grace Kelly	$ 2–4
	September 8	Cher and Gregg Allman	5–10
	September 15	Valerie Harper	2–4
	September 22	Rose Kennedy, David Niven, Phil Spector, Calvin Klein	1–2
	September 29	Howard Cosell	2–4
	October 6	Nancy Kissinger, Patty Hearst, Dennis Weaver, Natalie Cole	1–2
	October 13	Marlon Brando	2–4
	October 20	Julie and David Eisenhower	2–4
	October 27	Robert Redford, Elton John's New Hit Is Neil Sedaka	2–4
	November 3	Gene Hackman, Grand Ole Opry at 50, Gregg Allman	2–4
	November 10	Bob Dylan	4–8
	November 17	Bea Arthur	2–4
	November 24	Jennifer O'Neill	3–6
	December 1	Julia Child	2–4
	December 8	Jack Nicholson	2–4
	December 15	Roger Daltry of The Who	3–7
	December 22	Billy Graham	2–4
1976	January 5	25 Most Intriguing People Issue . . . Cher, Dolly Parton, Emmylou Harris, Lindsay Wagner	2–5
	January 12	Liza Minnelli	2–4
	January 19	Lee Majors and Farrah Fawcett	3–6
	January 26	Diana Ross	3–6
	February 9	Mary Tyler Moore in Moscow, Margot Kidder	3–6
	February 16	Chris Evert, Jack Ford	1–2
	February 23	Nancy Reagan, Maud Adams, Bob Dylan and Scarlet Rivera	2–4
	March 1	Michael Caine, Jill Clayburgh	1–2
	March 8	Marisa Berenson	1–2
	March 15	Elizabeth Taylor	2–4
	March 22	Rob Reiner and Penny Marshall, Phoebe Snow, Ginger Rogers	2–3

YEAR	ISSUE	DESCRIPTION	VALUE
1976	March 29	Glen Campbell	$ 2–4
	April 5	The Beatles: Will They Sing Again for $50 Million?	2–4
	April 12	Audrey Hepburn	2–4
	April 19	Telly Savalas, Robert Redford, Linda Blair, David Bowie Busted	2–4
	April 26	Barbra Streisand	2–4
	May 3	Dustin Hoffman, Robert Redford	2–4
	May 10	Truman Capote	1–2
	May 17	Goldie Hawn	2–4
	May 24	The Fonz: His Cult Grows, Fred Astaire, David Rockefeller, Elizabeth Taylor	2–4
	May 31	Frank Sinatra, Expectant Cher, Marilyn Monroe	2–4
	June 7	Paul McCartney: "What Will Daddy Do When He Grows Up?" . . . The Wings Tour, Jo-Jo Starbuck	3–6
	June 14	Jerry Brown	2–4
	June 21	Raquel Welch . . . What's New for JUGS, Bob Hope, Bruce Springsteen	3–6
	June 28	Rudolf Nureyev	1–2
	July 5	Louise Lasser . . . Mary Hartman, Jimmy Dean	2–4
	July 12	Celebs of '76 . . . Sonny Bono, Flip Wilson, etc., A Message from Jerry Garcia of The Grateful Dead, Ann-Margret, Elizabeth Taylor	3–6
	July 19	Jim and Amy Carter, Barney Miller, Stevie Wonder	1–3
	July 26	Lindsay Wagner	5–10
	August 2	The Carpenters	3–6
	August 9	Peter Falk	2–4

YEAR	ISSUE	DESCRIPTION	VALUE
1976	August 16	Carol Burnett	$ 2–4
	August 23	The Beach Boys . . . Still Riding the Crest 15 Hairy Years Later, Diahann Carroll, Sandy Dennis	4–8
	August 30	Princess Caroline	2–4
	September 6	David Bowie	4–8
	September 13	Paul Lynde	2–4
	September 20	Phyllis George	2–4
	September 27	Cher, Gregg Allman, and Children	4–8
	October 4	Woody Allen, Elton John's Songbird Is Kiki Dee	2–3
	October 11	Barbara Walters	2–4
	October 18	The Captain and Tennille	2–4
	October 25	Stevie Wonder: Life Offstage, Bernadette Peters	2–4
	November 1	Lee Radziwill	2–3
	November 8	Tony Randall	2–4
	November 15	Rosalynn Carter, Mel Tillis, Olivia Newton-John, Roger Moore	2–4
	November 22	Marjoe Wallace, Jimmy Connors, Dorothy Hamill the Star, Twiggy	2–4
	November 29	John Travolta	3–5
	December 6	Charlie's Angels . . . Farrah Fawcett, Jaclyn Smith, and Kate Jackson	5–10
	December 13	Robert Wagner and Natalie Wood	2–4
	December 20	Led Zeppelin	5–10
1977	January 3	25 Most Intriguing People of 1976 Issue . . . Farrah Fawcett, King Kong, Robert Redford, Jane Fonda	3–7
	January 10	Barbra Streisand and Kris Kristofferson	2–4

YEAR	ISSUE	DESCRIPTION	VALUE
1977	January 17	Ringo: His Tax Exile, His New Fiancée, His Rap on a Beatles Reunion, The Women in Gary Gilmore's Tormented Life	$2–4
	January 24	Claudine Longet	2–3
	January 31	Jessica Lange	3–5
	February 7	George C. Scott & Wife, Trish: A Fifth Marriage Mellows the Brawling Actor, Jerry Lewis's $1.25 Million Broadway Bomb, The Selling Of Gary Gilmore, Funky Music's Godfather	2–4
	February 14	Elizabeth Taylor and John Warner	2–4
	February 21	Rod Stewart & Britt Ekland ... A Sexy Swede Tames the Rascal of Rock, Paul Newman	3–6
	February 28	Ralph Nader, 15 Farrahs in Detroit, The Best Dressed, Lauren Bacall, Lesley Ann Warren	2–4
	March 7	Bjorn Borg, Bob Dylan, Larry Flint, Arnold Schwarzenegger	1–2
	March 14	Julie Andrews, Boston: Rock's Brainiest Band, Grace Jones	2–4
	March 21	David Carradine	2–4
	March 28	Faye Dunaway	2–4
	April 4	Dolly Parton	2–4
	April 11	Bruce Jenner and Chrystie	1–2
	April 18	Jackie Onassis	1–2
	April 25	Sally Field	3–5
	May 5	Bianca Jagger	3–5
	May 9	Alex Haley	1–2
	May 16	Jane Fonda	2–4
	May 23	David Frost and Richard Nixon, Dickey Betts on Cher and Gregg Allman, Yul Brynner	2–4

YEAR	ISSUE	DESCRIPTION	VALUE
1977	May 30	Cindy Williams	$ 2–4
	June 6	Fleetwood Mac	10–20
	June 13	John Travolta	2–4
	June 20	Elizabeth Taylor, Liza Minnelli	2–4
	June 27	Peter Frampton: More Alive Than Ever	3–5
	July 4	Farrah Fawcett and Lee Majors	3–5
	July 11	Linda (Exorcist II) Blair at 18, Michael Learned, Star Wars	5–10
	July 18	Star Wars . . . Talented Folks, Buck Owens	5–10
	July 25	Tom and Nancy Seaver	1–2
	August 1	Jacqueline Bisset, Emerson, Lake & Palmer Tour, Bette Davis	2–4
	August 8	Barry Manilow	3–6
	August 15	David Doyle, Jaclyn Smith, Cheryl Ladd, and Kate Jackson	5–10
	August 22	Sissy Spacek	2–4
	August 29	Mary Feldman and Ann-Margret, Miss Universe, The Late Elvis Presley	2–4
	September 5	Dan Rather	1–2
	September 12	Susan Saint James	2–3
	September 19	Robert Blake	2–3
	September 26	Cheryl Ladd	4–8
	October 3	Tony Orlando's Breakdown, Patty Hearst, Kristy McNichol	2–3
	October 10	Remembering Elvis Presley, Bernadette Peters, Wings	2–4
	October 17	O. J. Simpson, Dick Cavett, Debby Boone Lights Up the Pop Charts, Patty Duke and John Astin	2–4
	October 24	Linda Ronstadt: Rock's Hottest Flame, Farrah Fawcett Works Again, Diana Ross, Peter Frampton	4–8

YEAR	ISSUE	DESCRIPTION	VALUE
1977	October 31	Donny and Marie: At 18, She's Sexed Up Her TV Image . . . But All the Osmonds Still Check Out Her Dates, 007's Dazzling New Lady Spook . . . Barbara Bach, Cher, Tatum O'Neal	$5–10
	November 7	Suzanne Somers, Joyce DeWitt, and John Ritter	3–5
	November 14	Michelle Phillips	2–4
	November 21	Rolling Stones' Mick and Keith: Jagger's Genius Partner Richard Tells How He Kicked Heroin, But He's Not off the Hook in a Canadian Court, Susan Dey: Laurie Partridge in a Nude Movie?	5–10
	November 28	Al Pacino and Marthe Keller	2–3
	December 5	Gilda Radner Live, Freddie Mercury of Queen, Arlo Guthrie	2–4
	December 12	Crosby, Stills, and Nash	3–5
	December 19	Marlo Thomas	1–2
1978	January 2	25 Most Intriguing People Issue . . . Diane Keaton, Shaun Cassidy, Goldie Hawn, Stevie Nicks: Fleetwood Mac's Sexiest Symbol, Tony Orlando, etc.	4–8
	January 9	John Travolta, Karen Gorney	2–4
	January 16	The New Elton John: He's Given Up Those Nutty Glasses, But Not Lasses, Cocaine in Hollywood, Grizzly Adams's Close Shave, Linda Blair	4–8

YEAR	ISSUE	DESCRIPTION	VALUE
1978	January 23	Helen Reddy: The Woman Roars Softer Now . . . Family Comes First, and She's Got Jerry Brown's Ear, The Uppity Butler on Soap, Benny Goodman, Angela Davis	$2–4
	January 30	Penny Marshall, Mike McKean, David L. Lander, and Cindy Williams	2–4
	February 6	The Bee Gees	3–6
	February 13	Clint Eastwood and Sondra Locke	2–4
	February 20	Henry Winkler	1–2
	February 27	Mondale and Wife	1–2
	March 6	Goldie Hawn	2–4
	March 13	Richard Pryor	1–2
	March 20	Geneviève Bujold	1–2
	March 27	Carroll O'Connor, Jean Stapleton, Rob Reiner, and Sally Struthers of All in the Family	3–5
	April 3	Diane Keaton, Anne Bancroft, Shirley MacLaine, Jane Fonda, and Marsha Mason	2–4
	April 10	Cher, Gene Simmons	4–8
	April 17	Pat and Debby Boone	2–4
	April 24	Linda Lavin	2–4
	May 1	Steve Martin	2–4
	May 8	Sylvester Stallone	1–2
	May 15	Shaun Cassidy	3–5
	May 22	John Ritter	2–4
	May 29	Brooke Shields at 12 in Pretty Baby: Child Porn	4–8
	June 5	Loretta Lynn, Crystal Gayle	3–5
	June 12	Ron Howard	2–4
	June 19	Cheryl Tiegs	3–5
	June 26	Jane Fonda, Jon Voight	2–4

April 10, 1978   *June 5, 1978*   *October 6, 1980*

December 20, 1980   *October 20, 1986*   *May 18, 1987*

October 12, 1987   *January 25, 1988*   *September 9, 1991*

YEAR	ISSUE	DESCRIPTION	VALUE
1978	July 3	Princess Caroline and Philippe Junot	$2–4
	July 10	Ed Asner	1–2
	July 17	Carly Simon: She's Conquered Her Stage Fright, Paul Newman's Daughter, Alice Faye, Bob Dylan Tours	4–8
	July 24	Ali MacGraw and Kris Kristofferson	2–4
	July 31	Olivia Newton-John, How the Celebs Get Lured into Studio 54, Robert Klein, Bianca Jagger	3–6
	August 7	Joan Kennedy	1–2
	August 14	Carrie Fisher and Darth Vader	4–8
	August 21	The Elvis Presley Legend	2–4
	August 28	Ann-Margret	2–4
	September 4	Margaret Trudeau	2–3
	September 11	Michael Landon, Melissa Gilbert, and Melissa Sue Anderson	3–6
	September 19	Cheryl Ladd	4–8
	September 25	Joe Namath: Scouting Report, The Final Hours of The Who's Keith Moon, Pam Shriver, The Smothers Brothers, Mary Tyler Moore, Farrah Fawcett, Linda Ronstadt	3–5
	October 2	Battlestar Galactica	3–6
	October 9	Jaclyn Smith	4–8
	October 16	Chicago	3–6
	October 23	Elizabeth Taylor and John Warner	2–4
	October 30	Robin Williams and Pam Dawber	2–4
	November 6	Patty Hearst and Bernard Shaw	1–2
	November 13	Jackie Onassis	1–2
	November 20	Kristy McNichol and Jimmy McNichol	3–6

YEAR	ISSUE	DESCRIPTION	VALUE
1978	November 27	Angie Dickinson	$2–4
	December 4	Priscilla Presley	2–3
	December 11	Suzanne Somers, John Ritter, and Joyce DeWitt	3–5
	December 18	Ann-Margret	2–4
1979	January 1	25 Most Intriguing People Issue . . . John Travolta, John Belushi, Brooke Shields, Cheryl Tiegs, Meat Loaf, Donna Summer Cleans Up Her Act, Grace Slick, Elton John, Star Trek	3–6
	January 8	Christopher Reeve as Superman	2–4
	January 15	Diana Ross	3–6
	January 22	Neil Diamond, Barbra Streisand	3–6
	January 29	The Women of The Waltons	3–6
	February 5	Rod Stewart, Britt Ekland, Liz Treadwell, and Alana Hamilton	3–6
	February 12	Robin Wiliams, Pam Dawber	3–5
	February 19	Barbra Streisand and Jon Peters	2–4
	February 26	John Denver: The Unsung Story, Roots II, Sondra Locke, Brooke Shields, Phyllis George, Clint Eastwood, Loretta Lynn	2–4
	March 5	Farrah Fawcett: The Most Boring Woman on TV?, Jaclyn Smith: The Most Beautiful, Kiss: Most Disliked?, Billy Joel	3–6
	March 12	Loretta Swit	2–4
	March 19	Billy Joel Rocks Cuba, Blythe Danner, Rock Hudson, Sally Field, Johnny Mathis, Paul McCartney	3–6

YEAR	ISSUE	DESCRIPTION	VALUE
1979	March 26	The New Betty Ford, Miss America on Tour . . . Kylene Barker, Dire Straits: Rock's Sultans of Swing, Bee Gees	$2–4
	April 2	Robert De Niro, Warren Beatty, Jon Voight	1–2
	April 9	Donna Pescow, Marvin Gaye, Cheryl Ladd, Mick Jagger	2–4
	April 16	Jane Fonda, Michael Douglas	2–4
	April 23	Burt Reynolds	2–4
	April 30	Linda Ronstadt and Governor Brown, Paul Rogers of Bad Company, Faye Dunaway, Melba Moore, Art Garfunkel	4–8
	May 7	Battle of the Live-In Lovers . . . Lee Marvin, Peter Frampton, Nick Nolte, Keith Richards' Drug Rap Concert in Toronto, Gene Tierney, Cheryl Ladd, Suzanne Somers, Ali MacGraw	2–4
	May 14	Five's Company . . . Suzanne Somers, etc., Gary Coleman, Eric Clapton, Bob Dylan, Marilyn Monroe, Suzi Quatro, The Bee Gees	3–5
	May 21	Johnny Carson	2–3
	May 28	Morley Safer, Harry Reasoner, and Mike Wallace	1–2
	June 4	Kate Jackson	3–6
	June 11	Mariel Hemingway	3–5
	June 18	Rob Reiner and Father . . . Carl Reiner	2–4
	June 25	Paul Newman	2–4
	July 2	Ted Kennedy	1–2
	July 9	Olivia Newton-John	3–6
	July 17	Carly Simon and Motherhood, Bette Midler	3–6

YEAR	ISSUE	DESCRIPTION	VALUE
1979	July 23	Sylvester Stallone, Talia Shire	$1–2
	July 30	Stan Dragoti, Cheryl Tiegs	2–4
	August 6	Hanging Out with The Bee Gees: A Backstage Look at the Summer's Hottest Tour, the Boat People, Tanya Tucker, Paul and Linda McCartney	3–5
	August 13	Roger Moore, Lois Chiles, and Richard Kiel	3–6
	August 20	Farrah Fawcett	3–6
	August 27	Phil Donahue	1–2
	September 3	Miss Piggy, Erik Estrada, Conway Twitty, Sandy Duncan, Paul Stanley as a Father, Crystal Gayle, Deborah Harry Meets the Real Blondie, Roger Daltry, Teddy Pendergrass, Kiss	4–8
	September 10	Kenny Rogers, Donna Summer, Paul McCartney, Blondie's Debbie Harry and Peter Frampton	4–8
	September 17	Margot Kidder	2–4
	September 24	Shelley Hack ... The Classy New Angel, Ethel Merman	4–8
	October 1	Carol Burnett and Daughter, Jim Belushi, Peter Criss of Kiss: His Wife Talks, Debby Boone, Barbara Parkins, Elton John	3–6
	October 8	Nick Nolte, Bruce Springsteen Sparks the No-Nuke Rally, Elvis Presley's Doctor, Patty Duke Astin	2–4
	October 15	Suzanne Somers	3–5
	October 22	Cher	3–6
	October 29	Robin Williams	2–4
	November 6	Jill Clayburgh	2–4

YEAR	ISSUE	DESCRIPTION	VALUE
1979	November 12	Loni Anderson and Howard Hesseman: WKRP, Kate Jackson, Abba	$ 2–4
	November 19	The 10 Sexiest Bachelors in the World, Estrada, Andy Gibb, Bo Derek and Dudley Moore, Cathy Bach: Dazzling Duchess of Hazard, The Eagles, Mick and Bianca Jagger, Roger Daltry	3–6
	November 26	Fleetwood Mac	10–20
	December 3	Dick Van Patten, Grant Goodeve, Adam Rich, and Willie Aames	2–4
	December 10	Kenny Rogers and Marianne Gordon	2–4
	December 17	Those Women of Dallas . . . Linda Gray, Victoria Principal, Charlene Tilton, Anne Murray, the Angels' Charlie, Linda Ronstadt, Farrah Fawcett, Donny and Marie, Crystal Gayle	3–6
	December 24	25 Most Intriguing People Issue . . . Debbie Harry, Bo Derek, Olivia Newton-John, Bob Seger, Ellen Foley	5–10
1980	January 7	Bette Midler	2–4
	January 14	Lee Majors, Farrah Fawcett and Ryan O'Neal	2–4
	January 21	Steve Martin, Suzanne Somers: Why Did She Pose Nude?, The Police: Rock's New Hit Squad, Marilyn Monroe, Janis Joplin, Aerosmith, Natalie Cole, Jane Fonda	2–4

YEAR	ISSUE	DESCRIPTION	VALUE
1980	January 28	Elvis Presley: How Did He Die?, Cybill Shepherd's Blues, Lynda Carter, Pernell Roberts, Butterfly McQueen	$ 2–4
	February 4	Chris Evert Lloyd, Donna Summer: The Flip Side of Music's Bad Girl, Paul McCartney in the Clink, Deborah Harry	3–6
	February 11	Bo and John Derek, Lucille Ball	2–4
	February 18	Robert Redford, Patti Hansen, Liz Taylor, Cliff Richard, John Belushi and the Dead Boys	2–4
	February 25	Liza Minnelli, Goldie Hawn, Jihan Sadat	2–4
	March 3	Lindsay Wagner: The Bionic Woman Comes On Strong in Scruples, Dan Rather, Isaac Hayes, Meryl Streep, Neil Diamond, Jane Fonda	3–6
	March 10	Britt Ekland, Rod Stewart, Peter Sellers, Warren Beatty	2–4
	March 17	Mackenzie Phillips, Bonnie Franklin, Valerie Bertinelli, Jackie Onassis	2–4
	March 24	Bo Derek, Gilda Radner, Bruce Jenner, Dustin Hoffman, Jane Fonda, The Eagles	2–4
	March 31	Tatum O'Neal and Kristy McNichol, Alan King, Anne and Nancy Wilson of Heart: Alive and Well on the Road, The Knack	5–10
	April 7	Richard Gere	1–2
	April 14	Larry Hagman, Susan Anton	2–4
	April 21	Olivia Newton-John and Andy Gibb, Susan Strasberg	3–6

YEAR	ISSUE	DESCRIPTION	VALUE
1980	April 28	Penny Marshall, Erik Estrada and Larry Wilcox	$ 1–2
	May 5	Jacqueline Bisset and Paul Newman, Ursula Andress	2–4
	May 12	The Who: Pete Townshend Talks about Concert Tragedy	2–4
	May 19	Jodie Foster, Loretta Lynn and Sissy Spacek	3–5
	May 26	Mac Davis, Pogo	2–4
	June 2	Valerie Harper, Chuck Barris, Linda Ronstadt, Bernadette Peters	2–4
	June 9	The Empire Strikes Back, Yoda, Gloria Vanderbilt	3–6
	June 16	Soap Opera Stars Special	1–2
	June 23	John Travolta: Urban Cowboy, Bernie Taupin, Dolly Parton	2–4
	June 30	Tanya Roberts and Glen, the Richard Pryor Tragedy, Sean Connery	2–4
	July 7	The Empire's Fab Four . . . Harrison Ford, Billy Dee Williams, Carrie Fisher, and Mark Hamill, Elton John, Tanya Roberts: Charlie's Newest Angel	4–8
	July 14	Larry Hagman	1–2
	July 21	Nancy and Ronald Reagan, the Reagan Kids	1–2
	July 28	Jack Nicholson, Princess Caroline and Philippe Junot	2–3
	August 4	Dan Aykroyd and John Belushi: The Blues Brothers, Joyce DeWitt	2–4
	August 11	Brooke Shields and Chris Atkins, Dan Rather	3–5
	August 18	Kiss with Eric Carr, Ed McMahon	7–15

YEAR	ISSUE	DESCRIPTION	VALUE
1980	August 25	John Davidson	$1–2
	September 8	Airplane: The Summer's Silliest Movie, Ron Ely: Me Tarzan, Rachel Sweet: Rock Is Sweet on Rachel, The Rolling Stones' Emotional Rescue, Linda Ronstadt, Tina Turner	1–2
	September 15	Angie Dickinson: Dressed to Kill, Ron Reagan: His 53 Movies, Karen Carpenter's All-Star Wedding, Diana Ross, Elton John	2–4
	September 22	Richard Chamberlain, Cheech and Chong	1–2
	September 29	26 Best and Worst Dressed People . . . Debbie Harry, Cher, etc., Those Marilyn Monroe Years, Elton John, Matt Dillon	4–8
	October 6	Carly Simon Exclusive, Tony Geary, Lesley Ann Warren, Raquel Welch, Carrie Fisher, Bo Derek, Paul Simon	2–4
	October 13	Cathy Lee Crosby	1–2
	October 20	Liz Taylor: Life with Liz, Steve McQueen, Peter Criss: Post Kiss, Keith Richards, Bruce Lee, Ingrid Bergman	2–4
	October 27	Genie Francis, Marilyn Monroe	2–4
	November 3	Paul Simon Still Creative, Jackie Gleason, David Bowie, Carly Simon, Lynda Carter	2–4
	November 10	Linda Gray, John Wayne	2–4
	November 17	Nancy Reagan, Kliban Cat	1–2
	November 24	Melissa Gilbert as Anne Frank, Dorothy Hamill, Bruce Springsteen	2–4

YEAR	ISSUE	DESCRIPTION	VALUE
1980	December 1	Kenny Rogers, Ingrid Bergman	$ 2–3
	December 8	Mary Crosby, John Denver	2–4
	December 15	Mary Tyler Moore	2–4
	December 22	John Lennon: 1940–1980, a Tribute, Rudolph the Red-Nosed Reindeer, Sheree North, Tatum O'Neal, Rockpile	3–6
1981	January 5	25 Most Intriguing People Issue . . . Brooke Shields, Goldie Hawn, Robert Redford, Pat Benatar Sinks to the Top of the Rock Pile, Nancy Allen, Farrah Fawcett, Jane Seymour, Stevie Nicks Goes Solo, Barbara Bach, John Travolta, Ursula Andress	5–10
	January 12	Yoko Ono: How She Is Holding Up, Suzanne Somers, Susan Anton	2–4
	January 19	Dolly Parton, Lily Tomlin, Jane Fonda, Charlene Tilton	2–4
	January 26	Charlene Tilton, Truman Capote	1–2
	February 2	Frank Sinatra	1–2
	February 9	Tanya Roberts, Barbara Mandrell	2–4
	February 16	Sally Struthers and Daughter, Jane Seymor	2–3
	February 23	Ringo and Barbara Bach: Ringo Talks Movingly about John, the Reunion That Never Was, and His Saving Love for Barbara Bach, An Update on Paul, George and Yoko, Aretha Franklin Bounces Back, Barbra Streisand, The Blues Brothers, Faye Dunaway, Linda Ronstadt, Carly Simon, Jennifer O'Neill	2–4

YEAR	ISSUE	DESCRIPTION	VALUE
1981	March 2	Mackenzie Phillips and Dad, John Phillips, Jared Martin	$ 2–3
	March 9	Soap Stars Special	1–2
	March 16	Blondie's Debbie Harry: Pop's Sassy Lady Cleans Up Her Act and Aims for Hollywood, Shelley Duvall: Olive Oyl, The Stars Fight L.A. Crime	5–10
	March 23	Jackie Onassis, Loni Anderson	1–2
	March 30	Victoria Principal, Andy Gibb, William Hurt	3–5
	April 4	Cathy Bach, Elizabeth Taylor	2–4
	April 13	Ronald Reagan	1–2
	April 20	Jodie Foster	2–4
	April 27	Danielle Brisebois: Archie's Angel, Fred Astaire at 81, Tanya Tucker, Jessica Lange, Cathy Lee Crosby, Eric Clapton	2–3
	May 4	Tanya Tucker, Glen Campbell	2–4
	May 11	Farrah Fawcett, Ryan O'Neal, Jim Davis	2–4
	May 18	Victoria Principal, Robert Redford, Kenny Rogers, Nancy Reagan, Prince Charles, Barbra Streisand	2–4
	May 25	Billie Jean and Larry King, Barbara Cartland, Big Bird	1–2
	June 1	Phyllis George and Son, Burt Reynolds	1–2
	June 8	Lauren Bacall, Tony Geary	1–2
	June 15	Alan Alda, Jessica Lange	1–2
	June 22	Lady Diana Spencer, John Lennon	1–2
	June 29	Richard Pryor, Pam Dawber, Andy Gibb	1–2

YEAR	ISSUE	DESCRIPTION	VALUE
1981	July 6	Christopher Reeve as Superman: He Beds Lois in His Man of Steel Sequel, But in Film, and Fact, He Shuns Marriage Like Kryptonite, Kim Carnes Eyes Bette Davis, Barbi Benton, Harrison Ford, Liz Taylor	$2–4
	July 13	Morgan Fairchild, Doc Severinsen	2–4
	July 20	Harrison Ford and Karen Allen, Joyce Bartle's Legs and Roger Moore	2–4
	July 27	Bo Derek, Miles O'Keefe	2–4
	August 3	Prince Charles and Lady Diana	1–2
	August 10	Brooke Shields, Frank Sinatra	2–4
	August 17	John Travolta and Nancy Allen: Blow Out ... A Hot-Blooded Hollywood Dream Team Ignites a Diller of a Thriller, Rick Springfield: He's Rockin' General Hospital, Lynn Redgrave, Meat Loaf, Toni Tennille, Liza Minnelli, Foreigner, Carly Simon, Jennifer O'Neill	2–4
	August 24	Margot Kidder, James Taylor	2–3
	August 31	Mark Hamill, Elvis Presley	2–4
	September 7	Kris Kristofferson and Daughter, Andy Kaufman	1–2
	September 14	Dudley Moore and Susan Anton, Kim Carnes	2–3
	September 21	The 29 Best and Worst Dressed People ... Linda Gray, Bo Derek, Broadway's Glowing Goodbye to Elizabeth Taylor	1–2
	September 28	Pat Benatar, Rubik's Cube	4–8

YEAR	ISSUE	DESCRIPTION	VALUE
1981	October 5	Faye Dunaway and Joan Crawford	$2–4
	October 12	Justice Sandra Day O'Connor, Mick Jagger, Sorrell Booke	2–3
	October 19	Jaclyn Smith, Jackie Kennedy Onassis	2–4
	October 26	Lindsay Wagner, Princess Caroline	3–4
	November 2	Richard Simmons, Kristy McNichol	1–2
	November 9	Valerie Bertinelli, Henry Fonda	2–4
	November 16	Elizabeth Taylor, Tony Geary and Genie Francis	1–2
	November 23	Princess Diana, Ed Asner	1–2
	November 30	John and Caroline Kennedy	1–2
	December 7	Johnny Carson, Candice Bergen	1–2
	December 14	Cast from Three's Company, Natalie Wood	2–4
	December 21	Larry Hagman, Rod and Alana Stewart	2–3
1982	January 4	Elizabeth Taylor, President Reagan, Mick Jagger, Diana, Tom Selleck, John McEnroe, Barbara Mandrell	1–2
	January 11	Richard Thomas and Triplets	1–2
	January 18	Calvin Klein and Brooke Shields, Elvis Presley	2–4
	January 25	Cher	3–5
	February 1	Patty Hearst: Finally, Her Own Story, Donny Osmond: Tired of Being a Goody Two-Shoes, Peter Sellers's Kids, Liz Taylor, Tanya Tucker, Diana Rigg, Kenny Rogers, Johnny Lee	2–4

YEAR	ISSUE	DESCRIPTION	VALUE
1982	February 8	Timothy Hutton, Barry Manilow	$1–2
	February 15	Olivia Newton-John, Sally Field	3–5
	February 22	Daniel Travanti, Veronica Hamel, and Michael Conrad of Hill Street Blues, James Coco	1–2
	March 1	Suzanne Somers, Edward Kennedy	2–4
	March 8	Tom Selleck, Christie Brinkley: Supermodel and Billy Joel, Kate Jackson in Making Love, Janis Joplin, Jack Nicholson	2–4
	March 15	Liz Taylor and Richard Burton, An Osmond Ski Bash, William Shatner	2–4
	March 22	John Belushi: A Dangerous Life . . . A Tragic Death, Carol Burnett, Jane Fonda, Dean Jones, Julie Andrews, James Garner	2–4
	March 29	Kenny Rogers: A Neglectful Father Reforms, The Hollywood Drug Fad That Killed John Belushi, Bianca Jagger, Bernadette Peters, Bob Dylan, Kristy McNichol, Billie Holiday	2–4
	April 5	Princess Grace, Neil Diamond	2–3
	April 12	Henry Fonda, Kate Jackson	2–3
	April 19	Readers' Poll Issue . . . Tom Selleck, Brooke Shields, Stefanie Powers, Sean Connery, Debbie Allen, Lesley Ann Warren	2–4

YEAR	ISSUE	DESCRIPTION	VALUE
1982	April 26	Cheryl Tiegs . . . Fashion's $100 Million Lady, Ingrid Bergman, Those 36 Lost Beatles Tunes, Jessica Lange, Nastassja Kinski, Marie Osmond, Heart's Wilson Sisters, Jodie Foster, Brooke Shields	$3–6
	May 3	On Location with Tom Selleck, Shelley Bruce of Annie, Adrienne Barbeau, Ted Nugent, Sting, Catherine Bach, Sigourney Weaver Alarmed by Muslim Threats, Lee Remick	2–4
	May 10	Pamela Sue Martin and John James, Chariots of Fire	2–4
	May 17	Tony Geary, Nastassja Kinski	1–2
	May 24	Jane Fonda and Tom Hayden, Ken Marshall of Marco Polo	1–2
	May 31	Stefanie Powers	1–2
	June 7	Loni Anderson and Burt Reynolds, Pia Zadora, Sophia Loren	2–4
	June 14	Melody Thomas, Tristan Rogers, and Lisa Brown of the Soaps	1–2
	June 21	Sylvester Stallone and Son, Barbara Walters	1–2
	June 28	E.T. and Henry Thomas	1–2
	July 5	Princess Di, Marie Osmond a Bride	2–4
	July 12	Aileen Quinn and Sandy of Annie, Dyan Cannon	1–2
	July 19	Dan Aykroyd on John Belushi, E.T., A Family Reunion for the Rolling Stones, Drew Barrymore, Robert Redford	2–4

YEAR	ISSUE	DESCRIPTION	VALUE
1982	July 26	Richard Simmons and Mickey Mouse, Jane Fonda, Diana Ross, Star Trek's Tempestuous Kirstie Alley, Love Boat's Doc, Ozzy Osbourne Ties the Knot	$2–4
	August 2	Dolly Parton Talks, Monty Python, Valerie Bertinelli, The Beatles, Harrison Ford, Jill St. John, Charlton Heston	2–4
	August 9	Hollywood Kids . . . John Ritter and Wife, Paul McCartney: A $3 Million Love Affair?, Led Zep's Robert Plant, The Dukes of Hazzard, Marilyn Monroe Remembered, Eddie Money	2–4
	August 16	Princess Di, Sinatra, Jill St. John, Facts of Life, Joan Collins, REO Speedwagon, Victoria Principal, Andy Gibb, Huey Lewis	2–3
	August 23	All About E.T.: The Untold Story, John Travolta and the Summer Stock Stars, Elton John Salutes Yoko and Sean Lennon, Sly Stallone, Tanya Tucker, Chicago, Elvis Costello, Andy Gibb, Susan Anton	1–3
	August 30	Jill St. John and Robert Wagner, Lucie Arnaz, Richard Harris, Farrah, Morgan Fairchild, Drew Barrymore, Kenny Rogers	2–4
	September 9	Olivia Newton-John, Burt Reynolds and Goldie Hawn, Richard Pryor	3–5

YEAR	ISSUE	DESCRIPTION	VALUE
1982	September 13	Robin Williams, Dolly Parton	$1–2
	September 20	The Best and Worst Dressed ... Brooke Shields, Victoria Principal, Prince Charles, Sophia Loren, Nancy and Ronald Reagan	2–3
	September 27	Princess Grace	1–2
	October 4	Ted Knight, Nancy Dussault and Sitcom Son, Prince Andrew	1–2
	October 11	Scott Baio, Richard Chamberlain/Thorn Birds, Mary Martin, Patty Duke, Tanya Roberts, Carolyn Jones and The Addams Family, John Cougar, Cherry Boone, Brian Eno	2–4
	October 18	Falcon Crest Cast	1–2
	October 25	Why the Famous Date the Famous, Mia Farrow, Liz Taylor, Art Garfunkel, Kim Carnes, Bob Geldof, Richard Thomas	2–4
	November 1	Garfield the Cat, Christie Brinkley	2–3
	November 8	John Delorean and Family, Elizabeth Taylor	1–2
	November 15	Grimaldi Family	1–2
	November 22	Mick Jagger, Jerry Hall, Gregory Peck	3–6
	November 29	Christina Delorean, Phil Donahue	1–2
	December 6	Larry Hagman and Linda Gray	1–2
	December 13	Yoko Ono and Sean, Susan Lucci: The Sexiest Woman on the Soaps, Ricky Nelson's Daughter ... Tracy	2–4
	December 20	Joan Collins, Joan Kennedy	1–2

YEAR	ISSUE	DESCRIPTION	VALUE
1982	December 27	Barbra Streisand, Ted Koppel, Diana, Paul Newman	$1–2
1983	January 10	Clint Eastwood: A Surprising Look, Nancy Reagan, Billy Joel Drops In on Allentown, Simon & Simon, Jerry Lewis, Tony Basil, Liz Taylor, Nastassja Kinski, Elton John	2–4
	January 17	Dustin Hoffman, Marie Osmond	2–4
	January 24	Roxanne Pulitzer, The Hurt and Healing of the Soulful Marvin Gaye, Michael Jackson, Clint Eastwood, Ron Wood	1–2
	January 31	Princess Di, Eddie Murphy, Andy Gibb: Fired, Glen Campbell, Roy Orbison, Twiggy, Brooke Shields, Goldie Hawn	1–2
	February 7	Princess Stephanie, Beaver Is Back, Jerry Lewis, Snoopy, Mick Jagger Nails Down an Exotic Role, Heather Locklear	2–4
	February 14	Ali MacGraw and Robert Mitchum: The Winds of War, Dolly Parton, Willie Nelson, Waylon Jennings, Ric Ocasek of The Cars, Tina Turner, David Bowie, Keith Richards, Cher	2–4
	February 21	Karen Carpenter, Cheryl Ladd	3–5
	February 28	Brooke Shields: The Shock of Araby, Luther Vandross, Sonny Bono, Billy Joel, John Denver, Johnny Carson	3–5
	March 7	Sylvester Stallone and John Travolta, Queen Elizabeth II	1–2

YEAR	ISSUE	DESCRIPTION	VALUE
1983	March 14	Readers' Poll Issue . . . Victoria Principal, Linda Evans, Koo Stark, Dustin Hoffman, Jodie Foster, Linda Ronstadt, The Bee Gees	$ 2–3
	March 21	Bing Crosby, Linda Gray	1–2
	March 28	Richard Chamberlain: The Thorn Birds, Gary Coleman's Troubled Life, Sheena Easton, Margot Kidder	2–3
	April 4	The Oscars, E.T., Paul Newman, Pete Townshend, Shelley Long	1–2
	April 11	Linda Evans, Jon Voight	1–2
	April 18	The Crime of David Soul, Lois Chiles of Dallas, Tom Selleck, An Insider Look at the Beatles, Koo and the Royals	1–2
	April 25	Joan Rivers, Knight Rider, Oak Ridge Boys Feud, Nastassja Kinski, Jack Palance, Liz Taylor	1–2
	May 2	Dena Al-Fassi, Mariette Hartley, The Outsider's Teen Queen, Randy Newman Zings L.A., Mick Jagger, Julian Lennon	1–2
	May 9	Kristy McNichol, Bob Newhart	2–4
	May 16	Helen Reddy, Jamie Farr	2–4
	May 23	Victoria Principal, Adolf Hitler	3–5
	May 30	Mr. T, Richard Gere	1–2
	June 6	Carrie Fisher and Jabba the Hutt	5–10
	June 13	Tony Perkins of Psycho II, David Bowie and Stevie Nicks and a Rockfest Blowout, Genie Francis, Rickie Lee Jones, Lesley Ann Warren, Cher, Goldie Hawn, Connie Chung	3–6

YEAR	ISSUE	DESCRIPTION	VALUE
1983	June 20	Sally Ride, Return of the Jedi, Twiggy, Roger Moore, Elton, Menudo, WarGames's Ally Sheedy	$1–3
	June 27	Prince William, Love Boat's All-Star China Cruise, Patricia Neal, Loretta Lynn, Neil Young, Pete Townshend, Elton	1–3
	July 4	Robert Wagner . . . Superdad, John Lennon: The Sellout of Friends and Lovers, Twilight Zone's John Lithgow	1–2
	July 11	Richard Pryor and Eddie Murphy, Princess Daisy	1–2
	July 18	James Bond's Babes . . . Barbara Bach, etc., Spirited Shirley MacLaine, Burt Reynolds, Dolly Parton, Tom Selleck	2–4
	July 25	John Travolta: Two for Travolta, 3-D Movies and Jaws, Billy Joel, Diana Ross, Rod Stewart, Olivia Newton-John, Wendy O. Williams . . . The First Lady of Shock Rock, Kirstie Alley, Elizabeth Taylor	2–4
	August 1	Goldie Hawn, Mick Jagger at 40, Boy George, Styx, John Travolta, Brooke Shields, Cathy Bach	2–4
	August 8	Diana Ross: The Concert Controversy, Michael Jackson, Return of the Jedi: Behind the Magic, Flashdance Chic	3–5
	August 15	Ryan O'Neal and Farrah Fawcett, Griffin O'Neal	2–4

YEAR	ISSUE	DESCRIPTION	VALUE
1983	August 22	Kenny Rogers and Linda Evans, Jamie Lee Curtis, David Bowie, Stevie Nicks, Bruce Springsteen, Jackson Browne	$3–5
	August 29	Fall Preview Special, Cher, Olivia Newton-John, Kate Jackson, David Bowie, John Travolta, John Delorean, Martin Sheen, Jamie Farr, Harry Morgan	3–5
	September 5	Princess Grace, Sting	2–4
	September 12	Chevy Chase and Fatherhood, Barry Manilow, Tragedy Revisits Jerry Lee Lewis, Grace Kelly Part II, Liz Taylor, Marilyn Monroe, Marilu Henner, Dottie West	2–3
	September 19	Korean Airline Tragedy, Brooke Shields	2–3
	September 26	The Best and Worst Dressed . . . Princess Diana, Mr. T, John Travolta, Fidel Castro, Christie Brinkley, Donna Mills	2–3
	October 3	Bobby Kennedy Jr., Vanessa Williams	2–3
	October 10	Natalie Wood, Joan Collins	2–4
	October 17	Michael Jackson, Sean Connery and Kim Basinger, MTV	3–5
	October 24	M.A.S.H. Cast and Feature . . . After M.A.S.H.	2–4
	October 31	Pierce Brosnan, The Right Stuff Cast	1–2
	November 7	Jessica Savitch	1–2
	November 11	Princess Di, Brigitte Bardot, Til' Tuesday, Patsy Cline	2–3

YEAR	ISSUE	DESCRIPTION	VALUE
1983	November 14	Paul McCartney, Lindsay Wagner	$3–5
	November 21	Karen and Richard Carpenter, Mariel Hemingway	3–5
	November 28	The Kennedys: 20 Years Later, Linda Evans, Diane Keaton, Barry Manilow, Joan Collins, Kenny Rogers	1–2
	December 5	Jane Pauley, Mary Tyler Moore, Dr. Robert Levine	1–2
	December 12	Barbra Streisand	2–4
	December 19	Olivia Newton-John: Will Grease Lightning Strike Again?, Annie Lennox Makes Eurythmics Throb, Al Pacino, Yoko Ono, Jamie Lee Curtis Makes Ant Music with Adam, Mick Jagger Croons for Pregnant Jerry Hall, Linda Evans	2–4
1984	January 2	Year-End Double Issue Special, Richard Chamberlain, Mr. T, Ronald Reagan, Vanessa Williams, Jennifer Beals	2–4
	January 9	Princess Caroline, Keith Richards, Patti Hansen	2–4
	January 16	Dennis Wilson and the Beach Boys, Princess Caroline	3–6
	January 23	Cher, Jaclyn Smith	3–5
	January 30	Mr. T, Lindsay Wagner	2–4
	February 6	Debra Winger and Shirley MacLaine Talk about Mothers and Daughters, The Beatles' U.S. Invasion: The Insider's View, Mia Farrow, Boy George	1–2

YEAR	ISSUE	DESCRIPTION	VALUE
1984	February 13	Michael Jackson, Peter Jennings	$2–4
	February 20	John Lennon's Last Songs . . . Yoko's Bittersweet Story, Chris Evert and the Rock Star, Silkwood, Dyan Cannon, Michael Caine, Diane Keaton, Greta Garbo	1–3
	February 27	Bo Derek, Princess Diana	2–4
	March 5	People's First 10 Years . . . Farrah Fawcett: A New Kind of Love Goddess, John Travolta, John Lennon, Jane Fonda	2–3
	March 12	Tom Selleck	2–4
	March 19	Paul Newman	1–2
	March 26	Gary and Lee Hart, Linda Ronstadt	2–3
	April 2	Kevin Bacon, Footloose	1–2
	April 9	Daryl Hannah: Splash	2–4
	April 16	John Delorean and Children	1–2
	April 23	Boy George, Robert Duvall and Meryl Streep	3–5
	May 7	Michael Jackson, The Jackson Brothers	3–5
	May 14	Ethel and David Kennedy	1–2
	May 21	Dolly Parton, Willie Nelson, Kenny Rogers, Loretta Lynn, George Strait, Crystal Gayle	2–4
	May 28	Robert Redford	1–2
	June 4	Griffin O'Neal and Ryan, Andy Kaufman	1–2
	June 11	John Belushi, Michael Jackson	2–4
	June 18	Jackie Onassis, Boy George	2–3
	June 25	Princess Caroline and Son, Prince William	1–2
	July 2	Harrison Ford and Kate Capshaw, Jermaine Jackson	2–4

YEAR	ISSUE	DESCRIPTION	VALUE
1984	July 9	Dolly Parton and Sylvester Stallone, Elizabeth Taylor	$2–4
	July 16	People Poll Special . . . Boy George, Mick Jagger, Jerry Hall, Ronald Reagan, Christie Brinkley, Walter Mondale	2–4
	July 23	Michael Jackson: Magic . . . Behind the Scenes, Nastassja Kinski: A New Mom, Neil Diamond Plays for Di	2–4
	July 30	Geraldine Ferraro, Phoebe Cates, Billy Joel, Spinal Tap	1–2
	August 6	Vanessa Williams, Liza Minnelli	2–4
	August 13	Special Comedy Issue . . . David Letterman, Joan Rivers, Eddie Murphy, Bill Murray, Rodney Dangerfield	1–2
	August 20	Richard Burton, Prince: Rock's Reigning Prince . . . Loud, Lewd and #1, Mary Lou Retton	2–3
	August 27	Fall Preview Issue . . . Morgan Fairchild Dolls Up, Christie Brinkley and Billy Joel, Stefanie Powers, Tanya Roberts, etc.	3–5
	September 3	Bruce Springsteen, Bo Derek	2–4
	September 10	Vanessa Williams, Truman Capote	2–4
	September 17	Cyndi Lauper, Elizabeth Taylor	3–5
	September 24	The Best and Worst Dressed . . . Michael Jackson, Goldie Hawn, Geraldine Ferraro, Raquel Welch, Bo Derek, Bill Murray	2–3
	October 1	Princess Diana and Prince Henry, Mary Tyler Moore	1–2

YEAR	ISSUE	DESCRIPTION	VALUE
1984	October 8	Farrah Fawcett, John Delorean	$2–4
	October 15	Sally Field, Ryan O'Neal, Farrah Fawcett, Prince, Vanity	2–4
	October 22	Sophia Loren and Son, Barry Manilow	2–4
	October 29	David: The Bubble Boy, Jon-Erik Hexum, Princess Diana	1–2
	November 5	Diane Sawyer, Nick Nolte	1–2
	November 12	Kid Stars . . . Drew Barrymore, Ricky Schroder, and Henry Thomas, Joan Collins, Elton John	2–4
	November 19	Rock's Reclusive Prince: A Rare Look inside the Secret World of His Royal Badness, Princess Stephanie, Richard Burton, Baby Fae	2–4
	November 26	Liza Minnelli, Miss America, Sharlene Wells	1–2
	December 3	Baby Fae and Mother	1–2
	December 10	Joan Rivers and Husband, Bill Cosby and Baby Fae	1–2
	December 17	Linda Evans	1–2
	December 24	Double Issue Special, Mary Lou Retton, Farrah Fawcett, Tina Turner, Bruce Springsteen, Richard Gere	2–4
1985	January 7	New Brides Special . . . Jamie Lee Curtis, Olivia Newton-John, Mariel Hemingway, Bette Midler, Sally Field	2–4
	January 14	Princess Diana and Prince Harry, Sting	1–2

YEAR	ISSUE	DESCRIPTION	VALUE
1985	January 21	The 30 Hardest Working Celebs . . . Cyndi Lauper, Goldie Hawn, Eddie Murphy, Hall and Oates, etc., Amy Irving, Duran Duran, REO Speedwagon, the Real Charlotte Brontë	$2–4
	January 28	Ted Kennedy and Children	1–2
	February 4	Mel Gibson: The Sexiest Man Alive, Meredith Baxter-Birney's Family Ties, Gumby's Back, Clint Eastwood	2–3
	February 11	Cagney & Lacey, Van Halen's David Lee Roth Rocks Alone, Brash, Bratty Sean Penn, David Bowie in the Snow, Tina Turner, Bob Dylan, Harrison Ford	2–3
	February 18	Teen Suicide . . . Molly Ringwald cover, Christina O and Farrah, Kelly McGillis, Cyndi Lauper, Princess Caroline	2–3
	February 25	The Night Rock Cried . . . for Ethiopia: Michael Jackson, Diana Ross, Bob Dylan, Willie Nelson, Lionel Richie, Bruce Springsteen, Hollywood Wives's Angie Dickinson, Gloria Steinem versus Playboy, Michelle Pfeiffer, The Go-Go's	2–4
	March 4	TV's Rerun Madness . . . I Love Lucy, M.A.S.H., The Mary Tyler Moore Show, Star Trek, etc., Cyndi Lauper, The Who, Bruce Springsteen, Los Lobos, Mick Jagger, Matt Dillon	2–4

YEAR	ISSUE	DESCRIPTION	VALUE
1985	March 11	Madonna, Elizabeth Taylor	$3–5
	March 18	Cher and the True Story of Mask, Dynasty's Amanda, Tab Hunter, David Lee Roth, Tanya Tucker	2–3
	March 25	High-Salaried Celebs . . . Are They Worth It?	2–3
	April 1	Jacqueline Bisset and Alexander Godunov	2–3
	April 8	Christie Brinkley and Billy Joel's Wedding, Jackie Smith Shows Off Her Real-Life Angel, Diana Ross, Jimmy Page	2–4
	April 15	Dr. Ruth Westheimer, Princess Stephanie, Hall and Oates	1–2
	April 22	James Garner: The Last Real Man, Wham in China, Annie Lennox: Outrageous Hair, Crystal Gayle, Oliver Reed, Fish Farmer Ian Anderson, The Singing Nun	2–4
	April 29	Rape, Linda Evans, Tina Turner, Tom Selleck, Madonna and Rosanna Arquette, Pia Zadora	2–4
	May 6	Bette Dearest: Bette Davis's Daughter Talks, John Lennon: His Sister's Exclusive Story, Dynasty's Emma Samms	2–4
	May 13	Madonna, Patrick Duffy and Elizabeth Taylor	3–5
	May 20	Charles and Di, Ron and Nancy, Harlem's Apollo: The All-Night Jam, Britt Ekland, Diana Ross, Annie Lennox	2–3

YEAR	ISSUE	DESCRIPTION	VALUE
1985	May 27	Bruce Springsteen and Wife ... Who's the Boss Now?, Michael Landon, The Pointer Sisters	$2–4
	June 3	Sylvester Stallone's Silent Son, Chuck Norris, Bob Hope's Jokebag, Grace Jones Parties, Margaret Hamilton: A Beautiful Woman, Peter Sellers, Boy George, Bianca Jagger	2–4
	June 10	The Story of the Septuplets' Parents, Stacy Keach, John Travolta, Karen Black, Tyrone Power	1–2
	June 17	Von Bulow: A Shattered Family, Bruce Springsteen's Irish Gig, Don Johnson's Summer Job, Cybill Shepherd	2–3
	June 24	Josef Mengele, John Travolta and Jamie Lee Curtis, The Smiths, John Denver	1–2
	July 1	Cyndi Lauper, Warren Beatty, Elton John, Morgan Fairchild	2–4
	July 8	Jack Nicholson: The Strange, Sweet Love Story, Can Madonna Get Sean Penn to the Altar?, Rambo: America's Avenger, Phil Collins, Laraine Newman, Cher, Morgan Fairchild	2–4
	July 15	Tina Turner, Christina Onassis, Lorenzo Lamas	2–4
	July 22	Malice in the Palace: Forget Shy Di, Duran Duran: A Romp with the Idol Rich, Brigitte Nielsen	2–3

YEAR	ISSUE	DESCRIPTION	VALUE
1985	July 29	Live-Aid Special . . . Mick Jagger, Tina Turner, Madonna, Keith Richards, Ron Wood, Bob Dylan, Hall and Oates	$3–4
	August 5	Ali MacGraw, Bob Geldof and Nancy Reagan	1–2
	August 12	The Other Life of Rock Hudson, Michael J. Fox, Ratt, The Monkees, Cyndi Lauper	2–4
	August 19	Ann Jillian Exclusive, Bruce Springsteen: What's Next?	2–4
	August 26	Duran Duran's Simon LeBon: A Brush with Death at Sea	2–4
	September 3	Madonna and Sean Penn	2–4
	September 9	Priscilla Presley Exclusive . . . Life with Elvis, Samantha Smith	2–3
	September 16	Prince/Madonna/David Lee Roth, etc. . . . Has Rock Gone Too Far?, Priscilla Presley on Elvis Part II	2–4
	September 23	Rock Hudson	1–2
	September 30	Olivia Newton-John and Hubby, Billy Crystal, Princess Stephanie, Cher and Tina Turner, Boy George, Eddie Murphy	2–4
	October 7	Don Johnson, Backstage at Farm Aid, Bob Dylan	2–3
	October 14	Arnold Schwarzenegger, Heather Thomas Kicks Cocaine, Ringo's Grandchild, Aretha Franklin, Cybill Shepherd	2–3
	October 21	Marilyn Monroe and Rock Hudson: Their Last Days, Barbara Eden, John Schneider, Diana Ross Meets New Guy	2–3

YEAR	ISSUE	DESCRIPTION	VALUE
1985	October 28	The Best and Worst Dressed, Princess Stephanie, Madonna, Philip Michael Thomas	$ 2–3
	November 4	Cybill Shepherd: TV's Sexiest Spitfire, Clarence Clemons, Elvira: Mistress of the Macabre, Hall and Oates, John Cougar, Duran Duran's John Taylor, Bruce Springsteen	2–4
	November 11	What's Diana Worth to Britain?, Brigitte Bardot, Robert Wagner, Sissy Spacek	1–2
	November 18	AIDS: Every Parent's Nightmare, Rae Dawn Chong, Bill Cosby, Exotic Barbara Carrera	2–4
	November 25	Barbara Stanwyck and Linda Evans, Rock Hudson's Last Lover Talks, Mick Jagger, Marla Gibbs, Jerry Hall	2–3
	December 2	Raisa Gorbachev, Joan Rivers and Liz Taylor	.50–1
	December 9	Philip Michael Thomas, Sylvester Stallone, Katharine Hepburn Redefined, Whitney Houston's Big Break	2–4
	December 16	Baryshnikov: Ballet's Russian Romeo, Love Boat's Gopher, Joni Mitchell, Tracy Nelson: Rick's Daughter, Liz Taylor	2–3
	December 23	25 Most Intriguing People Issue . . . Don Johnson, Michael J. Fox, Bruce Springsteen and Wife, Madonna, Bob Geldof	2–3
1986	January 6	Donna Dixon, Barbi Benton, Madonna, Lindsay Wagner	2–4

YEAR	ISSUE	DESCRIPTION	VALUE
1986	January 13	Ingrid Bergman, Teddy Pendergrass, Michael Douglas, Kathleen Turner	$ 1–2
	January 20	Ricky Nelson, Meryl Streep, Robert Redford	3–5
	January 27	Mark Harmon: The Sexiest Man Alive, Donna Reed: It Was a Good Life	.50–1
	February 3	Bette Midler at 40, Liz Taylor and Stevie Wonder, Jessica Lange, Sade, Yoko Ono's Lost Daughter, Cher	2–4
	February 10	Christa McAuliffe, Julian and Sean Lennon, Madonna, Billy Joel, Keith Richards, Elvis, Chuck Berry, James Brown	2–3
	February 17	Diana Ross's Supreme Day, Brooke Shields, Pia Zadora	2–4
	February 24	The Rebel Reagan . . . Patti Davis, Michael J. Fox	1–2
	March 3	Michele Duvalier and Imelda Marcos: The Dragon Ladies, Night Court's Sassy Sidekick, Stevie Wonder	1–2
	March 10	Who Makes What Issue . . . Whoopi, Sade, Kim Basinger, Rosanna Arquette, Debra Winger, Grateful Dead, Phil Collins	2–3
	March 17	Caroline Kennedy, Katharine Hepburn, Clint Eastwood	1–2
	March 24	George Harrison: Madonna's Beatle Boss, Pouty Princess Molly Ringwald, Troy Beyer	2–4

YEAR	ISSUE	DESCRIPTION	VALUE
1986	March 31	Are These Old Maids? ... Donna Mills, Sharon Gless, Linda Ronstadt, and Diane Sawyer, Estelle Getty, Peter Sellers and Britt Ekland, Sally Field, Jacqueline Bisset, Diane Keaton	$2–4
	April 7	Sarah Ferguson, Mr. Mister, Joan Collins, Twisted Sister, Pia Zadora, Sly Stallone, Al Pacino	2–3
	April 14	Lionel Richie: Pop's #1 Hit Man, Opie and Andy Return to Mayberry, Farewell to James Cagney, Maureen O'Sullivan, Apollonia, Billy Crystal	2–4
	April 21	Ed McMahon and Family, Liz Taylor, Tony Danza, Madonna, Cher, LL Cool J, Mariel Hemingway	2–3
	April 28	Avenging Sergeant Ford, Moonlighting, The Bangles	2–3
	May 5	Dolly Parton: Peppery Talk, The Osmonds, Abbie Hoffman	2–4
	May 12	The Duke and Duchess of Windsor: Their Secret Love Letters, Arnold and Maria Shriver: A Splendid Wedding, Adam West: Batman	2–4
	May 19	Whitney Houston: America's Top New Star, How Sexy Is Cybill Shepherd?	3–5
	May 26	Joan Rivers, Heather Locklear and Her Motley Crue-Man, Neil Diamond, Johnny Carson, Sean Penn	2–4

YEAR	ISSUE	DESCRIPTION	VALUE
1986	June 2	Donna Mills, Tom Cruise: Top Gun	$2–4
	June 9	Rock Hudson's Story, Prince's Sneak Preview, Elvis Costello: More Smile, Less Bile, Kathleen Turner, Elle MacPherson, Robert Palmer	2–4
	June 16	The Rock Hudson Story: The Drama of His Final Days, Howie Mandel, Belinda Carlisle, Ozzy Osbourne, Tatum O'Neal	2–4
	June 23	John Kennedy Jr., Bruce Willis, Mikhail Baryshnikov, John James, The New Van Halen, Henry Ford in Love, Tony Bennett, Sammy Hagar	2–4
	June 30	Uncle Sam's Dirty Book, Ralph Macchio's Karate Master, Monika Scharre the Model, Anne Bancroft	1–2
	July 7	Prince William, Janet Jackson Scores High	2–4
	July 14	David Letterman, Tony Danza's Tony Wedding, Kate Collins, The Jets, Tatum O'Neal, Diana Ross, Connie Francis	2–4
	July 21	Prince, Robert Redford and Debra Winger, Boy George	2–3
	July 28	Hollywood Hunks '86 . . . Rodney Dangerfield and Danny DeVito, Christie Brinkley . . . A Salute to the Bikini . . . Joan Collins, Brigitte Bardot, Jayne Mansfield	2–4

YEAR	ISSUE	DESCRIPTION	VALUE
1986	August 4	Caroline Kennedy's Wedding, Dwight Yoakam	$1–2
	August 11	Pierce Brosnan . . . Remington Steele, Madonna's Man, Alien's Creator, Eric Clapton, Peter Townshend, Boy George	2–4
	August 18	Infidelity . . . Jack Nicholson, John McEnroe and Tatum O'Neal	2–4
	August 25	Vanna White, Paul Shaffer, Max Headroom, Willard Scott	2–4
	September 1	Farrah Fawcett, Eddie Murphy, Carol Burnett, Lucille Ball, Barbra Streisand, Tina Turner	2–4
	September 8	Priscilla Presley: "I'm Sick of Lies," Elton John, Alien's Sigourney Weaver, Peggy Lipton, Grace Jones	3–5
	September 15	Frank Sinatra: His Life and Loves, Liz Taylor, Diane Sawyer . . . 1963, The Pet Shop Boys, Joey Heatherton, The Monkees, Jan and Dean, Frankie Avalon, Bobby Rydell, Peter Noone	2–4
	September 22	Frank Sinatra and Women Part II . . . Victoria Principal, Natalie Wood, Lauren Bacall, Mia Farrow, etc., Barbra Streisand, Farrah Fawcett	2–4
	September 29	Patrick Duffy/Dallas, David Lee Roth: Rock's Sexy Road Warrior, Debra Winger, Jane Fonda, Tammy Wynette, Sissy Spacek	2–4
	October 6	Elizabeth Taylor and Robert Wagner, Paul Simon, Hollywood on Trial, Princess Di, David Rappaport	2–3

YEAR	ISSUE	DESCRIPTION	VALUE
1986	October 13	Princess Diana and Sarah Ferguson	$ 1–2
	October 20	Charlie's Angels . . . Look Homeward Angels: 10 Years Ago, Paul Hogan, Bruce Springsteen, Humphrey Bogart, John Wayne	7–15
	October 27	Joan Rivers, Ricky Nelson's Kids	2–4
	November 3	Kathleen Turner: Hollywood's Most Wanted Woman, Chuck Berry, The New Monkees, Johnny Cash, Keith Richards	2–4
	November 10	Princess Stephanie and Rob Lowe, Golden Girls's Sexpot, Betty Boop and Felix the Cat	2–4
	November 17	David and Julie Eisenhower, Tom Selleck, Angela Lansbury, Meredith Baxter-Birney, Huey Lewis, Bruce Hornsby, Diana Ross, Jimi Hendrix, Mary Wilson, Gregg Allman, Crosby, Stills, and Nash	2–4
	November 24	Carol Burnett, Troubled Boy George, Rock-Hot Bon Jovi, Anita Baker, Daryl Hannah, Jackson Browne	2–4
	December 1	The Best and Worst Dressed Issue . . . Cher, Cyndi Lauper, Liz Taylor, Cybill Shepherd, Elton John, Eric Clapton, Frank Zappa	2–4
	December 8	Bruce Springsteen: Bruce's Best, Dweezil Zappa, Elvis Presley in Leather, From Brando to Madonna	2–4

YEAR	ISSUE	DESCRIPTION	VALUE
1986	December 15	Cary Grant, Mae West, Ingrid Bergman, Sophia Loren, Dyan Cannon	$ 1–2
	December 22	25 Most Intriguing People Issue . . . Vanna White, Whitney Houston, Bette Midler, Run DMC, Diana Ross, Michael Jackson	2–4
1987	January 5	Bruce Willis and His Films, The Best of 1986, Cheers, Michael J. Fox, Liz Taylor, Snow White Turns 50, The Beverly Hillbillies, Marla Hanson, Kathleen Turner, Greta Garbo	2–4
	January 12	Oprah Winfrey, Billy Idol, Ellen Greene	1–2
	January 19	Huey Lewis: Rock's Best News, Howard Hesseman, Diane Sawyer, Ron Reagan, Leonard Nimoy	2–4
	January 26	Prince Edward, Shirley MacLaine, Sophia Loren	.50–1
	February 2	L.A. Law's . . . Susan Dey and Corbin Bernsen, Basil Rathbone As Sherlock Holmes, Chicago and Their Music, Mick Jagger, Cher	3–6
	February 9	The 100th Birthday of Hollywood . . . Marilyn Monroe, Liz Taylor, Bette Davis, Marlon Brando, The Wizard of Oz, Marlene Dietrich, Molly Ringwald, John Wayne, The Beastie Boys	3–6
	February 16	Liberace 1919–1987, Pam Dawber, Fergie, Ann-Margret	2–3

YEAR	ISSUE	DESCRIPTION	VALUE
1987	March 2	My Sister Sam's Pam Dawber Lands the Sexiest Man Alive, Jean Simmons, John Lennon Exclusive Part II	$ 2–4
	March 9	Charlie Sheen, Tom Berenger, Willem Dafoe	1–2
	March 16	Cybill Shepherd and Her Groom: The Wedding Album, Jill Ireland, Suzanne Somers, Goldie Hawn	2–4
	March 23	Mary Beth Whitehead, Elizabeth Stern and Baby	.50–1
	March 30	Harry Hamlin: The Sexiest Man	1–2
	April 6	Russia Special	.50–1
	April 13	Teen Sex Issue, Jane Fonda, Tina Turner, Paul Newman	.50–1
	April 20	Michael J. Fox, The Women of Designing Women	1–2
	April 27	David Crosby: The Confessions of a Coke Addict, Elizabeth Taylor Joins the Dash for the Duchess's Diamonds	2–4
	May 4	Michael Caine, Hill Street Blues, He-Man	.50–1
	May 11	Ted Danson, Madonna	1–2
	May 18	Gary Hart and Donna Rice, Sean Penn, Linda Purl	1–3
	May 25	Dustin Hoffman and Warren Beatty, Brigitte Nielsen	1–2
	June 1	Rita Hayworth Exclusive, Joan Rivers Fired, Diana and Charles Party at Cannes, Janis Joplin at 17	2–4
	June 8	Charles and Di, The Beatles, Susanna Hoffs Exclusive, Suzanne Vega	2–4

YEAR	ISSUE	DESCRIPTION	VALUE
1987	June 15	Donna Rice	$ 2–4
	June 22	Celebrating the '60s . . . A Summer of Love, Peter Max, Janis Joplin, Jimi Hendrix, Gurus, The Beatles, etc.	3–6
	June 29	Miss Amereica and Miss Wrong: The Bess Myerson Scandal, Robert De Niro, Peter O'Toole, Jenny Agutter	2–3
	July 6	Fred Astaire 1899–1987, John Travolta, Meat Loaf, Madonna	2–4
	July 13	Jackie Gleason: So Long Pal, Patty Duke, Tom Cruise	2–4
	July 20	Fergie and Di, Patty Duke, Mel Brooks, Howdy Doody	1–2
	July 27	Oliver North, People Poll Special . . . Donna Rice, Eddie Murphy, Ronald Reagan, Jim and Tammy Baker, Cybill Shepherd	1–2
	August 3	AIDS, Donovan, Annie Pujol, Liz Taylor, Fergie	2–4
	August 10	The Divorce Duels of Brigitte Nielsen and Joan Rivers, Marilyn Monroe: 25 Years Later, Frankie Avalon and Annette Funicello: Back on the Burning Sands	2–4
	August 17	Elvis Presley: 10 Years Later, Carly Simon's Victory over Paralyzing Stage Fright, Lou Diamond Phillips, Madonna on Tour, Whitney Houston, John Denver	2–4
	August 24	Jackie O, Boy George Back from a $1,000-a-Day Habit, 007's Maryam d'Abo	2–4

YEAR	ISSUE	DESCRIPTION	VALUE
1987	August 31	Joan Rivers's Tragedy, Fall Preview Issue, Dolly Parton, Emily Lloyd, Farrah Fawcett, Cher, The Cars	$ 2–4
	September 7	A Family at War ... The Nelsons, Carrie Fisher, Mary Hart	1–2
	September 14	Michael Jackson: He's Back and Bad, Lisa Lisa and Cult Jam	2–4
	September 21	Here Comes Fergie, Tom Selleck's Secret Tahoe Wedding, Madonna: A Sentimental Journey, Jump Street's Holly Robinson	2–3
	September 28	Princess Caroline: What Would Grace Say?, Matthew Broderick Faces Prison, Remembering Lorne Greene	1–2
	October 5	Jessica Hahn, Elizabeth Taylor	2–4
	October 12	Michael Jackson Exclusive: Message from Michael	2–4
	October 19	Pat Anthony: A Mother's Love, Valerie Harper Strikes Back, Bruce Springsteen Cutting Loose, A Beatle Coming Back, Jackson Browne, Roy Orbison, Elvis Costello, Jackson Five	2–4
	October 26	Glenn Close and Michael Douglas ... Real Life Fatal Attractions, Princess Ann in the U.S.A., Karen Carpenter, Spuds	2–4
	November 2	Baby Jessica McClure, Nancy Reagan	.50–1
	November 9	Princess Di, Barry Manilow Comeback, Paul Newman	1–2

YEAR	ISSUE	DESCRIPTION	VALUE
1987	November 16	The Best and Worst Dressed . . . Brigitte Nielsen, Elizabeth Taylor, Bruce Willis, Diane Keaton, Madonna, and others	$ 2–3
	November 23	Don Johnson and Sheena Easton, Staci Keanan, Michael Jackson	2–4
	November 30	Jay Leno, Kirstie Alley, Howdy Doody and Buffalo Bob	2–4
	December 7	Donald Trump, Courteney Cox	.50–1
	December 14	Madonna and Sean Penn: The Divorce of Madonna and Sean, Deidre Hall, Lillian Gish, Bette Davis	3–5
	December 21	Cybill Shepherd Exclusive: Cybill and Her Twins, Harry Chapin, Bruce Springsteen	2–4
	December 28	Double Issue Special, Princess Diana, Baby Jessica McClure, Michael Douglas, Oliver North, Brigitte Nielsen	2–3
1988	January 11	Bruce Willis, Mickey Mouse, Paul Hogan, Sarah Ferguson	1–2
	January 18	Elizabeth Taylor, Patrick Bissell: Cocaine and the Death of a Ballet Star, Meryl Streep, Bob Hope	2–4
	January 25	Cher: The Ultimate Liberated Woman, Liz Taylor Part II	2–4
	February 1	Broadcast News and Tom Brokaw	.50–1
	February 8	Margaux Hemingway, Sarah Ferguson, Mick Jagger, Bruce Springsteen	2–4
	February 15	The Story of a Test-tube Miracle, Priscilla Presley's Life after Elvis, Lana Turner's Daughter, Shirley Temple	2–3

YEAR	ISSUE	DESCRIPTION	VALUE
1988	February 22	Robin Williams, Marsha Garces	$ 1–2
	February 29	JFK and the Mob, Hugh Hefner and Carrie Leigh, Donna Rice	.50–1
	March 7	Jimmy Swaggart, Joan Severence, Steve Martin, Bette Davis, Barbra Streisand, Dudley Moore	.50–1
	March 14	AIDS and the Single Woman	.50–1
	March 21	The First Family, Grammy Awards, Dweezil Zappa	1–2
	March 28	Andy Gibb: A Superstar at 19, Prince Charles, Sting, Henry Winkler, Cybill Shepherd, Cher, Ziggy Marley	3–5
	April 4	Brigitte Nielsen: The Hot and the Heavy, Larry Hagman, Myrna Loy, Peggy Lipton, Yoko Ono	2–3
	April 11	Robert Chambers: The Preppy Murder Case, Happy Birthday Oscar, Sophia Loren, Jimmy Olsen	1–2
	April 18	Suzanne Somers/Susan Sullivan/Chuck Norris and others: Children of Alcoholics, Tiffany versus Her Mom	2–4
	April 25	Princess Diana, Eleanor Mondale	.50–1
	May 2	Leona Helmsley, Madonna and Sean Penn, Lita Ford, Denise Crosby: From Playboy to the Enterprise	2–4
	May 9	Love in Bloom . . . Don Johnson and Barbra Streisand and others, LaToya Jackson, Patricia Neal, Charlene Tilton, Terence Trent D'Arby	2–3

YEAR	ISSUE	DESCRIPTION	VALUE
1988	May 16	Loni Anderson and Burt Reynolds's Wedding, Duchess of York	$ 2–3
	May 23	Ron and Nancy Reagan and Astrology, 10,000 Maniacs, Eric Clapton, Patti Boyd, George Harrison, Fergie	2–4
	May 30	Amazing Grace . . . Ryan White, Debbie Gibson, Cher	2–4
	June 6	Laurie Dann, Bobby Kennedy	.50–1
	June 13	Paul Hogan and the Real Crocodile Dundee, Heather O'Rourke, Jade Jagger	1–2
	June 20	Bette Midler and Lily Tomlin, Morton Downey Jr., Diana	1–2
	June 27	Mike Tyson and Robin Givens, Bruce Springsteen	1–2
	July 4	Tawana Brawley, Jim and Tammy Bakker	.50–1
	July 11	Miracle at Sea, Jim and Tammy Bakker	.50–1
	July 18	The American Hostages	.50–1
	July 25	Michael and Kitty Dukakis, Eddie Murphy, Shari Headley	.50–1
	August 1	Charles and Diana: The Seven-Year Hitch, The Invisible Wedding of Michael J. Fox, Jane Fonda	1–2
	August 8	Eddie Murphy: Can't Buy Me Love	.50–1
	August 29	Fergie's Little Princess, Florence Griffith-Joyner	1–2
	October 18	Sally's Field Day, The Tyson-Givens Blowup, Charles Addams, Bob Dylan	2–4
1989	January 2	Liz Taylor, Jodie Foster, Jessica Rabbit, Michelle Pfeiffer, Lisa Marie Presley, Madonna	2–4

YEAR	ISSUE	DESCRIPTION	VALUE
1989	January 9	Preview Special, Cybill Shepherd and Ryan O'Neal, Dennis Quaid, Roy Orbison, Fergie, John Candy	$ 1–2
	January 16	Drew Barrymore, E.T.	.50–1
	January 23	Peter Bogdanovich, Louise and Dorothy Stratten	2–3
	January 30	Barbara and George Bush	.50–1
	February 5	Athena Onassis	.50–1
	February 13	Hedda Nussbaum	.50–1
	February 20	Ronald and Nancy Reagan, Princess Diana	.50–1
	February 27	Melanie Griffith and Don Johnson, Mike Tyson	1–2
	March 6	The First 15 Years of People Issue . . . Brooke Shields, Farrah, Cher: 15 Years Later, Kate Jackson, Madonna	2–4
	March 13	Elizabeth Taylor, Meredith Baxter-Birney and David Birney	1–2
	March 20	Sean Young, Athina and Thierry Rousell	.50–1
	March 27	John Gotti, Mary Martin: Peter Pan	.50–1
	April 3	Kristy McNichol, William Hurt	2–3
	April 10	Connie Chung and Maury Povich, Bobby Brown	1–2
	April 17	Tai Babilonia, Fred Savage, Kim Basinger: A Place of Her Own	2–3
	April 24	Princess Anne, Christine Keeler: A Torrid Film, Bonnie Raitt, Glenn Close, Morgan Fairchild, Donna Mills	2–4
	Summer '89 Special	TV's 50th Anniversary	2–4
	May 1	Abbie Hoffman	.50–1

YEAR	ISSUE	DESCRIPTION	VALUE
1989	May 8	Lucille Ball	$ 1–2
	May 15	Family Ties Cast, Andy Warhol, Clint Eastwood	1–2
	May 22	Night of the Wilding	.25–.50
	May 29	Children of Divorce	.25–.50
	June 5	Gilda Radner, Theresa Saldana	1–2
	June 12	Delta Burke and Gerald McRaney Wedding	.25–.50
	June 19	Lisa Marie Presley and Daughter	1–2
	June 26	Prince William, Dr. Joyce Brothers	.25–.50
	July 3	Conjoined Twins, Tyne Daly	.25–.50
	July 10	William Hurt, Sandra Jennings, Princess Diana	.25–.50
	July 17	Hugh Hefner and Kimberly Conrad Wedding	.50–1
	July 24	Laurence Olivier	.25–.50
	July 31	Rebecca Schaffer	.25–.50
	August 7	Clint Eastwood and Sondra Locke, Steven Spielberg and Amy Irving, Jane Fonda and Tom Hayden	1–2
	August 14	Lucille Ball, Carol Burnett, Joan Rivers, Betty White, Desi Arnaz Jr.	1–2
	August 21	Ordeal at Sea: The Janet Culver Story	.50–1
	August 28	Ringo Starr, Roger Daltry and Peter Townshend, The Rolling Stones	2–4
	September 4	Fall Preview Issue . . . Sally Field, Dolly Parton, Julia Roberts, Liz Taylor, Sting, Michael J. Fox	2–4
	September 11	Leona Helmsley, Laura San Giacomo	.25–.50
	September 18	Tammy and Jim Bakker, Princess Anne	.25–.50

YEAR	ISSUE	DESCRIPTION	VALUE
1989	September 25	Saturday Night Live: The Wild and Crazy Story Exclusive, Elton John, Jane Seymour, Bonnie Raitt, Justine Bateman	$ 2–3
	October 2	Roseanne Barr, Viscount Althorp and Victoria Lockwood	.25–.50
	October 9	Roseanne Barr, Jane Pauley	.25–.50
	October 16	Dr. Elizabeth Morgan, Zsa Zsa Gabor, Chris Burke	.25–.50
	October 23	Bette Davis	.50–1
	October 30	Heroes of the Quake	.25–.50
	November 6	Burt Reynolds, Loni Anderson and Son	.50–1
	November 13	Jane Pauley, Deborah Norville, John Travolta	.50–1
	November 20	Fergie, Amanda Blake	.25–.50
	November 27	Kitty Dukakis	.25–.50
	December 4	Michael J. Fox, Christina Applegate	2–3
	December 11	The Best and Worst Dressed . . . Madonna, Kim Basinger, Mel Gibson, Princess Di, Arsenio Hall	1–2
	December 18	The Sexiest Man Alive: Sean Connery, Ken Wahl, John Goodman, Michael Jordan	.50–1
1990	January 1	The 25 Most Intriguing People of the Year . . . Michelle Pfeiffer, Madonna: Another Typical Year, Paula Abdul	2–4
	January 9	Readers' Poll Special, Princess Diana, Jane Pauley, Rob Lowe, Tom Selleck, Zsa Zsa Gabor, Oprah Winfrey	.50–1
	January 15	Pat Sajak Wedding	.25–.50
	January 22	Stuart Boston Murder	.25–.50

YEAR	ISSUE	DESCRIPTION	VALUE
1990	January 29	Drew Barrymore: No Happy Ending, Jodie Foster, Annie II	$ 2–4
	February 5	McMartin Trial, Barbara Stanwyck	.25–.50
	February 12	Ava Gardner	.25–.50
	February 19	Kathleen Turner and Michael Douglas, Joan Rivers	1–2
	February 26	Ivana and Donald Trump, Marla Maples	.25–.50
	March 5	Marla Maples, Princess Diana	.25–.50
	March 12	Paula Abdul, TV's Elvis Presley: Michael St. Gerard	2–4
	March 19	Rob Lowe, Ivana Trump	.25–.50
	March 26	Murder in Beverly Hills, Menendez Family	.25–.50
	Spring Special	1990 Styles, Paula Abdul, Madonna, Dana Delany, Warren Beatty	1–2
	Summer Special	Michelle Pfeiffer, The 50 Most Beautiful People	1–2
	April 2	Mystery Lovers . . . Daryl Hannah, Michelle Pfeiffer, Kim Basinger and Prince, Tom Cruise, Whitney Houston	2–4
	April 9	Elizabeth Taylor, Liza Minnelli, Gloria Estefan	1–2
	April 16	Fergie and Eugene, Teenage Mutant Ninja Turtles	.25–.50
	April 23	Ryan White and Elton John	.25–.50
	April 30	Greta Garbo, Winona Ryder and Johnny Depp	1–2
	May 7	Marla Maples, Patricia Rose and John Kluge, Madonna	.50–1
	May 14	Children of the Dark, Jaime and Sherry	.25–.50
	May 21	John F. Kennedy Jr., Kathie Lee Gifford and Son	.25–.50
	May 28	Sammy Davis Jr., Athina Rousell	.25–.50

YEAR	ISSUE	DESCRIPTION	VALUE
1990	June 4	Christian Brando, Marlon Brando, Jill Ireland and Charles Bronson	$.25–.50
	June 11	Goldie Hawn and Mel Gibson, Jane Fonda and Ted Turner	.25–.50
	June 18	Jim Henson	.25–.50
	June 25	Gloria Estefan, Kerry Kennedy and Andrew Cuomo	2–3
	July 2	Madonna and Warren Beatty	2–4
	July 9	Donald Trump, Dick Tracy's Villains	.25–.50
	July 16	Princess Diana, Vanna White	.25–.50
	July 23	The Sexiest Man Alive: Tom Cruise	.25–.50
	July 30	Alison Gertz: Women with AIDS, Alex Trebek	.25–.50
	August 6	Patrick Swayze, Lucille Ball	.50–1
	August 13	New Kids on the Block, Jane Pauley	.25–.50
	August 20	Connie Chung, Princess Diana	.25–.50
	August 27	Lisa Steinberg, Michele Launders, Dan Rather	.25–.50
	September 3	Fall Preview Special, Tom Hanks, Bruce Willis, Melanie Griffith, Bart Simpson, Lucy and Desi, Sherilyn Fenn, Meryl Streep, Kirstie Alley, Sylvester Stallone	1–2
	September 10	Mom Goes to War Special, Stevie Ray Vaughan	1–2
	September 17	Julia Roberts, The Gainesville Murders	2–3
	September 24	Brian Watkins Murder	.25–.50
	October 1	Barbara Bush and Dog Millie, Sammy Davis Jr.	.25–.50
	October 8	Cybill Shepherd: Sexy, Saucy, and Outrageous, Shari Belafonte	2–4

YEAR	ISSUE	DESCRIPTION	VALUE
1990	October 15	Princess Caroline	$.25–.50
	October 22	Kimberly Bergalis, Princess Caroline	.25–.50
	October 29	Kirstie Alley, Leonard Bernstein	1–2
	November 5	Teens and Sex, Katharine Hepburn	.25–.50
	November 12	Demi Moore and Bruce Willis, Angie Dickinson	1–2
	November 19	Kevin Costner, Mary Martin	.25–.50
	November 26	Naomi and Wynonna Judd, Linda Evans	.50–1
	December 3	The Best and Worst Dressed of 1990 . . . Julia Roberts, Madonna, etc., Princess Caroline: The Grief That Will Not Go Away, Carly Simon: Beyond Dancing Bears	2–3
	December 10	Elizabeth Taylor, Yoko Ono and Sean Lennon	.50–1
	December 17	Rape on Campus, George Bush	.25–.50
	December 24	Patrick Swayze, Julia Roberts, Princess Caroline, Delta Burke, George Bush, MC Hammer, Claudia Schiffer	.50–1
1991	January 14	Oprah Winfrey, Tom Cruise and Nicole Kidman	.25–.50
	January 21	Cher, Arnold Schwarzenegger, John Travolta, Kelly Preston	1–2
	January 28	America Goes to War	.50–1
	February 4	Elizabeth Glaser, Paul Michael Glaser	.25–.50
	February 11	Princess Diana, Caroline Kennedy	.25–.50
	February 18	Lucille Ball and Desi Arnaz, Gloria Estefan	1–2

YEAR	ISSUE	DESCRIPTION	VALUE
1991	February 25	Julia Roberts and Kiefer Sutherland, Winona Ryder and Johnny Depp, Kirk Cameron and Chelsea Noble	$ 2–3
	March 4	Richard Dreyfuss and Wife, Anthony Hopkins, Jim and Tammy Faye Bakker	.25–.50
	March 11	Fergie, Jamie Lee Curtis, Kelly Emberg and Rod Stewart	1–2
	March 19	Sandra Dee, Val Kilmer	2–3
	March 25	Gary Coleman, Dana Plato and Todd Bridges of Different Strokes, Deborah Norville	2–3
	April 1	Reba McEntire, Jodie Foster, Anthony Hopkins	1–2
	April 8	Princess Caroline, Ivana Trump, Princess Anne	.25–.50
	April 15	Madonna and Michael Jackson, Donnie Wahlberg	2–4
	April 22	Ted Kennedy, Michael Landon	.50–1
	April 29	Nancy and Ronald Reagan, Merv Griffin, Ninja Turtles	.25–.50
	May 6	Michael Landon, Larry Hagman, Princess Diana	2–3
	May 13	Norman and Brenda Schwarzkopf, Dinosaurs	.50–1
	May 20	Michelle Phillips and Chynna Phillips, Jill Ireland, Jason Priestley	2–3
	May 27	Jackie Kennedy Onassis, Joan Kennedy, Patrick Swayze	.25–.50
	June 3	Gilda Radner, Gene Wilder, Sela Ward	1–2
	June 10	Marilyn Van Derbur, Princess Diana	.25–.50
	June 17	Princess Diana, Prince William and Prince Harry, Johnny Carson	.25–.50

YEAR	ISSUE	DESCRIPTION	VALUE
1991	June 24	Geena Davis, Susan Sarandon, Randy Travis	$ .50–1
	Spring Extra	Inside Hollywood: Women, Sex, and Power . . . Jodie Foster, Goldie Hawn, Julia Roberts, Sally Field, Carrie Fisher, Cher	2–4
	Spring/ Summer Special	Heroes of the Gulf War	2–3
	July 1	Julia Roberts, Kiefer Sutherland and Jason Patric, Di	1–2
	July 8	Sally Field, Johnny Carson, Martina Navratilova	1–2
	July 15	Michael Landon	1–2
	July 22	Prince Charles and Princess Diana, Lee Remick	.50–1
	July 29	Delta Burke, Cast of Designing Women, Annette Bening and Warren Beatty	.25–.50
	August 5	Matthew and Gunnar Nelson, Ricky Nelson, Ozzie and Harriet Nelson	2–3
	August 12	Jeffrey Dahmer, Elizabeth Taylor and Larry Fortensky	.25–.50
	August 19	Johnny Carson and Wife, Olivia Newton-John	1–2
	August 26	The Sexiest Man Alive: Patrick Swayze, Claudia Schiffer, Luke Perry	1–2
	September 2	Fall Preview Special, Barbra Streisand, Robin Williams and Dustin Hoffman, Steve Martin and Kimberley Williams, Nick Nolte, Suzanne Somers, Patrick Duffy, Anjelica Huston, Julia Roberts	2–3

YEAR	ISSUE	DESCRIPTION	VALUE
1991	September 9	Beverly Hills 90210 Cast, Princess Diana	$ 1–2
	September 16	Ann Jillian, Dottie West	1–2
	September 23	Texas Cheerleader Plot	.25–.50
	September 30	Regis Philbin and Kathie Lee Gifford, Miss America	.50–1
	October 7	Roseanne Barr, Garth Brooks	.25–.50
	October 14	Carolyn Sapp: Miss America, John Stamos	.50–1
	October 21	Elizabeth Taylor, Michael Jackson	1–2
	October 28	Anita Hill, Redd Foxx	.25–.50
	Summer Special	The 50 Most Beautiful People in the World	1–2
	Fall Special	Amazing Americans	1–2
	November 4	Luke Perry, Joan Rivers, Clint Black and Lisa Hartman	.25–.50
	November 11	Virginia and Clarence Thomas, Suzanne Somers	.50–1
	November 18	Fred MacMurray, The Cast of My Three Sons	1–2
	November 25	Chris Evert, Andy Mill and Baby, Magic Johnson	.25–.50
	December 2	Candice Bergen, Kirk Cameron and Chelsea Noble	.50–1
	December 9	Naomi and Wynonna Judd, Michael Landon	.50–1
	December 16	The Best and Worst Dressed . . . Madonna, Oprah Winfrey, JFK Jr., Jason Priestley, Andie MacDowell	1–2
	December 23	Dustin Hoffman, Julia Roberts, The Palm Beach Accuser	1–2
1992	January 2	Double Issue Special, Julia Roberts, Luke Perry, Magic Johnson, Elizabeth Taylor, Garth Brooks, Anita Hill, Princess Diana	1–2

YEAR	ISSUE	DESCRIPTION	VALUE
1992	January 13	Oprah Winfrey, Diet Wars, Elizabeth Taylor, Delta Burke, Ted Turner and Jane Fonda Wedding	$ .50–1
	January 20	Betty Rollin, Patty Duke and Maureen Stapleton, Deidre Hall	.25–.50
	January 27	Plastic Surgery of the Stars . . . Cher, Joan Rivers, Michael Jackson, Angela Lansbury	1–2
	February 3	Sally Jessy Rafael, Sarah Ferguson	.25–.50
	February 10	Cindy Landon and Children . . . Michael's Legacy	1–2
All other issues			1–2

People Extra

1984	November/ December	All about Michael Jackson, a Souvenir Issue	$3–5

People Parody

1986	Winter	A One-Shot Spoof . . . 25 Most Irritating People of 1985 . . . Madonna, Sly Stallone, Bette Davis	$3–6

US VALUES

YEAR	ISSUE	DESCRIPTION	VALUE
1977	June 28	Kate Jackson, Sylvester Stallone's Own Story, Linda Blair, Debbie Harry/Blondie	$5–10
	July 12	Glen Campbell, Mac Davis, Abba: The Rock Group That Pays 85% of Sweden's Taxes, Marty Feldman, Ann-Margret	5–10

March 7, 1978 · · · · · · · March 21, 1978 · · · · · · · January 8, 1980

January 22, 1980 · · · · · · · May 18, 1980 · · · · · · · June 10, 1980

November 11, 1980 · · · · · · · January 20, 1981 · · · · · · · April 14, 1981

YEAR	ISSUE	DESCRIPTION	VALUE
1977	August 9	Paul Michael Glaser: Alias Starsky, Peter Frampton Talks, Suzanne Somers	$5–10
	October 18	Sylvester Stallone: Rock's Back, Lesley Ann Warren's Sexy New Role, Mackenzie Phillips Gets a New Image, Kristy and Jimmy McNichol, Jamie Lee Curtis: A New Curtis Shows Her Petticoat, Keith Richards: Rock's Bad Boy Goes Straight, Bess Myerson	3–6
1978	January 10	Cher and Gregg Allman: The Untold Story of Their Loving Fight to Save a Marriage, Close Encounters's Richard Dreyfuss, Cindy Williams Family Snapshots, The Love Boat's Skipper, Donna Summer: Lust Lady	5–10
	March 7	Suzanne Somers: Sex on TV, Barry Manilow, Richard Burton, Behind Darth Vader's Mask, Madeline Kahn	3–6
	March 21	The Very Private Life of Paul and Linda McCartney, Fantasy Island's Little Man, Loretta Lynn: Her Struggle with Fame and Drugs, Reggie Jackson	3–5
	April 18	Elizabeth Taylor, Parker Stevenson: The Other Hardy Boy, James Taylor, The Gritty Humor of TV's Flo	2–4

YEAR	ISSUE	DESCRIPTION	VALUE
1978	May 30	Olivia Newton-John Photo Special: A Sneak Preview of Grease, The Search for Elvis Look-alikes, The Bee Gees' Kid Brother Fights Bad-Boy Image, John Travolta and Olivia Newton-John Talk, Barbara Walters	$3–6
	June 13	Anthony Quinn and Jackie Bisset: The Onassis Rip-Off, Rock's Carly Simon: Why Fans Terrify Me, Those Characters on One Day at a Time, The Man Behind the Dracula Boom, Patti Smith, Joe Namath	3–5
	July 11	TV's Hulk, Johnny Mathis Lucks in Again, Kris Kristofferson	3–5
	August 22	Goldie Hawn, Why Elvis Presley Lives, TV's McNichol Kids, Hard Rock's Boston Blast, Bonnie Tyler	3–6
	September 19	Who's Hot, Who's Not ... Battlestar Galactica, The Hulk, Wonder Woman, etc., The Who: Rock's Bad Boys Are Back	3–5
	October 3	Mick Jagger: Rock's Menace Is Now Calmer, Kate Jackson Marriage, Rocky Preview	3–6
	November 28	Raquel Welch and the Muppets, John Belushi, Chris Evert, Rod Stewart Makes Music out of Blond Trouble, Bob Urich, Angie Dickinson: Sexy and Alone, Heart: The Wilson Sisters	3–6

YEAR	ISSUE	DESCRIPTION	VALUE
1979	February 6	Kristy McNichol: TV's All-American Teen, The Bee Gees' Barry Gibb and Drugs, James Arness	$2–4
	February 20	Elvis Presley 10-Page Special, Darth Vader, Carpenters	2–4
	March 20	Cher on Her Own, Natalie Wood: Sexy Scenes	3–5
	April 17	Special Oscar Issue, Heaven Can Wait, Jane Fonda, The Deer Hunter	2–3
	May 1	Second Anniversary Issue, Cheryl Tiegs, Farrah Fawcett, the Blues Brothers, John Travolta, Mork and Mindy	2–3
	May 29	Rod Stewart and Alana Hamilton, Dawn of the Dead: The Most Gruesome Movie Ever, Dionne Warwick, Kate Jackson, Suzanne Somers, Jill Clayburgh, Jaclyn Smith	3–6
	June 26	The Village People, Ali MacGraw's Steamy Sex Scenes	2–4
	August 7	Cheryl Ladd, Rock's New Off-Screen Love, Tanya Tucker, Sissy Spacek, Sally Field, Charlie's Angels	4–8
	September 4	John Travolta Comes out of Hiding, Betty Ford, Marlon Brando on Sex and Money	2–4
	November 27	The Bee Gees: Why They're Breaking Up, Ann-Margret Fights Back After a Near Breakdown, Bo Derek: America's Newest Sex Symbol	3–6

YEAR	ISSUE	DESCRIPTION	VALUE
1980	January 8	The Sexy New Star Trek . . . Persis Khambatta, 1980's Preview Special, The Knack Leads Power Pop, Science Fiction Fashions	$5–10
	May 13	Kenny Rogers and Wife, Deborah Raffin, Jane Fonda, Rod Stewart	2–4
	June 10	Sally Field: A Survivor, The Urban Cowboy: John Travolta, Pam Dawber off the Tube, John Derek	2–4
	June 24	Cathy Lee Crosby, Billy Joel: The Bad Boy Is Back for More, The Hulk's New Image, Bo Derek's Kid Sister: Another 10, The Village People, Valerie Perrine and Alan Carr, Jane Fonda	2–4
	July 8	John Schneider: The Dukes of Hazzard, Clint Eastwood: Mr. Macho Reshapes His Image, Rock's Meat Loaf and Debbie Harry Seek Stardom Together, Jan Smithers of WKRP, Cher	2–4
	September 16	Toni Tennille: Blonde and Dynamite, The Rolling Stones Recharged by Emotional Rescue, Hart to Hart's Stefanie Powers, Gary Sandy: WKRP, Maud Adams, Jerry Reed, The Kinks Live On, Dave Davies	2–4
	September 30	The Chips Feud, Larry Hagman, The Who's Roger Daltry: Inside His Marriage	2–4

YEAR	ISSUE	DESCRIPTION	VALUE
1980	October 28	Barbra Streisand and Barry Gibb, Stevie Nicks: Fleetwood Mac's Rock Sorceress Talks about Men and Music, Paul Michael Glaser, Gregory Harrison, Melissa Gilbert, David Soul	$5–10
	November 11	The New Cher, Horror Flicks: Turning Blood into Bucks, Lynda Carter: Inside Her Million-Dollar Marriage, Loni Anderson As Jayne Mansfield	3–6
	December 23	Special Year-End Issue, Bo Derek, Kenny Rogers, Larry Hagman, The Empire Strikes Back, Cathy Lee Crosby	2–4
1981	January 6	Super Witches of the Soaps, Gutsy Goldie Hawn Goes It Alone, The Bellamy Brothers, Nina Hagen, Dire Straits, Rock's Pat Benatar: She's a Sexy Tinkerbell, Barbara Eden, Dolly Parton, Burt Reynolds	2–4
	January 20	Brooke Shields: Pants Cause Ripples, Kris Kristofferson's Gate Crash, Goldie Hawn Glitters, Cher's Black Rose Withers, Bruce Springsteen Bosses, Jane Fonda, Dolly Parton, Elizabeth Taylor's Daughter	2–4
	February 3	The 50 Hottest Couples, Farrah Fawcett, Tanya Tucker, Marlo Thomas, Kenny Rogers, Dallas, Flash Gordon's Spacy Women, Leo Sayer, Teddy Pendergrass Cleans Up His Act	2–4

April 28, 1981

June 9, 1981

July 7, 1981

August 18, 1981

October 19, 1981

April 27, 1982

August 3, 1982

March 28, 1983

June 20, 1983

YEAR	ISSUE	DESCRIPTION	VALUE
1981	March 17	Dynasty's Darling Linda Evans, Bo Derek, TV's Sexiest Hunks, Suzanne Somers, John Lennon Exclusive, My Secret Life with the Rolling Stones: A Special Feature	$2–4
	March 31	Sally Field Hits the Back Roads, Audrey Landers Vamps, The Police: Rock's Most Arresting Group, Todd Rundgren, Kris Kristofferson	2–4
	May 12	Greatest American Hero, Paul McCartney: Getting the Beatles Together, 007, This Is Elvis Presley: Old Home Movies and a New Film Reveal the Presley Nobody Knew	2–4
	June 9	Jaclyn Smith: The Devilish Angel, Dolly Parton, Paul Newman, Slim Whitman, Fantasy Island	3–6
	June 23	Kristy McNichol at 18, Burt Reynolds: What Women Have Taught Me, Foreigner: At Last on Radio, Shocking Chaka Khan, Sheena Easton, Dennis Quaid, Angie Dickinson	2–4
	July 7	Bodies Beautiful Issue . . . Victoria Principal: Red, Hot, and 31, Lois Lane Makes It with Superman, Linda Gray	2–4
	July 21	Eddie Van Halen, Olivia Newton-John, Brooke Shields, Tanya Tucker, Fleetwood Mac	3–5
	August 18	Bo Derek and Tarzan, Brooke Shields Is Tough: Making Endless Love, James Taylor, Britt Ekland	2–4

YEAR	ISSUE	DESCRIPTION	VALUE
1981	September 29	Priscilla Presley Fights for her Daughter's Future, JFK Jr., Mick Jagger: Jagger of the Jungle, Rocky Horror's Shocking Sequel, Meat Loaf Heats Up after His Breakdown, Bo's Swinging Tarzan, Keith Moon	$2–4
	November 10	Mick Jagger: Jagger Says Marriage Turns Him to Stone, John Belushi, TV's Gonzo, Jamie Lee Curtis: Hex, Sex, Creepy, and Weepy	3–6
	December 8	John Lennon and Yoko Ono: Their Struggle against Heroin and Each Other, Judy and Audrey Landers: Growing Up Sexy, Ronnie Milsap, Loni Anderson, Carly Simon, Dr. Hook, The Doors: On Fire, John Entwistle, Chris Atkins, Nastassja Kinski	3–6
1982	February 2	Dolly Parton and Burt Reynolds, Mick Jagger, Farrah Fawcett, Fred Astaire, Connie Francis, Jane Fonda	2–4
	February 16	Tony Geary, Maggie Eastwood: Life without Clint, Jerry Lee Lewis, Diane Keaton, Judy Collins	2–3
	March 2	Tom Selleck, Who's Hot, Who's Not, Olivia Newton-John, An Intimate Look at Elizabeth Taylor	2–4
	April 13	Couples of the Soaps, Joanie and Chachi, Paul McCartney by His Wife Linda, Debbie Harry as a Playboy Bunny	4–8

YEAR	ISSUE	DESCRIPTION	VALUE
1982	April 27	Best and Worst Dressed People Issue . . . Tom Selleck, Suzanne Somers, Liz Taylor, Linda Evans, Burt Reynolds	$2–4
	May 11	Charlene Tilton, Lindsay Wagner, Jaclyn Smith, Sissy Spacek, Julie Andrews, John Belushi's Last Party	2–5
	May 25	Christie Brinkley and Tom Selleck, Who Killed Sal Mineo?, Nastassja Kinski: Cat People's Untamed Sex Kitten, Nick Lowe, Willie Aames	2–4
	June 22	Linda Evans, Star Trek: The Death of Spock, Princess Grace, Johnny Mathis on Friends and Lovers, Charlene Tilton, Road Warrior, Annie, Pia Zadora	2–4
	July 6	Morgan Fairchild, Linda Evans, Sylvester Stallone: Rocky III, Sheena Easton: Sheena Shines, The Clash, Connie Stevens, Jamie Farr	2–4
	November 23	Tom Selleck, Faye Dunaway: Men, Movies, and Me, My Wild Life with David Bowie by His Ex-Wife, Bette Midler, Jodie Foster	2–4
1983	April 25	TV's Super Wives . . . Linda Evans and Linda Gray, Hot Suits Special . . . Shannon Tweed, Bruce Penhall, Tom Selleck	2–4
	May 23	Charlene Tilton, Diana Ross Rejoins the Supremes, Lindsay Wagner, Princess Di, John Schneider	1–2

YEAR	ISSUE	DESCRIPTION	VALUE
1983	June 20	Return of the Jedi, Farrah Fawcett's Two Lovers	$3–6
	October 10	Christina Delorean, JFK, Carol Burnett: Serious Talk, Jodie Foster Since Hinkley, Led Zeppelin's Robert Plant Flies Solo	2–4
	October 24	Kate Jackson: Kate's Back, Tom Selleck: The Next James Bond?, MTV's Naughty Nina, John Travolta, Natalie Wood	2–4
1984	January 30	The Odd Couples . . . Caroline Kennedy, Joan Collins, Billy Joel and Christie Brinkley, Goldie Hawn, Adam Ant and Jamie Lee Curtis, Joanna Carson, Shelley Long	2–4
	February 13	Lisa Marie Presley at 16, Donna Mills, The Beatles 20th Anniversary Tribute, Bette Davis: Beating Cancer	2–4
	February 27	The Stars' Biggest Lie . . . Ageless Victoria Principal, Shari Belafonte, Landers Sisters, Veronica Hamel, Nancy Reagan, Joan Collins, David Hasselhoff	2–3
1985	March 25	Farrah Fawcett and Son . . . Love Babies, Charles and Diana, Melissa Gilbert, Lionel Richie, Clint Eastwood, Michelle Pfeiffer, David Lee Roth	2–4
	May 6	Bill Cosby, JFK and the Mafia, Phil Collins's Noisy Bedroom, Nashville Wives, The New Edition	1–2
	July 1	Cher	2–4

April 22, 1985

July 15, 1985

July 29, 1985

August 12, 1985

September 9, 1985

March 10, 1986

November 17, 1986

February 23, 1987

October 31, 1988

YEAR	ISSUE	DESCRIPTION	VALUE
1985	July 15	Jamie Lee Curtis	$2–4
	July 29	Sylvester Stallone in Love, The Future of Michael J. Fox, Cybill Shepherd, Bruce Jenner at Home, Christie Hefner, Return to Oz, Prince's Birthday	2–4
	August 12	Tina Turner	2–3
	August 26	Tony Danza, Madonna and Sean: Cool for Marriage, Carly Simon's Home Pleasures, Pee-Wee Herman, Teri Copley	2–3
	September 9	Joan Collins: The US Interview, Robert Blake's Toughest Mission, The Double Life of Jennifer Beals, Bob Hope, Kevin Costner: Silverado Sex Symbol, Mickey Mouse	2–4
	September 23	1985 Fall Preview Special . . . Miami Vice, Dustin Hoffman, Dynasty, Moonlighting, Robert Wagner, Cagney & Lacey	2–3
	October 7	Hollywood Faces AIDS, Elvis's Other Women, Michael Douglas, Madonna's Honeymoon, Tom Selleck	2–3
	October 21	Bill Cosby After Hours, Billy Crystal's Double Play, Jane Seymour's Country Castle, Rachel Ward, Jenilee Harrison	2–3
	November 4	The Irresistible Robert Wagner, Why Rona Barrett Hates Barbara Walters, John and Yoko's TV Bio, Being Brooke Shields, The Last Days of Jon-Erik Hexum, Whitney Houston	2–3

YEAR	ISSUE	DESCRIPTION	VALUE
1985	November 18	Shirley MacLaine: Her Many Lives, Arnold Schwarzenegger, Patrick Swayze, Michele Lee, Morgan Fairchild	$1–2
	December 2	John James, Family Ties's Other Fox, Bruce Willis: Moonlighting's Mystery Man, Simon LeBon on Board	1–2
	December 16	Charles and Diana: The Di-namic Duo, Betty White, Mitch Gaylord, Sinatra at His Frankest	1–2
	December 30	Michael Douglas and Danny DeVito, Morgan Fairchild's Mating Call, Barbi Benton, Heather Locklear	1–2
1986	January 13	Cybill Shepherd Rating Men, The Trouble with Saturday Night Live, Whoopi Goldberg, Meet the Equalizer	2–4
	January 27	Michael J. Fox	1–2
	February 10	Barbra Streisand	1–2
	February 24	Robert Redford, Dean Paul Martin, Mary Tyler Moore	1–2
	March 10	Goldie Hawn: Solid Goldie . . . A Wildcat Lands on Her Feet, Stacy Keach, Chuck Norris, Julian Lennon	2–4
	March 26	Oscar Fever, Cher, Donna Reed, Molly Ringwald, Madonna	2–4
	April 4	Clint Eastwood	2–3
	April 21	Don Johnson	1–2
	May 5	Dynasty	1–2
	May 19	Tony Danza, Hands across America	1–2
	June 6	Alan Alda	1–2
	June 16	Richard Pryor	1–2

YEAR	ISSUE	DESCRIPTION	VALUE
1986	June 30	Tom Cruise Interview, David Bowie: Mr. Cool Warms Up, Down Home with Dolly Parton, Cloris Leachman, Michelle Phillips: The Last Red-Hot Mama	$2–4
	July 14	Arnold Schwarzenegger	1–2
	July 28	Bette Midler	1–2
	August 8	Whitney Houston	2–4
	August 25	Bruce Willis	1–2
	September 8	Tina Turner	2–3
	September 22	Cybill Shepherd	2–3
	October 6	Patrick Duffy	1–2
	October 20	The 10 Sexiest Men and Women	2–4
	November 3	Elizabeth Taylor	2–4
	November 17	Loni Anderson	2–4
	December 1	Tom Cruise, Paul Newman	1–2
	December 15	Eddie Murphy	1–2
	December 29	Entertainment Yearbook Double Issue Special	2–4
1987	January 26	Clint Eastwood	2–3
	February 9	Don Johnson and Philip Michael Thomas	2–3
	February 23	Bruce Willis and Cybill Shepherd, 30 Famous Couples Talk, Sophia Loren, Michael Jackson	2–3
	March 9	Valerie Bertinelli	2–4
	March 23	Why We Love Family Ties, Burt Reynolds, Vanna White, Garry Shandling, Kathleen Turner, Christie Brinkley	2–4
	April 6	The Oscars: Who Will Win	1–2
	April 20	The 10 Sexiest and the 10 Richest	1–2
	May 4	Harry Hamlin	1–2

YEAR	ISSUE	DESCRIPTION	VALUE
1987	May 18	Shelley Long . . . Celebrity Moms and Kids	$2–3
	June 1	Diana Ross	2–4
	June 15	Summer Sneak Preview Special	1–2
	July 13	10th Anniversary Double Issue Special	1–2
	August 10	The Private Life of Mark Harmon, Jessica Hahn, Madonna	2–4
	August 24	Elvis Presley: The Last Days	2–4
	September 7	Madonna Talks	2–4
	September 21	Cybill Shepherd and Bruce Willis, Fall Preview	2–3
	October 5	Worrying about Whitney Houston	2–4
	October 19	Who's the Sexiest in 1987?	2–3
	November 2	Bruce Willis	1–2
	November 16	Princess Diana	1–2
	November 30	Farrah Fawcett	2–4
	December 14	Tom Selleck	2–4
	December 28	Year-End Double Issue Special	2–3
1988	January 25	Charlie Sheen, The 10 Most Beautiful Women	2–3
	February 8	Who's In and Who's Out Special	1–2
	February 22	Patrick Swayze and Wife, Lisa Niemi	1–2
	March 7	Tom Selleck, Readers' Poll Special	2–3
	March 21	Brigitte Nielsen	2–4
	April 4	Rob Lowe	1–2
	April 18	Michael J. Fox	1–2
	May 2	The 10 Sexiest Bachelors	1–2
	May 16	Demi Moore, Mother's Day Special	2–4
	May 30	Marlee Matlin, The Hottest Couples	2–3

YEAR	ISSUE	DESCRIPTION	VALUE
1988	June 13	Sylvester Stallone	$1–2
	June 27	Jane Seymour Gets Personal ... The Frantic, Romantic World of Jane, Chevy Chase Interview, Gloria Estefan	3–6
	July 11	The Boys of Summer Double Issue Special	1–2
	August 8	Tom Cruise	1–2
	August 22	Julianne Phillips	1–2
	September 5	Jeff Bridges	1–2
	September 19	The 10 Most Stylish Celebs, Fashion Issue Special	2–3
	October 3	Don Johnson on Love, Sexy John Stamos	1–2
	October 17	The 10 Sexiest	2–3
	October 31	Valerie Bertinelli	2–4
	November 14	Kirstie Alley, Whoopi Goldberg	2–4
	November 28	Jason and Justine Bateman, Betty White	2–3
	December 12	Mel Gibson	1–2
	December 26	Year-End Double Issue Special	2–3
1989	January 23	Sexy Talk from Kim Basinger: interview, photos and cover, Melanie Griffith: Working Mom, Cruising with the Bangles, Bianca Jagger, Bette Midler, Anita Baker, Madonna	2–4
	February 6	Who's In and Who's Out	1–2
	February 20	Hollywood's Red-Hot Couples	2–4
	March 6	Suddenly Single ... Madonna, Julianne Phillips, Robin Givens, Cybill Shepherd, Michelle Pfeiffer, Tom Selleck on Bringing Up Baby	2–4
	March 20	Oprah Winfrey	1–2
	April 3	The 10 Most Beautiful Women	2–3
	April 17	Ken Wahl	1–2

YEAR	ISSUE	DESCRIPTION	VALUE
1989	May 1	Roseanne Barr	$.50–1
	May 29	Patrick Swayze	1–2
	June 12	Madonna	3–5
	June 26	Johnny Depp	2–3
	July 10	Summer Double Issue Special	2–3
	August 7	Rob Lowe Special	2–3
	August 21	Michael J. Fox	2–3
	September 4	Kevin Costner	1–2
	September 18	Arsenio Hall	1–2
	October 2	Bruce Willis	1–2
	October 16	Those Hollywood Feuds	1–2
	October 30	Candice Bergen, Al Pacino's Comeback, Bon Jovi	2–4
	November 13	The 10 Sexiest	2–3
	November 27	Mick Jagger	2–4
	December 11	Paula Abdul	2–4
1990	January 8	1989 Yearbook Issue . . . Kim Basinger, Madonna, Paula Abdul, The Stones, The Who, Michelle Pfeiffer, Meg Ryan, Andie MacDowell, Cher, John Travolta, Jack Nicholson	2–4
	January 22	Tom Cruise	1–2
	February 5	Who's In and Who's Out	1–2
	February 19	Paul and Linda McCartney	2–4
	March 5	Janet Jackson	2–4
	March 19	Elvis Presley . . . TV's Portrait, Fashion Issue	2–4
	April 2	Michelle Pfeiffer, New Goddesses	2–4
	April 16	The 10 Sexiest Bachelors	1–2
	April 30	Richard Gere	1–2
	May 14	The 10 Most Beautiful Women	2–4
	May 28	Inside Twin Peaks	2–4
	June 11	Richard Grieco, Judy Belushi	1–2
	June 25	Annual Readers' Poll Special	1–2
	July 9	Summer Double Issue Special	2–3

YEAR	ISSUE	DESCRIPTION	VALUE
1990	August 6	Tom Cruise, Andrew Dice Clay	$1–2
	August 20	Harrison Ford	2–4
	September 3	Mel Gibson	1–2
	September 17	Demi Moore	2–4
	October 1	Ken Olin	1–2
	October 15	Arsenio Hall, Madonna: The Struggle to Stay on Top, Backstage with the Hottest Girl Groups . . . Seduction, En Vogue, The Allure of James Dean, Kim Basinger, Paula Abdul	2–4
	October 29	The 10 Sexiest Stars	2–4
	November 12	Patrick Swayze	1–2
	November 26	The US Heavy 100	2–4
	December 10	Dennis Quaid	1–2
1991	January 7	US Entertainment Yearbook Double Issue Special	2–4
	January 24	Who's In and Who's Out for 1991 . . . Johnny Depp, Julia Roberts, Patrick Swayze, Kevin Costner, Whitney Houston, George Michael Exclusive Interview	1–2
	February 7	The New Nice Guys	2–3
	February 21	Hollywood's Hottest Couples	2–3
	March 7	Kevin Costner	1–2
	March 21	The 10 Sexiest Bachelors	1–2
	April 4	Michael J. Fox	1–2
	April 18	The Portraits Special Double Issue	2–4
	May 16	Alec Baldwin, Sting	1–2
	May 30	Readers' Poll	1–2
	June 13	Madonna	2–4
	June 27	Paula Abdul	2–4
	July 11	The Hot Men of Summer Double Issue Special	2–3

YEAR	ISSUE	DESCRIPTION	VALUE
1991	August	Julia Roberts	$2–3
	September	Fall Entertainment Preview	2–3
	October	Who's the Sexiest, Cher Interview	2–3
	November	Don Johnson and Melanie Griffith	2–3
All other issues			1–3

TV Guide

For most people, *TV Guide* spends a week atop their TV set, or by the remote, and then is discarded. But to collectors this weekly chronicle of TV history is revered like bars of gold. Why do people collect *TV Guide*? The reasons are varied. For many people, vintage *TV Guide*s evoke happy feelings of the simpler days of youth. They are willing to pay a price to recapture these fond memories. They also hunger for information on television shows not found in reference books and are willing to pay a price for this information. People also want memorabilia from their favorite shows. A *TV Guide* may contain a cover article on the subject, an inside article, a program blurb, a *TV Guide* Close-Up, or a full- or half-page program ad. Video collectors may want the *TV Guide* for a week of shows they have on tape. There are some collectors who are trying to complete an entire run of the magazine. Other collectors may want only a full set of Fall Previews; a copy from their birthdate each year; only cowboys on the cover; animals; Emmy Award issues; Olympic issues; and so on. The subjects of interest are virtually limitless. The current popular collecting trend is issues of *TV Guide* featuring pop culture show covers. Such shows as "Superman," "Batman," "Bonanza," "Star Trek," "Lost in Space," "I Love Lucy," "The Green Hornet," "I Dream of Jeannie," "The Dick Van Dyke Show," "The Munsters," and "The Fugitive" are but a few. Due to the popularity of cable, particularly Nickelodeon's Nick at Nite, some subjects may be popular one year but actually drop in price the next. For instance, "Route 66" issues were very popular when the show was on Nick at Nite in the mid-1980s, but are not so now. When Ronald Reagan was president, the November 22, 1958, issue with him and Nancy on the cover was extremely in demand. Today there is little interest in this issue.

The history of *TV Guide* magazine actually goes back to before World

War II when TV stations would send out weekly program schedule cards to TV set owners. As TV programming grew there became a need for publications that specialized in TV programming listings. The digest size became the norm because of its convenient size. The first of these digest-size TV log magazines was *TV Forecast,* based in Chicago, which began on May 16, 1948. Within a few weeks *Television Guide,* based in New York City, and *Teleguide,* based in the Washington-Baltimore area, began on June 14, 1948. During the next five years, similar publications sprang up in other cities with two or more stations. Among these included the following:

TV Forecast (later *TV Guide*) of New England

Local Televisor (later *TV Digest*) of Philadelphia

TV Image of Los Angeles

TV Digest of Pittsburgh

TV Digest of Atlanta

TV News of Indianapolis

Tele-Views (later *TV Forecast*) of Davenport–Rock Island–Moline

TV Today of Michigan-Ohio-Ontario

TV Dial of Cincinnati-Dayton-Columbus

TV Life of Portland, Oregon

TV Press of Louisville, Kentucky

TV Preview of Dallas, Texas

TV Showtime of Omaha, Nebraska

TV Times (later *TV Forecast*) of Minneapolis–St. Paul

TV Weekly of Denver, Colorado

TV Review of St. Louis, Missouri

For the advanced collector, these pre-Lucy's-baby issues, called "pre-nationals," are the major focus of interest. In many ways this pre-1953 era is still unexplored, as new titles are discovered all the time. One title recently discovered, although not of digest size, is *Phillipp's Television Weekly,* of New York City. This issue is dated January 26, 1948 (Vol. 1, No. 1), which predates the original *TV Forecast* by almost four months. It is still not known how long this publication lasted. The first issue of

New York's *Television Guide* and the first issue of Chicago's *TV Forecast* were sent out free to all TV set owners. *TV Forecast*'s first issue's circulation was 16,000 copies; five years later it had climbed to 192,549. New York City's *Television Guide*'s average circulation in 1948 was just 8,557. In 1949 it was 42,972; in 1950, 157,461; in 1951, 292,341; and in 1952, 359,297. Compare this to 1992's average circulation of just a little over 18,000,000.

The first "national" *TV Guide* was dated April 3, 1953, and had Lucy's baby on the cover. Lucille Ball had combined the birth of her son and the plot of her popular TV show, and this seemed to be the obvious point to start the national publication. *TV Guide*'s average circulation in 1953 was 1,481,564. Circulation of *TV Guides* peaked in 1974–1975 at around 19,000,000, and *TV Guides* from these years are very common. Circulation started to dip after that, to a low of about 15,000,000, but by 1992 it had climbed to around 18,000,000. The person appearing on the most national *TV Guide* covers is Lucille Ball, with twenty-nine covers to her credit.

In 1990 *TV Guide* experimented with different cover layouts on the same issue in different cities. For example, the November 3, 1990, issue out of Chicago had only the "Cheers" cast on the cover, while the western Illinois edition had the cast of "Cheers" and three other subjects on the cover. In 1991 *TV Guide* tested a larger format (7½" by 10") from March 30 to November 30 in only three cities; Nashville; Rochester, New York; and Pittsburgh. Sixteen of these covers were different from the digest-size national edition.

Related *TV Guide*–type collectibles would include foreign *TV Guide*–type magazines. Australia's *TV Week* and *TV Times* have published many gorgeous covers from the 1960s of "Star Trek," "The Saint," "The Man from U.N.C.L.E.," "Bonanza," "Batman," and "The Avengers," not found in the United States. Other collectibles would include the *TV Guide* game published by Trivia, Inc. in 1984; the promotional 45 rpm record "*TV Guide* Presents Elvis Presley" from 1956; *TV Guide* cookbooks, crossword puzzle books, aprons, swizzle sticks, and other items. A recent collectible is a 1991 *TV Guide* 200th Issue Commemorative Edition with Lucille Ball on the cover.

Value of vintage *TV Guides* is based on a number of variables. Purists would want the cardboard centerfold intact, as it is counted in the page-numbering sequence. Crossword puzzles that are filled in, particularly in pen, lower values, as do address labels on the covers for some collectors. In the 1950s this was less of a problem because most cities used address labels on the back cover. New York City editions tend to bring higher prices due to their more detailed program listings. It is difficult to find mint copies of early *TV Guides* as most were usually used for one week and then discarded. Common cover flaws would include torn-off address label marks, fingerprinting, coffee mug marks, rodent chewing, staple tears, heavy creases, and water damage. The issues from the 1950s and early 1960s seem to hold up best due to heavier cover stock. Some issues from the mid and later 1960s are extremely hard to find in near-mint condition due to the flimsy paper and type of printing used on some covers. An example of this is the Green Hornet cover; dated October 29, 1966, it is virtually impossible to find in near-mint condition due to its inferior cover paper. In contrast, the March 26, 1966, issue, with Batman on the cover, was printed on a heavier cover stock and with a different printing process, and copies of this issue in the higher grades are not difficult to find. Professionally bound volumes were given to many TV stations in the 1950s and 1960s. Although these volumes contain complete *TV Guides*, often in mint condition, demand for them is surprisingly limited.

Where can vintage *TV Guides* be found? Collectors in Boise, Idaho, or even locales like Miami or Phoenix should know that they are not going to find a "Lucy's Baby" issue at a neighborhood garage sale. The original ten cities to carry national *TV Guide,* on April 3, 1953, were Boston, Chicago, Cincinnati-Dayton-Columbus, Davenport–Rock Island–Moline, Los Angeles, Minneapolis–St. Paul, New York City, Philadelphia, Washington–Baltimore, and Wilkes Barre–Scranton–Binghamton. Sources for locating old *TV Guides* include flea markets, garage sales, estate auctions, trade papers, and retail dealers. One of the most respected mail-order dealers is TV Guide Specialists, Box 20, Macomb, Illinois 61455. This company boasts a complete inventory of every issue at all times and offers a sixty-six-page illustrated catalog for $3.

Note: In this guide we have listed the values for *TV Guide* (pre-nationals and nationals). There are many, many spin-off titles, encompassing thousands of issues, that have not been listed. For values on these issues, our guide offers you our *TV Guide* Collector's Hotline. For any question you may have regarding the most current *TV Guide* values or values on the spin-offs call 1-309-833-1809 (during regular EST business hours please).

TV GUIDE VALUES
(PRE-NATIONAL)

YEAR	ISSUE	NUMBER	DESCRIPTION	VALUE
1948	VOLUME I			
	June 14–20	#1	Gloria Swanson and Lois Wilson cover	$150–300
	June 21–27	#2		50–100
	June 28	#3	Video Venus	30–60
	July 5–11	#4	Angel (wrestler) and poet cover, Howdy Doody	30–60
	July 12–18	#5	Pixie Playtime	30–60
	July 19–25	#6		30–60
	July 26	#7		30–60
	August 2–8	#8		30–60
	August 9–15	#9		30–60
	August 16–22	#10		25–50
	August 23–29	#11	Harness Racing, Television Facts	25–50
	August 30	#12		25–50
	September 6–12	#13	Dance cover	25–50
	September 13–19	#14	Ed Sullivan's Toast of the Town	25–50
	September 20–26	#15	Football	25–50
	September 27	#16	Gene Autry cover and feature	25–50
	October 2–8	#17	1948 World Series issue	30–60
	October 9–15	#18	Milton Berle cover and feature	25–50
	October 16–22	#19	Eddie Condon Jam Session	25–50
	October 23–29	#20	Fashions on Parade	25–50
	October 30	#21	Nature of Things	25–50

#52, 1951

#109, 1955

#112, 1955

#522, 1963

#533, 1963

#658, 1965

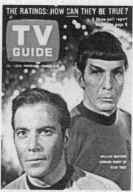

#678, 1966

#709, 1966

#727, 1967

YEAR	ISSUE	NUMBER	DESCRIPTION	VALUE
1948	November 6–12	#22	Bob Howard cover, contains feature story on Bob Smith and Howdy Doody	$50–100
	November 13–19	#23	Hockey at the Garden	25–50
	November 20–26	#24	Bert Lytell/ Television Playhouse cover	25–50
	November 27	#25	Goldberg by Goldberg	25–50
	December 4–10	#26	Lanny Ross	25–50
	December 11–17	#27	Danny Webb	25–50
	December 18–24	#28	Phil Silvers cover	25–50
	December 25	#29	Christmas issue	25–50
1949	VOLUME II			
	January 1–7	#1	Happy New Year issue	25–50
	January 8–14	#2	Cliff-hangers issue	25–50
	January 15–21	#3	Basketball at the Garden	25–50
	January 22–28	#4	Arthur Godfrey cover, Sid Caesar, Ed Sullivan	25–50
	January 29	#5	Kyle MacDonnell cover	20–40
	February 5–11	#6	Harry Conover cover	20–40
	February 12–18	#7	Jerry Mahoney cover	20–40
	February 19–25	#8	Morey Amsterdam cover, Ted Mack, Imogene Coca	20–40
	February 26	#9	Howdy Doody's Flub-a-Dub Feature	20–40

YEAR	ISSUE	NUMBER	DESCRIPTION	VALUE
1949	March 5–11	#10	Howdy Doody's Flub-a-Dub Feature	$ 20–40
	March 12–18	#11	Joe DiMaggio and Mel Allen cover, Howdy Doody's Flub-a-Dub feature	50–100
	March 19–25	#12	Mahattan Spotlight	20–40
	March 26	#13	Boxing: Chicago versus New York	20–40
	April 2–8	#14	Mother's Incorporated	20–40
	April 9–15	#15	Douglas Edwards and the News	20–40
	April 16–22	#16	Foodini's Easter Bunny cover	20–40
	April 23–29	#17	Roller Derby cover, Howdy Doody feature	20–40
	April 30	#18	Farmer's Daughter cover	20–40
	May 7–13	#19	TV Mother's Day cover, Boris Karloff: Ford Theater	20–40
	May 14–20	#20	TV Ballet	20–40
	May 21–27	#21	Gigi Durston cover	20–40
	May 28	#22	General Dwight Eisenhower cover, Imogene Coca	20–40
	June 4–10	#23	Morton Downey cover	20–40
	June 11–17	#24	Charlie Chaplin cover	20–40

YEAR	ISSUE	NUMBER	DESCRIPTION	VALUE
1949	June 18–24	#25	First Anniversary issue, The Year in TV	$ 25–50
	June 25	#26	Olsen and Johnson cover	20–40
	July 2–8	#27	Bert Parks cover	20–40
	July 9–15	#28	Mama and Family cover	20–40
	July 16–22	#29	Mary Kay and Johnny cover	20–40
	July 23–29	#30	Peter W. Pixie cover, Ted Mack, Cliff Edwards	25–50
	July 30	#31	The Flying Man and the Helmet	20–40
	August 6–12	#32	Captain Video cover, Candid Camera	200–500+
	August 13–19	#33	Quiz Kids cover	20–40
	August 20–26	#34	Joan Diener cover, TV This Fall	25–50
	August 27	#35	Miss Reingold cover, Ed Sullivan, Art Carney	20–40
	September 3–9	#36	Cover of Kukla, Fran, and Ollie	25–50
	September 10–16	#37	Rita Colton cover	20–40
	September 17–23	#38	TV Football cover	20–40
	September 24–30	#39	Ted Mack cover, women wrestlers	20–40
	October 1–7	#40	Joan Barton cover	20–40
	October 8–14	#41	Frankie Lane cover, Uncle David	15–30
	October 15–21	#42	Perry Como cover	15–30
	October 22–28	#43	Wendy Barrie cover	12–25

YEAR	ISSUE	NUMBER	DESCRIPTION	VALUE
1949	October 29	#44	Bowling cover, Henry Aldrich feature	$ 12–25
	November 5–11	#45	Gregg Sherwood cover, Victor Borge feature	12–25
	November 12–18	#46	Auction-Aire Show cast cover, Ralph Bellamy	12–25
	November 19–25	#47	Jack Carter cover, Howdy Doody feature	20–40
	November 26	#48	Ed Wynn cover, Chuck Wagon feature	15–30
	December 3–9	#49	The Truex cover	12–25
	December 10–16	#50	Jackie Gleason cover from The Life of Riley	100–300
	December 17–23	#51	Jimmy Powers cover	12–25
	December 24–30	#52	Milton Berle cover	20–40
	December 31	#53	Arthur Godfrey cover, Zero Mostel feature	20–40
1950	VOLUME III			
	January 7–13	#1	Kay Kyser cover	12–25
	January 14–20	#2	Bill Lawrence cover, Oliver Dragon feature	12–25
	January 21–27	#3	Dave Garroway cover	12–25
	January 28	#4	Bert Parks cover, Mr. Magic feature	12–25
	February 4–10	#5	Katharine Hepburn cover, The Lone Ranger feature	50–100

YEAR	ISSUE	NUMBER	DESCRIPTION	VALUE
1950	February 11–17	#6	Ed Sullivan cover, Uncle Fred feature	$12–25
	February 18–24	#7	Junior Frolics' Farmer Gray cover	12–25
	February 25	#8	Wrestling on TV cover, The Lone Ranger feature, Dorothy Kilgallen	25–50
	March 4–10	#9	Golden Gloves cover, Magic Cottage feature	12–25
	March 11–17	#10	Morey Amsterdam cover, Howdy Doody feature	15–30
	March 18–24	#11	Pinhead cover, Captain Video feature	25–50
	March 25–31	#12	Eleanor Roosevelt cover, Robert Montgomery feature	12–25
	April 1–7	#13	Sid Caesar cover, Baseball, Mr. I. Magination	12–25
	April 8–14	#14	Happy Easter issue, Molly Goldberg feature	12–25
	April 15–21	#15	Jackie Robinson cover, Bob Hope, Judy Splinters	40–80+
	April 22–28	#16	Linda Danson cover, Kukla feature, Alan Young	12–25
	April 29	#17	Women of Wrestling cover, Imogene Coca, Dizzy Dean	12–25

YEAR	ISSUE	NUMBER	DESCRIPTION	VALUE
1950	May 6–12	#18	Hopalong Cassidy cover, Howdy Doody, Henry Aldrich	$150–300+
	May 13–19	#19	Milton Berle and his mother cover, Foodini	12–25
	May 20–26	#20	Viera Monkeys cover, Ed Sullivan, Snarky Parker	12–25
	May 27	#21	Roller Derby issue, Wilmethe Pigeon feature	12–25
	June 3–9	#22	Fay Emerson cover, Dennis James feature	12–25
	June 10–16	#23	Sam Renick and the Kentucky Derby cover, Cavalcade of Stars feature, Junior Talent Time	12–25
	June 17–23	#24	Kay Kyser cover, Second Anniversary issue	12–25
	June 24–30	#25	Laraine Day cover, Morey Amsterdam, Children's Hour, Baseball	12–25
	July 1–7	#26	Marion Morgan cover, Happy Felton, Wendy Barrie	12–25

YEAR	ISSUE	NUMBER	DESCRIPTION	VALUE
1950	July 8–14	#27	Ted Williams and Joe DiMaggio cover, Ripley's Believe It or Not, Ted Mack, Alan Young	$ 75–150+
	July 15–21	#28	Magnificant Menasha cover, Mystery Rider, Joan Diener	12–25
	July 22–28	#29	Lynn Bari cover, Gene Autry, Jackie Gleason	12–25
	July 29	#30	Eva Marie Saint cover, Mr. Magic feature	12–25
	August 5–11	#31	Fred Allen and Jack Haley cover, TV Yesterday and Today, Big Top	15–30
	August 12–18	#32	Grace Kelly cover, Captain Video feature, Mama	50–100
	August 19–25	#33	Miss Reingold cover, Captain Video feature	50–100
	August 26	#34	Tennis cover, Rosie the Duck, Bob Emery feature	12–25
	September 2–8	#35	Howdy Doody cover, Ed Sullivan, Time for Beany	100–200+
	September 9–15	#36	Eddie Cantor cover, Fireside Theatre	12–25

YEAR	ISSUE	NUMBER	DESCRIPTION	VALUE
1950	September 16–22	#37	Groucho Marx, Frank Sinatra and Gang cover, TV's Golden Age, Sheriff Bob Dixon feature	$35–75
	September 23–29	#38	Baseball issue, Rumpus Room, Edie Adams feature, Zoo Parade	12–25
	September 30	#39	Football issue, Danny Kaye, Bing Crosby	12–25
	October 7–13	#40	Alan Young cover, TV Rodeo, Fred Allen, Gabby Hayes feature	12–25
	October 14–20	#41	Miss TV 1950 cover, Max Liebman, Arthur Godfrey	12–25
	October 21–27	#42	Robert Montgomery cover, Space Cadet feature, Leslie Nielsen	15–30
	October 28	#43	Jack Benny cover, Jerry Lester, Ed Herlihy	12–25
	November 4–10	#44	Imogene Coca cover, Sid Caesar, Panhandle Pete	12–25
	November 11–17	#45	Dean Martin and Jerry Lewis cover, Ted Steele, Can You Top This? feature	40–80

YEAR	ISSUE	NUMBER	DESCRIPTION	VALUE
1950	November 18–24	#46	The McCrays cover, Faye Emerson, Sheriff Bob Dixon feature	$ 12–25
	November 25	#47	Howdy Doody and Gang cover, TV Kid Shows, The Merry Mailman feature	50–100+
	December 2–8	#48	Gertrude Berg cover, Break the Bank, Bob Emery	12–25
	December 9–15	#49	Walter Winchell cover, Danny Thomas, Dave Garroway	12–25
	December 16–22	#50	Marguerite Piazza cover, Captain Glenn	10–20
	December 23–29	#51	Jimmy Durante cover, Rosemary Clooney, Frank Sinatra feature	15–30
	December 30	#52	Happy New Year issue, Snooky Lanson, Bill Hayes	10–20
1951	VOLUME IV			
	January 12	#1	Milton Berle cover, Beat the Clock, Magic Clown	12–25
	January 13–19	#2	Roller Derby issue, Groucho Marx, Dr. Wesley Young feature	12–25

YEAR	ISSUE	NUMBER	DESCRIPTION	VALUE
1951	January 20–26	#3	Sheriff Bob Dixon cover, Jackie Gleason, Charlton Heston	$10–20
	January 27	#4	Jerry Lester cover, We the People, The Jolly Roger	10–20
	February 3–9	#5	Leave It to the Girls cast cover, Perry Como	10–20
	February 10–16	#6	Bert Parks cover, Buddy Rogers, Captain Video	20–40
	February 17–23	#7	Lili Palmer cover, Space Barton, Arlene Francis	12–25
	February 24	#8	Big Town cast cover, Garry Moore, Howdy Doody's Princess Summer Fall Winter Spring feature	20–40
	March 3–9	#9	Jack Carter cover, Art Linkletter feature	10–20
	March 10–16	#10	Sid Caesar cover, How the Lone Ranger Found Silver	25–50
	March 17–23	#11	Jack McCarthy, Buster Crabbe, Hopalong Cassidy	10–20
	March 24–30	#12	Arthur Godfrey cover, Truth or Consequences	10–20

YEAR	ISSUE	NUMBER	DESCRIPTION	VALUE
1951	March 29	#13	Horse Racers' issue, Sam Levenson, Gene Autry	$10–20
	April 7–13	#14	Super Circus's Mary Hartline, Bill Stern	10–20
	April 14–20	#15	Joe DiMaggio and Ted Williams cover, Steve Allen, Fireside Theatre	40–80+
	April 21–27	#16	Eddie Cantor cover, Captain Roots, Arthur Murray	10–20
	April 28	#17	Dagmar and Jerry Lester cover, Buster Crabbe	10–20
	May 5–11	#18	Nature Boy Rogers cover	7–15
	May 12–18	#19	Perry Como cover, Dennis James, John Conte	7–15
	May 19–25	#20	Ken Murray cover, Douglas Edwards, Jerry Mahoney	7–15
	May 26	#21	Frank Sinatra cover, Morton Downey, Roller Derby	25–50
	June 2–8	#22	Ralph Bellamy in Man Against Crime cover, Lady Wrestlers feature, Alan Dale	10–20

YEAR	ISSUE	NUMBER	DESCRIPTION	VALUE
1951	June 9–15	#23	Groucho Marx cover, Amos 'n' Andy feature	$25–50
	June 16–22	#24	Milton Berle cover, Third Anniversary special	15–30
	June 23–29	#25	Dean Martin and Jerry Lewis cover, Bob Howard	25–50
	June 30	#26	Judy Raben . . . Miss WNBT cover, Ben Grauer	7–15
	July 7–13	#27	Sid Caesar and Imogene Coca cover, Color TV	12–25
	July 14–20	#28	How to Get a Baby on TV, Sheriff Bob Dixon	7–15
	July 21–27	#29	Roxanne cover, Freddy Martin, Hal Tunis	5–10
	July 28	#30	Bathing Suit cover, Story Theatre	5–10
	August 4–10	#31	My Friend Irma's Marie Wilson cover, Sammy Kaye, Is TV Too Sexy?	10–20
	August 11–17	#32	Kathy Norris cover, Strike It Rich, Star of the Family feature	5–10
	August 18–24	#33	Dagmar cover, Peggy Lee, Mel Torme, the Children's Hour feature	5–10

YEAR	ISSUE	NUMBER	DESCRIPTION	VALUE
1951	August 25	#34	Jerry Lester cover, Captain Video, New TV Shows	$ 7–15
	August 31	#35	Special Kids' Shows cover, Twenty Questions	17–35
	September 7–13	#36	Sid Caesar and Imogene Coca cover, Fall Preview 1951–1952 Season Part I	30–60
	September 14–20	#37	Milton Berle cover, Fall Preview 1951–1952 Season Part II	30–60
	September 21–27	#38	Arthur Godfrey cover, Dennis James, TV Theme Song Titles	10–20
	September 28	#39	Groucho Marx and Red Skelton cover, The Lone Ranger, Somerset Maugham	25–50
	October 5–11	#40	Jimmy Durante as a New York Yankee cover, The Big Top, Herb Shriner	20–40
	October 12–18	#41	Bob Hope, Lucille Ball and Danny Thomas cover, Fall Preview 1951–1952 Season Part III	30–60

YEAR	ISSUE	NUMBER	DESCRIPTION	VALUE
1951	October 19–25	#42	Martin Kane as Private Investigator cover, Lloyd Nolan, Tropical Fish on TV	$ 10–20
	October 26	#43	Bert Parks cover, Hopalong Cassidy's Horse	15–30
	November 2–8	#44	Jack Benny, Dean Martin, Jerry Lewis, and others on cover, Laura Weber, Football	25–50
	November 9–15	#45	Jackie Gleason cover, Miss New York City TV	25–50
	November 16–22	#46	Frank Sinatra and Milton Berle cover, Johnny Olsen, Roller Derby	25–50
	November 23–29	#47	Howdy Doody cover, The Birthplace of TV, The 10 Most Exciting Men on TV	50–100+
	November 30	#48	Does TV Think You're Stupid, Bud Palmer	7–15
	December 7–13	#49	Agathon of the Jerry Lester Show cover, Ralph Bellamy feature	7–15
	December 14–20	#50	Cathy Hild cover, Ed Sullivan, Foreign Intrigue	7–15

YEAR	ISSUE	NUMBER	DESCRIPTION	VALUE
1951	December 21–27	#51	Annual Awards Special, Walt Disney feature, the Crime Photographer	$ 17–35
	December 28	#52	Roy Rogers cover, TV's 10 Most Exciting Men	25–50
1952	VOLUME V			
	January 4–10	#1	Groucho Marx, Milton Berle, Arthur Godfrey, Sid Caesar, and Ed Sullivan cover, What's My Line	10–20
	January 11–17	#2	Red Skelton cover, Amos 'n' Andy feature	12–25
	January 18–24	#3	My Friend Irma's Marie Wilson, You Asked for It	10–20
	January 25–31	#4	A wonderful cover of Lucille Ball and Desi Arnaz: The Marriage That Fooled Hollywood, Ellery Queen	75–200+
	February 1–7	#5	Molly Goldberg cover, Mike Wallace, Donald O'Connor feature	10–20
	February 8–14	#6	Frances Langford cover, Carl Reiner, Mr. Wizard, Don Ameche	10–20

YEAR	ISSUE	NUMBER	DESCRIPTION	VALUE
1952	February 15–21	#7	Harry Truman and Dwight Eisenhower cover, Bob and Ray, Dragnet	$10–20
	February 22–28	#8	Captain Video cover, Tom Corbett, Space Patrol, Morey (George Washington) Amsterdam, Guy Mitchell, great full-page+ advertisement for Beany & Cecil	40–80
	February 29	#9	Sid Caesar cover, Molly Goldberg, Dagmar, Tony Bennett feature	10–20
	March 7–13	#10	Arthur Godfrey cover, Little Ton-Ton	7–15
	March 14–20	#11	Dean Martin and Jerry Lewis cover, Buster Crabbe, TV Crime Shows	20–40
	March 21–27	#12	Bess Myerson cover, Robert Q. Lewis	5–10
	March 28	#13	Video's Dancing Daughters cover, The Whistling Wizard, Daytime Soap Operas	5–10

YEAR	ISSUE	NUMBER	DESCRIPTION	VALUE
1952	April 4–10	#14	Marion Marlowe and Frank Parker cover, The Celanese Theatre, Kukla, Fran, and Ollie	$ 5–10
	April 11–17	#15	Baseball cover, Sky King, Joe DiMaggio, Bishop Sheen feature	10–20
	April 18–24	#16	Jimmy Durante cover, Kid Shows	10–20
	April 25	#17	Dagmar cover, Elizabeth Montgomery, Sky King	20–40
	May 2–8	#18	Strike It Rich's Warren Hull, Groucho Marx, Bud Collyer, Bill Cullen	10–20
	May 9–15	#19	Peggy Wood of Mama cover, Alan Dale	10–20
	May 16–22	#20	Gene Autry cover, Garry Moore, Foreign Intrigue	50–100
	May 23–29	#21	Milton Berle cover, Martha Raye, Rootie Kazootie	15–30
	May 30	#22	Johnnie Ray cover, Irene Dunne, What's My Line	15–30

YEAR	ISSUE	NUMBER	DESCRIPTION	VALUE
1952	June 6–12	#23	Lucille Ball and Desi Arnaz cover, Allen Funt, Joe Bolton, Arthur Godfrey	$100–200+
	June 13–19	#24	Jackie Gleason cover, Robert Stack, Wally Cox, Charles Ruggles	20–40
	June 20–26	#25	Special Fourth Anniversary issue, Gabby Hayes	20–40
	June 27	#26	Jerry Mahoney and Paul Winchell cover, Art Carney	20–40
	July 4–10	#27	Bob Hope cover, Julius LaRosa, Larry Storch, Babe Ruth feature	10–20
	July 11–17	#28	Jerry Lewis and Lou Costello cover, Ozzie and Harriet, Danny Thomas, Willie Mays	15–30
	July 18–24	#29	Groucho Marx cover, Dave Garroway, Jack Barry, the Chordettes	25–50
	July 25–31	#30	Sandra Spence of Pantomime Quiz, Robert Stack, Howdy Doody feature	10–20

YEAR	ISSUE	NUMBER	DESCRIPTION	VALUE
1952	August 1–7	#31	Don Russell and Lee Joyce cover, Quick Trick Magic, Robert Q. Lewis	10–20
	August 8–14	#32	The Cisco Kid, Roy Rogers, and Hopalong Cassidy cover, The Cowboy Hall of Fame special feature, Al Pearce	50–100+
	August 15–21	#33	Cast of What's My Line cover, Space Patrol contest issue, Fred Astaire	10–20
	August 22–28	#34	Perry Como and Dinah Shore cover, Fall Preview Special Part I . . . 1952–1953 season	25–50
	August 29	#35	Dorothy Collins cover, Morey Amsterdam, Space Patrol contest	10–20
	September 5–11	#36	Imogene Coca cover, Fall Preview Special Part II . . . 1952–1953 season	25–50
	September 12–18	#37	Lucille Ball and Milton Berle cover, Fall Preview Special Part III . . . 1952–1953 season	50–100

YEAR	ISSUE	NUMBER	DESCRIPTION	VALUE
1952	September 19–25	#38	Dean Martin and Jerry Lewis, Jackie Gleason and Jimmy Durante cover, Fall Preview Special Part IV . . . 1952–1953 season	$ 25–50
	September 26	#39	Roy Rogers cover, Jack Lemmon, Zoo Parade	50–100
	October 3–9	#40	My Friend Irma's Marie Wilson, Jim McKay, Paul Dixon show	5–10
	October 10–16	#41	Al Capp and his cartoon characters cover, the history of TV Guide, Tallulah Bankhead, Captain Video feature	10–20
	October 17–23	#42	Arthur Godfrey cover, Your Show of Shows, Captain Video feature	10–20
	October 24–30	#43	Ed Sullivan and Walter Winchell cover, Arthur Godfrey, Ted Brown, Gabby Hayes	10–20
	October 29	#44	Marion Marlowe cover, Howdy Doody, Dennis Day	10–20

YEAR	ISSUE	NUMBER	DESCRIPTION	VALUE
1952	November 7–13	#45	Reed Hadley of Racket Squad cover, Irene Wicker, Roller Derby	$ 10–20
	November 14–20	#46	TV detectives cover special, Imogene Coca, Lady Wrestlers	15–30
	November 21–27	#47	Howdy Doody and Rootie Kazootie cover, Uncle David, Bishop Sheen, Groucho Marx	50–100
	November 28	#48	Perry Como, Eddie Fisher, Julius LaRosa and Patti Page, Terry and the Pirates, Italians on TV feature	10–20
	December 5–11	#49	Lucy Knoch cover, Wally Cox, Red Skelton, the heroes of Space Patrol	10–20
	December 12–18	#50	Arthur Godfrey cover, Lucille Ball's baby, Dragnet, Space Patrol feature	10–20
	December 19–25	#51	Special annual awards issue, Howdy Doody	10–20
	December 26	#52	Jack Russell cover, Ricky and David Nelson, Gale Storm	20–40

YEAR	ISSUE	NUMBER	DESCRIPTION	VALUE
1953	VOLUME VI			
	January 2–8	#1	Jackie Gleason cover, Carl Reiner, Mr. Wizard, Don Ameche	$ 20–40
	January 9–15	#2	Dinah Shore cover, Joan Davis, Eve Arden, Gene Autry feature	10–20
	January 16–22	#3	Ed Sullivan cover, Abbott and Costello, Milton Berle feature	15–30
	January 23–29	#4	Marilyn Monroe cover	150–300+
	January 30	#5	Mary Hartline of Super Circus, Red Buttons, Bob Cummings, Jack Barry	10–20
	February 6–12	#6	Roxanne cover, the stars' most embarrassing moments special feature	12–25
	February 13–19	#7	Kukla, Fran, and Ollie cover, John Cameron Swayze	15–30
	February 20–26	#8	Julius LaRosa and Lu Ann Simms cover, Slick Trick Quigley, The Macy's TV Party	7–15

YEAR	ISSUE	NUMBER	DESCRIPTION	VALUE
1953	February 27	#9	Groucho Marx and George Fenneman cover, June Valli, Johnnie Ray, George Jessel	$15–30
	March 6–12	#10	Jimmy Durante cover, daytime soap operas, the women of Space Patrol	15–30
	March 13–19	#11	Janette Davis cover, George Burns and Gracie Allen, Academy Awards	10–20
	March 20–26	#12	I Love Lucy's Fred and Ethel Mertz cover, Joe Bolton feature	50–100
	March 27	#13	John Forsythe cover, Betty Furness, Range Rider	10–20

TV Guide Values
(National)

Note: First nationwide distribution begins with April 3, 1953, issue.

YEAR	ISSUE	NUMBER	DESCRIPTION	VALUE
1953	April 3–9	#1	Lucille Ball's $50,000,000 Baby	$150–300+
	April 10–16	#2	Jack Webb cover, You Asked for It, The Star Theatre	35–75

YEAR	ISSUE	NUMBER	DESCRIPTION	VALUE
1953	April 17–23	#3	Milton Berle, Lucille Ball, Sid Caesar and Imogene Coca cover, See It Now	$ 40–80
	April 24–30	#4	Ralph Edwards cover, Wally Cox and Mr. Peepers, Howdy Doody's Princess Summer Fall Winter Spring	30–60
	May 1–7	#5	Eve Arden cover, The Homicide Squad, Dick Tracy, Lucille Ball	15–30
	May 8–14	#6	Arthur Godfrey cover, Your Hit Parade, Roy Rogers	15–30
	May 14–21	#7	Ricky and David Nelson, The Fireside Theatre	50–100
	May 22–28	#8	Red Buttons cover, Howdy Doody, Ted Mack	25–50
	May 29	#9	England's Queen Elizabeth, Mickey Mantle, Roy Campanella, Bob Hope: Quick Change Artist, Ralph Edwards, Donald O'Connor: Old-time Song and Dance Man, Bishop Sheen	20–40

YEAR	ISSUE	NUMBER	DESCRIPTION	VALUE
1953	June 5–11	#10	Dean Martin and Jerry Lewis cover, Beat the Clock	$20–40
	June 12–18	#11	Eddie Fisher cover, Bob and Ray	12–25
	June 19–25	#12	Ed Sullivan cover, My Friend Irma, Douglas Edwards	10–20
	June 26	#13	Dinah Shore cover, Dean Martin and Jerry Lewis	15–30
	July 3–9	#14	Perry Como cover, TV Playhouse, Mary Stewart	12–24
	July 10–16	#15	Dave Garroway cover, TV's oddest jobs	10–20
	July 17–23	#16	Lucille Ball and Desi Arnaz cover, Kukla, Fran, and Ollie, House Party	35–75
	July 24–30	#17	Groucho Marx cover, The Goldbergs, Hopalong Cassidy	25–50
	July 31	#18	Sid Caesar and Imogene Coca cover, Gene Autry, TV's top tunes	10–20
	August 7–13	#19	Ray Milland cover, Gale Storm and My Little Margie, Roy Rogers	10–20

YEAR	ISSUE	NUMBER	DESCRIPTION	VALUE
1953	August 14–20	#20	Patti Page cover, Martin Kane, The Range Rider	$ 15–30
	August 21–27	#21	Super Circus cover, Fred Allen, Teresa Brewer, Kit Carson	10–20
	August 28	#22	Jayne and Audrey Meadows cover, Bert Parks, Jimmy Durante, Milton Berle, Bob Hope, Tales of the City	15–30
	September 4–10	#23	Mr. Peepers's Wally Cox cover, Juvenile Jury, The Medallion Theater	10–20
	September 11–17	#24	Joan Caulfield and Ralph Edwards cover, Betty Furness, What's My Line, Marlin Perkins	10–20
	September 18–24	#25	First National Fall Preview issue for 1953–1954 TV season	50–100
	September 25	#26	George Reeves as Superman cover, Bob and Ray	200–400+
	October 2–8	#27	Red Skelton cover, Video Theatre, Gene Autry	10–20
	October 9–15	#28	Bishop Sheen cover, Dorothy Kilgallen, George Jessel	10–20

February 28, 1952

#9, 1953

#40, 1954

#45, 1954

#385, 1960

#452, 1961

#760, 1967

#763, 1967

#765, 1967

YEAR	ISSUE	NUMBER	DESCRIPTION	VALUE
1953	October 16–22	#29	Beauty contest winners cover, Dean Martin and Jerry Lewis, Paul Winchell	$10–20
	October 23–29	#30	Arthur Godfrey cover, Howdy Doody, David Selznick	15–30
	October 30	#31	Kukla and Buelah Witch cover, Joan Davis and I Married Joan, My Favorite Husband	15–30
	November 6–12	#32	Warren Hull cover, Leo G. Carroll and Topper, The Life of Riley	15–30
	November 13–19	#33	Jimmy Durante cover, Ray Bolger, Mary Martin, Ed Sullivan, Carl Reiner	10–20
	November 20–26	#34	Julius LaRosa and Dorothy McGuire cover, Ted Mack's Amateur Hour, Danny Thomas and Make Room for Daddy	15–30
	November 27	#35	Lugene Sanders as Babs Riley, Julius LaRosa, Natalie Wood	15–30
	December 4–10	#36	Loretta Young cover, The Dave Garroway Show	15–30

YEAR	ISSUE	NUMBER	DESCRIPTION	VALUE
1953	December 11–17	#37	Dragnet's Jack Webb cover, Jungle Jim, Ramar of the Jungle	$15–30
	December 18–24	#38	Bob Hope cover, The Jack Paar Show	10–20
	December 25–31	#39	Perry Como, Eddie Fisher and Patti Page Christmas special, The Big Top, Doctor I.Q.	15–30
1954	January 1–7	#40	Bing Crosby cover, TV forecast for '54, Captain Video: "I'll be down to get you in a space ship, honey," Bing Crosby's TV Debut, Jackie Gleason's dancing girls, Ray Bloch, Eddie Fisher	15–30
	January 8–14	#41	Joan Caulfield cover, Foreign Intrigue, Twenty Questions	7–15
	January 15–21	#42	Martha Raye cover, Red Skelton, Hopalong Cassidy, Paul Winchell	7–15
	January 22–28	#43	Jayne Meadows and Joan Bennett cover, Your Show of Shows, Kate Smith	10–20

YEAR	ISSUE	NUMBER	DESCRIPTION	VALUE
1954	January 29	#44	Robert Montgomery cover, Maria Riva, Jack Palance, Elizabeth Montgomery	$10–20
	February 5–11	#45	Jack Benny cover, Jack Benny May Quit Radio, The Pied Piper of TV, Rocky Graziano, Brandon De Wilde: TV's Jamie, The Jackie Gleason Show, Perry Como	10–20
	February 12–18	#46	Red Skelton cover, Buick Berle Show, the Lucille Ball/Desi Arnaz movie	10–20
	February 19–25	#47	Ann Southern cover, Racket Squad	5–10
	February 26	#48	Liberace cover, I Love Lucy, TV Circus, I Remember Mama	10–20
	March 5–11	#49	Frank Parker and Marion Marlowe cover, Danny Thomas and Make Room for Daddy, Lassie	7–15

YEAR	ISSUE	NUMBER	DESCRIPTION	VALUE
1954	March 12–18	#50	Maria Riva cover, Jack Palance, Ronald Reagan: Death Valley Days, Eve Arden: Our Miss Brooks	$10–20
	March 19–25	#51	Groucho Marx cover, The Spike Jones Show	12–25
	March 26	#52	Jackie Gleason cover, Space Cadet	12–25
	April 2–8	#53	Eve Arden cover: Our Miss Brooks, Inner Sanctum, Rocket Rangers	15–30
	April 9–15	#54	Milton Berle and Charlie Applewhite cover, Private Secretary	7–15
	April 16–22	#55	TV Guide awards annual, Duffy's Tavern	10–20
	April 23–29	#56	Lucille Ball cover, Arnold Stang, Milton Berle, Arlene Francis, Public Defender	25–50
	April 30	#57	Jack Webb and Ben Alexander cover, The Spike Jones Show	5–10
	May 7–13	#58	Ozzie and Harriet, Ricky and David Nelson cover, Annie Oakley	30–60

YEAR	ISSUE	NUMBER	DESCRIPTION	VALUE
1954	May 14–20	#59	Frank Sinatra cover, Your Show of Shows, Jonathan Winters	$12–25
	May 21–27	#60	Wally Cox and Patricia Benoit cover, Martin Manulis, Mr. and Mrs. North	10–20
	May 28	#61	My Little Margie's Gale Storm cover, Wally Cox and Mr. Peepers, Imogene Coca	15–30
	June 4–10	#62	Arthur Godfrey cover, Topper, Gene Autry	7–15
	June 11–17	#63	Allen Young and Ben Blue cover, The Roy Rogers Show, Douglas Fairbanks, Jr.	7–15
	June 18–24	#64	Ed Sullivan and Rise Stevens cover, Bud Abbott and Lou Costello	10–20
	June 27	#65	Buffalo Bob and Howdy Doody cover, You Asked for It, Mr. District Attorney	30–60
	July 2–8	#66	I Married Joan's Jim Backus and Joan Davis cover, The Joe Palooka Story, Pat Brady	15–30

YEAR	ISSUE	NUMBER	DESCRIPTION	VALUE
1954	July 9–16	#67	Arlene Francis cover, Mr. District Attorney, Ray Bolger	$10–20
	July 17–23	#68	Roy Rogers cover, The Big Top, horror shows on TV	30–60
	July 24–30	#69	Jack Webb and Ann Robinson cover, Jack Paar, Pinky Lee	5–10
	July 31	#70	Life of Riley's William Bendix cover, I Love Lucy, Merv Griffin	15–30
	August 7–13	#71	Perry Como cover, Elizabeth Montgomery, Jackie Gleason, Jimmy and Tommy Dorsey	15–30
	August 14–20	#72	Dean Martin and Jerry Lewis cover, Laurel and Hardy, Bud Abbott and Lou Costello	25–50
	August 21–27	#73	Steve Allen and Jayne Meadows cover, Jack Paar, Dorothy McGuire	15–30
	August 28	#74	Roxanne cover, Red Skelton, Liberace	10–20
	September 4–10	#75	Eddie Fisher cover, Dragnet, Mickey Rooney	10–20

YEAR	ISSUE	NUMBER	DESCRIPTION	VALUE
1954	September 11–17	#76	Betty Hutton cover, Wrestling	$ 5–10
	September 18–24	#77	Liberace cover, TV Westerns, Private Secretary	10–20
	September 25	#78	Special Fall Preview Issue	30–60
	October 2–8	#79	Dick Powell and Teresa Wright cover, Polly Bergen	5–10
	October 9–15	#80	Lucille Ball cover, Richard Boone, Private Secretary	20–40
	October 16–22	#81	Red Buttons cover, Meet Corliss Archer, Ginger Rogers	10–20
	October 23–29	#82	Walt Disney and his creations cover: Why Walt Disney Changed His Mind About TV, Peter Lawford	20–40
	October 30	#83	Joan Caulfield and Barry Nelson, Anne Francis, Grace Kelly	15–30
	November 6–12	#84	George Burns and Gracie Allen cover, Marilyn Monroe, People Are Funny	15–30
	November 13–19	#85	Liberace and Joanne Rio cover, Captain Video, Space Patrol	10–20

YEAR	ISSUE	NUMBER	DESCRIPTION	VALUE
1954	November 20–26	#86	This Is Your Life's Ralph Edwards cover, Vivian Vance, Father Knows Best	$ 7–15
	November 27	#87	Peter Lawford cover, Lassie, Steve Allen	5–10
	December 4–10	#88	George Gobel cover, December Bride, Walt Disney, Howdy Doody	15–30
	December 11–17	#89	Marion Marlowe cover, December Bride, Ronald Reagan	5–10
	December 18–24	#90	Imogene Coca cover, Joyce Randolph, Sherlock Holmes	10–20
	December 25–31	#91	Ozzie and Harriet, David and Ricky Nelson Christmas cover, Lucille Ball, Space Patrol, Elizabeth Montgomery	25–50
1955	January 1–7	#92	Loretta Young cover, Jackie Gleason, Disneyland	10–20
	January 8–14	#93	Arthur Godfrey cover, George Gobel, Disneyland	10–20

YEAR	ISSUE	NUMBER	DESCRIPTION	VALUE
1955	January 15–21	#94	I've Got A Secret cast cover, Johnny Carson, Disneyland	$10–20
	January 22–28	#95	Ed Sullivan cover, Disneyland	10–20
	January 29	#96	Martha Raye cover, Sherlock Holmes	7–15
	February 5–11	#97	Edward R. Murrow cover, Milton Berle, Vampira	7–15
	February 12–18	#98	Your Hit Parade cast cover, Tennessee Ernie Ford, Dagmar	7–15
	February 19–25	#99	Sid Caesar cover, Faye Emerson, Make Room for Daddy	7–15
	February 26	#100	Steve Allen and Judy Holliday cover, Rin Tin Tin	10–20
	March 5–11	#101	Liberace cover, Lucille Ball, Mary Martin, Disneyland	10–20
	March 12–18	#102	Dinah Shore cover, Bob Cummings, Henry Fonda	10–20

YEAR	ISSUE	NUMBER	DESCRIPTION	VALUE
1955	March 19–25	#103	The Honeymooners's Ed Norton (Art Carney) cover, Tennessee Ernie Ford, Richard Boone, Ozzie and Harriet, David and Ricky Nelson	$30–60+
	March 26	#104	Eve Arden and Gale Gordon cover, The Millionaire, Rin Tin Tin	10–20
	April 2–8	#105	Tony Martin cover, Marilyn Monroe, Lone Wolf	15–30
	April 9–15	#106	Bob Cummings and Gloria Marshall cover, Donald O'Connor, Eddie Cantor	5–10
	April 16–22	#107	Garry Moore cover, I Love Lucy, Walt Disney's Mickey Mouse	12–25
	April 23–29	#108	My Little Margie's Gale Storm cover, Liberace, Stan Laurel and Oliver Hardy	12–25

YEAR	ISSUE	NUMBER	DESCRIPTION	VALUE
1955	April 30	#109	Walt Disney's Davy Crockett, Fess Parker cover, Lucille Ball, Harpo Marx, June Lockhart	$25–50
	May 7–13	#110	Peggy Wood cover, Captain Midnight, Captain Gallant	7–15
	May 14–20	#111	Perry Como cover, The Little Rascals, Steve Allen	12–25
	May 21–27	#112	Jackie Gleason and Audrey Meadows cover, Jayne and Audrey Meadows	25–50
	May 28	#113	Ralph Edwards cover, Dean Martin and Jerry Lewis, Humphrey Bogart	10–20
	June 4–10	#114	Eddie Fisher cover, Roy Rogers	10–20
	June 11–17	#115	Annie Oakley's Gail Davis cover, Liberace	10–20
	June 18–24	#116	Danny Thomas cover and story	10–20
	June 25	#117	Sid Caesar cover, Gale Storm, the Whiting Sisters	10–20
	July 2–8	#118	Lassie and Rin Tin Tin cover, Soldiers of Fortune	12–25

YEAR	ISSUE	NUMBER	DESCRIPTION	VALUE
1955	July 9–15	#119	Patti Page cover, Captain Gallant, Desi Arnaz	$10–20
	July 16–22	#120	Julius LaRosa cover, Marilyn Monroe	12–25
	July 23–29	#121	Jack Webb and Janet Leigh cover, Ed Sullivan, Make Room for Daddy	12–25
	July 30	#122	Lucille Ball and Desi Arnaz cover, Wally Cox: Mr. Peepers, Tony Randall	15–30
	August 6–12	#123	House Party's Art Linkletter cover, Julius LaRosa, Buddy Ebsen	10–20
	August 13–19	#124	Bud Collyer cover, Mel Blanc, The Cisco Kid	5–10
	August 20–26	#125	The $64,000 Question's Hal March cover, Hopalong Cassidy, Johnny Carson	5–10
	August 27	#126	Groucho Marx cover, Jack Benny's Rochester	15–30
	September 3–9	#127	Johnny Carson cover, Father Knows Best, My Little Margie	10–20
	September 10–16	#128	Arthur Godfrey cover, Patti Page, Garry Moore, The Ames Brothers	10–20

YEAR	ISSUE	NUMBER	DESCRIPTION	VALUE
1955	September 17–23	#129	Milton Berle and Esther Williams cover, Frank Sinatra, Judy Garland	$10–20
	September 24–30	#130	1955–1956 Fall Preview special, Andy Devine: Andy's Gang, Jackie Gleason and The Honeymooners	25–50
	October 1–7	#131	Mickey Mouse Club cover, The Honeymooners, December Bride	25–50
	October 8–14	#132	George Burns and Gracie Allen cover . . . How Gracie Allen Gets That Way, Ed Murrow Comes to Call, The younger set loves TV . . . TV toys: Howdy Doody, Davy Crockett, Superman, Pinky Lee, and others	15–30
	October 15–21	#133	The Medic's Richard Boone cover, The Honeymooners, Pinky Lee	10–20

YEAR	ISSUE	NUMBER	DESCRIPTION	VALUE
1955	October 22–28	#134	George Gobel cover, Mary Martin, Jackie Gleason, Perry Como, Milton Berle	$10–20
	October 29	#135	Sergeant Bilko's Phil Silvers cover, The Millionaire, Robin Hood	12–25
	November 5–11	#136	Nanette Fabray cover, Jack Paar	5–10
	November 12–18	#137	Liberace cover, Phil Silvers: Sergeant Bilko, Our Miss Brooks: Eve Arden	5–10
	November 19–25	#138	Jack Benny cover, The $64,000 Question, Peggy King	7–15
	November 26	#139	Martha Raye cover, I Love Lucy, Gunsmoke	6–12
	December 3–9	#140	Peter Lind Hayes and Mary Healy cover, Alfred Hitchcock Presents, TV's horses	5–10
	December 10–16	#141	Lucille Ball cover, The Ding Dong School	10–20
	December 17–23	#142	Robert Montgomery cover, Sheena of the Jungle	5–10

YEAR	ISSUE	NUMBER	DESCRIPTION	VALUE
1955	December 24–30	#143	Special Christmas issue, Ricky and David Nelson, Disneyland	$12–25
	December 31	#144	The People's Choice's Dog, Cleo cover, Lassie	6–12
1956	January 7–13	#145	Arthur Godfrey cover, Long John Silver, The Mickey Mouse Club	6–12
	January 14–20	#146	Loretta Young cover, Dragnet, Highway Patrol	6–12
	January 21–27	#147	Lawrence Welk cover, Tony Randall, Wyatt Earp	5–10
	January 28	#148	Janis Paige cover, Disney animation	5–10
	February 4–10	#149	Ed Sullivan and Judy Tyler cover, Sergeant Preston of the Yukon	5–10
	February 11–17	#150	Perry Como cover, The Honeymooners	10–20
	February 18–24	#151	Jimmy Durante cover, Fireside Theatre, Death Valley Days	5–10
	February 25	#152	Gisele Mackenzie cover, Liberace, Sergeant Bilko	5–10

YEAR	ISSUE	NUMBER	DESCRIPTION	VALUE
1956	March 3–9	#153	Hal March and Lynn Dollar cover, Ann Sothern, Eve Arden: Our Miss Brooks	$ 5–10
	March 10–16	#154	Spring Byington and Frances Rafferty cover, Julius LaRosa, Super Circus	5–10
	March 17–23	#155	Lilli Palmer and Maurice Evans cover, Captain Kangaroo, Meet the Press	5–10
	March 24–30	#156	Dave Garroway cover, Brave Eagle, Ernie Kovacs	5–10
	March 31	#157	Arlene Francis and John Daly cover, Wyatt Earp, Dragnet, Beat the Clock Show	5–10
	April 7–13	#158	Garry Moore and Jayne Meadows cover, Groucho Marx, Lassie, Rin Tin Tin, Sid Caesar	5–10
	April 14–20	#159	Grace Kelly, Princess of Monaco cover, Alfred Hitchcock, Sheena of the Jungle	12–25

YEAR	ISSUE	NUMBER	DESCRIPTION	VALUE
1956	April 21–27	#160	Nanette Fabray cover, Fred Allen, I Love Lucy, Lawrence Welk	$ 5–10
	April 28	#161	Red Skelton cover, Annie Oakley, Our Miss Brooks	5–10
	May 4–11	#162	Mitzi Gaynor and George Gobel cover, Ernie Kovacs, You Asked for It	5–10
	May 12–18	#163	Robin Hood's Richard Green cover, Oscar Levant	5–10
	May 19–25	#164	Sergeant Bilko's Phil Silvers cover, Your Hit Parade, Death Valley Days	10–20
	May 26	#165	Lawrence Welk and Alice Lon cover, Sergeant Preston of the Yukon, Liberace	5–10
	June 2–8	#166	Sid Caesar and Janet Blair cover, The Mickey Mouse Club, Annie Oakley	5–10
	June 9–15	#167	Patti Page cover, Your Hit Parade, Ernie Kovacs, Disneyland	10–20

YEAR	ISSUE	NUMBER	DESCRIPTION	VALUE
1956	June 16–22	#168	Father Knows Best cast cover, Sheena of the Jungle	$15–30
	June 23–29	#169	Steve Allen cover, Jayne Mansfield, Roy Rogers	10–20
	June 30	#170	Love That Bob's Robert Cummings cover, The Lone Ranger	10–20
	July 7–13	#171	Lassie cover, Robin Hood, Elvis Presley feature	15–30
	July 14–20	#172	Sheila MaCrae cover, Johnny Carson	5–10
	July 21–27	#173	Bill Lundigan and Mary Costa, Mickey Dolenz: Circus Boy, Red Skelton, Groucho Marx	10–20
	July 28	#174	Annie Oakley's Gail Davis cover, Cheyenne, Super Circus	10–20
	August 4–10	#175	The People's Choice's Jackie Cooper and Cleo cover, Milton Berle	6–12
	August 11–17	#176	The 1956 Democratic Convention special	5–10

YEAR	ISSUE	NUMBER	DESCRIPTION	VALUE
1956	August 18–24	#177	The 1956 Republican Convention special	$ 5–10
	August 25–31	#178	Esther Williams cover, George Burns and Gracie Allen, I Love Lucy, Tennessee Ernie Ford	10–20
	September 1–7	#179	Alice Lon cover, Rosemary DeCamp, Wyatt Earp	5–10
	September 8–14	#180	Elvis Presley cover, Elvis in the Army, Ernie Kovacs	50–100+
	September 15–21	#181	1956–1957 Fall Preview special	20–40
	September 22–28	#182	Hal March cover, Elvis Presley Part II, Child Actors special feature	25–50
	September 29	#183	Jackie Gleason cover, The Lone Ranger, Elvis Presley in the Army Part III	25–50
	October 6–12	#184	My Little Margie's Gale Storm cover, The NBC Bandstand, Harry Morgan	10–20
	October 13–19	#185	Ozzie and Harriet, David and Ricky Nelson cover, I Love Lucy	25–50

YEAR	ISSUE	NUMBER	DESCRIPTION	VALUE
1956	October 20–26	#186	Perry Como and Phyllis Goodkind cover, Cheyenne, Private Secretary	$ 5–10
	October 27	#187	Alfred Hitchcock cover, Arlene Francis, Mary Martin	10–20
	November 3–9	#188	Edward R. Murrow cover, Hit Parade, Clint Walker	5–10
	November 10–16	#189	Loretta Young cover, Lucille Ball, Milton Berle	5–10
	November 17–23	#190	Buddy Hackett cover, Sir Lancelot	5–10
	November 24–30	#191	Nanette Fabray cover, Phil Silvers: Sergeant Bilko, Mickey Dolenz: Circus Boy, Lawrence Welk	15–20
	December 1–7	#192	George Burns and Gracie Allen cover, The Mickey Mouse Club, Broken Arrow	10–20
	December 8–14	#193	Victor Borge cover, Dobie Gillis: Dwayne Hickman, Bob Cummings: Love That Bob	6–12

YEAR	ISSUE	NUMBER	DESCRIPTION	VALUE
1956	December 15–21	#194	Dinah Shore cover, Joan Caulfield, The 77th Bengal Lancers	$ 6–12
	December 22–28	#195	Christmas special. Groucho Marx	6–12
	December 29	#196	Jeannie Carson cover, Sir Lancelot, The Life of Riley	6–12
1957	January 5–11	#197	Arthur Godfrey cover, My Little Margie's Gale Storm, Loretta Young Theatre	6–12
	January 12–18	#198	Lucille Ball cover, The 77th Bengal Lancers	10–20
	January 19–25	#199	Jerry Lewis cover, The Buccaneers, Sergeant Bilko	10–20
	January 26	#200	Bob Hope cover, Mickey Dolenz: Circus Boy, Cheyenne	12–25
	February 2–8	#201	Jane Wyman cover, Groucho Marx, Phil Silvers: Sergeant Bilko, Buddy Hackett	5–10
	February 9–15	#202	Wyatt Earp's Hugh O'Brian cover, Broken Arrow, Douglas Fairbanks Jr. feature	12–25

YEAR	ISSUE	NUMBER	DESCRIPTION	VALUE
1957	February 16–22	#203	Father Knows Best's Jane Wyatt and Robert Young cover, You Bet Your Life, Captain Gallant	$12–25
	February 23	#204	Charles Van Doren cover, Mike Wallace	5–10
	March 2–8	#205	Dorothy Collins and Gisele Mackenzie cover, Broken Arrow, Sir Lancelot	5–10
	March 9–15	#206	Pat Boone and Arthur Godfrey cover, Zane Grey, Jim Bowie	10–20
	March 16–22	#207	The Emmy Awards special, Barbara Hale	5–10
	March 23–29	#208	Tennessee Ernie Ford cover, Sergeant Bilko, Superman, Dragnet	5–10
	March 30	#209	Julie Andrews cover, Jonathan Winters, Broken Arrow	10–20
	April 6–12	#210	Lawrence Welk cover, Sergeant Preston of the Yukon	5–10
	April 13–19	#211	Nanette Fabray cover, Dean Martin, Ronald Reagan	5–10

YEAR	ISSUE	NUMBER	DESCRIPTION	VALUE
1957	April 20–26	#212	Loretta Young cover, Ida Lupino, Tommy Sands	$ 5–10
	April 27	#213	Groucho Marx cover, Highway Patrol	5–10
	May 4–10	#214	Hal March and Robert Strom cover, Tales of Wells Fargo, Andy Devine	5–10
	May 11–17	#215	Gunsmoke's James Arness cover, Rod Serling	15–30
	May 18–24	#216	Esther Williams cover, Sal Mineo, Ronald Reagan	5–10
	May 25–31	#217	Sid Caesar cover, Spike Jones, The Lone Ranger	6–12
	June 1–7	#218	Ida Lupino and Howard Duff cover, The Mickey Mouse Club, Judy Garland	7–15
	June 8–14	#219	Lassie cover, Elvis Presley, Debra Paget	10–20
	June 15–21	#220	Red Skelton cover, Jackie Gleason, Nina Foch	5–10
	June 22–28	#221	Queen for a Day's Jack Bailey, Maverick, Ed Sullivan, Jack Palance	5–10

YEAR	ISSUE	NUMBER	DESCRIPTION	VALUE
1957	June 29	#222	Oh Susanna's Gale Storm, The Whirlybirds, Jane Wyman, Wyatt Earp	$ 5–10
	July 6–12	#223	What's My Line's cast cover, June Havoc	5–10
	July 13–19	#224	Annie Oakley's Gale Davis cover, Ida Lupino, Vincent Price	10–20
	July 20–26	#225	Julius LaRosa cover, Ann Sothern, Tales of Wells Fargo, Blondie	5–10
	July 27	#226	Garry Moore cover, Shirley MacLaine, Lassie	5–10
	August 3–9	#227	The People's Choice's Cleo cover, Jackie Cooper, Rita Moreno	5–10
	August 10–16	#228	Bob Cummings cover, The Restless Gun, Spike Jones	5–10
	August 17–23	#229	Phil Silvers cover, Jim Bowie	10–20
	August 24–30	#230	Danny Thomas and Marjorie Lord cover, Jack Paar	6–12
	August 31	#231	Cheyenne's Clint Walker cover, Ed Wynn, Vic Damone, The Whiting Sisters	10–20

YEAR	ISSUE	NUMBER	DESCRIPTION	VALUE
1957	September 7–13	#232	Arthur Godfrey and Janette Davis cover, Nat King Cole, Betty White	$10–20
	September 14–20	#233	1957–1958 Fall Preview special	20–40
	September 21–27	#234	Pat Boone cover	5–10
	September 28	#235	George Burns and Gracie Allen cover, Dick Clark and American Bandstand	12–25
	October 5–11	#236	Joan Caulfield cover, Broken Arrow, John Cassavetes	5–10
	October 12–18	#237	Richard Boone: Have Gun Will Travel, Louis Nye	5–10
	October 19–25	#238	Loretta Young cover, Rin Tin Tin, Dick Clark and American Bandstand	12–25
	October 26	#239	Phyllis Kirk and Peter Lawford cover, Wagon Train, Hit Parade	5–10
	November 2–8	#240	Lucille Ball cover, Tony Curtis, Robin Hood	15–30
	November 9–15	#241	Maverick's James Garner cover, You Asked for It, Robin Hood	15–30
	November 16–22	#242	Patti Page cover, Barbara Eden, Steve Allen	15–30

YEAR	ISSUE	NUMBER	DESCRIPTION	VALUE
1957	November 23–29	#243	Mary Martin cover, Captain Kangaroo's Mr. Green Jeans, Eddie Fisher	$ 5–10
	November 30	#244	Alfred Hitchcock cover, Eve Arden	5–10
	December 7–13	#245	Dinah Shore cover, Tallulah Bankhead, Steve Allen	5–10
	December 14–20	#246	Walt Disney and his creations cover, horror pictures on television, Broken Arrow	7–15
	December 21–27	#247	Christmas special, Peter Lawford, Jack Lemmon	5–10
	December 28	#248	Ricky Nelson cover, Howdy Doody, Eve Arden	25–50
1958	January 4–10	#249	Lawrence Welk cover, Guy Williams: Zorro, Cochise, Woody Woodpecker	10–20
	January 11–17	#250	Gisele Mackenzie cover, Shirley Temple, Boris Karloff	10–20
	January 18–24	#251	The Restless Gun's John Payne cover, Wild Bill Hickok	10–20

YEAR	ISSUE	NUMBER	DESCRIPTION	VALUE
1958	January 25–31	#252	Sid Caesar and Imogene Coca cover, Dennis Weaver	$ 6–12
	February 1–7	#253	Walter Winchell cover, Leave It to Beaver's Jerry Mathers, Perry Mason	10–20
	February 8–16	#254	Tab Hunter and Peggy King cover, Frank Sinatra	10–20
	February 17–21	#255	Walter Brennan, Jerry Lewis	6–12
	February 22–28	#256	Rosemary Clooney cover, The Millionaire, Perry Mason	5–10
	March 1–7	#257	Lassie cover, E. G. Marshall, Sugarfoot	6–12
	March 8–14	#258	Arthur Godfrey cover, Richard Boone and Have Gun Will Travel, William Bendix: The Life of Riley	6–12
	March 15–21	#259	Gunsmoke's James Arness and Amanda Blake cover, The Pat Boone Show, Dick Clark	10–20
	March 22–28	#260	Perry Como cover, TV Westerns, Claude Rains	5–10

YEAR	ISSUE	NUMBER	DESCRIPTION	VALUE
1958	March 29	#261	Tennessee Ernie Ford cover, Rin Tin Tin, Horror shows	$ 6–12
	April 5–11	#262	Gale Storm cover, Where Westerns are made	6–12
	April 12–8	#263	Wyatt Earp's Hugh O'Brian cover, Barbara Eden, Wagon Train	12–25
	April 19–25	#264	Polly Bergen cover, Howdy Doody, Richard Diamond	5–10
	April 26	#265	Zorro's Guy Williams cover, Have Gun Will Travel, Gunsmoke	15–30
	May 3–9	#266	Shirley Temple cover, Liberace, Playhouse 90	15–30
	May 10–16	#267	Have Gun Will Travel's Richard Boone, Alfred Hitchcock Presents	15–30
	May 17–23	#268	Make Room for Daddy's Danny Thomas and cast cover, Maverick	15–30
	May 24–30	#269	American Bandstand's Dick Clark cover, Lassie, Annette Funicello	25–50

YEAR	ISSUE	NUMBER	DESCRIPTION	VALUE
1958	May 31	#270	The Thin Man's Phyllis Kirk cover, John Forsythe, Bette Davis	$ 6–12
	June 7–13	#271	Pat Boone cover, Maverick	6–12
	June 14–20	#272	Father Knows Best's Robert Young and Jane Wyatt cover, George Burns and Gracie Allen, Wagon Train's Ward Bond	10–20
	June 21–27	#273	Ed Sullivan cover, Rod Cameron, Perry Mason	5–10
	June 28	#274	Leave It to Beaver's Jerry Mathers cover, Wayde Preston	25–50
	July 5–11	#275	The Price Is Right's Bill Cullen cover, Sky King, Lee Marvin, Barbara Hale	3–6
	July 12–18	#276	Lucille Ball cover, Peter Lawford, John Russell	10–20
	July 19–25	#277	Tales of Wells Fargo's Dale Robertson cover, Polly Bergen, Doris Day	10–20

YEAR	ISSUE	NUMBER	DESCRIPTION	VALUE
1958	July 26	#278	The Millionaire's Marvin Miller cover, Groucho Marx, Clint Walker, TV Westerns	$10–20
	August 2–8	#279	The Real McCoys' Walter Brennan cover, Wyatt Earp, Richard Nixon, Benny Goodman	10–20
	August 9–15	#280	Steve Lawrence and Eydie Gorme cover, Guy Williams: Zorro, Lassie, Shirley Temple	10–20
	August 16–22	#281	Wagon Train's cast cover, Harpo Marx, John Forsythe	10–20
	August 23–29	#282	Edie Adams and Janet Blair cover, Jayne Meadows, Bill Cullen	3–6
	August 30	#283	To Tell the Truth cast cover, Lloyd Bridges: Sea Hunt, Gray Ghost	3–6
	September 6–12	#284	Arthur Godfrey cover, Perry Mason, Cheyenne, Milton Berle	3–6
	September 13–19	#285	The Lennon Sisters cover, Spike Jones	5–10

YEAR	ISSUE	NUMBER	DESCRIPTION	VALUE
1958	September 20–26	#286	Fall Preview special	$15–30
	September 27	#287	Garry Moore cover, Sea Hunt's Lloyd Bridges, The Rifleman's Chuck Connors	7–15
	October 4–10	#288	American Bandstand's Dick Clark cover, Guy Williams: Zorro, Robert Culp	15–30
	October 11–17	#289	Fred Astaire and Barrie Chase cover, Naked City, Liberace	5–10
	October 18–24	#290	Perry Como cover, Like Elvis, Ann Sothern, Clayton Moore: The Lone Ranger, Amanda Blake	5–10
	October 25–31	#291	George Burns cover, The Texan, Barbara Eden	9–18
	November 1–7	#292	Jack Paar cover, Lou Costello Plays It Straight, Robert Horton, TV studios	6–12
	November 8–14	#293	Loretta Young cover, Western heroes ... John Wayne, Tom Mix, and others, Anne Francis, TV wives	6–12

YEAR	ISSUE	NUMBER	DESCRIPTION	VALUE
1958	November 15–21	#294	The Lineup's cast cover, Walt Disney's Westerns, Bob Hope, Davy Crockett	$ 5–10
	November 22–28	#295	Ronald and Nancy Reagan cover, 77 Sunset Strip, Barbara Stanwyck	5–10
	November 29	#296	Victor Borge cover, Ellery Queen, Dobie Gillis's Tuesday Weld	7–15
	December 6–12	#297	Gunsmoke's James Arness cover, Gale Storm, Monster Makeup, Swiss Family Robinson, Shari Lewis	10–20
	December 13–19	#298	Danny Thomas cover, Donna Reed, Fred Astaire, Barrie Chase, George Fenneman	5–10
	December 20–26	#299	Christmas issue special, Ed Wynn, Shirley Temple	10–20
	December 27	#300	David and Ricky Nelson cover, TV Cowboys special, Garry Moore	25–50

YEAR	ISSUE	NUMBER	DESCRIPTION	VALUE
1959	January 3–9	#301	Peter Gunn cast cover, George Burns and Carol Channing, Julia Meade, Jimmy Durante, Steve Canyon	$ 5–10
	January 10–16	#302	Milton Berle cover, Hanna-Barbera's Huckleberry Hound, Jack Webb	5–10
	January 17–23	#303	Maverick's James Garner and Jack Kelly cover, Lucille Ball and Desi Arnaz, Captain Kangaroo, Hit Parade	7–15
	January 24–30	#304	Red Skelton cover, Have Gun Will Travel, Cimmaron Strip, Playhouse 90	6–12
	January 31	#305	George Gobel cover, Gunsmoke's Doc Adams, Carl Reiner, Rory Calhoun	6–12
	February 7–13	#306	The Rifleman's Chuck Connors and Johnny Crawford cover, Naked City	12–25

YEAR	ISSUE	NUMBER	DESCRIPTION	VALUE
1959	February 14–20	#307	Alfred Hitchcock cover, The Donna Reed Show, Tony Randall	$ 6–12
	February 21–27	#308	Perry Mason's Raymond Burr and Barbara Hale cover, Annette Funicello, Bat Masterson, Northwest Passage	10–20
	February 28	#309	Have Gun Will Travel's Richard Boone cover, The Lawman, Bing Crosby, Bachelor Father, The Peter Lind Hayes Show	10–20
	March 7–13	#310	The Real McCoys' Walter Brennan cover, The Restless Gun, The Marx Brothers	10–20
	March 14–20	#311	Arthur Godfrey cover, Ann Sothern, Yancy Derringer, Wyatt Earp, Spring Byington	3–6
	March 21–27	#312	Ann Sothern cover, The Three Stooges, Tales of Wells Fargo, Western sets	10–20

YEAR	ISSUE	NUMBER	DESCRIPTION	VALUE
1959	March 28	#313	Tennessee Ernie Ford cover, Patricia Barry, Lloyd Bridges, Naked City, TV females, Mary Martin special: Peter Pan, Dodge City	$15–30
	April 4–10	#314	77 Sunset Strip cover, Tombstone Territory, Hugh Downs	5–10
	April 11–17	#315	Wagon Train's Ward Bond cover, The Thin Man	7–15
	April 18–24	#316	Dinah Shore cover, Charley Weaver, Rawhide	7–15
	April 25	#317	Dick Powell cover, Steve McQueen, Cheyenne, June Lockhart	5–10
	May 2–8	#318	Wyatt Earp's Hugh O'Brian cover, The Lawman, Jack Webb, Barbara Stanwyck	5–10
	May 9–15	#319	77 Sunset Strip's Edd "Kookie" Burns cover, The Rifleman's Johnny Crawford, Gunsmoke	10–20
	May 16–22	#320	Loretta Young cover, Sergeant Bilko, Naked City	7–15

YEAR	ISSUE	NUMBER	DESCRIPTION	VALUE
1959	May 23–29	#321	Bob Hope cover, You Asked for It	$ 5–10
	May 30	#322	Steve McQueen cover, Mary Tyler Moore, Tony Dow of Leave It to Beaver	7–15
	June 6–12	#323	Gale Storm cover, female Western Stars	5–10
	June 13–19	#324	Pat Boone cover	7–15
	June 20–26	#325	Robert Young and Lauren Chapin cover, Connie Stevens, Annette Funicello, The Three Stooges	20–40
	June 27	#326	Sea Hunt's Lloyd Bridges, The Death of TV's Superman George Reeves, Piper Laurie, Patty McCormack, U.S. Marshal	20–40
	July 4–10	#327	Jon Provost and Lassie cover, Connie Francis	7–15
	July 11–17	#328	Peter Gunn cast, Father Knows Best	5–10
	July 18–24	#329	Janet Blair cover, Perry Mason, Leave It to Beaver	5–10
	July 25–31	#330	The Lawman's John Russell cover, Jayne Meadows, Faye Emerson	5–10

YEAR	ISSUE	NUMBER	DESCRIPTION	VALUE
1959	August 1–7	#331	Dave Garroway cover, Maverick, June Lockhart, The Real McCoys	$ 5–10
	August 8–14	#332	Donna Reed cover, Gene Autry and Roy Rogers, 77 Sunset Strip, Diane Ladd	5–10
	August 15–21	#333	Lawrence Welk cover, Clint Eastwood/ Rawhide, Mary Tyler Moore	7–15
	August 22–28	#334	I've Got a Secret cast cover, Jerry Mathers of Leave It to Beaver, Johnny Carson	5–10
	August 29	#335	Dick Clark cover, Jerry Lewis, Broderick Crawford	10–20
	September 5–11	#336	Maverick's James Garner and Jack Kelly cover, Clint Eastwood, Bachelor Father	10–20
	September 12–18	#337	Arthur Godfrey cover, Gunsmoke	5–10
	September 19–25	#338	Fall Preview special	20–40
	September 26	#339	Hennesey cast cover, Dobie Gillis, Men into Space	5–10

YEAR	ISSUE	NUMBER	DESCRIPTION	VALUE
1959	October 3–9	#340	June Allyson cover, Dick Clark: American Bandstand	$ 7–15
	October 10–16	#341	The Detectives's Robert Taylor cast cover, Dobie Gillis, Bette Davis	5–10
	October 17–23	#342	Ingrid Bergman cover, The Rifleman, Sid Caesar	5–10
	October 24–30	#343	Dennis the Menace's Jay North cover, Groucho Marx, Tales of Wells Fargo	15–30
	October 31	#344	Fred Astaire cover, Rawhide	5–10
	November 7–13	#345	Jack Benny cover, The Twilight Zone, Bonanza	10–20
	November 14–20	#346	Perry Como cover, Gunsmoke, Maverick	5–10
	November 21–27	#347	Cheyenne's Clint Walker cover, Dobie Gillis	10–20
	November 28	#348	Art Carney cover, Johnny Cash	25–50
	December 5–11	#349	Dobie Gillis's cast cover, Robert Stack: The Untouchables	12–25
	December 12–18	#350	Danny Thomas cover, The Wizard of Oz	10–20

YEAR	ISSUE	NUMBER	DESCRIPTION	VALUE
1959	December 19–25	#351	Christmas issue special, Ernie Kovacs, Wagon Train, Art Carney	$ 6–12
	December 26	#352	Loretta Young cover, Charley Weaver, Bobby Darin	7–15
1960	January 2–8	#353	Gunsmoke cast cover, Tales of the Vikings	10–20
	January 9–15	#354	Father Knows Best's Jane Wyatt and Elinor Donahue cover, Tuesday Weld, Maverick	7–15
	January 16–22	#355	Charley Weaver cover, The Rebel's Nick Adams	7–15
	January 23–29	#356	The Real McCoys cover, The Deputy, Men into Space	10–20
	January 30	#357	Garry Moore cover, Tony Randall	5–10
	February 6–12	#358	Paladin's Richard Boone cover, Fred MacMurray: My Three Sons, Connie Stevens	7–15
	February 13–19	#359	Peter Gunn cast cover, Hawaiian Eye, The Texans	5–10

YEAR	ISSUE	NUMBER	DESCRIPTION	VALUE
1960	February 20–26	#360	Red Skelton cover, Bob Denver: Dobie Gillis, Dennis the Menace	$ 5–10
	February 27	#361	The Untouchables' Robert Stack cover, The Twilight Zone, Milburn Stone	5–10
	March 5–11	#362	Dennis the Menace's Jay North cover, Bonanza's Dan Blocker	7–15
	March 12–18	#363	The Rifleman's Chuck Connors cover	10–20
	March 19–25	#364	Perry Mason cast cover, Nick Adams: The Rebel, Bob Cummings	5–10
	March 26	#365	Donna Reed cover, The Untouchables, Lee Marvin	5–10
	April 2–8	#366	Tennessee Ernie Ford cover, Robert Conrad	4–8
	April 9–15	#367	77 Sunset Strip's Efrem Zimbalist Jr., Ed Wynn, Eva Gabor	5–10
	April 16–22	#368	Ann Sothern cover, Shelley Fabares: The Donna Reed Show	10–20

YEAR	ISSUE	NUMBER	DESCRIPTION	VALUE
1960	April 23–29	#369	Laramie cast cover, Tony Randall, Groucho Marx	$ 5–10
	April 30	#370	Lassie and June Lockhart cover, Broken Arrow, Jackie Gleason, Arthur Godfrey	7–15
	May 7–13	#371	Elvis Presley and Frank Sinatra cover, Steve Allen, Westerns on TV	20–40
	May 14–20	#372	Ernie Kovacs and Edie Adams cover, What's My Line, Carl Reiner	5–10
	May 21–27	#373	Bat Masterson's Gene Barry cover, The Untouchables, Ross Martin	10–20
	May 28	#374	Hawiian Eye's Connie Stevens cover, Father Knows Best	5–10
	June 4–10	#375	Riverboat's Darren McGavin cover, The Lawman	4–8
	June 11–17	#376	Bachelor Father cast cover, The Alaskans, Roger Moore	4–8

YEAR	ISSUE	NUMBER	DESCRIPTION	VALUE
1960	June 18–24	#377	Adventures in Paradise cover, Rod Serling: The Twilight Zone, The Deputy, Shelley Fabares	$ 7–15
	June 25	#378	Bonanza cast cover, Annette Funicello, Fabian, Bob Denver	20–40
	July 2–8	#379	Lawrence Welk cover, Johnny Ringo	4–8
	July 9–15	#380	David Brinkley and Chet Huntley cover, The Untouchables	4–8
	July 16–22	#381	Lucille Ball cover, The Untouchables, Connie Stevens	10–20
	July 23–29	#382	John Charles Daly cover, Richard Nixon	4–8
	July 30	#383	Tightrope's Mike Connors cover, Tuesday Weld, Howdy Doody	7–15
	August 6–12	#384	Esther Williams cover, Bert Parks	3–6
	August 13–19	#385	The Rebel's Nick Adams cover, 77 Sunset Strip	15–30
	August 20–26	#386	Betsy Palmer cover, Merv Griffin	3–6

YEAR	ISSUE	NUMBER	DESCRIPTION	VALUE
1960	August 27	#387	77 Sunset Strip cast cover, Popeye, Bob Denver, Spike Jones	$ 5–10
	September 3–9	#388	Arlene Francis cover, The Lawman	3–6
	September 10–16	#389	American Bandstand's Dick Clark cover, Tom Poston, Rawhide	12–25
	September 17–23	#390	Dick Powell and June Allyson cover, Bonanza's Pernell Roberts, Charlie Chaplin	4–8
	September 24–30	#391	Fall Preview special	20–40
	October 1–7	#392	Dinah Shore cover, The Andy Griffith Show	5–10
	October 8–14	#393	Arthur Godfrey cover, Leave It to Beaver, Maverick	5–10
	October 15–21	#394	Carol Burnett and Marion Lorne cover, Dobie Gillis, Boris Karloff: Thriller	5–10
	October 22–28	#395	Debbie Reynolds cover, The Untouchables, Gail Davis	5–10
	October 29	#396	Danny Kaye cover, Thriller, Tab Hunter, Route 66	5–10

YEAR	ISSUE	NUMBER	DESCRIPTION	VALUE
1960	November 5–11	#397	Loretta Young cover, The Twilight Zone	$ 5–10
	November 12–18	#398	Fred MacMurray cover, Jack Benny, Death Valley Days	5–10
	November 19–25	#399	Wagon Train's Ward Bond cover, Dina Merrill	5–10
	November 26	#400	Abby Dalton cover, Tab Hunter, James Garner: Maverick	5–10
	December 3–9	#401	Shirley Temple cover, Perry Como	10–20
	December 10–16	#402	Gunsmoke's James Arness and Amanda Blake cover, James Garner	10–20
	December 17–23	#403	Checkmate cast cover, Harpo Marx, Walt Disney	3–6
	December 26–30	#404	Christmas issue special, June Allyson	3–6
	December 31	#405	The Roaring Twenties' Dorothy Provine cover, Perry Mason, The Aquanauts	3–6
1961	January 7–13	#406	Richard Boone cover, The Islanders	3–6

YEAR	ISSUE	NUMBER	DESCRIPTION	VALUE
1961	January 14–20	#407	Perry Como cover, Have Gun Will Travel's Richard Boone	$ 3–6
	January 21–27	#408	Barbara Stanwyck cover, Shirley Temple	3–6
	January 28	#409	Andy Griffith and Ronnie Howard (Opie) cover, Adventures in Paradise	10–20
	February 4–10	#410	Clint Eastwood cover, The Andy Griffith show	10–20
	February 11–17	#411	Peter Gunn cast cover, Wally Cox, Disneyland	3–6
	February 18–24	#412	Nanette Fabray cover, Jackie Gleason, Route 66	3–6
	February 25	#413	Allen Funt and the cast of Candid Camera cover, The Tall Man, Leave It to Beaver	5–10
	March 4–10	#414	Perry Mason's Raymond Burr cover, Danny Thomas: Make Room for Daddy, The Roaring Twenties	3–6

YEAR	ISSUE	NUMBER	DESCRIPTION	VALUE
1961	March 11–17	#415	The Untouchables' Robert Stack cover, Lee Remick, Raymond Burr: Perry Mason	$3–6
	March 18–24	#416	The Danny Thomas Show's Marjorie Lord, The Flintstones, Loretta Young, Jane Wyatt	3–6
	March 25–31	#417	Alfred Hitchcock cover, The Untouchables, Maverick	3–6
	April 1–7	#418	77 Sunset Strip's Roger Smith cover, Sea Hunt's Lloyd Bridges, Tarzan through the years	3–6
	April 8–14	#419	National Velvet cast cover, The Naked City, 77 Sunset Strip	3–6
	April 15–31	#420	Mitch Miller cover, Surfside Six	3–6
	April 22–28	#421	Garry Moore cover, Perry Como, George Burns	3–6
	April 29	#422	Hong Kong's Rod Taylor cover, Garry Moore	3–6

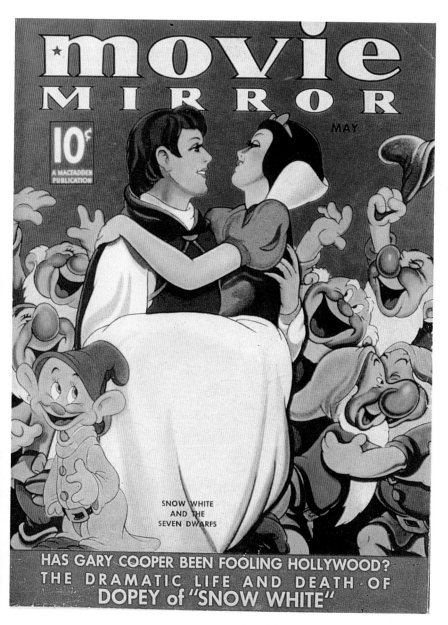

Movie Mirror
May 1938

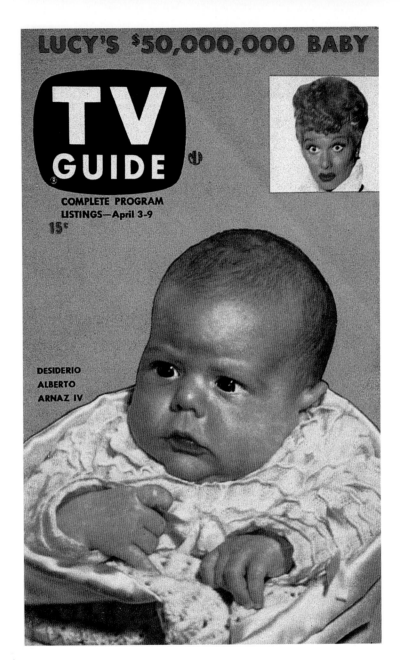

TV Guide
April 3, 1953, #1

TV Guide
September 25, 1953, #26

TV Guide
(clockwise from top left)
#614, #641, #605, #657

Movie Classic
August 1936

Photoplay
November 1937

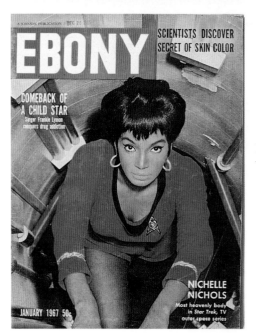

Ebony
January 1967

Life Magazine
March 15, 1968

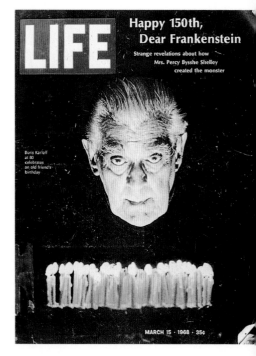

Pic
May 15, 1940

Pic
September 15, 1942

Pic
October 27, 1942

Pic
December 19, 1944

Various issues of Illustrated Horror Magazines featuring the now-popular grotesque cover art

YEAR	ISSUE	NUMBER	DESCRIPTION	VALUE
1961	May 6–12	#423	Donna Reed cover, Mr. Ed, Boris Karloff: Thriller	$ 3–6
	May 13–19	#424	Bonanza's Ben Cartwright cover, Walt Disney	10–20
	May 20–26	#425	The Real McCoys cover, Walt Disney, Andy Williams	5–10
	May 27	#426	Ronald Reagan and Dorothy Malone cover, Walt Disney, Jim Backus	5–10
	June 3–9	#427	The Naked City's cast cover, Perry Mason	3–6
	June 10–16	#428	Efrem Zimbalist Jr. cover, The Naked City	3–6
	June 17–23	#429	Lawrence Welk cover, Bonanza's Michael Landon	10–20
	June 24–30	#430	Wagon Train cast cover, Nanette Fabray	3–6
	July 1–7	#431	The Flintstones cover, Colt .45, Peggy Lee	12–25
	July 8–14	#432	Harry Morgan and Cara Williams cover, Peter Gunn	3–6
	July 15–21	#433	Gardner McKay cover, Julie London, Dennis the Menace	3–6

YEAR	ISSUE	NUMBER	DESCRIPTION	VALUE
1961	July 22–28	#434	Route 66 cast cover, Donna Reed's Paul Petersen	$ 5–10
	July 29	#435	Captain Kangaroo cover, Ozzie and Harriet and boys	10–20
	August 5–11	#436	My Three Sons cast cover, Captain Kangaroo, Adventures in Paradise	5–10
	August 12–18	#437	Soap Opera special, Bob Cummings	3–6
	August 19–25	#438	Troy Donahue cover, Elizabeth Montgomery, The Untouchables	7–15
	August 26	#439	Hugh Downs cover, My Three Sons, Charley Weaver	3–6
	September 2–8	#440	Dobie Gillis's Dwayne Hickman and Bob Denver cover, Clint Eastwood: Rawhide, Perry Mason	12–25
	September 9–15	#441	Checkmate cast cover, Robert Fuller, Shari Lewis	3–6
	September 16–22	#442	Fall Preview special	20–40

YEAR	ISSUE	NUMBER	DESCRIPTION	VALUE
1961	September 23–29	#443	Mitch Miller cover, Jack Benny, Mary Tyler Moore	$ 3–6
	September 30	#444	Carol Burnett cover, Mickey Spillane	3–6
	October 7–13	#445	Walter Cronkite and President Eisenhower cover, Candid Camera's Allen Funt, 77 Sunset Strip, Hazel	3–6
	October 14–20	#446	Red Skelton cover, Michael Rennie	3–6
	October 21–27	#447	Car 54 Where Are You cast cover, Red Skelton, 77 Sunset Strip	15–30
	October 28	#448	The Twilight Zone, Alfred Hitchcock Presents	5–10
	November 4–10	#449	Dorothy Provine cover, The Defenders, Perry Mason's Raymond Burr	3–6
	November 11–17	#450	Robert Stack and wife cover, Sid Caesar, Anne Baxter	3–6
	November 18–24	#451	Garry Moore and Durward Kirby cover, Howdy Doody	3–6

YEAR	ISSUE	NUMBER	DESCRIPTION	VALUE
1961	November 25	#452	Gunsmoke's James Arness and Amanda Blake, Adventures in Paradise	$ 7–10
	December 2–8	#453	Joey Bishop cover, National Velvet, Gunsmoke's Dennis Weaver	3–6
	December 9–15	#454	Dick Van Dyke and Mary Tyler Moore cover, Gloria Swanson	10–20
	December 16–22	#455	Dr. Kildare's Richard Chamberlain and Raymond Massey cover, 77 Sunset Strip	3–6
	December 23–29	#456	Christmas issue special, Fabian, Car 54 Where Are You?	5–10
	December 30	#457	Cynthia Pepper cover, Checkmate	3–6
1962	January 6–12	#458	American Bandstand's Dick Clark cover, Bonanza's Michael Landon	10–20
	January 13–19	#459	Hazel cast cover, Sex on TV, Robert Young	3–6

YEAR	ISSUE	NUMBER	DESCRIPTION	VALUE
1962	January 20–26	#460	The Rifleman's Chuck Connors cover, Dr. Kildare's Richard Chamberlain, Rocky & Bullwinkle, Robert Young	$12–25
	January 27	#461	Myrna Fahey cover, Leave It to Beaver's Jerry Mathers, The Dick Van Dyke Show	6–12
	February 3–9	#462	Mark Richmond cover, 77 Sunset Strip's Connie Stevens	3–6
	February 10–16	#463	Jackie Kennedy cover, Gunsmoke's Amanda Blake, Route 66	3–6
	February 17–23	#464	Danny Thomas cover, The 87th Precinct	3–6
	February 24	#465	Troy Donahue cover, Johnny Carson, Ben Casey, Huckleberry Hound	3–6
	March 3–9	#466	Perry Mason cast cover, Danny Thomas, Surfside Six	3–6

YEAR	ISSUE	NUMBER	DESCRIPTION	VALUE
1962	March 10–16	#467	Jack Paar cover, Zorro's Guy Williams, Rawhide's Clint Eastwood	$ 6–12
	March 17–23	#468	The Defenders cast cover, Dobie Gillis, Maverick's James Garner	4–8
	March 24–30	#469	Dick Powell cover, Leave It to Beaver's Jerry Mathers, Johnny Carson	6–12
	March 31	#470	Mr. Ed and Wilbur (Alan Young) cover, Bachelor Father, Inger Stevens: The Farmer's Daughter	12–25
	April 7–13	#471	Wagon Train's John McIntire cover, The Real McCoys, Dick Powell	5–10
	April 14–20	#472	Route 66 cast cover, Dr. Kildare	3–6
	April 21–27	#473	Connie Stevens cover, The Twilight Zone's Rod Serling, Route 66	3–6
	April 28	#474	The 87th Precinct cast cover, Don Adams	3–6
	May 5–11	#475	Dobie Gillis cast cover, Abby Dalton, The Law and Mr. Jones	10–20

YEAR	ISSUE	NUMBER	DESCRIPTION	VALUE
1962	May 12–18	#476	The Andy Griffith Show's Don Knotts, Candid Camera's Allen Funt, The Danny Thomas Show's Marjorie Lord	$10–20
	May 19–25	#477	The Naked City's Paul Burke cover, Dr. Kildare, Password, Marlo Thomas	3–6
	May 26	#478	My Three Sons' Fred MacMurray, Bud Collyer, Hazel	3–6
	June 2–8	#479	Mary Tyler Moore cover, Maverick, The Corruptors	5–10
	June 9–15	#480	77 Sunset Strip's Efrem Zimbalist Jr. cover, Julie Andrews, Bob Newhart	3–6
	June 16–22	#481	Dr. Kildare's Dick Chamberlain and Raymond Massey cover, Paul Anka	5–10
	June 23–29	#482	Arlene Francis cover, Ed Sullivan, Mr. Ed, Bonanza	5–10
	June 30	#483	Mitch Miller cover, The Twilight Zone	5–10
	July 7–13	#484	David Brinkley cover, Dobie Gillis's Tuesday Weld	5–10

YEAR	ISSUE	NUMBER	DESCRIPTION	VALUE
1962	July 14–20	#485	Checkmate cast cover, Jackie Cooper, Gunsmoke's Dennis Weaver	$ 3–6
	July 21–27	#486	Donna Reed cover, Perry Mason, Bonanza	5–10
	July 28	#487	The Price Is Right's Bill Cullen cover, Adventures in Paradise	3–6
	August 4–10	#488	Dennis the Menace cast cover, Ann-Margret, Clint Walker	10–20
	August 11–17	#489	The Untouchables' Robert Stack cover, Sid Caesar, Bullwinkle	5–10
	August 18–24	#490	I've Got a Secret cast cover, Ozzie and Harriet, Robert Conrad	3–6
	August 25–31	#491	Lawrence Welk cover, Beverly Garland	3–6
	September 1–7	#492	Troy Donahue and Connie Stevens cover	3–6
	September 8–14	#493	Bonanza cast cover, Dr. Kildare Meets Ben Casey, Inger Stevens	17–35

YEAR	ISSUE	NUMBER	DESCRIPTION	VALUE
1962	September 15–21	#494	Fall Preview special	$20–40
	September 22–28	#495	Ben Casey's Vince Edwards cover, My Three Sons	3–6
	September 29	#496	Lucille Ball cover, The Untouchables	10–20
	October 6–12	#497	Hazel cast cover, Danny Thomas, Mr. Ed	3–6
	October 13–19	#498	Jackie Gleason cover, Dinah Shore, Merv Griffin	3–6
	October 20–26	#499	Loretta Young cover, Jackie Gleason	3–6
	October 27	#500	Sam Benedict cast cover, Fred Astaire, The Virginian	3–6
	November 3–9	#501	Our Man Higgins cover, Charles Boyer, The Virginian	3–6
	November 10–16	#502	The Beverly Hillbillies cast cover, Car 54, The Rifleman, Stoney Burke	25–50
	November 17–23	#503	Stoney Burke's Jack Lord cover, The Eleventh Hour, Bob Hope	3–6
	November 24–30	#504	Jackie Kennedy cover, Milburn Stone	3–6

YEAR	ISSUE	NUMBER	DESCRIPTION	VALUE
1962	December 1–7	#505	I'm Dickens, He's Fenster cover, Jackie Gleason, Clint Eastwood	$ 3–6
	December 8–14	#506	Dick Van Dyke cover, The Virginian, Roy Rogers	3–6
	December 15–21	#507	The Nurses cast cover, The Beverly Hillbillies, Route 66	5–10
	December 22–28	#508	Christmas issue special, Judy Carnes	3–6
	December 29	#509	Edie Adams cover, Shari Lewis, The Naked City	3–6
1963	January 5–11	#510	Ben Casey cast cover, Terry Moore, Leave It to Beaver, Our Man Higgins	3–6
	January 12–18	#511	Arnold Palmer cover, Perry Como, Marjorie Lord	3–6
	January 19–25	#512	Car 54 Where Are You? cast cover, Leave It to Beaver's Tony Dow, It's a Man's World	15–30

YEAR	ISSUE	NUMBER	DESCRIPTION	VALUE
1963	January 26	#513	Route 66 cast cover, The Alfred Hitchcock Hour, Bette Davis on Perry Mason	$ 5–10
	February 2–8	#514	Jack Webb cover, Yogi Bear, Julie Newmar	5–10
	February 9–15	#515	McHale's Navy's Ernest Borgnine cover, Vivian Vance off camera	1–20
	February 16–22	#516	Princess Grace (Kelly) cover, Pebbles on The Flintstones, Sid Caesar	10–20
	February 23	#517	Carol Burnett cover, Sid Caesar, Mary Tyler Moore	3–6
	March 2–8	#518	The Eleventh Hour cast cover, The Lucy Show, Lloyd Bridges	3–6
	March 9–15	#519	The Beverly Hillbillies' Donna Douglas and Buddy Ebsen cover, Car 54 Where Are You?, Cyd Charisse	10–20
	March 16–22	#520	Richard Chamberlain cover, Phil Silvers, Judy Garland, Hazel, Ed Sullivan	3–6

YEAR	ISSUE	NUMBER	DESCRIPTION	VALUE
1963	March 23–29	#521	Andy Williams cover, Charles Bronson of Empire, Jack Benny, Hope Lange	$ 3–6
	March 30	#522	Bonanza cast cover	17–35
	April 6–12	#523	Lucille Ball cover, The Dakotas, anniversary issue	10–20
	April 13–19	#524	Empire's Richard Egan cover, Garry Moore	2–4
	April 20–26	#525	Red Skelton cover, George Gobel, Dinah Shore	2–4
	April 27	#526	Perry Mason cover, Liz Taylor, Mary Tyler Moore	2–4
	May 4–10	#527	The Virginian cast cover, President Kennedy	2–4
	May 11–17	#528	The Andy Griffith Show's Don Knotts and Ron Howard cover, special color pages on Ann-Margret, Stoney Burke	10–20
	May 18–24	#529	The Defenders cast cover, Dr. Kildare	2–4

YEAR	ISSUE	NUMBER	DESCRIPTION	VALUE
1963	May 25–31	#530	Lawrence Welk cover, Burt Reynolds of Gunsmoke, Ben Casey	$ 2–4
	June 1–7	#531	Garry Moore and Dorothy Loudon cover, Barbara Bain, Combat	3–6
	June 8–14	#532	Johnny Carson cover, The Naked City	3–6
	June 15–21	#533	Combat cast cover, Mary Tyler Moore, Jerry Lewis	15–30
	June 22–28	#534	Candid Camera's Allen Funt and Durward Kirby cover, Route 66	10–20
	June 29	#535	Donna Reed and Carl Betz cover, Cloris Leachman	2–4
	July 6–12	#536	Route 66 cast cover, The Beverly Hillbillies	5–10
	July 13–19	#537	The Lively Ones cast cover, McHale's Navy, The Andy Griffith Show's Ronnie Howard	2–4
	July 20–26	#538	Gunsmoke's James Arness and Dennis Weaver cover, Ben Casey's Vince Edwards	7–15

YEAR	ISSUE	NUMBER	DESCRIPTION	VALUE
1963	July 27	#539	Game show issue	$ 2–4
	August 3–9	#540	Morey Amsterdam cover, The New York Mets, Combat	2–4
	August 10–16	#541	I've Got a Secret cast cover, Johnny Carson	2–4
	August 17–23	#542	My Three Sons' Fred MacMurray cover, Mickey Rooney	3–6
	August 24–30	#543	Lassie cast cover, Jack Lemmon, Carol Burnett	5–10
	August 31	#544	Have Gun Will Travel's Richard Boone, Joey Heatherton	5–10
	September 7–13	#545	The Beverly Hillbillies' Donna Douglas and Irene Ryan cover, Ann-Margret	10–20
	September 14–20	#546	Fall Preview special	20–40
	September 21–27	#547	Dr. Kildare's Richard Chamberlain cover, Edie Adams, Ozzie and Harriet	4–8
	September 28	#548	Inger Stevens cover, Ben Casey, Lucille Ball	3–6
	October 5–11	#549	Phil Silvers cover, Willie Mays, Elizabeth Taylor	2–4

YEAR	ISSUE	NUMBER	DESCRIPTION	VALUE
1963	October 12–18	#550	Chuck Connors and Ben Gazzara cover, Jayne Mansfield, Phil Silvers	$10–20
	October 19–25	#551	Judy Garland cover, McHale's Navy's Tim Conway, The Rifleman's Johnny Crawford	7–15
	October 26	#552	The Virginian cover, Breaking Point	2–4
	November 2–8	#553	My Favorite Martian cast cover, The Fugitive	25–50
	November 9–15	#554	Carol Burnett cover, The Jerry Lewis Show	2–4
	November 16–22	#555	Mr. Novak cast cover, The Beverly Hillbillies, My Favorite Martian, Meredith MacRae	6–12
	November 23–29	#556	Burke's Law's Gene Barry cover, David Suskind	2–4
	November 30	#557	George C. Scott cover, Danny Kaye, The Twilight Zone, Jack Palance, The Greatest Show on Earth	3–6

YEAR	ISSUE	NUMBER	DESCRIPTION	VALUE
1963	December 7–13	#558	Wagon Train cast cover, Yvette Mimieux, Dr. Kildare	$ 5–10
	December 14–20	#559	Bing Crosby, Frank Sinatra and Dean Martin cover, The Outer Limits, Jerry Lewis	10–20
	December 21–27	#560	Christmas issue special, Lassie, Arthur Godfrey	2–4
	December 28	#561	Patty Duke cover, Inger Stevens, Lassie	10–20
1964	January 4–10	#562	The Dick Van Dyke Show cast cover, Petticoat Junction, Gunsmoke	5–10
	January 11–17	#563	June Lockhart and other women of TV cover, Jeffrey Hunter, Rip Cord, The Fugitive	3–6
	January 18–24	#564	Bonanza's Pernell Roberts cover, The Patty Duke Show, The Andy Griffith Show's Don Knotts, Burke's Law	10–20
	January 25–31	#565	Assassination of President Kennedy special	5–10

YEAR	ISSUE	NUMBER	DESCRIPTION	VALUE
1964	February 1–7	#566	Danny Kaye cover, Combat, My Favorite Martian's Bill Bixby	$10–20
	February 8–14	#567	Petticoat Junction's leading young females cover, Jonathan Winters	10–20
	February 15–21	#568	Andy Williams cover, The Dick Van Dyke Show, Bess Myerson	2–4
	February 22–28	#569	The Fugitive's David Janssen cover, The Outer Limits, Alfred Hitchcock, Red Skelton	15–30
	February 29	#570	The Nurses cast cover, Mae West, Mr. Ed	2–4
	March 7–13	#571	Dr. Kildare's Richard Chamberlain cover, Animals on TV	2–4
	March 14–20	#572	The Beverly Hillbillies cast cover, Gunsmoke, Bonanza, Have Gun Will Travel, Joseph Cotten	15–30
	March 21–27	#573	The Andy Griffith Show cast cover, Judy Garland, The Outer Limits	15–30

YEAR	ISSUE	NUMBER	DESCRIPTION	VALUE
1964	March 28	#574	Lawrence Welk cover, color photos of The Beverly Hillbillies' Donna Douglas, George C. Scott, Petticoat Junction	$10–20
	April 4–10	#575	Ben Casey's Vince Edwards cover, The Farmer's Daughter, Inger Stevens	2–4
	April 11–17	#576	My Favorite Martian cast cover, Bob Hope, Burt Reynolds, Suzy Parker	12–25
	April 18–24	#577	Mr. Novak cast cover, The Beatles on The Ed Sullivan Show/ The Beatles back in Britain	5–10
	April 25	#578	Danny Thomas cover, Shari Lewis, Jack Palance	2–4
	May 2–8	#579	The Farmer's Daughter cast cover, Angie Dickinson, Judy Garland	2–4
	May 9–15	#580	Combat cast cover, The Avengers, Jack Benny	12–25

YEAR	ISSUE	NUMBER	DESCRIPTION	VALUE
1964	May 16–22	#581	Alfred Hitchcock cover, McHale's Navy, Carol Burnett	$ 2–4
	May 23–29	#582	Mary Tyler Moore cover, Judy Garland	2–4
	May 30	#583	McHale's Navy cast cover, Petticoat Junction	5–10
	June 6–12	#584	Gunsmoke's Amanda Blake cover, Milton Berle, Steve Allen, The Fugitive, Ozzie and Harriet	2–4
	June 13–19	#585	The Flintstones cover, Candid Camera	7–15
	June 20–26	#586	The Donna Reed Show cover, McHale's Navy	2–4
	June 27	#587	Johnny Carson and wife cover, The Farmer's Daughter, Inger Stevens, Barbara Bain, Gunsmoke	2–4
	July 4–10	#588	Perry Mason cover, Mr. Novak	2–4
	July 11–17	#589	Walter Cronkite and other TV anchormen cover, Red Skelton	2–4
	July 18–24	#590	The Virginian cover, George C. Scott	2–4

YEAR	ISSUE	NUMBER	DESCRIPTION	VALUE
1964	July 25–31	#591	My Three Sons cover, Eva Marie Saint	$ 5–10
	August 1–7	#592	Today cast cover, The Beverly Hillbillies, Donna Reed	4–8
	August 8–14	#593	Burke's Law cast cover, Mike Wallace, Anna Maria Alberghetti	2–4
	August 15–21	#594	Wagon Train cast cover, Perry Mason	2–4
	August 22–28	#595	The Defenders cover, Rudy Vallee, General Hospital	2–4
	August 29	#596	Patty Duke Show cover, Carol Lynley, Fred Astaire	10–20
	September 5–11	#597	Lucille Ball cover, Peter Lawford	4–8
	September 12–18	#598	The Fugitive cover, Bonanza's Ben Cartwright, Gypsy Rose Lee	10–20
	September 19–25	#599	Fall Preview special	20–40
	September 26	#600	Bonanza's Dan Blocker cover, Gomer Pyle, Sophia Loren	10–20
	October 3–9	#601	Peyton Place's Mia Farrow, Jill St. John	2–4

YEAR	ISSUE	NUMBER	DESCRIPTION	VALUE
1964	October 10–16	#602	The Rogues cast cover, My Favorite Martian, Combat	$ 5–10
	October 17–23	#603	Lassie cover, The Man from U.N.C.L.E., The Patty Duke Show	7–15
	October 24–30	#604	The Man from U.N.C.L.E. cover, Bewitched, Gunsmoke	25–50
	October 31	#605	Addams Family's Gomez and Morticia cover, The Smothers Brothers, Gilligan's Island	25–50+
	November 7–13	#606	Dr. Kildare's Richard Chamberlain cover, Wagon Train, Leslie Caron	2–4
	November 14–20	#607	Cara Williams cover, Petticoat Junction, Tony Franciosa	2–4
	November 21–27	#608	Gomer Pyle U.S.M.C. cover, Margaret Rutherford	5–10
	November 28	#609	Bewitched's Elizabeth Montgomery cover, Lauren Bacall, Winston Churchill, The Addams Family	10–20

YEAR	ISSUE	NUMBER	DESCRIPTION	VALUE
1964	December 5–11	#610	No Time for Sergeants cover, Tina Louise, Gomer Pyle	$ 2–4
	December 12–18	#611	My Living Doll's Julie Newmar cover, Bing Crosby	5–10
	December 19–25	#612	Christmas issue special, The Munsters	10–20
	December 26	#613	Juliet Prowse cover, Fess Parker, Jack Klugman	2–4
1965	January 2–8	#614	The Munsters cast cover, The Mickey Mouse Club, Rawhide	30–60+
	January 9–15	#615	Broadside cast cover, Carol Burnett, Danny Kaye	2–4
	January 16–22	#616	Bob Hope cover, The Man from U.N.C.L.E., Peyton Place	5–10
	January 23–29	#617	Chuck Connors cover, Everything from Cinderella to Peyton Place	3–6
	January 30	#618	Inger Stevens cover, Voyage to the Bottom of the Sea	10–20
	February 6–12	#619	Jackie Gleason cover, Bing Crosby, The Man from U.N.C.L.E.	5–10

YEAR	ISSUE	NUMBER	DESCRIPTION	VALUE
1965	February 13–19	#620	Andy Williams cover, Popeye, Ben Casey, Harry Belafonte, Jim Backus	$ 2–4
	February 20–26	#621	Mr. Novak cast cover, The Addams Family	10–20
	February 27	#622	The Beverly Hillbillies cover, Mae West, Flipper, The Fugitive	15–30
	March 6–12	#623	The Fugitive cover, Three Stooges, Johnny Carson	10–20
	March 13–19	#624	Bonanza cast cover, Ron Howard	10–20
	March 20–26	#625	Peyton Place cover, Anne Bancroft, Petticoat Junction, Mitch Miller	2–4
	March 27	#626	Dick Van Dyke Show cover, The Munsters, Carol Burnett	10–20
	April 3–9	#627	Ben Casey's Vince Edwards cover, The King Family	2–4
	April 10–16	#628	The Tycoon's Walter Brennan cover, The Fugitive's one-armed man	3–6

YEAR	ISSUE	NUMBER	DESCRIPTION	VALUE
1965	April 17–23	#629	The Man from U.N.C.L.E. cover, Sally Kellerman	$15–30
	April 24–30	#630	The Andy Griffith Show cover, June Lockhart, Barbra Streisand, Gilligan's Island	5–10
	May 1–7	#631	Wendy and Me's Connie Stevens cover, Voyage to the Bottom of the Sea, George Burns	6–12
	May 8–14	#632	Gilligan's Island's Bob Denver cover, The Man from U.N.C.L.E.	10–20
	May 15–21	#633	Twelve O'clock High's Robert Lansing cover, The Man from U.N.C.L.E.'s David McCallum, Chuck Connors: Branded, Gilligan's Island	5–10
	May 22–28	#634	Julie Andrews cover, Voyage to the Bottom of the Sea: The making of the Seaview, Harvey Korman, The Beverly Hillbillies	6–12
	May 29	#635	Bewitched's Elizabeth Montgomery and Dick York cover, Dick Van Dyke	10–20

YEAR	ISSUE	NUMBER	DESCRIPTION	VALUE
1965	June 5–11	#636	Flipper cover, Gardner McKay, The Fugitive	$ 5–10
	June 12–18	#637	Gunsmoke's Amanda Blake and Milburn Stone cover, The Rogues, Janet Margolin	2–4
	June 19–25	#638	Voyage to the Bottom of the Sea cover, Bonanza	20–40
	June 26	#639	Hullabaloo cover, Gomer Pyle, TV dog actors	2–4
	July 3–9	#640	Jimmy Dean cover, Shelley Winters	2–4
	July 10–16	#641	The Munsters's Yvonne DeCarlo and Fred Gwynne cover, Julie Newmar, The King Family	15–30+
	July 17–23	#642	McHale's Navy cast cover, Gilligan's Island, Bewitched, Walt Disney	10–20
	July 24–30	#643	Raymond Burr cover, The Munsters, I Spy, Daniel Boone, Jimmy Dean	10–20

YEAR	ISSUE	NUMBER	DESCRIPTION	VALUE
1965	July 31	#644	My Three Sons cast cover, The Man from U.N.C.L.E., Barbara Eden: I Dream of Jeannie	$ 6–12
	August 7–13	#645	Burke's Law cover, Daniel Boone, Hazel, Al Hirt	2–4
	August 14–20	#646	Lassie cover, Sally Field, The Lennon Sisters, Hazel's Shirley Booth	2–4
	August 21–27	#647	Daniel Boone's Fess Parker cover, Eileen Fulton, Discover, Mel Blanc	2–4
	August 28	#648	Lucille Ball cover, Jack Benny, Peyton Place, The Virginian	3–6
	September 4–10	#649	Bonanza cast cover, Lawrence Welk, The Addams Family's Lurch	10–20
	September 11–17	#650	Fall Preview special	20–40
	September 18–24	#651	Honey West's Anne Francis cover, Dawn Wells	10–20

YEAR	ISSUE	NUMBER	DESCRIPTION	VALUE
1965	September 25	#652	Jackie Gleason cover, Tony Curtis: Run for Your Life, The Flintstones	$ 2–4
	October 2–8	#653	Get Smart's Don Adams and Barbara Feldon cover, Rawhide, Combat	12–25
	October 9–15	#654	Honey West's Anne Francis cover, My Three Sons, I Spy, Soupy Sales	10–20
	October 16–22	#655	Red Skelton cover, Juliet Prowse, Trials of O'Brian, Roaring Chicken	2–4
	October 23–29	#656	Branded's Chuck Connors cover, Honey West, Gunsmoke, I Spy's Bill Cosby	7–15
	October 30	#657	Addams Family cover, Get Smart	20–40+
	November 6–12	#658	Lost in Space cover, Jackie Cooper	40–80+
	November 13–19	#659	Joey Heatherton cover, Richard Crenna, Frank Sinatra	5–10
	November 20–26	#660	The F.B.I. cover, F Troop, Rod Serling	2–4

YEAR	ISSUE	NUMBER	DESCRIPTION	VALUE
1965	November 27	#661	Hogan's Heroes' Bob Crane cover, Liza Minnelli, Green Acres	$10–20
	December 4–10	#662	Juliet Prowse cover, The Wild, Wild West, My Mother the Car	6–12
	December 11–17	#663	F-Troop cover, Peter Falk, Gidget	7–15
	December 18–24	#664	Gomer Pyle, U.S.M.C. cover, Mr. Ed	5–10
	December 25–31	#665	Christmas issue special, Bewitched, Hogan's Heroes	5–10
1966	January 1–7	#666	Carol Channing cover, The F.B.I., Ben Casey	2–4
	January 8–14	#667	Green Acres' Eva Gabor and Eddie Albert cover, Petticoat Junction, Gilligan's Island	5–10
	January 15–21	#668	I Spy's Robert Culp and Bill Cosby cover, The Loner	10–20
	January 22–28	#669	The Fugitive's David Janssen cover, Hogan's Heroes' Werner Klemperer	10–20
	January 29	#670	Please Don't Eat the Daisies cast cover, Get Smart, Mr. Roberts, Garry Moore	2–4

YEAR	ISSUE	NUMBER	DESCRIPTION	VALUE
1966	February 5–11	#671	I Dream of Jeannie's Barbara Eden and Larry Hagman cover, Lost in Space, The Smothers Brothers	$12–25
	February 12–18	#672	Peyton Place's Barbara Parkins and Ryan O'Neal cover, The Virginian, Batman, Cousteau	3–6
	February 19–25	#673	Run for Your Life's Ben Gazzara, The Big Valley's Lee Majors, Dr. Kildare	2–4
	February 26	#674	The Big Valley's Barbara Stanwyck cover, The Dick Van Dyke Show	7–15
	March 5–11	#675	Get Smart's Barbara Feldon cover, My Favorite Martian, Andy Warhol	10–20
	March 12–18	#676	Beverly Hillbillies cast cover, I Dream of Jeannie	10–20
	March 19–25	#677	The Man from U.N.C.L.E.'s David McCallum and Robert Vaughn cover, The Donna Reed Show's last episode	12–25

YEAR	ISSUE	NUMBER	DESCRIPTION	VALUE
1966	March 26	#678	Batman's Adam West cover, Flipper, Secret Agent	$20–40
	April 2–8	#679	Dean Martin cover, Honey West, The Man from U.N.C.L.E., Get Smart	7–15
	April 9–15	#680	The Long Hot Summer's Roy Thinnes cover, My Mother the Car	2–4
	April 16–22	#681	Petticoat Junction cover, The Wild, Wild West	10–20
	April 23–29	#682	Andy Williams cover, Wide World of Sports, Barbara McNair	2–4
	April 30	#683	Lucille Ball cover, My Mother the Car, Jesse James	2–4
	May 7–13	#684	President Johnson cover, My Three Sons	2–4
	May 14–20	#685	Frank Sinatra cover and special, The Avengers	5–10
	May 21–27	#686	The Wild, Wild West's Robert Conrad and Ross Martin cover, Get Smart, The Dick Van Dyke Show's last episode	15–30

YEAR	ISSUE	NUMBER	DESCRIPTION	VALUE
1966	May 28	#687	Gidget's Sally Field cover, Red Skelton	$ 5–10
	June 4–10	#688	Mayberry's Andy Griffith, The Man from U.N.C.L.E., Batman	5–10
	June 11–17	#689	Gilligan's Island cast cover, Dragnet	10–20
	June 18–24	#690	Bewitched cast cover, Arlene Francis, Willie Mays	10–20
	June 25	#691	Laredo cast cover, Batman's Batmobile	5–10
	July 2–8	#692	Walter Cronkite cover, Sarah: Napoleon Solo's secretary from The Man from U.N.C.L.E.	5–10
	July 9–15	#693	Flipper cover, The Soupy Sales Show, Sammy Davis Jr.	5–10
	July 16–22	#694	My Three Sons' Fred MacMurray and William Demarest cover, Voyage to the Bottom of the Sea's David Hedison, The Fugitive	5–10
	July 23–29	#695	The F.B.I. cover, Laredo, The Munsters	5–10

YEAR	ISSUE	NUMBER	DESCRIPTION	VALUE
1966	July 30	#696	Johnny Carson cover, The Beatles, Bette Davis	$ 5–10
	August 6–12	#697	Daktari cover, Bonanza's Pernell Roberts, The Wild, Wild West	5–10
	August 13–19	#698	F-Troop's Larry Storch cover, TV game shows, Fess Parker	5–10
	August 20–26	#699	Red Skelton cover, TV nostalgia, Robert Goulet	2–4
	August 27	#700	Get Smart cast cover, The Dating Game, The Beverly Hillbillies	10–20
	September 3–9	#701	Green Acres' Eva Gabor cover, Jack Jones, Alan Arkin	5–10
	September 10–16	#702	Fall Preview special, Star Trek	30–60
	September 17–23	#703	Joey Heatherton cover, Boris Karloff, The Girl from U.N.C.L.E.'s Stefanie Powers	5–10
	September 24–30	#704	I Dream of Jeannie's Barbara Eden cover, Lost in Space's Guy Williams, The Tijuana Brass	25–50
	October 1–7	#705	The Vietnam War cover and special, Family Affair	5–10

YEAR	ISSUE	NUMBER	DESCRIPTION	VALUE
1966	October 8–14	#706	Gomer Pyle's Jim Nabors cover, The Virginian, That Girl's Marlo Thomas	$ 5–10
	October 15–21	#707	Love on a Rooftop's Judy Carne cover, Red Skelton, Vincent Price, Star Trek's William Shatner: "No one ever upsets the star"	15–30
	October 22–28	#708	Lucille Ball in London cover and special, Bewitched, Bozo the Clown	5–10
	October 29	#709	Green Hornet cast cover, The Time Tunnel	35–75
	November 5–11	#710	The Man from U.N.C.L.E. cast cover, The Bell Telephone Hour	15–30
	November 12–18	#711	That Girl's Marlo Thomas cover, Gene Arthur, Mission Impossible, Roger Miller	2–4
	November 19–25	#712	Hogan's Heroes cover, The Monkees, Merv Griffin	10–20
	November 26	#713	Tarzan's Ron Ely cover, Frank Sinatra	2–4

YEAR	ISSUE	NUMBER	DESCRIPTION	VALUE
1966	December 3–9	#714	Rat Patrol cast cover, Dark Shadows	$15–30
	December 10–16	#715	Gunsmoke's James Arness cover, Mickey Rooney, Milton Berle, The Rat Patrol	4–8
	December 17–23	#716	Occasional Wife cover, Tina Louise, The Girl from U.N.C.L.E., David Carradine	4–8
	December 24–30	#717	Christmas issue special, Linda Evans in 1976, Pistols and Petticoats, The Wild, Wild West's Robert Conrad, Disney	7–15
	December 31	#718	The Girl from U.N.C.L.E.'s Stefanie Powers cover, Larry Hagman	10–20
1967	January 7–13	#719	Run for Your Life's Ben Gazzara cover, The Avengers' Diana Rigg, Love on a Rooftop	5–10
	January 14–20	#720	Art Carney cover, Dom DeLuise, Pistols and Petticoats	2–4

YEAR	ISSUE	NUMBER	DESCRIPTION	VALUE
1967	January 21–27	#721	The Avengers' Diana Rigg and Patrick Macnee cover, Petula Clark, The Iron Horse	$20–40
	January 28	#722	The Monkees cover, Jackie Gleason	15–30
	February 4–10	#723	The Iron Horse's Dale Robertson cover, Candid Camera, Lauren Bacall, Captain Nice	2–4
	February 11–17	#724	Mission Impossible's Barbara Bain and Martin Landau cover, Mr. Terrific, Captain Nice, TV cartoons, Batman, The Girl from U.N.C.L.E.	10–20
	February 18–24	#725	Dean Martin cover, Lana Wood, Diahann Carroll, The Invaders	4–8
	February 25	#726	Phyllis Diller cover, Laredo, Alan King	2–4
	March 4–10	#727	Star Trek's William Shatner and Leonard Nimoy cover, The Road West, Ingrid Bergman	25–50+

YEAR	ISSUE	NUMBER	DESCRIPTION	VALUE
1967	March 11–17	#728	Dorothy Malone cover, The Girl from U.N.C.L.E.'s Noel Harrison, Jane Fonda, Daniel Boone	$ 4–8
	March 18–24	#729	Jackie Gleason cover, Sea Hunt, Dragnet	4–8
	March 25–31	#730	I Spy's Robert Culp and Bill Cosby cover, Star Trek, Batman's Robin, The Boy Wonder	10–20
	April 1–7	#731	Daktari cover, Rango's Tim Conway, T.H.E. Cat	2–4
	April 8–14	#732	Dick Van Dyke cover, The Girl from U.N.C.L.E., Phil Silvers	3–6
	April 15–21	#733	The Starlet 1967 cover and special, The Beverly Hillbillies' Irene Ryan, The Felony Squad	3–6
	April 22–28	#734	Family Affair cast cover, Lucille Ball, Tijuana Brass, Smothers Brothers	5–10
	April 29	#735	Lawrence Welk cover, Star Trek's Mr. Spock, The Avengers	10–20

YEAR	ISSUE	NUMBER	DESCRIPTION	VALUE
1967	May 6–12	#736	Dragnet's Jack Webb and Harry Morgan cover, Jack Banner	$ 3–6
	May 13–19	#737	Bewitched's Elizabeth Montgomery cover, Greg Morris	5–10
	May 21–26	#738	Andy Griffith cover, Gilligan's Island's Dawn Wells	4–8
	May 27	#739	F-Troop cast cover, T.H.E. Cat, Mr. Terrific	5–10
	June 3–9	#740	The Felony Squad's Howard Duff cover, The Emmy Awards, Vic Damone	2–4
	June 10–16	#741	The Smothers Brothers cover, The Avengers' Diana Rigg and the Emma Peeler, The Time Tunnel	10–20
	June 17–23	#742	Ed Sullivan cover, Tim Conway, What's My Line's last show	2–4
	June 24–30	#743	Get Smart's Barbara Feldon and Don Adams cover, Disney	10–20

YEAR	ISSUE	NUMBER	DESCRIPTION	VALUE
1967	July 1–7	#744	David Brinkley and Chet Huntley cover, The Man from U.N.C.L.E., Elizabeth Taylor and Richard Burton	$ 4–8
	July 8–14	#745	The F.B.I. cover, Michael Dunn	2–4
	July 15–21	#746	Lucille Ball cover, Star Trek	10–20
	July 22–28	#747	Bonanza cast cover, The Rat Patrol, Lost in Space	17–35
	July 29	#748	The Rat Patrol cast cover, Steve Allen	10–20
	August 5–11	#749	Today's Barbara Walters cover, The Saint's Roger Moore, Hogan's Heroes	5–10
	August 12–18	#750	Mike Douglas cover, Coronet Blue, George Carlin	2–4
	August 19–25	#751	The Fugitive's David Janssen and Barry Morse cover and special . . . The Fugitive Stops Running	12–25
	August 26	#752	Gomer Pyle's Jim Nabors cover, Lee Remick, Get Smart, Dark Shadows	5–10

YEAR	ISSUE	NUMBER	DESCRIPTION	VALUE
1967	September 2–8	#753	Green Acres's Eva Gabor and Eddie Albert cover, Tarzan's Ron Ely	$ 5–10
	September 9–15	#754	Fall Preview special, Star Trek	25–50
	September 16–22	#755	Ironside's Raymond Burr cover, Claire Bloom, The Beverly Hillbillies, Tarzan	3–6
	September 23–29	#756	The Monkees cover, I Dream of Jeannie's Barbara Eden, Rock Hudson	12–25
	September 30	#757	The Flying Nun's Sally Field cover, The Time Tunnel, The Man from U.N.C.L.E.	10–20
	October 7–13	#758	He and She's Jack Cassidy cover, Cimmaron Strip, Marlo Thomas	2–4
	October 14–20	#759	Johnny Carson cover, Star Trek's androids, Daktari	10–20
	October 21–27	#760	Mia Farrow cover, Don Knotts, The High Chaparral	2–4
	October 28	#761	Who Killed Hollywood special, John Wayne, Henry Fonda, Paula Prentiss, Carol Burnett	2–4

YEAR	ISSUE	NUMBER	DESCRIPTION	VALUE
1967	November 4–10	#762	Cimmaron Strip cover, Batman's Batgirl . . . Yvonne Craig	$10–20
	November 11–17	#763	Yvette Mimieux cover, TV specials, Mothers-in-law, Harry Reasoner	3–6
	November 18–24	#764	Star Trek's William Shatner and Leonard Nimoy cover, Ironside, Hippies	25–50+
	November 25	#765	Garrison's Gorillas cover, Mel Blanc, Who Killed Hollywood	10–20
	December 2–8	#766	Danny and Marlo Thomas cover, Barbara Stanwyck, Jack Paar	2–4
	December 9–15	#767	The Mothers-in-law's Eve Arden cover, Gomer Pyle's Frank Sutton, Carol Burnett	2–4
	December 16–22	#768	Sebastian Cabot cover, Pat Paulsen, Ed McMahon	2–4
	December 23–29	#769	Christmas issue special, Bonanza, Hogan's Heroes's Richard Dawson	4–8

YEAR	ISSUE	NUMBER	DESCRIPTION	VALUE
1967	December 30	#770	Carol Burnett cover, Lynn Redgrave, Cousteau	$ 2–4
1968	January 6–12	#771	The Wild, Wild West's Robert Conrad cover	15–30
	January 13–19	#772	Bob Hope cover, Marlo Thomas, Mannix, The High Chaparral	2–4
	January 20–26	#773	High Chaparral cover, Garrison's Gorillas, Mission Impossible	5–10
	January 27	#774	Bewitched's Elizabeth Montgomery cover, Cowboy in Africa's Chuck Connors	7–15
	February 3–9	#775	Run for Your Life's Ben Gazzara cover, N.Y.P.D., Winter Olympics	2–4
	February 10–16	#776	The Smothers Brothers cover	2–4
	February 17–23	#777	The F.B.I. Cover, My Three Sons, Jonathan Winters	2–4
	February 24	#778	Joey Bishop cover, It Takes a Thief, The Man from U.N.C.L.E.'s Robert Vaughn	3–6

YEAR	ISSUE	NUMBER	DESCRIPTION	VALUE
1968	March 2–8	#779	Bonanza's Lorne Greene and David Canary cover, The Avengers, The Newlywed Game	$ 7–15
	March 9–15	#780	Jackie Gleason cover, Lucille Ball, The Dating Game, Jack Benny	3–6
	March 16–22	#781	The Flying Nun's Sally Field cover, Don Rickles, Bill Cosby, Mannix	10–20
	March 23–29	#782	I Spy's Robert Culp and Bill Cosby, Zsa Zsa Gabor, Laugh-In, Petticoat Junction	7–15
	March 30	#783	Lucille Ball cover, Ed Ames, Walter Brennan	2–4
	April 6–12	#784	Ironside cover, Daktari, Tarzan	2–4
	April 13–19	#785	Carl Betz cover, Angie Dickinson photos	2–4
	April 20–26	#786	Get Smart's Barbara Feldon cover, The Jerry Lewis Show, Beverly Hillbillies' Irene Ryan	10–20
	April 27	#787	Leslie Uggams cover, The High Chaparral's Cameron Mitchell	2–4

YEAR	ISSUE	NUMBER	DESCRIPTION	VALUE
1968	May 4–10	#788	Mission Impossible cast cover, Vicki Lawrence	$ 5–10
	May 11–17	#789	Daniel Boone's Fess Parker cover, Dragnet	2–4
	May 18–24	#790	Mannix's Mike Connors cover, Lucille Ball, Vivian Vance	2–4
	May 25–31	#791	Peyton Place's Diana Hyland cover, Raquel Welch, The Prisoner	7–15
	June 1–7	#792	Ed Sullivan cover, Richard Burton and Elizabeth Taylor, The Wild, Wild West	5–10
	June 8–14	#793	Hugh Downs cover, Salvador Dali on TV	2–4
	June 15–21	#794	High Chaparral cover, Glen Campbell, Abby Dalton	3–6
	June 22–28	#795	Toni Helfer cover, Star Trek's William Shatner	12–25
	June 29	#796	It Takes a Thief's Robert Wagner cover, Goldie Hawn, Gunsmoke	5–10
	July 6–12	#797	I Dream of Jeannie's Barbara Eden cover, Johnny Carson	10–20

#774, 1968

#783, 1968

#788, 1968

#790, 1968

#799, 1968

#808, 1968

#809, 1968

#818, 1968

#832, 1969

YEAR	ISSUE	NUMBER	DESCRIPTION	VALUE
1968	July 13–19	#798	Andy Griffith, Don Knotts and Jim Nabors cover, Hawaii Five-O	$ 5–10
	July 20–26	#799	The Big Valley cast cover, Laugh-In's Kaye Ballard, Andy Griffith	10–20
	July 27	#800	Frank Sinatra Jr. and Joey Heatherton cover, Cher, Dom DeLuise	5–10
	August 3–9	#801	TV Anchormen cover, Hogan's Heroes's Bob Crane, The Avengers's Diana Rigg	5–10
	August 10–16	#802	Gentle Ben cast cover, Mannix, Joan Rivers	3–6
	August 17–23	#803	Gunsmoke cast cover, Frank Gifford, Merv Griffin	5–10
	August 24–30	#804	Star Trek cast cover, Edd Byrnes, Clint Eastwood	25–50+
	August 31	#805	Johnny Carson cover, The Prisoner	5–10
	September 7–13	#806	Family Affair cast cover	5–10
	September 14–20	#807	Fall Preview special	20–40

YEAR	ISSUE	NUMBER	DESCRIPTION	VALUE
1968	September 21–27	#808	Laugh-In's Rowan and Martin cover, Art Carney, Anthony Quinn	$ 5–10
	September 28	#809	Dean Martin cover, Peyton Place, Lee Marvin	2–4
	October 5–11	#810	My Three Sons cast cover, Dragnet, Carol Burnett, The Mod Squad	5–10
	October 12–18	#811	Olympics cover, Tiny Tim, Raymond Burr, TV monsters	5–10
	October 19–25	#812	Jim Nabors cover, Charlie Brown, The Ghost and Mrs. Muir, Mannix, Dragnet	3–6
	October 26	#813	The Ghost and Mrs. Muir's Hope Lange, Gomer Pyle, Jay Silverheels	5–10
	November 2–8	#814	The Mod Squad cover, Jackie Gleason, The High Chaparral	7–15
	November 9–15	#815	Special Get Smart wedding cover and feature, Johnny Carson, James Garner	12–25
	November 16–22	#816	The Good Guys cast cover, Patrick Macnee	5–10

YEAR	ISSUE	NUMBER	DESCRIPTION	VALUE
1968	November 23–29	#817	Frank Sinatra cover, Woody Allen, Peggy Fleming	$ 3–6
	November 30	#818	Ann-Margret cover, Brigitte Bardot, Elvis Presley	5–10
	December 7–13	#819	That's Life cover, Diana Ross, Hawaii Five-O	5–10
	December 14–20	#820	Diahann Carroll cover, Green Acres's Arnold the Pig, John Wayne, Adam 12	5–10
	December 21–27	#821	Christmas issue special, Mayberry R.F.D., Walt Disney's Mickey Mouse	5–10
	December 28	#822	Doris Day cover, Michael Caine	3–6
1969	January 4–10	#823	Here Come the Brides's Bobby Sherman and cast cover, Hawaii Five-O	10–20
	January 11–17	#824	Bob Hope cover, Cousteau, Peyton Place	2–4
	January 18–24	#825	The Outsider's Darren McGavin cover, The Prisoner, The Land of the Giants	10–20

#840, 1969

#856, 1969

#865, 1969

#883, 1971

#953, 1971

#963, 1971

#501, 1972

#539, 1973

#543, 1973

YEAR	ISSUE	NUMBER	DESCRIPTION	VALUE
1969	January 25–31	#826	Land of the Giants cast cover, 60 Minutes, Judy Carne	$20–40+
	February 1–7	#827	High Chaparral cover, David McCallum, Dark Shadows	5–10
	February 8–14	#828	Mission Impossible cast cover, Stella Stevens	7–15
	February 15–21	#829	Ironside's Raymond Burr cover, Land of the Giants, Jimmy Durante	5–10
	February 22–28	#830	Lancer cast cover, Land of the Giants	5–10
	March 1–7	#831	Lucille Ball and her children cover, The Outcasts, Dean Martin	3–6
	March 8–14	#832	Laugh-In cast cover, Jonathan Winters	5–10
	March 15–21	#833	Mayberry R.F.D. cover, Tom Jones, Hawaii Five-O, Lancer	5–10
	March 22–28	#834	Bewitched's Elizabeth Montgomery cover, Isaac Asimov, Mission Impossible	10–20

YEAR	ISSUE	NUMBER	DESCRIPTION	VALUE
1969	March 29	#835	The Name of the Game cast cover, Get Smart's Don Adams, The Felony Squad	$ 5–10
	April 5–11	#836	The Smothers Brothers cover, Kate Smith, I Dream of Jeannie	5–10
	April 12–18	#837	Mary Tyler Moore cover, Dick Van Dyke, Goldie Hawn	5–10
	April 19–25	#838	Lawrence Welk cover, Joan Blondell, The Beatles	3–6
	April 26	#839	Jack Paar cover, Pierre Salinger, The F.B.I.	2–4
	May 3–9	#840	The Flying Nun's Sally Field cover, Ray Bradbury	10–20
	May 10–16	#841	Space special, Richard Chamberlain	2–4
	May 17–23	#842	Marlo Thomas cover, Wayne Newton, Pogo, The Ghost and Mrs. Muir	3–6
	May 24–30	#843	Today cast cover, Tom Jones, Mayberry R.F.D.	2–4
	May 31	#844	Family Affair cast cover, Walter Brennan	5–10

YEAR	ISSUE	NUMBER	DESCRIPTION	VALUE
1969	June 7–13	#845	The Hollywood Dancers cover, Robert Mitchum	$ 2–4
	June 14–20	#846	Glen Campbell cover, Playboy After Dark, Green Acres	5–10
	June 21–27	#847	Jackie Gleason cover, TV's soap As the World Turns	3–6
	June 28	#848	Julia cast cover, Joyce Van Patten	3–6
	July 5–11	#849	Adam 12 cast cover, Rosemary DeCamp, That Girl	5–10
	July 12–18	#850	Mod Squad cast cover, Petticoat Junction, Frank Sinatra	7–15
	July 19–25	#851	Apollo 11 cover and special moon telecast, Paul Lynde	4–8
	July 26	#852	Petticoat Junction cast cover, Carol Burnett, Lucille Ball	7–15
	August 2–8	#853	Lancer cover, Mission Impossible's Peter Graves, Laugh-In's Ruth Buzzi	4–8
	August 9–15	#854	Sports cover and feature, The Mod Squad's Peggy Lipton, Liberace, Don Murray	5–10

YEAR	ISSUE	NUMBER	DESCRIPTION	VALUE
1969	August 16–22	#855	Merv Griffin cover, Night Gallery, Robert Culp	$ 5–10
	August 23–29	#856	High Chaparral cover, The Beverly Hillbillies, Lassie	5–10
	August 30	#857	Johnny Cash cover, Bing Crosby, Lassie, Milton Berle	3–6
	September 6–12	#858	Green Acres cover, The King Family	5–10
	September 13–19	#859	Fall issue special	15–30
	September 20–26	#860	Jim Nabors cover, Room 222, Lassie	3–6
	September 27	#861	Marcus Welby, M.D. cover, Gina Lollobrigida	3–6
	October 4–10	#862	Bill Cosby cover, Sesame Street, Bill Bixby	2–4
	October 11–17	#863	TV and children special issue, Buddy Ebsen, Then Came Bronson	2–4
	October 18–24	#864	Mission Impossible cast cover, Richard Burton	5–10
	October 25–31	#865	My World and Welcome to It cover, Walt Disney, Land of the Giants, Room 222	5–10

YEAR	ISSUE	NUMBER	DESCRIPTION	VALUE
1969	November 1–7	#866	Room 222 cast cover, Marcus Welby, Ann-Margret	$ 3–6
	November 8–14	#867	Andy Williams cover, Leslie Uggams, Bill Cosby	2–4
	November 15–21	#868	The Governor and J.J. cover, Star Trek's William Shatner	5–10
	November 22–28	#869	I Dream of Jeannie special marriage issue . . . Barbara Eden on cover wearing wedding gown, Medical Center, The Mod Squad	10–20
	November 29	#870	Bonanza cast cover, The Ghost and Mrs. Muir	10–20
	December 6–12	#871	Doris Day cover, Bracken's World, Mission Impossible	3–6
	December 13–19	#872	Then Came Bronson cover, David Frost, Simon and Garfunkel	3–6
	December 20–26	#873	Christmas issue special, The Courtship of Eddie's Father, Julia	3–6

YEAR	ISSUE	NUMBER	DESCRIPTION	VALUE
1969	December 27	#874	Remembering 1969 special issue, The Avengers's Diana Rigg, Adam 12	$5–10
1970	January 3–9	#875	TV in the 'Seventies special issue, My World and Welcome to It	3–6
	January 10–16	#876	My Three Sons cover, Susan Saint James, Henry Fonda, Land of the Giants	5–10
	January 17–23	#877	Ironside cover, Flip Wilson, Jack Benny	2–4
	January 24–30	#878	Tom Jones cover, Bette Davis, Ricardo Montalban	2–4
	January 31	#879	Debbie Reynolds cover, John Wayne, The Bold Ones, Room 222	2–4
	February 7–13	#880	Bewitched cover, The Brady Bunch, Bobby Sherman	7–15
	February 14–20	#881	Bracken's Girls cover, Soap operas, Dick Clark, John Wayne	2–4
	February 21–27	#882	Medical Center cast cover, Hee Haw, Room 222	2–4

YEAR	ISSUE	NUMBER	DESCRIPTION	VALUE
1970	February 28	#883	Mod Squad cost cover, Jimmy Durante, Engelbert Humperdinck	$ 5–10
	March 7–13	#884	Hee Haw cover, Pat Paulsen	2–4
	March 14–20	#885	Diahann Carroll cover, Tim Conway, Oz	2–4
	March 21–27	#886	Jackie Gleason cover, Ringo Starr, Bill Cosby, Harry Belafonte and Lena Horne	2–4
	March 28	#887	Rowan and Martin cover, Ringo on Laugh-In	2–4
	April 4–10	#888	The Brady Bunch cast cover, Laugh-In, Green Acres	10–20
	April 11–17	#889	Carol Burnett cover, Robert Wagner, Fred Astaire	2–4
	April 18–24	#890	The Bold Ones cover, Burl Ives, Lawrence Welk, Art Linkletter, Dean Martin	2–4
	April 25	#891	John Wayne and Raquel Welch cover and special, Leonard Nimoy, Terry-Thomas	5–10
	May 2–8	#892	Glen Campbell cover, Love American Style, The Nelsons, Isaac Asimov	2–4

YEAR	ISSUE	NUMBER	DESCRIPTION	VALUE
1970	May 9–15	#893	David Frost cover, The Avengers's Diana Rigg, Robert Vaughn	$5–10
	May 16–22	#894	Vice President Agnew cover, James Stewart, Muppets	2–4
	May 23–29	#895	Tricia Nixon cover and her tour of the White House special with Mike Wallace, The Lennon Sisters, Liberace, Lancer	2–4
	May 30	#896	The Governor and J.J. cover, The Forsythe Saga	2–4
	June 6–12	#897	Robert Young cover, Doc Severinsen, Captain Kangaroo	2–4
	June 13–19	#898	Johnny Cash cover, The Forsythe Saga, Laugh-In	3–6
	June 20–26	#899	To Rome with Love cover, The Lone Ranger, Room 222	2–4
	June 27	#900	Liza Minnelli cover and special, The Hollywood Squares	2–4
	July 4–10	#901	The Courtship of Eddie's Father cover, Bill Bixby, Carol Burnett	2–4

YEAR	ISSUE	NUMBER	DESCRIPTION	VALUE
1970	July 11–17	#902	The Beverly Hillbillies cover, Sesame Street, Bewitched	$ 5–10
	July 18–24	#903	The Golddiggers cover, Peter Graves, Gunsmoke's James Arness	5–10
	July 25–31	#904	Mayberry R.F.D. cast cover, Juliet Mills, Love American Style	2–4
	August 1–7	#905	Chet Huntley cover, The Odd Couple, Laugh-In	2–4
	August 8–14	#906	That Girl cover, Hogan's Heroes	2–4
	August 15–21	#907	Johnny Carson cover, Female stars, General Hospital	2–4
	August 22–28	#908	Gunsmoke cover, Jo Anne Worley, Mae West	3–6
	August 29	#909	Green Acres's Eddie Albert cover, Barefoot in the Park, Joel Grey	5–10
	September 5–11	#910	Lucille Ball and Liz Taylor cover, Miss America	10–20
	September 12–18	#911	Fall issue special	7–15
	September 19–25	#912	Mary Tyler Moore cover, The Young Lawyers, Chad Everett	3–6

YEAR	ISSUE	NUMBER	DESCRIPTION	VALUE
1970	September 26	#913	Room 222 cast cover, The Partridge Family	$ 5–10
	October 3–9	#914	Red Skelton cover, Lesley Ann Warren, Dinah Shore	2–4
	October 10–16	#915	Arnie cover, Anne Francis, Flip Wilson	2–4
	October 17–23	#916	The Partridge Family cover, Arnie	10–20
	October 24–30	#917	Don Knotts cover, Hee Haw, Tim Conway	2–4
	October 31	#918	Mannix cover, Robert Stack, Dark Shadows	5–10
	November 7–13	#919	Nancy cast cover, Buck Owens	2–4
	November 14–20	#920	The Immortals cover, Christopher George, Lily Tomlin, The Odd Couple	2–4
	November 21–27	#921	Sally Marr cover, The Cisco Kid, Laugh-In	2–4
	November 28	#922	John Wayne cover and special, Yvette Mimeux	5–10
	December 5–11	#923	Dick Cavett cover, John Wayne, Mannix	3–6

YEAR	ISSUE	NUMBER	DESCRIPTION	VALUE
1970	December 12–18	#924	Ed Sullivan and the Muppets cover, McCloud, The Mary Tyler Moore Show	$ 3–6
	December 19–25	#925	Christmas issue special, Stewart Granger, Green Acres's Eva Gabor	2–4
	December 26	#926	Julia cast cover, Yvette Mimieux, The Interns	3–6
1971	January 2–8	#927	Remember 1970 special, The Odd Couple's Tony Randall, The Partridge Family	5–10
	January 9–15	#928	Andy Griffith cover, Pinky Lee	2–4
	January 16–22	#929	Johnny Cash and June Carter cover, Make Room for Daddy, Green Acres's Arnold the Pig	2–4
	January 23–29	#930	Flip Wilson cover, Lassie, Dark Shadows	5–10
	January 30	#931	Gunsmoke's James Arness cover, Loretta Swit	3–6
	February 6–12	#932	The Odd Couple cover and feature	4–8
	February 13–19	#933	Goldie Hawn cover, The Immortals	3–6

YEAR	ISSUE	NUMBER	DESCRIPTION	VALUE
1971	February 20–26	#934	Doris Day cover, The Interns, Hawaii Five-O, Carol Burnett	$ 2–4
	February 27	#935	Hal Holbrook cover, All in the Family	2–4
	March 6–12	#936	The Interns's Broderick Crawford cover, Alias Smith and Jones, Dinah Shore	5–10
	March 13–19	#937	The Name of the Game cover, Secret Storm	2–4
	March 20–26	#938	Harry Reasoner cover, The Interns, George C. Scott	2–4
	March 27	#939	Bonanza cast cover, The Partridge Family, Pearl Bailey	5–10
	April 3–9	#940	Cable TV special feature, Lee Meriwether, Firing Line	2–4
	April 10–16	#941	Bob Hope cover, Merv Griffin	2–4
	April 17–23	#942	Paul Newman cover, The Young Lawyers, Allan Sherman	2–4
	April 24–30	#943	Marcus Welby, M.D. cover, Mission Impossible, Lesley Ann Warren, The Beverly Hillbillies	3–6

YEAR	ISSUE	NUMBER	DESCRIPTION	VALUE
1971	May 1–7	#944	Mary Tyler Moore cover, Lloyd Bridges, Tony Randall	$ 4–8
	May 8–14	#945	Henry Fonda cover, The Smith Family, High Chaparral	2–4
	May 15–21	#946	TV Journalism special, Alias Smith and Jones's Peter Duel	10–20
	May 22–28	#947	The Partridge Family's David Cassidy cover and feature . . . David's Teenage World, The Mary Tyler Moore Show's Ed Asner, Stiller and Meara	10–20
	May 29	#948	All in the Family cast cover, James Komack, American TV in China	5–10
	June 5–11	#949	Rowan and Martin cover, All My Children, Isaac Asimov	2–4
	June 12–18	#950	Lucille Ball cover, The Hollywood Squares	2–4
	June 19–25	#951	The Courtship of Eddie's Father cover, Dark Shadows	5–10

YEAR	ISSUE	NUMBER	DESCRIPTION	VALUE
1971	June 26	#952	Adam 12 cover, Christine Crawford, Annie, Laugh-In	$ 2–4
	July 3–9	#953	The Mod Squad cast cover, Old-time radio	10–20
	July 10–16	#954	Sesame Street's Cookie Monster cover, All in the Family's Sally Struthers, Mel Torme	3–6
	July 17–23	#955	Medical Center's Chad Everett cover, Dick Cavett	2–4
	July 24–30	#956	Walt Disney's Dingaling Lynx cover, Arthur Fiedler	2–4
	July 31	#957	Henry the VIII on TV cover and special, Mr. Ed's Alan Young	3–6
	August 7–13	#958	As the World Turns cast cover, Mary Tyler Moore Show's Ted Knight, Gene Wilder	2–4
	August 14–20	#959	Bonanza cover, The Carpenters, Bewitched	5–10
	Augut 21–27	#960	Henry Fonda cover, Public TV, Connie Stevens, The Mod Squad	3–6

YEAR	ISSUE	NUMBER	DESCRIPTION	VALUE
1971	August 28	#961	Announcers of Monday Night Football cover, Walter Cronkite	$ 2–4
	September 4–10	#962	Hawaii Five-O's Jack Lord cover, Robert Morley, Ed Sullivan	7–15
	September 11–17	#963	Fall Preview special	5–10
	September 18–24	#964	Sandy Duncan cover, Funny Face, Bearcats, Howdy Doody	3–6
	September 25	#965	Shirley MacLaine cover, Richard Boone, Cher	2–4
	October 2–8	#966	James Stewart cover, Mission Impossible's Barbara Bain, Rex Humbard	3–6
	October 9–15	#967	Dick Van Dyke and Hope Lange cover, Bonanza, Sandy Duncan	3–6
	October 16–22	#968	Mia Farrow cover and special . . . Then and Now, John Wayne, Sesame Street, The Partridge Family, Gidget	5–10
	October 23–29	#969	Longstreet's James Franciscus cover, Rod Taylor, Bearcats, Lynda Day George	2–4

YEAR	ISSUE	NUMBER	DESCRIPTION	VALUE
1971	October 30	#970	The Good Life's Larry Hagman cover, Glen Campbell, Longstreet	$ 2–4
	November 6–12	#971	Cannon's William Conrad cover, Anthony Eisley	2–4
	November 13–19	#972	The Partners's Don Adams cover, Sue Ane Langdon, Ann-Margret	2–4
	November 20–26	#973	All in the Family cast cover, Funny Face, Nichols	5–10
	November 27	#974	Joanne Woodward cover, Modern-day monster makers, Night Gallery	5–10
	December 4–10	#975	Special issue ... John Wayne, Bob Hope, Julie Andrews and Carol Burnett cover and feature, Dick Van Dyke, George Kennedy	3–6
	December 11–17	#976	James Garner cover, Hope Lange, Cannon, TV wrestling	3–6
	December 18–24	#977	The Partridge Family cast cover, Patricia Neal, McCloud	10–20

YEAR	ISSUE	NUMBER	DESCRIPTION	VALUE
1971	December 25–31	#978	Christmas issue special, Bobby Sherman, Lucille Ball	$ 3–6
1972	January 1–7	#979	1971 Remembered, McMillan and Wife	2–4
	January 8–14	#980	Flip Wilson cover, McMillan and Wife	1–3
	January 15–21	#981	European TV, John Wayne, Bette Davis	1–3
	January 22–28	#982	Mission Impossible cast cover, Nichols, Raymond Burr	4–8
	January 29	#983	David Janssen cover, Columbo	1–3
	February 5–11	#984	Ironside's cast cover, Buddy Ebsen, Night Gallery	4–8
	February 12–18	#985	Owen Marshall cover, Attorney At Law, Marilyn Monroe, Sonny and Cher	3–6
	February 19–25	#986	TV Journalism special, Alias Smith and Jones, Don Rickles	5–10
	February 26	#987	Mary Tyler Moore cover, Susan Hayward, Sanford and Son	4–8

YEAR	ISSUE	NUMBER	DESCRIPTION	VALUE
1972	March 4–10	#988	Johnny Carson cover, Vera Miles, Alex Karras	$ 1–3
	March 11–17	#989	Marcus Welby M.D. cast cover, Morris the Cat	1–3
	March 18–24	#990	Sonny and Cher cover, Gunsmoke, James Garner	5–10
	March 25–31	#991	Columbo's Peter Falk cover, Star Trek	5–10
	April 1–7	#992	Glenn Ford cover, Julie Adams, Emergency	1–3
	April 8–14	#993	TV Political Coverage special, Jerry Lewis, Roger Moore, The Story of the Oscar	1–3
	April 15–21	#994	Moon Spectacular special, All in the Family's Rob Reiner, David Frost	2–4
	April 22–28	#995	Don Rickles cover, Hope Lange, The Muppets, Hank Aaron	2–4

Note: April 29–May 5 issue begins *TV Guide's* change in issue numbering.

	April 29	#496 (#996)	McMillan and Wife cover, Longstreet, TV's Golddiggers	2–4

YEAR	ISSUE	NUMBER	DESCRIPTION	VALUE
1972	May 6–12	#497 (#997)	Funny Face's Sandy Duncan cover, Peter Marshall, General Hospital	$ 1–3
	May 13–19	#498 (#998)	Sanford and Son cover, Janet Blair, Jennifer O'Neill	3–6
	May 20–26	#499 (#999)	F.B.I cover, Brenda Vaccaro, Gary Collins	1–3
	May 27	#500 (#1000)	All in the Family cast cover, The future of Bonanza, Lloyd Bridges	5–10
	June 3–9	#501 (#1001)	Night Gallery's Rod Serling cover, Ruth Buzzi, Carroll O'Connor	10–20
	June 10–16	#502 (#1002)	Doris Day cover, Susan Hampshire, Lassie, Mel Blanc, Dr. Who	2–4
	June 17–23	#503 (#1003)	Emergency's Julie London cover, Melba Moore, Marty Feldman	2–4
	June 24–30	#504 (#1004)	Mannix's Mike Connors cover, Sherry Bain, Mary Tyler Moore	2–4
	July 1–7	#505 (#1005)	Carol Burnett cover, Room 222	2–4
	July 8–14	#506 (#1006)	Merv Griffin cover, Susan Sullivan, Lucille Ball	2–4

YEAR	ISSUE	NUMBER	DESCRIPTION	VALUE
1972	July 15–21	#507 (#1007)	The Partridge Family's David Cassidy cover, Curt Gowdy, British TV	$10–20
	July 22–28	#508 (#1008)	Adam 12 cast cover, Phil Donahue	2–5
	July 29	#509 (#1009)	Love American Style cover, Emergency, Sandy Duncan	2–4
	August 5–11	#510 (#1010)	War and Peace on TV special, William Shatner, David Steinberg	5–10
	August 12–18	#511 (#1011)	Leonardo da Vinci TV special, Alan King	1–3
	August 19–25	#512 (#1012)	Medical Center's Chad Everett cover, As the World Turns	1–3
	August 26	#513 (#1013)	Olympics issue special, Bobby Darin	2–4
	September 2–8	#514 (#1014)	The Odd Couple cover, Liza Minnelli, David Niven	5–10
	September 9–15	#515 (#1015)	Fall Preview special	10–20
	September 16–22	#516 (#1016)	Yul Brynner, The King and I cover, Laugh-In, Goldie Hawn	2–4

YEAR	ISSUE	NUMBER	DESCRIPTION	VALUE
1972	September 23–29	#517 (#1017)	Banacek's George Peppard cover, Ed McMahon, Dr. Joyce Brothers	$ 1–3
	September 30	#518 (#1018)	Bridget Loves Bernie cover, Doctor in the House, Bill Cosby	2–4
	October 7–13	#519 (#1019)	Bonanza cast cover, Mission Impossible, Groucho Marx	7–15
	October 14–20	#520 (#1020)	Assignment Vienna's Robert Conrad cover, The Protectors, The Mod Squad	5–10
	October 21–27	#521 (#1021)	Carroll O'Connor and Cloris Leachman in Of Thee I Sing cover and special, Lee Majors, The Rookies	2–4
	October 28	#522 (#1022)	Charlie Brown cover and special, Julie Andrews, Jacqueline Scot	5–10
	November 4–10	#523 (#1023)	John Wayne cover, The Little People, President Richard Nixon	2–4
	November 11–17	#524 (#1024)	America's Alistair Cooke cover, Patton, David Carradine	2–4

YEAR	ISSUE	NUMBER	DESCRIPTION	VALUE
1972	November 18–24	#525 (#1025)	Maude's Bea Arthur cover, James Caan, The Waltons, Henry Mancini	$ 2–4
	November 25	#526 (#1026)	Search cast cover, Orson Welles, Lassie, Paul Lynde	1–3
	December 2–8	#527 (#1027)	Mike Douglas cover, Banacek	1–3
	December 9–15	#528 (#1028)	Julie Andrews cover, Ghost Story, Alice Cooper	5–10
	December 16–22	#529 (#1029)	The Duke and Duchess of Windsor cover and special, Bridget Loves Bernie	3–6
	December 23–29	#530 (#1030)	Christmas issue special, The Partridge Family, Gavin MacLeod	5–10
	December 30	#531 (#1031)	Barbara Walters cover, Isaac Asimov, Assignment Vienna	1–3
1973	January 6–12	#532 (#1032)	1972 Reviewed, Shelley Winters	1–3
	January 13–19	#533 (#1033)	China special, Susan Dey, Robert Vaughn	10–20
	January 20–26	#534 (#1034)	Bob Newhart Show cast cover, Dr. Kildare	4–8

YEAR	ISSUE	NUMBER	DESCRIPTION	VALUE
1973	January 27	#535 (#1035)	The Rookies cast cover, The Waltons, Mission Impossible	$ 4–8
	February 3–9	#536 (#1036)	Bill Cosby cover, Elizabeth Taylor: The Burtons, Hawaii Five-O	2–4
	February 10–16	#537 (#1037)	The Paul Lynde Show cover, Maude's Adrienne Barbeau, M.A.S.H.	5–10
	February 17–23	#538 (#1038)	McMillan and Wife's Susan Saint James and Rock Hudson cover, Diana Rigg, Larry Hagman	5–10
	February 24	#539 (#1039)	M.A.S.H. cast cover, John Wayne, Kate Jackson	5–10
	March 3–9	#540 (#1040)	Cannon's William Conrad cover, Dr. Jekyl and Mr. Hyde, Kung Fu	2–4
	March 10–16	#541 (#1041)	Marlo Thomas cover and special, Gene Wilder	2–4
	March 17–23	#542 (#1042)	Sanford and Son cover, Mission Impossible	5–10
	March 24–30	#543 (#1043)	Ann-Margret cover and special, Admiral Perry, M.A.S.H., Bette Davis	5–10

YEAR	ISSUE	NUMBER	DESCRIPTION	VALUE
1973	March 31	#544 (#1044)	Lucille Ball and Desi Arnaz Jr. cover and special	$5–10
	April 7–13	#545 (#1045)	Children's TV special, The Partridge Family, Kim Novak	5–10
	April 14–20	#546 (#1046)	The Little People's Shelley Fabares and Brian Keith cover, Barnaby Jones	5–10
	April 21–27	#547 (#1047)	Raymond Burr as Pope John cover and special, Bobby Darin	2–4
	April 28	#548 (#1048)	The Waltons cast cover, TV Western plots, Cleavon Little	5–10
	May 5–11	#549 (#1049)	Columbo's Peter Falk cover, Paul Lynde, Star Trek	5–10
	May 12–18	#550 (#1050)	Shirley Booth cover, Skylab, Peyton Place, Jayne Kennedy	1–3
	May 19–25	#551 (#1051)	Mary Tyler Moore cover, The Brady Bunch, Isaac Asimov	5–10
	May 26	#552 (#1052)	Streets of San Francisco cover, Jimmy Breslin, Kung Fu	2–4
	June 2–8	#553 (#1053)	All in the Family cover, Fannie Flagg, Mark Spitz	4–8

YEAR	ISSUE	NUMBER	DESCRIPTION	VALUE
1973	June 9–15	#554 (#1054)	Madigan's Richard Widmark cover, The Bob Newhart Show, Lee Meriwether	$ 2–4
	June 16–22	#555 (#1055)	Maude cast cover, American Bandstand, M.A.S.H.	2–4
	June 23–29	#556 (#1056)	Kung Fu's David Carradine cover, Lola Falana	10–20
	June 30	#557 (#1057)	McCloud's Dennis Weaver cover, Bridget Loves Bernie	2–4
	July 7–13	#558 (#1058)	Dick Cavett cover, Jacqueline Susann	1–2
	July 14–20	#559 (#1059)	Sonny and Cher cover, Michael Tilson-Thomas	5–10
	July 21–27	#560 (#1060)	Marcus Welby and Medical Center cover, Helen Reddy, Peter Graves	2–4
	July 28	#561 (#1061)	TV sex movies special, Monty Hall, General Hospital	2–4
	August 4–10	#562 (#1062)	Adam 12 cover, Julie Harris	2–4
	August 11–17	$563 (#1063)	Hee Haw's Roy Clark cover, Anne Meara, Hank Aaron	2–4

YEAR	ISSUE	NUMBER	DESCRIPTION	VALUE
1973	August 18–24	#564 (#1064)	Emergency's Robert Fuller cover, Bill Cosby, Mary Tyler Moore	$ 2–4
	August 25–31	#565 (#1065)	Barnaby Jones's Buddy Ebsen cover, Secret Storm	2–4
	September 1–7	#566 (#1066)	Miss America contest special, Bert Parks	1–3
	September 8–14	#567 (#1067)	Fall Preview Special	10–20

Note: Beginning with the September 15–21 issue, *TV Guide* returns to the original issue numbering.

	September 15–21	#1068	Football special	1–2
	September 22–28	#1069	Hawaii Five-O cover, Paul Winchell, Peter Pan	5–10
	September 29	#1070	Vietnam War special issue, Diana Rigg, Gunsmoke, The Waltons	5–10
	October 6–12	#1071	Diana's Diana Rigg, Wolfman Jack, Bilko	5–10
	October 13–19	#1072	TV's Limits special, Sally Field, Burt Reynolds	2–4
	October 20–26	#1073	Kojak's Telly Savalas cover, 60 Minutes, Randy Mantooth	2–4

#556, 1973   #1071, 1973   #1074, 1973

#1086, 1974   #1098, 1974   #1107, 1974

#1124, 1974   #1128, 1974   #1132, 1974

YEAR	ISSUE	NUMBER	DESCRIPTION	VALUE
1973	October 27	#1074	Adam's Rib cover, Barbra Streisand, Steve McQueen	$2–4
	November 3–9	#1075	Needles and Pins cover, Alfred Hitchcock	1–2
	November 10–16	#1076	A Week of Specials, Adam's Rib, Sammy Davis Jr.	1–2
	November 17–23	#1077	Frank Sinatra cover, Natalie Wood, My Fair Lady	2–4
	November 24–30	#1078	Cousteau cover and Antarctica special, Milton Berle, The Waltons, Frankenstein	2–4
	December 1–7	#1079	The Magician's Bill Bixby cover, Perry Mason	2–4
	December 8–14	#1080	Mary Tyler Moore cast cover, Buck Taylor, The Magician	2–4
	December 15–21	#1081	Katharine Hepburn cover, 3-D TV, Darren McGavin	2–4
	December 22–28	#1082	Christmas issue special, The Rockefellers, Susan Strasberg	2–4

YEAR	ISSUE	NUMBER	DESCRIPTION	VALUE
1973	December 29	#1083	Mason Reese cover, Miss World, The Guiding light	$ 2–4
1974	January 5–11	#1084	Reviewing 1973, Richard Chamberlain	1–3
	January 12–18	#1085	Maude cast cover	1–3
	January 19–25	#1086	Bob Hope cover, Larry Hagman	1–3
	January 26	#1087	Kung Fu's David Carradine cover, W. C. Fields, The Diary of Jane Pittman	7–15
	February 2–8	#1088	Lotsa Luck's Dom DeLuise cover, Jason Robards, The Magician, Isaac Asimov	1–3
	February 9–15	#1089	M.A.S.H. cast cover	5–10
	February 16–22	#1090	The Streets of San Francisco cast cover	2–4
	February 23	#1091	Hec Ramsey's Richard Boone cover, Gloria Swanson, Upstairs, Downstairs	1–3
	March 2–8	#1092	Hawkins's James Stewart cover, Alice Cooper, Lloyd Bridges	5–10
	March 9–15	#1093	TV news and show-biz special, Martin Sheen, Shirley Jones	4–8

YEAR	ISSUE	NUMBER	DESCRIPTION	VALUE
1974	March 16–22	#1094	Carol Burnett and Vicki Lawrence cover, The Six Million Dollar Man, Upstairs, Downstairs	$ 3–6
	March 23–29	#1095	Doc Elliot cover, Oscar Wild, Carl Sagan, Gunsmoke	1–3
	March 30	#1096	Toma cast cover, The Oscar, Happy Days	2–4
	April 6–12	#1097	Norman Lear, Redd Foxx and Carroll O'Connor cover, Good Times, Tarzan	2–4
	April 13–19	#1098	The Waltons cast cover, The Odd Couple, Sally Field	5–10
	April 20–26	#1099	Columbo's Peter Falk cover, Richard Roundtree, Isaac Asimov, Andy Griffith	2–4
	April 27	#1100	QB VII cover, Liza Minnelli	1–3
	May 4–10	#1101	The Rookies cast cover, Firehouse, Isaac Asimov	3–5
	May 11–17	#1102	The Bob Newhart Show cover, Nova	3–5
	May 18–24	#1103	The Six Million Dollar Man's Lee Majors cover, Johnny Carson	5–10

YEAR	ISSUE	NUMBER	DESCRIPTION	VALUE
1974	May 25–31	#1104	McCloud cast cover, Soul Train, Robert Morley	$ 2–4
	June 1–7	#1105	Cher and Cher cover, Carl Sagan	5–10
	June 8–14	#1106	KQED TV San Francisco cover, John Davidson, Columbo	1–3
	June 15–21	#1107	Happy Days's Ron Howard and Kathy O'Dare cover, All in the Family	4–8
	June 22–28	#1108	John Chancellor cover, Japanese TV, Nancy Walker	1–3
	June 29	#1109	Good Times cover, The Six Million Dollar Man	4–8
	July 6–12	#1110	Lucille Ball cover, Japanese TV	2–4
	July 13–19	#1111	Johnny Carson cover, Cannon, Mannix, Barnaby Jones	2–4
	July 20–26	#1112	Made-for-TV films special, Betty White, Mac Davis	1–3
	July 27	#1113	Apple's Way cover, Sherlock Holmes, Columbo	1–2
	August 3–9	#1114	Emergency cast cover, The Hudson Brothers	2–4

YEAR	ISSUE	NUMBER	DESCRIPTION	VALUE
1974	August 10–16	#1115	TV Game shows, M.A.S.H.	$ 2–4
	August 17–23	#1116	Police Story cover, Good Times, Johnny Carson	1–3
	August 24–30	#1117	Susan Blakely cover, Tom Snyder, M.A.S.H.	2–4
	August 31	#1118	Kojak's Telly Savalas cover, Evil Knievel, Henry Fonda	2–4
	September 7–13	#1119	Fall Preview special	5–10
	September 14–20	#1120	New Show winners special, Connie Stevens, O. J. Simpson	2–4
	September 21–27	#1121	Football 1974 special, Barbara Walters	1–2
	September 28	#1122	Friends and Lovers cover, Bill Cosby, Shazam	1–2
	October 5–11	#1123	Sanford and Son cover, Demond Wilson	3–6
	October 12–18	#1124	Rhoda's Valerie Harper cover, James Earl Jones, That's My Mama	3–6
	October 19–25	#1125	Chico and the Man's Freddie Prinze cover, Born Free, Robert Culp	5–10
	October 26	#1126	The Waltons cast cover, Columbo, Elvis Presley	5–10

YEAR	ISSUE	NUMBER	DESCRIPTION	VALUE
1974	November 2–8	#1127	M.A.S.H. cast cover, Clint Eastwood, Born Free, The Jeffersons	$5–10
	November 9–15	#1128	Sophia Loren cover, Lucas Tanner, Isaac Asimov	2–4
	November 16–22	#1129	The Godfather on TV special, Marlon Brando, Jodie Foster	3–5
	November 23–29	#1130	What a Week special, Chico and the Man	3–5
	November 30	#1131	Get Christie Love's Teresa Graves cover, Paul Newman, John Denver, Police Woman	3–5
	December 7–13	#1132	Little House on the Prairie's Michael Landon cover, The Planet of the Apes	5–10
	December 14–20	#1133	Good Times cast cover, Harry-O	2–4
	December 21–27	#1134	Christmas issue special, The Rockford Files	2–4
	December 28	#1135	TV Bowling special, Upstairs, Downstairs, Citizen Kane	1–2

YEAR	ISSUE	NUMBER	DESCRIPTION	VALUE
1975	January 4–10	#1136	Police Woman's Angie Dickinson cover, Richard Chamberlain, Little House on the Prairie	$5–10
	January 11–17	#1137	Harry-O's David Janssen cover, Little House on the Prairie	2–4
	January 18–24	#1138	That's My Mama cast cover, Maureen Stapleton	2–4
	January 25–31	#1139	Today cover, Upstairs, Downstairs, Tony Orlando	2–4
	February 1–7	#1140	The Rockford Files's James Garner cover, TV's old shows, Mac Davis	5–10
	February 8–14	#1141	Bob Newhart cover, Linda Blair, Another World	5–10
	February 15–21	#1142	The Rookies cast cover, Superman	5–10
	February 22–28	#1143	Kojak's Telly Savalas cover, The Jeffersons, Isaac Asimov	2–4
	March 1–7	#1144	Chico and the Man cover, The Smothers Brothers, Karen Black—**Note:** This issue is dated March 1–8 on the cover	3–6

YEAR	ISSUE	NUMBER	DESCRIPTION	VALUE
1975	March 8–14	#1145	Medical Center's Chad Everett cover, David McCallum	$ 2–4
	March 15–21	#1146	Karen Valentine cover, TV Hockey	2–4
	March 22–28	#1147	Streets of San Francisco cast cover, Arnold Palmer	2–4
	March 29	#1148	Maude cover, The Gong show, Baretta, Medical Center	3–6
	April 5–11	#1149	TV Baseball special, Cher, Stacy Keach	3–6
	April 12–18	#1150	Cher cover, Barney Miller	5–10
	April 19–25	#1151	Movin' On cast cover, Nevada Smith, Connie Chung	2–4
	April 26	#1152	McCloud cover, Animation special, Karen	3–5
	May 3–9	#1153	Rhoda cast cover, S.W.A.T.	2–4
	May 10–16	#1154	Muhammad Ali cover, The Untouchables, Dinah Shore, Baretta	2–4
	May 17–23	#1155	Petrocelli cover, Monty Python, The Lawyers	1–2

YEAR	ISSUE	NUMBER	DESCRIPTION	VALUE
1975	May 24–30	#1156	Jason Robards and Colleen Dewhurst cover, A Moon for the Misbegotten, 25 years of What's My Line, Sanford and Son	$5–10
	May 31	#1157	The Bob Newhart Show cast cover, The Smothers Brothers, William Conrad	5–10
	June 7–13	#1158	Little House on the Prairie cast cover, Cloris Leachman: Sooner, S.W.A.T.	5–10
	June 14–20	#1159	TV Violence issue special, Isaac Asimov	1–2
	June 21–27	#1160	The Jeffersons cast cover, TV shows of the 'fifties, Mickey Mouse Club, 1976 Olympics	4–8
	June 28	#1161	Bicentennial issue special, M.A.S.H.	1–3
	July 5–11	#1162	Tony Orlando and Dawn cover, The new faces of Space 1999, Aliens, Lucy, Lassie	5–10
	July 12–18	#1163	Apollo/Soyuz space mission special, Gladys Knight, Stacy Keach	2–4

YEAR	ISSUE	NUMBER	DESCRIPTION	VALUE
1975	July 19–25	#1164	Barney Miller cast cover, Good Times, Rod Serling death story	$ 3–6
	July 26	#1165	Howard K. Smith and Harry Reasoner cover, Pay TV	1–2
	August 2–8	#1166	Mike Douglas cover, Pat Finley, The Bob Newhart Show	2–4
	August 9–15	#1167	Buddy Ebsen cover, Liza Minnelli, Emergency	2–4
	August 16–22	#1168	Emergency cast cover, M.A.S.H.'s Loretta Swit, McCloud, The Waltons	3–5
	August 23–29	#1169	The Waltons cast cover, Gunsmoke's Chester, The Beverly Hillbillies' Donna Douglas	5–10
	August 30	#1170	Carroll O'Connor cover, Isaac Asimov, M.A.S.H.	1–2
	September 6–12	#1171	Fall Preview special	5–10
	September 13–19	#1172	NFL Winners special, Gene Shalit	1–2
	September 20–26	#1173	Barbara Walters cover, Beacon Hill	1–2

YEAR	ISSUE	NUMBER	DESCRIPTION	VALUE
1975	September 27	#1174	Howard Cosell cover, M.A.S.H.'s Jamie Farr	$ 1–2
	October 4–10	#1175	Jennie's Lee Remick cover	1–2
	October 11–17	#1176	The Family Holvak cover, Far-out space nuts, Marcus Welby, Ellery Queen	1–2
	October 18–24	#1177	TV's sex crisis special, The Bionic Woman, Cher	3–6
	October 25–31	#1178	Cloris Leachman cover, Martin Sheen, Barbary Coast	2–4
	November 1–7	#1179	Lloyd Bridges cover, The crash experts, Morgan Fairchild	3–6
	November 8–14	#1180	Rhoda cover, James Arness, All in the Family	3–6
	November 15–21	#1181	Starsky and Hutch cast cover, Trekkies	5–10

Note: The following four issues of *TV Guide* were printed with improper issue numbering.

| | November 22–28 | #1181 | A Week of Specials, Doctors' Hospital, Matt Helm | 1–2 |
| | November 29 | #1182 | Tony Curtis cover, To Tell the Truth, Ellery Queen | 1–2 |

YEAR	ISSUE	NUMBER	DESCRIPTION	VALUE
1975	December 6–12	#1183	Family Viewing special, John Denver, Harry-O, Welcome Back Kotter	$ 1–2
	December 13–19	#1184	Switch cover, When Things Were Rotten	1–2

Note: Issue numbering returns to proper sequence

	December 20–26	#1186	Christmas issue special, Andy Williams, Switch	1–2
	December 27	#1187	Baretta's Robert Blake cover, Mickey Mouse, Starsky and Hutch	2–4
1976	January 3–9	#1188	Kojak's Telly Savalas cover, Saturday Night Live, Bob Barker	2–4
	January 10–16	#1189	Happy Days cover, Medical Center	3–6
	January 17–23	#1190	Police Woman cover, The Super Bowl, The Adams Chronicles	5–10
	January 24–30	#1191	M.A.S.H. cover, Louis Armstrong, The Honeymooners	4–8
	January 31	#1192	S.W.A.T. cover, Desi Arnaz Remembers Part I	3–5
	February 7–13	#1193	Barney Miller cover, Desi Arnaz Remembers Part II	3–5

#1170, 1975

#1171, 1975

#1181, 1975

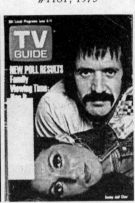

#1203, 1976

#1209, 1976

#1210, 1976

#1221, 1976

#1415, 1976

#1251, 1977

YEAR	ISSUE	NUMBER	DESCRIPTION	VALUE
1976	February 14–20	#1194	Sanford and Son's Redd Foxx cover, The Waltons	$ 3–5
	February 21–27	#1195	Cannon's William Conrad cover, Redd Foxx, One Day at a Time	1–3
	February 28	#1196	Bob Hope cover, The Addams Family, Space 1999	5–10
	March 6–12	#1197	The Rockford Files's James Garner cover, Johnny Carson	3–6
	March 13–19	#1198	Chico and the Man cover, The Batmobile, The Bionic Woman	4–8
	March 20–26	#1199	Danny Thomas cover, Laverne & Shirley, Harry-O	1–3
	March 27	#1200	Bronk's Jack Palance cover, Donny and Marie	3–6
	April 3–9	#1201	Baseball 1976 special	1–2
	April 10–16	#1202	Police Story cover, Russian TV	1–2
	April 17–23	#1203	Welcome Back Kotter cover, The Jeffersons	1–2
	April 24–30	#1204	Maude cover, Rich Little, Cousteau and the Calypso	2–4

YEAR	ISSUE	NUMBER	DESCRIPTION	VALUE
1976	May 1–7	#1205	The Blue Knight's George Kennedy cover, Mary Hartman, Mary Hartman, Happy Days's Marion Ross	$ 2–4
	May 8–14	#1206	The Bionic Woman's Lindsay Wagner cover, Sonny and Cher, Tom Snyder	10–20
	May 15–21	#1207	On the Rocks cover, Peter Ustinov and Zero Mostel, British TV	1–2
	May 22–28	#1208	Laverne & Shirley cover, Soap Opera Queens	3–5
	May 29	#1209	Little House on the Prairie cast cover, Saturday Night Live	5–10
	June 5–11	#1210	Sonny and Cher cover, The Donny and Marie Show	5–10
	June 12–18	#1211	Harry-O cover, Gail Christian	2–4
	June 19–25	#1212	Mary Hartman, Mary Hartman cover, Sylvia Chase	1–2
	June 26	#1213	Mary Tyler Moore cover and her Moscow special, Rich Little	5–10

YEAR	ISSUE	NUMBER	DESCRIPTION	VALUE
1976	July 3–9	#1214	Bicentennial special, TV from Mars	$ 1–2
	July 10–16	#1215	Convention special, Jimmie Walker, Wayne Rogers	1–2
	July 17–23	#1216	The Olympics special, Welcome Back Kotter	1–2
	July 24–30	#1217	One Day at a Time's Bonnie Franklin cover, Mary Tyler Moore, Isaac Asimov	2–4
	July 31	#1218	Terrorism on TV, The Beach Boys, Maude's Adrienne Barbeau	5–10
	August 7–13	#1219	Donny and Marie Osmond cover, Female boxing	10–20
	August 14–20	#1220	Columbo cover, TV in South Africa, The Muppets	2–4
	August 21–27	#1221	The Waltons cast cover, Frankie Avalon, Lily Tomlin	5–10
	August 28	#1222	The Bionic Woman cover, M.A.S.H.	5–10
	September 4–10	#1223	Annual Football Predictions issue, Neil Sedaka	1–2

YEAR	ISSUE	NUMBER	DESCRIPTION	VALUE
1976	September 11–17	#1224	Bob Dylan cover and feature: Bob Dylan Today, British TV	$ 5–10
	September 18–24	#1225	Fall Preview special	5–10
	September 25	#1226	Charlie's Angels cover, Barney Miller	10–20
	October 2–8	#1227	Serpico's David Birney cover, Paul Michael Glaser	1–2
	October 9–15	#1228	All's Fair's Bernadette Peters cover, The Gong Show	2–4
	October 16–22	#1229	World Series issue special, Cher, Sherlock Holmes	2–4
	October 23–29	#1230	Alice's Linda Lavin cover, Isis, TV Wrestling	2–4
	October 30	#1231	The Election special, M.A.S.H.'s helicopter pilot, The Jeffersons	2–4
	November 6–12	#1232	Gone with the Wind cover and special first TV showing, The Six Million Dollar Man, The Bionic Woman	5–10

YEAR	ISSUE	NUMBER	DESCRIPTION	VALUE
1976	November 13–19	#1233	Dorothy Hamill cover, John Denver, Happy Days's Tom Bosley, Charlie's Angels	$ 3–6
	November 20–26	#1234	NBC's 50th Birthday special, Kojak, Carol Burnett	1–2
	November 27	#1235	Starsky and Hutch cover, George C. Scott, Rhoda	5–10
	December 4–10	#1236	Tony Randall cover, Chico and the Man, Nancy Walker	2–4
	December 11–17	#1237	Rhoda's Valerie Harper cover, Peter Pan, The Streets of San Francisco	3–5
	December 18–24	#1238	John Chancellor and David Brinkley cover, Alice, Rich Man, Poor Man Part II	1–2
	December 25–31	#1239	Christmas issue special, Dick Van Dyke, General Hospital	1–2
1977	January 1–7	#1240	John Travolta cover, The Captain and Tennille	3–5
	January 8–14	#1241	Super Bowl special, Lesley-Anne Down	2–4

YEAR	ISSUE	NUMBER	DESCRIPTION	VALUE
1977	January 15–21	#1242	Jimmy Carter special, Dinah Shore, Charlie's Angels	$ 2–4
	January 22–28	#1243	Roots cover, Robert Stack, Dolly Parton	1–2
	January 29	#1244	Wonder Woman cover, Tony Randall	5–10
	February 5–11	#1245	Barbara Walters cover, James Arness, Phil Donahue, Roots	1–2
	February 12–18	#1246	Kojak cast cover, Barbara Walters, Bob Hope, Roots	2–4
	February 19–25	#1247	Nancy Walker cover, Grammy Awards, What's Happening, Roots	1–2
	February 26	#1248	McMillan and Wife cover, Welcome Back Kotter, Baa Baa Black Sheep	3–6
	March 5–11	#1249	Liv Ullmann cover, The Rockford Files	2–4
	March 12–18	#1250	Lauren Hutton cover, Rich Man, Poor Man	2–4
	March 19–25	#1251	Mary Tyler Moore cover, The Wizard of Oz, Catherine Schell of Space 1999, The Hobbit	5–10

YEAR	ISSUE	NUMBER	DESCRIPTION	VALUE
1977	March 26	#1252	Quincy's Jack Klugman cover, Happy Days's Erin Moran, TV Comics	$ 3–6
	April 2–8	#1253	Dinah Shore cover, Hee Haw, Fred Berry	1–2
	April 9–15	#1254	Baseball special, Fish, Ernie Kovacs	1–2
	April 16–22	#1255	Frank Sinatra cover, Fantastic Journey	2–4
	April 23–29	#1256	60 Minutes cover, Baa Baa Black Sheep, Charlie's Angels	3–5
	April 30	#1257	David Frost and Richard Nixon cover, Barbara Parkins, Stefanie Powers, Chevy Chase	3–5
	May 7–13	#1258	One Day at a Time cast cover	2–4
	May 14–20	#1259	Today's Tom Brokaw cover, The New Mickey Mouse Club	2–4
	May 21–28	#1260	Charlie's Angels's Farrah Fawcett cover, Quincy	5–10
	May 29	#1261	Baretta's Robert Blake cover, All in the Family, Roots, Grizzly Adams	3–5

YEAR	ISSUE	NUMBER	DESCRIPTION	VALUE
1977	June 4–10	#1262	M.A.S.H.'s Alan Alda cover, Queen Elizabeth	$ 3–6
	June 11–17	#1263	Grizzly Adams cover, Fish, The Hardy Boys, Nancy Drew	3–6
	June 18–24	#1264	Laverne & Shirley cover, TV News	3–6
	June 25	#1265	The Waltons cast cover, David Brenner, Charlie's Angels's Farrah Fawcett	5–10
	July 2–8	#1266	Alice cover, Star Trek, Mushroom magic	5–10
	July 9–15	#1267	C.P.O. Sharkey cover, Fernwood Tonight	1–2
	July 16–22	#1268	Barney Miller cast cover, Victor Hugo	2–4
	July 23–29	#1269	Public TV special, TV's Money Movies, King Kong	2–4
	July 30	#1270	Johnny Carson cover, Daniel Boone, Soap	2–4
	August 6–12	#1271	The Muppets cover and feature: Behind the Scenes on the Muppet Show, Jackie Robinson	2–4

#1258, 1977

#1260, 1977

#1263, 1977

#1271, 1977

#1275, 1977

#1284, 1977

#1295, 1978

#1298, 1978

#1299, 1978

YEAR	ISSUE	NUMBER	DESCRIPTION	VALUE
1977	August 13–19	#1272	Starsky and Hutch's David Soul cover, TV Boxing	$ 5–10
	August 20–26	#1273	The Rockford Files cover, Ed Bradley	4–8
	August 27	#1274	Hollywood Fights Back . . . sex and violence, Jane Pauley	2–4
	September 3–9	#1275	Jason Robards and Andy Griffith cover and feature: Washington, Behind Closed Doors, Laugh-In '77, Charlie's Angels	3–5
	September 10–16	#1276	Fall Preview special	5–10
	September 17–23	#1277	Football issue special, John Wayne, M.A.S.H., Patrick McGoohan	2–4
	September 24–30	#1278	The Betty White Show cover, Rhoda, Soap	2–4
	October 1–7	#1279	Rosetti and Ryan cover, The Gong Show, Isaac Asimov	1–2
	October 8–14	#1280	Donny and Marie Osmond cover, Hee Haw, X-rated Pay TV, Soap	10–20

YEAR	ISSUE	NUMBER	DESCRIPTION	VALUE
1977	October 15–21	#1281	Lou Grant's Ed Asner cover, The Love Boat, Little House on the Prairie, CHiPs	$ 2–4
	October 22–28	#1282	Welcome Back Kotter cast cover, Rafferty	2–4
	October 29	#1283	We've Got Each Other cover, Space Academy, Mark Hamill	2–4
	November 5–11	#1284	The Hardy Boys cover, Happy Days, On Our Own, The Addams Family Cartoon Show	5–10
	November 12–18	#1285	The Godfather on TV special, All in the Family, I Claudius, Soap	2–4
	November 19–25	#1286	Frank Sinatra cover, Charlie's Angels, Betty White	2–4
	November 26	#1287	Soap cast cover, Doonesbury	1–2
	December 3–9	#1288	Man from Atlantis's Patrick Duffy cover, Happy Days, Bette Midler, The Love Boat	5–10

YEAR	ISSUE	NUMBER	DESCRIPTION	VALUE
1977	December 10–16	#1289	The Censors special, Marlo Thomas, The World of Magic, The Man from Atlantis	$ 3–5
	December 17–23	#1290	One Day at a Time cast cover, We've Got Each Other, The Grand Ole Opry	4–8
	December 24–30	#1291	Christmas issue special, Kristy McNichol, Star Wars and Star Trek, Isaac Asimov	5–10
	December 31	#1292	Kojak cover, I Claudius, Julia Child, Soap	2–4
1978	January 7–13	#1293	Happy Days cover and feature	2–4
	January 14–20	#1294	Super Bowl cover by Charles Addams	1–3
	January 21–27	#1295	Cast of Family cover and feature	2–4
	January 28	#1296	Life and Times of Grizzly Adams	2–4
	February 4–10	#1297	The Love Boat	2–4
	February 11–17	#1298	Jack Klugman: Quincy	2–4
	February 18–24	#1299	Charlie's Angels	3–7
	February 25	#1300	Cast of M.A.S.H. cover and feature	3–5
	March 4–10	#1301	On Our Own cover and feature	1–2
	March 11–17	#1302	Carter Country	1–2

YEAR	ISSUE	NUMBER	DESCRIPTION	VALUE
1978	March 18–24	#1303	Lindsay Wagner of The Bionic Woman cover and feature	$3–7
	March 25–31	#1304	Mary Tyler Moore and Walter Cronkite	2–3
	April 1–7	#1305	Baseball	1–2
	April 8–14	#1306	Alice cast cover	2–4
	April 15–21	#1307	Holocaust	1–2
	April 22–28	#1308	Changing the Shape of Television	1–2
	April 29	#1309	Laverne & Shirley cast cover	2–4
	May 6–12	#1310	Barnaby Jones's Buddy Ebsen cover and feature	1–3
	May 13–19	#1311	Little House on the Prairie cast cover and feature	3–6
	May 20–26	#1312	Three's Company cast cover	2–4
	May 27	#1313	Phil Donahue	1–2
	June 3–9	#1314	Starsky and Hutch	2–4
	June 10–16	#1315	UFOs on TV	1–2
	June 17–23	#1316	Rhoda's Valerie Harper	1–3
	June 24–30	#1317	Can You Believe the Ratings?	1–2
	July 1–7	#1318	Fantasy Island cast cover	2–4
	July 8–14	#1319	The Young and the Restless cast cover	1–3
	July 15–21	#1320	Black Sheep Squadron's Robert Conrad cover	3–6

YEAR	ISSUE	NUMBER	DESCRIPTION	VALUE
1978	July 22–28	#1321	Love Boat's Gavin MacLeod	$ 2–4
	July 29	#1322	Saturday Night Live cast cover	3–6
	August 5–11	#1323	The Jeffersons cast cover	3–5
	August 12–18	#1324	Good Morning America's David Hartman	1–2
	August 19–25	#1325	Sport on TV	1–2
	August 26	#1326	Charlie's Angels's Cheryl Ladd	5–10
	September 2–8	#1327	Pro Football 1978	1–2
	September 9–15	#1328	Fall Preview special	2–4
	September 16–22	#1329	Battlestar Galactica cast cover	5–10
	September 23–29	#1330	Mary Tyler Moore	2–4
	September 30	#1331	Centennial cast cover	1–2
	October 7–13	#1332	World Series	1–2
	October 14–20	#1333	Robert Urich of Vegas	1–3
	October 21–27	#1334	WKRP cast cover	2–5
	October 28	#1335	Mork & Mindy	2–4
	November 4–10	#1336	Welcome Back Kotter's John Travolta	2–4
	November 11–17	#1337	Ron Leibman of Kaz	1–2
	November 18–24	#1338	Foreign lobbyists and TV	1–2
	November 25	#1339	Suzanne Somers cover and feature	2–5
	December 2–8	#1340	Benji	1–2
	December 9–15	#1341	Lou Grant	1–2

YEAR	ISSUE	NUMBER	DESCRIPTION	VALUE
1978	December 16–22	#1342	Eight Is Enough cast cover	$ 2–4
	December 23–29	#1343	Christmas issue special	1–2
	December 30	#1344	Dick Clark	1–2
1979	January 6–12	#1345	All in the Family by Hirschfeld	2–5
	January 13–19	#1346	Network News Chiefs	1–2
	January 20–26	#1347	Super Bowl XIII	1–2
	January 27	#1348	Katharine Hepburn	2–4
	February 3–9	#1349	CHiPs cast cover	1–3
	February 10–16	#1350	William Shakespeare	1–2
	February 17–23	#1351	Roots II	1–2
	February 24	#1352	James Arness	2–4
	March 3–9	#1353	Gary Coleman	1–2
	March 10–16	#1354	60 Minutes cast cover	1–2
	March 17–23	#1355	M.A.S.H.	2–5
	March 24–30	#1356	Fantasy Island	2–4
	March 31	#1357	Baseball '79	1–2
	April 7–13	#1358	Battlestar Galactica's Maren Jensen	5–10
	April 14–20	#1359	Quincy cast cover	2–4
	April 21–27	#1360	Walter Cronkite	1–2
	April 28	#1361	Taxi	2–4
	May 5–11	#1362	Paper Chase	1–2
	May 12–18	#1363	What Viewers Hate About TV	1–2
	May 19–25	#1364	Laverne & Shirley cast cover	2–4
	May 26	#1365	Ken Howard of White Shadow	1–2
	June 2–8	#1366	Rockford Files's James Garner	2–4

YEAR	ISSUE	NUMBER	DESCRIPTION	VALUE
1979	June 9–15	#1367	Donna Pescow of Angie	$ 1–2
	June 16–22	#1368	Dallas	2–4
	June 23–29	#1369	Johnny Carson	1–3
	June 30	#1370	Dukes of Hazzard	2–4
	July 7–13	#1371	Barney Miller	2–4
	July 14–20	#1372	Little House on the Prairie cast cover	3–6
	July 21–27	#1373	B.J. and the Bears	1–3
	July 28	#1374	The Incredible Hulk	3–6
	August 4–10	#1375	Joyce DeWitt of Three's Company	2–4
	August 11–17	#1376	Soap idol Rod Arrants	1–2
	August 18–24	#1377	Lou Grant cast cover	2–3
	August 25–31	#1378	Pro Football '79	1–2
	September 1–7	#1379	Miss America	1–3
	September 8–14	#1380	Fall Preview special	2–5
	September 15–21	#1381	Benson	1–2
	September 22–28	#1382	Carroll O'Connor	2–4
	September 29	#1383	Pope John Paul II	1–2
	October 6–12	#1384	World Series	1–2
	October 13–19	#1385	Tom Snyder	1–2
	October 20–26	#1386	WKRP cast cover	2–4
	October 27	#1387	Muhammad Ali in Freedom Road	1–2
	November 3–9	#1388	Hart to Hart	2–4
	November 10–16	#1389	The Bee Gees	5–10
	November 17–23	#1390	The Associates cast cover	1–2
	November 24–30	#1391	Trapper John	2–4
	December 1–7	#1392	Barbara Walters	1–2
	December 8–14	#1393	Talk show hosts	1–2
	December 15–21	#1394	The Fonz	1–3

YEAR	ISSUE	NUMBER	DESCRIPTION	VALUE
1979	December 22–28	#1395	Christmas issue special	$ 1–2
	December 29	#1396	Charlie's Angels cast cover	4–7
1980	January 5–11	#1397	M.A.S.H. cast cover	2–5
	January 12–18	#1398	CHiPs	1–3
	January 19–25	#1399	Super Bowl '80	1–2
	January 26	#1400	Soap	1–2
	February 2–8	#1401	Diff'rent Strokes cast cover	2–4
	February 9–15	#1402	Olympics	1–2
	February 16–22	#1403	Barnaby Jones cast cover	2–4
	February 23–29	#1404	Campaign '80	1–2
	March 1–7	#1405	Fantasy Island cover by Hirschfeld	2–4
	March 8–14	#1406	Dallas	2–4
	March 15–21	#1407	Family cast cover	2–4
	March 22–28	#1408	Misadventures of Sheriff Lobo	1–2
	March 28	#1409	Archie Bunker's Place	2–4
	April 5–11	#1410	1980 Baseball	1–2
	April 12–18	#1411	Olivia Newton-John	5–10
	April 19–25	#1412	Alice cast cover	2–4
	April 26	#1413	United States	1–2
	May 3–9	#1414	Mork & Mindy	2–4
	May 10–16	#1415	One Day at a Time cast cover	2–5
	May 17–23	#1416	The Jeffersons cast cover	2–4
	May 24–30	#1417	Situation Comedies	1–2
	May 31	#1418	Vegas cast cover	1–2
	June 7–13	#1419	Knot's Landing	1–2

#1382, 1979

#1392, 1979

#1416, 1980

#1419, 1980

#1421, 1980

#1482, 1981

#1485, 1981

#1564, 1983

#1566, 1983

YEAR	ISSUE	NUMBER	DESCRIPTION	VALUE
1980	June 14–20	#1420	House Calls's Lynn Redgrave	$1–2
	June 21–27	#1421	Hart to Hart cast cover	1–3
	June 28	#1422	Trapper John, M.D. cast cover	2–3
	July 5–11	#1423	Little House on the Prairie cast cover	3–6
	July 12–18	#1424	Dukes of Hazzard cast cover	2–4
	July 19–25	#1425	The Love Boat cast cover	2–4
	July 26	#1426	Taxi	2–3
	August 2–8	#1427	Real People	1–2
	August 9–15	#1428	Children's Television	1–2
	August 16–22	#1429	TV's Hunks	1–3
	August 23–29	#1430	General Hospital's Genie Francis	2–4
	August 30	#1431	Pro Football '80	1–2
	September 6–12	#1432	Richard Chamberlain of Shogun	1–3
	September 13–19	#1433	Fall Preview special	2–4
	September 20–26	#1434	Priscilla Presley	2–4
	September 27	#1435	Cosmos	1–2
	October 4–10	#1436	Lou Grant	1–2
	October 11–17	#1437	World Series	1–2
	October 18–24	#1438	Sophia Loren	1–3
	October 25–31	#1439	Barney Miller cover by Hirschfeld	1–3
	November 1–7	#1440	Reagan, Carter, and Anderson cover	1–2

YEAR	ISSUE	NUMBER	DESCRIPTION	VALUE
1980	November 8–14	#1441	Flo's Polly Holliday	$1–3
	November 15–21	#1442	Dallas's Larry Hagman	2–3
	November 22–28	#1443	Mork & Mindy's Pam Dawber	2–4
	November 29	#1444	Monday Night Football	1–2
	December 6–12	#1445	Diff'rent Strokes	2–4
	December 13–19	#1446	I'm a Big Girl Now	1–2
	December 20–26	#1447	Christmas issue special	2–3
	December 27	#1448	Magnum, P.I.	2–5
1981	January 3–9	#1449	Too Close for Comfort	2–4
	January 10–16	#1450	Good Morning America	1–2
	January 17–23	#1451	Ronald Reagan	1–2
	January 23–30	#1452	Super Bowl '81	1–2
	January 31	#1453	Johnny Carson, Bob Hope, and George Burns cover	1–2
	February 7–13	#1454	Jane Seymour of East of Eden	2–4
	February 14–20	#1455	WKRP	2–4
	February 21–27	#1456	Faye Dunaway as Eva Peron	2–4
	February 28	#1457	Hollywood's Cocaine Connection	1–2
	March 7–13	#1458	Dukes of Hazzard cast cover	2–4
	March 14–20	#1459	Suzanne Somers cover and feature	2–4
	March 21–27	#1460	House Calls	1–2

YEAR	ISSUE	NUMBER	DESCRIPTION	VALUE
1981	March 28	#1461	Johnny Carson cover by Amsel	$1–3
	April 4–10	#1462	Baseball 1981	1–2
	April 11–17	#1463	Ed Asner of Lou Grant	1–2
	April 18–24	#1464	Ted Koppel of ABC News	1–2
	April 25	#1465	Alan Alda cover by Hirschfeld	2–4
	May 2–8	#1466	That's Incredible	1–3
	May 9–15	#1467	Dallas	2–4
	May 16–22	#1468	Hart to Hart cast cover	1–3
	May 23–29	#1469	Harper Valley P.T.A.'s Barbara Eden	2–5
	May 30	#1470	Dan Rather	1–2
	June 6–12	#1471	Taxi	2–3
	June 13–19	#1472	Trapper John, M.D.	2–3
	June 20–26	#1473	Real People hosts cover	1–2
	June 27	#1474	Linda Evans of Dynasty	2–4
	July 4–10	#1475	Diff'rent Strokes's Dana Plato and Gary Coleman	2–5
	July 11–17	#1476	Prime Time Vixens	2–4
	July 18–24	#1477	B.J. and the Bear	2–4
	July 25–31	#1478	Prince Charles and Diana Spencer	1–2
	August 1–7	#1479	Miss Piggy	1–2
	August 8–14	#1480	Carroll O'Connor	2–4
	August 15–21	#1481	The Day Elvis Died	2–5
	August 22–28	#1482	Ann Jillian of It's a Living	2–5

YEAR	ISSUE	NUMBER	DESCRIPTION	VALUE
1981	August 29	#1483	Pro Football '81	$1–2
	September 5–11	#1484	Backstage with Miss America	1–2
	September 12–18	#1485	Fall Preview special issue	2–4
	September 19–25	#1486	Kate Mulgrew as Rachel Manion	1–2
	September 26	#1487	The Battle for Northern Ireland	1–2
	October 3–9	#1488	Valerie Bertinelli of One Day at a Time	2–5
	October 10–16	#1489	Jaclyn Smith as Jacqueline Kennedy	2–4
	October 17–23	#1490	World Series	1–2
	October 24–30	#1491	Middle East News Coverage	1–2
	October 31	#1492	Hill Street Blues cast cover	1–3
	November 7–13	#1493	The Two of Us	1–2
	November 14–20	#1494	Loretta Lynn	2–5
	November 21–27	#1495	John Lennon cover and feature	4–8
	November 28	#1496	Merlin Olsen of Father Murphy	2–3
	December 5–11	#1497	Private Benjamin	1–3
	December 12–18	#1498	Video Games	1–2
	December 19–25	#1499	Christmas issue special	1–2
	December 26	#1500	Henry Fonda	2–3
1982	January 2–8	#1501	Magnum, P.I.	2–4
	January 9–15	#1502	Michael Landon	3–6
	January 16–22	#1503	Bending the Rules in Hollywood	1–2
	January 23–29	#1504	Football Issue	1–2
	January 30	#1505	CHiPs	2–3
	February 6–12	#1506	The Jeffersons	2–4

YEAR	ISSUE	NUMBER	DESCRIPTION	VALUE
1982	February 13–19	#1507	TV's Holocaust Films	$1–2
	February 20–26	#1508	60 Minutes cast cover	1–2
	February 27	#1509	Dynasty cast cover	2–4
	March 6–12	#1510	Love, Sidney cast cover	1–2
	March 13–19	#1511	Three's Company cast cover	2–5
	March 20–26	#1512	President Reagan	1–2
	March 27	#1513	Dallas's Larry Hagman	2–4
	April 3–9	#1514	Baseball	1–2
	April 10–16	#1515	Today's Tom Brokaw	1–2
	April 17–23	#1516	Happy Days cast cover	3–6
	April 24–30	#1517	Ingrid Bergman as Golda Meir	1–2
	May 1–7	#1518	Dukes of Hazzard cast cover	2–3
	May 8–14	#1519	Goldie Hawn	2–4
	May 15–21	#1520	Marco Polo	1–2
	May 22–28	#1521	Falcon Crest	1–3
	May 29	#1522	Anatomy of a Smear	1–2
	June 5–11	#1523	Love Boat	2–4
	June 12–18	#1524	Foreign Disinformation on U.S. TV	1–2
	June 19–25	#1525	Hill Street Blues	1–3
	June 26	#1526	Knot's Landing's Michele Lee	2–4
	July 3–9	#1527	Too Close for Comfort	2–3
	July 10–16	#1528	Facts of Life cast cover	2–4

YEAR	ISSUE	NUMBER	DESCRIPTION	VALUE
1982	July 17–23	#1529	Rick Springfield of General Hospital	$2–4
	July 24–30	#1530	Greatest American Hero	2–3
	July 31	#1531	Father Murphy cast cover	2–3
	August 7–13	#1532	Archie Bunker's Place cast cover	2–4
	August 14–20	#1533	T.J. Hooker's William Shatner	2–4
	August 21–27	#1534	Gimme a Break	1–3
	August 28	#1535	Laverne & Shirley	2–4
	September 4–10	#1536	Almost Miss America	3–5
	September 11–17	#1537	Fall issue special	2–4
	September 18–24	#1538	Victoria Principal	2–4
	September 25	#1539	Ratings of TV newspeople	1–2
	October 2–8	#1540	Genie Francis	2–4
	October 9–15	#1541	World Series	1–2
	October 16–22	#1542	Honey Boy	1–2
	October 23–29	#1543	Dynasty	2–4
	October 30	#1544	Trapper John, M.D.	1–2
	November 6–12	#1545	Fame	1–2
	November 13–19	#1546	The Blue and the Gray	2–4
	November 20–26	#1547	Three's Company cast cover	2–5
	November 27	#1548	Family Ties's Meredith Baxter-Birney	2–4
	December 4–10	#1549	1982's Best Video Games	1–2
	December 11–17	#1550	Sally Struthers and daughter	1–3

YEAR	ISSUE	NUMBER	DESCRIPTION	VALUE
1982	December 18–24	#1551	Too Close for Comfort cast cover	$2–4
	December 25–31	#1552	Christmas issue special	1–2
1983	January 1–7	#1553	Bob Newhart and Mary Frann	3–5
	January 8–14	#1554	John Madden	1–2
	January 15–21	#1555	Nine to Five cast cover	1–2
	January 22–28	#1556	TV's Investigative Reporters	1–2
	January 29	#1557	The Winds of War	2–3
	February 5–11	#1558	Cheryl Ladd as Grace Kelly	3–6
	February 12–18	#1559	The final M.A.S.H. episode issue	3–6
	February 19–25	#1560	Jaclyn Smith and Ken Howard	1–3
	February 26	#1561	All My Children cast cover	1–2
	March 5–11	#1562	Valerie Bertinelli	2–5
	March 12–18	#1563	Hill Street Blues	1–3
	March 19–25	#1564	Gary Coleman and Nancy Reagan	1–3
	March 26	#1565	Thorn Birds	4–8
	April 2–8	#1566	Donna Mills of Knots Landing	3–5
	April 9–15	#1567	Elvis Presley	3–6
	April 16–22	#1568	60 Minutes cast cover	2–4
	April 23–29	#1569	Happy Days	3–6
	April 30	#1570	Tom Selleck	3–5
	May 7–13	#1571	Silver Spoons cast cover	3–5
	May 14–20	#1572	Dynasty	2–4
	May 21–27	#1573	Bob Hope	1–3

YEAR	ISSUE	NUMBER	DESCRIPTION	VALUE
1983	May 28	#1574	Dallas	$2–4
	June 4–10	#1575	The Fall Guy cast cover	2–5
	June 11–17	#1576	Alan Alda, Linda Evans, Valerie Bertinelli	2–4
	June 18–24	#1577	Simon & Simon cast cover	3–6
	June 25	#1578	Knight Rider	3–6
	July 2–8	#1579	M.A.S.H., Dynasty, Thorn Birds	1–2
	July 9–15	#1580	Falcon Crest cast cover	2–3
	July 16–22	#1581	TV's Hunks	1–2
	July 23–29	#1582	Knots Landing cast cover	3–5
	July 30	#1583	The Jeffersons	2–4
	August 6–12	#1584	Network Newswomen	1–2
	August 13–19	#1585	Days of Our Lives	1–2
	August 20–26	#1586	Hart to Hart	2–4
	August 27	#1587	White House News Coverage	1–2
	September 3–9	#1588	All in the Family final episode	4–8
	September 10–16	#1589	Fall Preview special	3–5
	September 17–23	#1590	Miss America Pageant	2–3
	September 24–30	#1591	Three's Company cast cover	3–5
	October 1–7	#1592	Gregory Harrison	1–2
	October 8–14	#1593	Willie Nelson and Anne Murray	4–8
	October 15–21	#1594	Larry Hagman and Joan Collins	3–5
	October 22–28	#1595	Mr. Smith	1–2

#1569, 1983

#1602, 1983

#1603, 1983

#1875, 1989

July 24, 1953

October 2, 1953

November 13, 1953

January 15, 1954

March 12, 1954

YEAR	ISSUE	NUMBER	DESCRIPTION	VALUE
1983	October 29	#1596	Hotel cast cover	$1–3
	November 5–11	#1597	Princess Daisy	1–3
	November 12–18	#1598	President Kennedy	2–4
	November 19–25	#1599	The Day After	1–2
	November 26	#1600	Linda Evans and Kenny Rogers cover	3–5
	December 3–9	#1601	Johnny Carson and Barbara Walters cover	2–4
	December 10–16	#1602	Tom Selleck	2–4
	December 17–23	#1603	Silver Spoons's Erin Gray	3–5
	December 24–30	#1604	The Love Boat cast cover	3–5
	December 31	#1605	Farrah Fawcett	3–6
1984	January 7–13	#1606	After M.A.S.H. cast cover	2–4
	January 14–20	#1607	Emmanuel Lewis	1–2
	January 21–27	#1608	TV Game Show Hosts	1–2
	January 28	#1609	Cybill Shepherd	3–5
	February 4–10	#1610	Winter Olympics	1–3
	February 11–17	#1611	Scarecrow and Mrs. King	3–6
	February 18–24	#1612	Cheers cast cover	3–6
	February 25	#1613	60 Minutes cast cover	2–3
	March 3–9	#1614	Ann-Margret and Treat Williams	2–5
	March 10–16	#1615	The A-Team cast cover	3–6
	March 17–23	#1616	Priscilla Presley	3–5
	March 24–30	#1617	Hill Street Blues	2–4
	March 31	#1618	Teri Copley	2–4
	April 7–13	#1619	George Washington	1–3
	April 14–20	#1620	Knight Rider	3–6

YEAR	ISSUE	NUMBER	DESCRIPTION	VALUE
1984	April 21–27	#1621	The Far Pavilions	$1–3
	April 28	#1622	Happy Days 1974–1984	3–6
	May 5–11	#1623	Lesley-Anne Downs	2–3
	May 12–18	#1624	Crystal Gayle	3–7
	May 19–25	#1625	Morgan Fairchild	3–5
	May 26	#1626	Hardcastle & McCormick	3–6
	June 2–8	#1627	Victoria Principal	3–5
	June 9–15	#1628	Remington Steele cast cover	2–5
	June 16–22	#1629	Larry Hagman, Stefanie Powers, Joan Collins	2–4
	June 23–29	#1630	Connie Sellecca	2–4
	June 30	#1631	Review of 1983–1984 Season	2–4
	July 7–13	#1632	Valeri Bertinelli	3–5
	July 14–20	#1633	Johnny Carson	1–3
	July 21–27	#1634	Knots Landing cast cover	2–4
	July 28	#1635	Olympics	1–2
	August 4–10	#1636	Simon & Simon	3–6
	August 11–17	#1637	Call to Glory cast cover	1–2
	August 18–24	#1638	Jane Pauley	1–2
	August 25–31	#1639	Mike Hammer	1–2
	September 1–7	#1640	Who Shot Dallas's Bobby?	2–4
	September 8–14	#1641	Fall Preview special	4–8
	September 15–21	#1642	George Burns and Catherine Bach	2–4
	September 22–28	#1643	Mistral's Daughter	1–2
	September 29	#1644	Heartsounds	1–2
	October 6–12	#1645	Paper Dolls	1–2
	October 13–19	#1646	Cosby Show	1–2

YEAR	ISSUE	NUMBER	DESCRIPTION	VALUE
1984	October 20–26	#1647	Aurora by Night	$1–2
	October 27	#1648	Brooke Shields	3–5
	November 3–9	#1649	Election Night Drama	1–2
	November 10–16	#1650	Dynasty	1–3
	November 17–23	#1651	Top Models	1–3
	November 24–30	#1652	Kate & Allie	3–5
	December 1–7	#1653	Hotel	1–3
	December 8–14	#1654	Falcon Crest	1–3
	December 15–21	#1655	Connie Sellecca, Priscilla Presley, Jaclyn Smith	2–4
	December 22–28	#1656	Webster cast cover	2–4
	December 29	#1657	Dallas	2–4
1985	January 5–11	#1658	Elvis Presley	3–6
	January 12–18	#1659	Knots Landing	2–3
	January 19–25	#1660	President Reagan	1–2
	January 26	#1661	Riptide	1–3
	February 2–8	#1662	Cagney & Lacey cover by Amsel	4–8
	February 9–15	#1663	Night Court	2–3
	February 16–22	#1664	Hollywood Wives cast cover	1–2
	February 23	#1665	Bruce Springsteen, Prince, Michael Jackson	4–8
	March 2–8	#1666	Michael Landon	3–6
	March 9–15	#1667	Angela Lansbury	2–4
	March 16–22	#1668	Lauren Tewes	1–2
	March 23–29	#1669	Dynasty's Diahann Carroll	2–3
	March 30	#1670	A.D. cast cover	1–2
	April 6–12	#1671	Richard Chamberlain	1–2
	April 13–19	#1672	Space cast cover	1–3
	April 20–26	#1673	Dallas's Deborah Shelton	1–2

YEAR	ISSUE	NUMBER	DESCRIPTION	VALUE
1985	April 27	#1674	Family Ties cast cover	$3–6
	May 4–10	#1675	Phoebe Cates in Lace II	3–6
	May 11–17	#1676	Cheryl Ladd	3–6
	May 18–24	#1677	Christopher Columbus	1–2
	May 25–31	#1678	Cover Up	1–2
	June 1–7	#1679	Hill Street Blues	2–4
	June 8–14	#1680	Simon & Simon	3–6
	June 15–21	#1681	Summer TV Surprises	1–2
	June 22–28	#1682	Nancy Reagan	1–2
	June 29	#1683	The Best and Worst We Saw	1–2
	July 6–12	#1684	Cheers cast cover	3–6
	July 13–19	#1685	The Fall Guys's Heather Thomas	3–6
	July 20–26	#1686	Hottest Soap Couples	1–2
	July 27	#1687	Miami Vice	3–5
	August 3–9	#1688	Romance on the Set	1–2
	August 10–16	#1689	Madonna	3–6
	August 17–23	#1690	Real Men versus the Wimps	1–2
	August 24–30	#1691	Knots Landing	1–2
	August 31	#1692	The A-Team	2–4
	September 7–13	#1693	The Cosby Show	1–3
	September 14–20	#1694	Fall Preview special	4–8
	September 21–27	#1695	Michael J. Fox	3–5
	September 28	#1696	Howard Cosell	1–2
	October 5–11	#1697	Don Johnson and Cybill Shepherd	2–4
	October 12–18	#1698	Victoria Principal	2–4
	October 19–25	#1699	Golden Girls cast cover	2–4

YEAR	ISSUE	NUMBER	DESCRIPTION	VALUE
1985	October 26	#1700	Network Newscasters	$1–2
	November 2–8	#1701	North and South cast cover	1–3
	November 9–15	#1702	Prince Charles and Princess Diana	1–2
	November 16–22	#1703	Dynasty II . . . The Colbys	1–2
	November 23–29	#1704	Who's the Boss cast cover	2–4
	November 30	#1705	Is Knots Landing Better?	1–2
	December 7–13	#1706	Cybill Shepherd	2–4
	December 14–20	#1707	Hell Town's Robert Blake	2–3
	December 21–27	#1708	Highway to Heaven cast cover	3–7
	December 28	#1709	Crazy Like a Fox	1–2
1986	January 4–10	#1710	Connie Sellecca	2–3
	January 11–17	#1711	Scarecrow and Mrs. King	3–7
	January 18–24	#1712	Night Court cast cover	2–3
	January 25–31	#1713	Joan Collins	2–4
	February 1–7	#1714	Peter the Great	1–2
	February 8–14	#1715	Hollywood Love Scenes	2–4
	February 15–21	#1716	Angela Lansbury	2–4
	February 22–28	#1717	Crossings	2–4
	March 1–7	#1718	Dynasty's Linda Evans	2–4
	March 8–14	#1719	Miami Vice	2–4
	March 15–21	#1720	If Tomorrow Comes	1–2
	March 22–28	#1721	Bill Cosby	1–2
	March 29	#1722	Sexual Harassment	1–2

YEAR	ISSUE	NUMBER	DESCRIPTION	VALUE
1986	April 5–11	#1723	Family Ties cast cover	$2–4
	April 12–18	#1724	Dream West	1–2
	April 19–25	#1725	10 Most Attractive Men on TV	2–4
	April 26	#1726	Kate & Allie cast cover	2–4
	May 3–9	#1727	Del Stranger versus North and South	1–2
	May 10–16	#1728	Cheers cast cover	3–5
	May 17–23	#1729	Burt Lancaster	2–4
	May 24–30	#1730	Larry Hagman	2–3
	May 31	#1731	MacGyver	2–4
	June 7–13	#1732	10 Most Talented TV Stars	2–4
	June 14–20	#1733	Webster	1–3
	June 21–27	#1734	Knots Landing's Teri Austin	2–3
	June 28	#1735	Ronald and Nancy Reagan	1–3
	July 5–11	#1736	The Goodwill Games	1–2
	July 12–18	#1737	The Worst and Best on TV	2–4
	July 19–25	#1738	Spencer: For Hire cast cover	2–4
	July 26	#1739	TV's Top Moneymakers	2–4
	August 2–8	#1740	TV's Macho Men	2–4
	August 9–15	#1741	Growing Pains cast cover	2–4
	August 16–22	#1742	Suzanne Somers	2–4
	August 23–29	#1743	Valerie Harper	2–3
	August 30	#1744	Dallas . . . The Mystery of Bobby's Return	2–4

YEAR	ISSUE	NUMBER	DESCRIPTION	VALUE
1986	September 6–12	#1745	Miss America, NFL Football	$1–2
	September 13–19	#1746	Fall Preview special	3–6
	September 20–26	#1747	George Washington	1–2
	September 27	#1748	Perfect Strangers	1–2
	October 4–10	#1749	Lucille Ball and Andy Griffith	4–8+
	October 11–17	#1750	L.A. Law cast cover	3–5
	October 18–24	#1751	Family Ties	3–5
	October 25–31	#1752	Falcon Crest	2–3
	November 1–7	#1753	Rage of Angels	1–2
	November 8–14	#1754	Joan Collins and George Hamilton	2–3
	November 15–21	#1755	Fresno cast cover	1–2
	November 22–28	#1756	Farrah Fawcett	3–6
	November 29	#1757	Jack and Mike	1–2
	December 6–12	#1758	Designing Women's Delta Burke	2–4
	December 13–19	#1759	Promise	1–2
	December 20–26	#1760	Our House cast cover	2–3
	December 27	#1761	Dynasty's Heather Locklear	3–5
1987	January 3–9	#1762	Angela Lansbury	2–3
	January 10–16	#1763	Nightline's Ted Koppel	1–2
	January 17–23	#1764	Amen	2–3
	January 24–30	#1765	Knots Landing	1–2
	January 31	#1766	Golden Girls cast cover	2–4
	February 7–13	#1767	Ann-Margret	2–4
	February 14–20	#1768	Controversy over Amerika	1–2

YEAR	ISSUE	NUMBER	DESCRIPTION	VALUE
1987	February 21–27	#1769	Tom Selleck and Frank Sinatra	$2–4
	February 28	#1770	Valerie Bertinelli	2–4
	March 7–13	#1771	Justine Bateman and Michael J. Fox	3–4
	March 14–20	#1772	Dallas's Victoria Principal	2–4
	March 21–27	#1773	Miami Vice	2–4
	March 28	#1774	Growing Pains	2–4
	April 4–10	#1775	L.A. Law	2–4
	April 11–17	#1776	Bob Newhart cast cover	2–4
	April 18–24	#1777	Who's the Boss's Tony Danza	2–3
	April 25	#1778	Hunter	1–2
	May 2–8	#1779	Cheers cast cover	3–5
	May 9–15	#1780	My Sister Sam	2–4
	May 16–22	#1781	Head of the Class cast cover	2–4
	May 23–29	#1782	The Equalizer	3–6
	May 30	#1783	Moonlighting's Cybill Shepherd	2–4
	June 6–12	#1784	Grading TV's Child Stars	2–4
	June 13–19	#1785	Cagney & Lacey	2–4
	June 20–26	#1786	Night Court's Markie Post	2–4
	June 27	#1787	The Best and Worst We Saw	2–4
	July 4–10	#1788	Barbara Walters	1–2
	July 11–17	#1789	Cosby Show	1–2
	July 18–24	#1790	Kate Jackson, Victoria Principal, Oprah Winfrey	2–3
	July 25–31	#1791	Molly Dodd	1–2
	August 1–7	#1792	The Young and the Restless	1–2

YEAR	ISSUE	NUMBER	DESCRIPTION	VALUE
1987	August 8–14	#1793	Is TV Getting Bolder?	$1–2
	August 15–21	#1794	Alf	3–4
	August 22–28	#1795	Soviet Bloc Nations' TV	1–2
	August 29	#1796	Amen	1–3
	September 5–11	#1797	Dynasty's Terri Garber	2–4
	September 12–18	#1798	Fall Preview special	3–6
	September 19–25	#1799	Brooke Shields	3–8
	September 26	#1800	L.A. Law	2–4
	October 3–9	#1801	Victoria Principal	2–4
	October 10–16	#1802	TV's Best and Worst Sitcoms	2–4
	October 17–23	#1803	Dolly Parton	3–5
	October 24–30	#1804	Moonlighting cast cover	2–4
	October 31	#1805	Family Ties	2–4
	November 7–13	#1806	Napoleon	2–4
	November 14–20	#1807	Cheers	2–4
	November 21–27	#1808	Gambler	1–2
	November 28	#1809	David and Meredith Baxter-Birney	2–4
	December 5–11	#1810	Connie Sellecca	2–3
	December 12–18	#1811	Hooperman's John Ritter	1–2
	December 19–25	#1812	Keshia Knight Pulliam	1–2
	December 26	#1813	A Year in the Life cast cover, Star Trek	3–6
1988	January 2–8	#1814	Falcon Crest cast cover	2–3
	January 9–15	#1815	Emma Samms	3–5
	January 16–22	#1816	Cagney & Lacey cast cover	3–4

YEAR	ISSUE	NUMBER	DESCRIPTION	VALUE
1988	January 23–29	#1817	Campaign '88	$1–2
	January 30	#1818	Elvis and Priscilla Presley	2–5
	February 6–12	#1819	Jaclyn Smith and Robert Wagner	2–4
	February 13–19	#1820	Winter Olympics	1–2
	February 20–26	#1821	Noble House	1–2
	February 27	#1822	Cheryl Ladd	2–4
	March 5–11	#1823	Oprah Winfrey	1–2
	March 12–18	#1824	Is TV Getting Better or Worse?	1–2
	March 19–25	#1825	Miami Vice	2–4
	March 26	#1826	Sheree J. Wilson	1–2
	April 2–8	#1827	Growing Pains	2–4
	April 9–15	#1828	Harry Hamlin	1–2
	April 16–22	#1829	Frank's Place	1–2
	April 23–29	#1830	Jason Bateman	1–2
	April 30	#1831	Dr. Ruth, Golden Girls	2–4
	May 7–13	#1832	Richard Chamberlain, Jaclyn Smith	2–4
	May 14–20	#1833	Beat the Press	1–2
	May 21–27	#1834	Prince Charles and Princess Diana	1–3
	May 28	#1835	Family Ties	2–4
	June 4–10	#1836	ABC Sports	1–2
	June 11–17	#1837	Thirtysomething cast cover	2–4
	June 18–24	#1838	1988 Network News All-Stars	1–2
	June 25	#1839	The Best and the Worst	2–3
	July 2–8	#1840	Designing Women cast cover	2–3
	July 9–15	#1841	Head of the Class cast cover	2–4
	July 16–22	#1842	The Six Most Beautiful Women	2–4

YEAR	ISSUE	NUMBER	DESCRIPTION	VALUE
1988	July 23–29	#1843	TV and the American Family	$1–2
	July 30	#1844	Leann Hunley	1–2
	August 6–12	#1845	The Best Daytime Soaps	1–2
	August 13–19	#1846	The Alfer	2–4
	August 20–26	#1847	21 Jump Street	2–4
	August 27	#1848	Mariel Hemingway	3–5
	September 3–9	#1849	Fall Survivor's Guide	1–2
	September 10–16	#1850	Kaye Lani	1–2
	September 17–23	#1851	Olympics	1–2
	September 24–30	#1852	Cosby Show cast cover	1–2
	October 1–7	#1853	Fall Preview special	3–6
	October 8–14	#1854	Brandon Tartikoff and Stars	1–2
	October 15–21	#1855	Bull Durham	1–2
	October 22–28	#1856	The AIDS Scare	1–2
	October 29	#1857	Harry Hamlin, Linda Kozlowski	1–2
	November 5–11	#1858	Election	1–2
	November 12–18	#1859	War and Remembrance cast cover	1–2
	November 19–25	#1860	Remembering JFK	1–2
	November 26	#1861	Barbara Walter's Specials	1–2
	December 3–9	#1862	Guide to Holiday Specials	1–2
	December 10–16	#1863	Empty Nest cast cover	1–2
	December 17–23	#1864	Kramer, Wilson, Belafonte	1–2
	December 24–30	#1865	Angela Lansbury	2–3
	December 31	#1866	Sandy Duncan, Jason Bateman	2–3

YEAR	ISSUE	NUMBER	DESCRIPTION	VALUE
1989	January 7–13	#1867	8th Annual J. Fred Muggs Awards	$1–2
	January 14–20	#1868	Moonlighting cast cover	2–3
	January 21–27	#1869	Elvis Presley	3–5
	January 28	#1870	Roseanne cast cover	2–4
	February 4–10	#1871	Hot February	1–2
	February 11–17	#1872	Jr. on the Couch	1–2
	February 18–24	#1873	The Best Children's Shows	1–2
	February 25	#1874	Victoria Principal	2–3
	March 4–10	#1875	Vanna White	2–4
	March 11–17	#1876	What's In	1–2
	March 18–24	#1877	Oprah, Jackie, Robin Givens	1–2
	March 25–31	#1878	Oscars	1–2
	April 1–7	#1879	Women of L.A. Law	2–4
	April 8–14	#1880	The Busy Person's TV Guide	1–2
	April 15–21	#1881	Joan Collins	1–2
	April 22–28	#1882	Jason Bateman, Kirk Cameron	2–3
	April 29	#1883	May Is Bustin' Out	1–2
	May 6–12	#1884	TV Is 50	1–2
	May 13–19	#1885	Dynasty's Tracy Scoggins	1–2
	May 20–26	#1886	Roseanne's Roseanne Barr	2–3
	May 27	#1887	Cheers's Kirstie Alley	2–4
	June 3–9	#1888	Oprah Winfrey	1–2
	June 10–16	#1889	Fred Savage	1–3
	June 17–23	#1890	Knots Landing's Donna Mills	2–3
	June 24–30	#1891	Soap Couples	1–2

YEAR	ISSUE	NUMBER	DESCRIPTION	VALUE
1989	July 1–7	#1892	TV Stars in the Movies	$1–2
	July 8–14	#1893	The Best and the Worst	1–2
	July 15–21	#1894	Network News All-Stars	1–2
	July 22–28	#1895	Roseanne Barr, Nicollette Sheridan	1–2
	July 29	#1896	Married with Children cast cover	2–4
	August 5–11	#1897	Tabloid TV	1–2
	August 12–18	#1898	TV's News Queens	1–2
	August 19–25	#1899	Hollywood's Drug Scene	1–2
	August 26	#1900	Oprah Winfrey's Head on Ann-Margret's Body cover	1–2
	September 2–8	#1901	Miss America, Football	1–2
	September 9–15	#1902	Fall Preview special	3–5
	September 16–22	#1903	Roseanne Barr, Bill Cosby	1–2
	September 23–29	#1904	Foster, Haje, Tyson	1–2
	September 30	#1905	Elizabeth Taylor, Mark Harmon	1–2
	October 7–13	#1906	Delta Burke and Gerald McRaney	1–2
	October 14–20	#1907	World Series	1–2
	October 21–27	#1908	Anything But Love's Jamie Lee Curtis	2–4
	October 28	#1909	The Final Days	1–2

YEAR	ISSUE	NUMBER	DESCRIPTION	VALUE
1989	November 4–10	#1910	Farrah, Bateman, Bertinelli	$2–4
	November 11–17	#1911	Richard Chamberlain	1–2
	November 18–24	#1912	Courtney Cox, Barry Bostwick	1–2
	November 25	#1913	Victoria Principal	2–3
	December 2–8	#1914	Holiday special	1–2
	December 9–15	#1915	The 80s	1–2
	December 16–22	#1916	Doogie Howser	1–2
	December 23–29	#1917	Murphy Brown's Candice Bergen	2–4
	December 30	#1918	Julia Duffy, Jean Smart	2–4
1990	January 6–12	#1919	Rock Hudson	2–4
	January 13–19	#1920	Roseanne	1–2
	January 20–26	#1921	Arsenio Hall, Dana Delany	1–2
	January 27	#1922	Super Bowl, Indiana Jones	2–4
	February 3–9	#1923	Lesley Ann Warren	1–2
	February 10–16	#1924	The Hottest TV Couples	1–2
	February 17–23	#1925	Elvis Presley	2–4
	February 24	#1926	Challenger Disaster	2–3
	March 3–9	#1927	Children's TV	1
	March 10–16	#1928	L.A. Law cast cover	2–4
	March 17–23	#1929	The Simpsons	2–4
	March 24–30	#1930	Oscar Night, Billy Crystal	1
	March 31	#1931	America's Funniest Videos	1
	April 7–13	#1932	Valerie Bertinelli, Carol Burnett	1–2

YEAR	ISSUE	NUMBER	DESCRIPTION	VALUE
1990	April 14–20	#1933	What's In/What's Out	$ 1
	April 21–27	#1934	Arnold Schwarzenegger	1
	April 28	#1935	May Sweeps	1
	May 5–11	#1936	Oprah Winfrey	1
	May 12–18	#1937	Growing Pains cast cover	1–2
	May 19–25	#1938	Carol Burnett cover by Hirschfeld	1–2
	May 26	#1939	TV Goes to the Movies	1
	June 2–8	#1940	Steve Bond, Barbara Crampton	1
	June 9–15	#1941	Bart Simpson, Ninja Turtles	1–2
	June 16–22	#1942	Dana Delany	1
	June 23–29	#1943	Arsenio Hall	1
	June 30	#1944	Summer Survival Guide	1
	July 7–13	#1945	The Best and the Worst	1
	July 14–20	#1946	A Different World	1
	July 21–27	#1947	TV's Top Teen Stars	2–3
	July 28	#1948	Guide to New Home Video	1
	August 4–10	#1949	Candice Bergen, Kirstie Alley, Nicollette Sheridan	1–2
	August 11–17	#1950	TV Sports and Money	1
	August 18–24	#1951	Designing Women cast cover	1–2
	August 25–31	#1952	Delaney, Smith, Sheridan	1

YEAR	ISSUE	NUMBER	DESCRIPTION	VALUE
1990	September 1–7	#1953	Madonna, Paula Abdul, Janet Jackson	$2–4
	September 8–14	#1954	The Women of Twin Peaks	2–4
	September 15–21	#1955	Fall Preview special	3–6
	September 22–28	#1956	Fall Preview special II	1–2
	September 29	#1957	Fall Preview special III	1–2
	October 6–12	#1958	Fall Preview special IV	1–2
	October 13–19	#1959	New Teen Shows	1–2
	October 20–26	#1960	The Best and Worst Dressed	1
	October 27	#1961	Horror on TV	1–2
	November 3–9	#1962	November to Remember	1
	November 10–16	#1963	Susan Lucci	1–2
	November 17–23	#1964	The Muppets	1
	November 24–30	#1965	Linda Evans	1–3
	December 1–7	#1966	Guide to the Holidays	1
	December 8–14	#1967	Full House cast cover	1
	December 15–21	#1968	Designing Women's Dixie Carter	1
	December 23–28	#1969	Batman, The Flash, Dick Tracy	1–2
	December 29	#1970	Murphy Brown cast cover	1–2
1991	January 5–11	#1971	Jane Pauley	1–2
	January 12–18	#1972	Farrah Fawcett and Ryan O'Neal	1–2
	January 19–25	#1973	The Best Stories of 60 Minutes	1

YEAR	ISSUE	NUMBER	DESCRIPTION	VALUE
1991	January 26	#1974	Cybill Shepherd	$1–2
	February 2–8	#1975	Julia Roberts, MC Hammer, Gary Cole	1–2
	February 9–15	#1976	Lucy and Desi	1–2
	February 16–22	#1977	Watching the War	1
	February 23	#1978	Roseanne, War News, Mr. Rogers	1
	March 2–8	#1979	Jaleel White of Family Matters	1
	March 9–15	#1980	Empty Nest	1
	March 16–22	#1981	Teenage Mutant Ninja Turtles	2–3
	March 23–29	#1982	Costner, Goldberg, Julia Roberts	1–2
	March 30	#1983	Cheryl Ladd, Whitney Houston	2–4
	April 6–12	#1984	Baseball TV Preview	1
	April 13–19	#1985	Designing Women's Delta Burke	1–2
	April 20–26	#1986	Burt Reynolds and Marilu Henner	1–2
	April 27	#1987	Dinosaurs	1–3
	May 4–10	#1988	Larry Hagman: Adios Dallas	1–2
	May 11–17	#1989	L.A. Law cast cover	1–2
	May 18–24	#1990	Murphy Brown cast cover	1–2
	May 25–31	#1991	Julia Roberts, Arnold Schwarzennegger	1–2
	June 1–7	#1992	A Different World	1
	June 8–14	#1993	Michael Landon	2–4

YEAR	ISSUE	NUMBER	DESCRIPTION	VALUE
1991	June 15–21	#1994	The Wizard of Oz, 50 Best Videos	$1–2
	June 22–28	#1995	Gerald McRaney and Delta Burke	1
	June 29	#1996	The Battle for Johnny Carson's Crown	1
	July 6–12	#1997	The Best and the Worst	1
	July 13–19	#1998	Michael Landon	2–4
	July 20–26	#1999	Michael Landon	2–4
	July 27	#2000	2,000 Issue Special	1–3
	August 3–9	#2001	Madonna: MTV's 10th Anniversary	2–4
	August 10–16	#2002	TV's Most Beautiful Women	1
	August 17–23	#2003	Kevin Costner, Macauley Culkin	1
	August 24–30	#2004	Beverly Hills 90210's Shannen Doherty	2–3
	August 31	#2005	Star Trek: Kirk versus Picard	2–4
	September 7–13	#2006	Northern Exposure's Janine Turner	1–3
	September 14–20	#2007	Fall Preview special	4–5
	September 21–27	#2008	Jan Hooks and Julia Duffy	1–2
	September 28	#2009	Parents' Guide to New Kids' Shows	1
	October 5–11	#2010	Best and Worst Dressed	1
	October 12–18	#2011	Jacqueline Kennedy	1

September 15, 1963   November 17, 1963   February 23, 1964

March 8, 1964   January 31, 1965   December 12, 1965

January 16, 1966   February 6, 1966   January 15, 1967

YEAR	ISSUE	NUMBER	DESCRIPTION	VALUE
1991	October 19–25	#2012	Dynasty's Linda Evans and Joan Collins	$1–2
	October 26	#2013	Joan Rivers	1
	November 2–8	#2014	Michael Landon	2–4
	November 9–15	#2015	Is Network News Crumbling?	1
	November 16–22	#2016	Valerie Bertinelli	1–2
	November 23–29	#2017	Madonna	2–4
	November 30	#2018	The Judds	2–3
	December 7–13	#2019	Holiday Viewing Guide	1
	December 14–20	#2020	Beverly Hills 90210	1–2
	December 21–27	#2021	Northern Exposure	1–2
	December 28	#2022	John Goodman	1–2
All other issues				1–2
Fall Preview issues (1992–Present)				2–5

Illustrated Magazines

Old magazines are much in demand in today's collectible marketplace. They are fascinating paper time machines that propel one into other times and ages. They unfold for you attitudes, fashions, illustrations, advertising, photographica, and a slice of history—they cover the spectrum from yellow journalism to slick high fashion.

It would be an impossible task to price each and every issue ever published in the past hundred years, as there have been thousands of American publications and millions of different issues. Values for old magazines also vary a great deal. For example, say you find a pile of old magazines and they are fifty to sixty years old; most of these magazines will be worth only $2 or $5, other issues may have retail values of $10 to $100 each. What makes some of the issues more valuable than others is something on it or in it that is salable to a collector, dealer, or general buyer. Many old magazines have multiple value. For instance: a mid-1920s *Ladies' Home Journal* may have a cover by Norman Rockwell, an advertisement by Maxfield Parrish, a Mavis Perfume ad, an article by F. Scott Fitzgerald, a paper doll page, auto ads, and on and on . . . each of these separate items has value to the specialized collector looking for that certain type of old paper.

During the Golden Age of Illustration (about 1895 to 1930) magazine covers, ads, and story illustrations were created by a large variety of highly paid illustrators. It is mostly these illustrated items that make up most of an old magazine's value. Illustrator-oriented items are sought nationwide.

Today the best source for buying, selling, or just learning about old magazines is *The Illustrator Collector's News,* located at P.O. Box 1958, Sequim, Washington 98382. A one-year subscription to this most interesting publication is $17 for first-class posting. *The Illustrator Collec-*

tor's News also offers various free price guides to subscribers on related subject matter. For more information, feel free to call our special Collector's Hotline at 201-641-7212.

THE 12 MOST-COLLECTIBLE ILLUSTRATORS

ILLUSTRATOR	YEARS WORKED	MAGAZINE VALUES
Maxfield Parrish	1895–1936	$10–175
Norman Rockwell	1914–1975	1–500
Varga	1920–1974	3–100
Petty	1932–1955	5–100
Rose O'Neal	1896–1935	3–100
Harrison Fisher	1890–1935	5–65
Erté	1916–1936	10–80
Coles Phillips	1907–1927	2–40
Rolf Armstrong	1914–1932	8–75
J. C. Leyendecker	1896–1951	3–90
F. X. Leyendecker	1886–1924	3–90
Jessie Wilcox Smith	1900–1934	4–35

There are also hundreds of other minor illustrators who are becoming more popular with the collecting world daily. This trend will continue, causing an ever-growing demand for their works. Because these old magazines are no longer being published, demand will continue to outpace supply, and values will rise steadily.

October 1927

August 3, 1918

August 1908

June 1926

April 25, 1914

March 20, 1915

Alberto Varga
Magazines Featuring Varga Work
(A Sampling)

YEAR	ISSUE	DESCRIPTION	VALUE
Airbrush Action			
1988	March/April	Article	$2–5
Dance			
1931	June	Cover: Pavlova	$50–100
	August	Cover: Spanish Girl	50–100
Esquire			
1940	October	Centerfold: Love at Second Sight	$25–50
1941	January	Centerfold: Double Trouble	20–40
	February	Centerfold: Lullabye for a Dream	20–40
1943	January	6-Page Calendar Special	25–75
	February	Centerfold: Song for a Soldier	20–40
1946	January	Centerfold: Miss January	25–50
	February	Centerfold: Saints Be Praised	20–40
Ladies' Home Journal			
1942	November	¼-Page Sealy Ad	$5–10
1943	November	Jergens Ad	10–20
Mademoiselle			
1941	December	Calendar Ad	$7–15
Motion Picture			
1924	February	Leatrice Joy	$30–60
Newsweek			
1940	October 23	Article	$5–10

Rose O'Neal
Magazines Featuring O'Neal Work
(A Sampling)

Rose O'Neal is the most famous woman illustrator of all time. Rose is primarily known for her Kewpie art, though her talents were much broader than just Kewpies. Her old paper items sell very well, and there is a large number of faithful followers who avidly hunt for her old illustrations, advertising, and magazine covers.

Delineator (Kewpie pages)

YEAR	ISSUE	DESCRIPTION	VALUE
1928	July	Kewpieville Civil Pride	$10–20

Good Housekeeping
(most containing 4 pages of Kewpie illustrations)

YEAR	ISSUE	DESCRIPTION	VALUE
1914	May	Kewpies Are Coming	$12–25
	August	Kewpies and Little Tibby's Tree	10–20
	September	Kewpies and Young McShanes	10–20
1915	January	Kewpies and Old Father Time	9–18
1916	April	Kewpies and Little Tommy Todd	9–18
1917	December	Kewpies and Forgotten Toys	10–20
1918	January	Kewpies and Their Winter Industry	9–18
	July	Kewpies and Liberty's Birthday	8–16
1919	May	Kewpies and the Haunted House	10–20

Puck

YEAR	ISSUE	DESCRIPTION	VALUE
1897	September 15	Black-and-white cover	$45–90
	December 22	Black-and-white illustration	10–20
1898	January 5	Black-and-white illustration	10–20
	February 9	Illustration	30–60

YEAR	ISSUE	DESCRIPTION	VALUE
1900	January 9	Black-and-white illustrations	$10–20
	April 11	Illustration	20–40
1903	March 11	Black-and-white illustrations	15–30
1904	March 30	Black-and-white illustration	10–20
1926	April	Black-and-white illustration	10–20
1927	February	Black-and-white illustration	7–15

Woman's Home Companion (Dotty Darling and Kewpies)

YEAR	ISSUE	DESCRIPTION	VALUE
1910	September	Just How It Happened	$15–30
1911	February	D.D.'s Kewpish Valentine	10–20
	March	Kewpies Teach D.D. to Fly	10–20

GEORGE PETTY
MAGAZINES FEATURING PETTY WORK
(A SAMPLING)

Esquire

YEAR	ISSUE	DESCRIPTION	VALUE
1933	August	Pinups: Darling and Pardon Me, Miss	$15–35
1934	June	Pinup: Oh, Mr. Feinberg	20–40
1935	February	Old Gold cigarette ad: Stymied by a Stupid	10–20
	March	Old Gold cigarette ad: Wearied by a Windbag	10–20
	April	Old Gold cigarette ad: Pawed by a Pudgy-Widgy	10–20
	May	Old Gold cigarette ad: Shanghaied by a Silly Salt	10–20
	June	Old Gold cigarette ad: Tortured by a Tele-Phoney	8–15
	July	Old Gold cigarette ad: Bothered by a Beach Bore Pinup: Tired Folks	25–50

YEAR	ISSUE	DESCRIPTION	VALUE
1935	August	Old Gold cigarette ad: No-Noed by a Nifty Number	$ 8–15
	September	Old Gold cigarette ad: Marooned with a Mental Mummy	8–15
	October	Old Gold cigarette ad: Hitched to a Humrummy	8–15
	November	Old Gold cigarette ad: Riled by a Racoon Rah-Rah	8–15
	December	Old Gold cigarette ad: Smacked by a Sappy Santa	8–15
1939	December	Pinup: Well	25–50
1940	January	Pinup: So He Pointed Out	20–40
1941	January	Pinup: Remember Me	20–40
	February	Pinup: Yes, Yes, Yes	20–40
	March	Pinup: No It Isn't That	20–40
1946	September	½-page Springmaid Fabrics ad	4–8
1955	January	Pinup: Lady Fair	10–25
1971	October	Girl on Swing cover illustration	5–10

True

1945	January	Pinup: Miss Pouty	$15–30
	February	Pinup: Miss Athlete	10–25
	March	Pinup: Miss Clinging Vine	10–25
	April	Pinup: Miss Career Girl	10–25
	June	Pinup: Miss Bashful	10–25
	July	Pinup: Miss She Wolf	10–25
	August	Pinup: Miss Pixie	10–25
	September	Pinup: Miss Self Salesman	10–25
	October	Pinup: Miss Exclusive	10–25
	November	Pinup: Miss Bewitching	15–25
	December	Pinup: Miss Wrong Number	10–25

Norman Rockwell
Magazines Featuring Rockwell Covers
(A Sampling)

YEAR	ISSUE	DESCRIPTION	VALUE
American Magazine			
1918	November	Cover	$25–50
1923	March	Cover	15–30
Boys Life			
1913	November	Cover	$25–50
	December	Cover	25–50
1914	February	Cover	25–50
	March	Cover	25–50
1915	May	Cover	30–60
	August	Cover	30–60
1919	July	Cover	25–50
Child Life			
1954	December	Cover	$10–15
Country Gentleman			
1917	August 25	Cover	$20–40
	September 8	Cover	20–40
Leslie's			
1916	October 5	Cover	$10–35
1918	March 30	Cover	10–35
Literary Digest			
1919	February 8	Cover	$10–25
	June 14	Cover	10–30
	July 26	Cover	10–30
McCall's			
1964	December	Cover	$5–8

YEAR	ISSUE	DESCRIPTION	VALUE

People's Popular Monthly

YEAR	ISSUE	DESCRIPTION	VALUE
1917	May	Cover	$25–60
	June	Cover	25–60
1920	May 15	Cover	25–40
1923	August	Cover	20–40
1962	November 3	Cover	5–10
1963	March 2	Cover	5–10

Youth's Companion

YEAR	ISSUE	DESCRIPTION	VALUE
1916	February 24	Cover	$20–40
1917	April 26	Cover	20–40

MAXFIELD PARRISH
MAGAZINES FEATURING PARRISH WORK
(A SAMPLING)

YEAR	ISSUE	DESCRIPTION	VALUE

Atlantic Monthly

YEAR	ISSUE	DESCRIPTION	VALUE
1921	June	Hires ad	$20–40

Book Buyer

YEAR	ISSUE	DESCRIPTION	VALUE
1897	December	Cover	$50–100+
1899	December	Cover and black-and-white illustration	50–100

Bookseller, The

YEAR	ISSUE	DESCRIPTION	VALUE
1914	May 1	Illustration	$12–25

Century

YEAR	ISSUE	DESCRIPTION	VALUE
1900	December	Black-and-white Fisk Tire ad	$20–40
1914	December	Cover	25–50
1921	September	Jell-O ad	20–40

YEAR	ISSUE	DESCRIPTION	VALUE

Collier's

1904	December 3	Cover	$30–60
1906	November 17	Frontispiece	25–50
1908	January 25	Frontispiece	35–75
1909	July 24	Cover	40–80
1929	January 5	Cover	40–80

Harper's Bazaar

1895	December	Cover	$75–125
1922	March	Jell-O ad	40–60

Nebraska Educational Journal

1928	October	Cover	$20–40

Pictorial Review

1922	January	Jell-O ad	$60–100

Progressive Farmer

1952	June	Cover	$20–30

St. Nicholas

1898	December	Black-and-white illustration	$10–20
1900	November	Black-and-white illustration	10–20

Town and Country

1918	May	Fisk Tire ad	$30–60
1919	August	Fisk Tire ad	40–80

Vanity Fair

1922	February	Jell-O ad	$35–70

Vogue

1917	September 1	Fisk Tire ad	$35–70

YEAR	ISSUE	DESCRIPTION	VALUE
Woman's Home Companion			
1918	March	Djer-Kiss ad	$40–80
1921	April	Ferry Seed ad	45–90
Worlds Work			
1919	December	Fisk Tire ad	$20–40
1921	June	Hires ad	15–30
Yankee			
1935	December	Cover	$20–40
1968	December	Cover	10–20
1977	May	Cover	5–10
1979	December	Cover	3–6

JOSEPH CHRISTIAN AND FRANK XAVIER LEYENDECKER
MAGAZINES FEATURING LEYENDECKER WORK
(A SAMPLING)

Joseph Christian Leyendecker (1896–1951) and Frank Xavier Leyendecker (1886–1924) covers their known illustrated works. Both brothers today have a large following of collectors. Joseph Christian did more published illustration work than almost anyone, with the exception of Norman Rockwell. In the early years Norman Rockwell emulated Leyendecker's style. In the first quarter of this century Leyendecker art was predominant in the form of magazine covers, advertising, story illustrations, books, and posters.

Joseph Christian Leyendecker had a rather large cult/art following of Americans who framed his magazine art to hang in their homes in the 'teens and the 'twenties of this century. Many of the colorful ads Joseph Christian created adorned the walls in the rooms of many college men of those days. His strong and bold art helped create the fashion trends that influenced millions of men and women. There are still those who remember the days of the steel-jawed Arrow Shirt Man and the Kuppenheimer Man. These fantasy men were women's answers to the Gibson Girl.

Both brothers were born in Germany and traveled with their family to Chicago in 1882. There they both displayed an extraordinary talent for drawing at an early age. By the time they were teenagers and had acquired some formal training, the doors to small ad agencies opened up to them in Chicago. After a few years of art training in Paris—at the Academie Du Julian—the brothers returned home with newly honed skills and began illustrating for many of the high-paying magazines of the day. Frank died early in his career (1924); much of his early work was as good if not better than his older brother's. Many experts believe his true potential was never fully realized.

YEAR	ISSUE	DESCRIPTION	VALUE
Arts and Decoration			
1922	November	Frank Xavier cover	$20–30
Collier's			
1901	Anniversary issue	Frank Xavier cover	$40–75
1902	July 5	Frank Xavier cover	25–50
	December 20	Frank Xavier cover	25–50
1903	February 20	Frank Xavier cover	25–50
	June 27	Frank Xavier cover	25–50
	July 25	Frank Xavier cover	25–50
1904	February 13	Frank Xavier cover	35–60
	March 5	Joseph Christian cover	35–60
	May 7	Joseph Christian cover	30–40
	May 14	Frank Xavier cover	20–30
	June 18	Joseph Christian cover	20–40
	July 4	Frank Xavier cover	30–40
	August 4	Frank Xavier cover	30–40
1906	January 13	Frank Xavier cover	30–40
	March 24	Joseph Christian cover	40–60
	May 5	Joseph Christian cover	40–60
	October 27	Frank Xavier cover	30–40
	December 29	Frank Xavier cover	20–40
1907	January 19	Joseph Christian cover	20–40
	February 23	Joseph Christian cover	20–40

December 18, 1937 *October 20, 1939* *November 1939*

December 23, 1939 *December 30, 1939* *January 6, 1940*

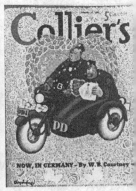

January 27, 1940 *February 7, 1940* *February 17, 1940*

March 2, 1940

March 16, 1940

March 23, 1940

May 1929

April 1940

September 1928

June 1939

July 1946

October 1946

YEAR	ISSUE	DESCRIPTION	VALUE
1907	March 23	Joseph Christian cover	$25–50
	April 27	Joseph Christian cover	25–50
	May 25	Joseph Christian cover	25–40
	August 17	Frank Xavier cover	30–40
	August 31	Frank Xavier cover	20–35
	September 14	Joseph Christian cover	20–40
	September 19	Joseph Christian cover	20–40
	October 26	Joseph Christian cover	20–45
	November 9	Frank Xavier cover	20–40
	December 7	Joseph Christian cover	17–35
	December 21	Joseph Christian cover	30–50
1908	April 18	Frank Xavier cover	30–40
1909	January 9	Frank Xavier cover	20–40
	August 28	Joseph Christian cover	20–40
	October 16	Joseph Christian cover	20–40
1910	January 29	Frank Xavier cover	20–40
	February 26	Frank Xavier cover	30–50
	March 12	Frank Xavier cover	30–40
	April 30	Frank Xavier cover	30–40
	December 10	Frank Xavier cover	30–40
1912	June 19	Frank Xavier cover	25–40
1914	May 30	Frank Xavier cover	20–40
	September 12	Joseph Christian cover	30–45
	November 28	Joseph Christian cover	30–40
1915	February 20	Frank Xavier cover	25–45
	May 29	Frank Xavier cover	25–45
	June 19	Joseph Christian cover	20–40
	September 11	Frank Xavier cover	20–40
	October 9	Joseph Christian cover	20–40
	December 11	Joseph Christian cover	20–40
1916	January 8	Joseph Christian cover	20–40
	April 22	Joseph Christian cover	25–50
	June 24	Joseph Christian cover	20–40
	September 23	Joseph Christian cover	20–45
	October 23	Joseph Christian cover	20–40
1917	January 6	Joseph Christian cover	20–40
	April 14	Joseph Christian cover	20–40

YEAR	ISSUE	DESCRIPTION	VALUE
1917	April 28	Joseph Christian cover	$20–40
	July 7	Joseph Christian cover	20–40
	November 10	Joseph Christian cover	20–40

Inland Printer

1896	November	Joseph Christian cover	$100–150
1897	January	Joseph Christian cover	100–150
	February	Joseph Christian cover	100–150
	March	Joseph Christian cover	100–150
	August	Joseph Christian cover	100–150
	September	Joseph Christian cover	100–150

Saturday Evening Post

1899	May 20	Joseph Christian cover	$25–50
1900	May 26	Frank Xavier cover	20–35
1901	March 23	Frank Xavier cover	15–30
	June 22	Frank Xavier cover	15–30
1902	May 31	Frank Xavier cover	15–30
1910	January 1	Joseph Christian cover	20–30
	February 12	Joseph Christian cover	20–30
1912	April 6	Joseph Christian cover	20–30
	May 25	Joseph Christian cover	20–30
	June 22	Joseph Christian cover	15–25
	July 6	Joseph Christian cover	20–30
	September 28	Frank Xavier cover	15–25
	October 12	Frank Xavier cover	15–25
1914	January 3	Joseph Christian cover	15–25
	June 13	Joseph Christian cover	15–30
	July 4	Joseph Christian cover	15–30
	August 22	Frank Xavier cover	20–30
	September 19	Joseph Christian cover	20–30
	October 3	Joseph Christian cover	20–30
	October 24	Joseph Christian cover	15–30
	November 21	Joseph Christian cover	20–30
	November 28	Joseph Christian cover	20–30
	December 19	Joseph Christian cover	20–30

YEAR	ISSUE	DESCRIPTION	VALUE
1915	January 2	Joseph Christian cover	$20–30
	April 3	Joseph Christian cover	20–30
	May 22	Joseph Christian cover	15–30
	June 12	Joseph Christian cover	15–30
	July 24	Joseph Christian cover	15–30
	August 7	Joseph Christian cover	20–30
	November 20	Joseph Christian cover	15–30
	December 11	Joseph Christian cover	15–30
	December 25	Joseph Christian cover	15–30
1916	January 1	Joseph Christian cover	15–25
	March 11	Joseph Christian cover	15–25
	April 15	Joseph Christian cover	15–25
	April 22	Joseph Christian cover	20–30
	May 6	Joseph Christian cover	15–25
	June 17	Joseph Christian cover	20–40
	July 1	Joseph Christian cover	20–30
	August 26	Joseph Christian cover	15–30
	December 8	Joseph Christian cover	20–30
1921	January 1	Joseph Christian cover	20–30
	March 26	Joseph Christian cover	20–30
	June 11	Joseph Christian cover	20–30
	December 10	Joseph Christian cover	20–30
	December 24	Joseph Christian cover	12–25
	December 31	Joseph Christian cover	12–25
1929	March 30	Joseph Christian cover	20–30
	June 8	Joseph Christian cover	20–30
1934	March 10	Joseph Christian cover	20–30
	March 31	Joseph Christian cover	20–30
	July 7	Joseph Christian cover	20–30
	December 1	Joseph Christian cover	20–35
	December 29	Joseph Christian cover	20–30
1937	January 2	Joseph Christian cover	10–20
	February 20	Joseph Christian cover	12–25
	May 15	Joseph Christian cover	12–25
	July 3	Joseph Christian cover	12–25
	December 18	Joseph Christian cover	15–30

Media Magazines

❈

A media magazine is any magazine that features news of the day on its cover and in its stories. Such titles as *Newsweek, Time, Pic, Click,* and *Look* fall into this category. Below we have valued average media issues—that is, issues that do not feature an outstanding cover or feature. Exceptional issues will be issues that feature major national or worldwide events, such as catastrophes (the sinking of the *Titanic* or the *Lusitania,* the San Francisco earthquake, and so on), historic events or people (Lindbergh crossing the Atlantic, gangster news, the sinking of the *Bismark,* reports on Hitler or major war events). These issues will have a value from 100 to 500 percent of the listed average issue value for that time period.

Average Media Magazine Values

ISSUES	VALUE
Pre-1918	$10–20
1919–1930	10–15
1931–1938	8–12
1939–1945	10–20
1946–1955	4–8
1956–1965	2–5
1965–1975	1–3
1976–Present	1–2

Monster Magazines: Illustrated Horror, Monster/Science Fiction TV/Movie and Related Magazines

In 1958 James Warren published *Famous Monsters of Filmland*; today it is known as the Granddaddy of All Monster Magazines. With the very first issue, Editor Forrest J. Ackerman set the spark that has become a glowing flame in the hearts of collectors, both young and old. Monster magazine collectors take their hobby very seriously, and quite often branch out into collecting monster models, figures, gum cards, buttons, posters, photos, horror videos, and countless other related memorabilia. This hobby has shown tremendous growth in the past two decades. This is clearly attested to by the increasing number of monster conventions being held throughout the United States and other countries. Values are rising and the number of new collectors entering the field is tremendous.

To the new collector, welcome to the hobby. To all seasoned collectors, sit back in a soft chair and enjoy viewing the values on all those magazines you saved despite the many voices advising you to throw them out.

WHAT ARE MONSTER MAGAZINES?

The term monster magazine covers a wide assortment of magazine types, such as magazines specializing in a monster, horror, or science fiction theme. However the "true" monster magazine in its purest form is a publication dedicated solely to monster and horror films of the movies and television. Examples of these "true" monster magazines are ... *Famous Monsters of Filmland, Castle of Frankenstein, Mad Monsters, The Monster Times, Horror Monsters, Monster Parade, Mon-*

sters and Things, Movie Monsters, World Famous Creatures, and *The Journal of Frankenstein.* These monster magazines generally have excellent stories packed with photos on all the classic horror films from the past, right up to the film reviews of current releases. Quite often biographies and interviews are included about the stars, directors, and the makeup and production people. A currently published magazine that nearly falls into this category is *Filmfax.* This publication has been received quite well by collectors and has seen its back issues climb in value in a very short period of time. Not only are the classic horror films covered in *Filmfax,* but it includes the TV shows of the 'fifties and 'sixties.

Next come the science fiction/horror magazines. Titles such as *Starlog, Starburst, Fantastic Films, Science/Fantasy Film Classics,* and others specialize mainly in science fiction movies and TV with an occasional story on monsters or classic horror. These magazines, for the most part, are very well done and service the collector's need to keep up on the current and upcoming science fiction movies.

Monster magazine collectors are often interested in science fiction and monster related magazines. A related science fiction monster magazine is any non-horror/science fiction magazine that contains a feature story with a horror, science fiction, or monster theme. Very often the cover of the magazine depicts its theme.

The following are examples of some magazines and issues that fall into this category:

YEAR	ISSUE/NUMBER	DESCRIPTION	VALUE
American Cinematographer			
1981	March	Altered States cover and feature: The Filming of	$2–4
1983	January	E.T. the Extra-Terrestrial cover and feature	2–4
1989	October	Phantom of the Opera cover and feature: The Legend Continues	3–6
Bananas (Scholastic Magazines Inc.)			
1979	#33	Star Trek the Movie cover and feature	$3–6

YEAR	ISSUE/NUMBER	DESCRIPTION	VALUE

Dynamite (Scholastic Magazines Inc.)

1975	#15	Christopher Lee cover and feature: The Monster Hall of Fame . . . an exclusive interview with Christopher Lee, issue includes a free Christopher Lee poster	$3–6
1981	#83	Interview with Don Post, Christopher Lee, Bride of Frankenstein	2–4

Film Comment

1979	November/December	Nosferatu cover and feature	$3–5
1981	January/February	Altered States cover and feature	2–4
	July/August	Raiders of the Lost Ark cover and feature	3–6
	November/December	Time Bandits cover and feature	2–4

Films Illustrated

1976	October	Logan's Run cover and feature	$5–10

Jump Cut (tabloid)

1979	#21	Alien cover and feature	$5–10

Rolling Stone

1989	#553	Sigourney Weaver and Ghostbusters II cover and feature	$3–6

Wow (Scholastic Inc.)

1983	#67	Star Wars cover and feature	$3–6

Most science fiction monster related magazines fall into the $2 to $4 price range, with some selling for as high as $10. Higher prices are based on the current popularity of a show or star and the issue's availability.

A fanzine, as the name implies, is a fan magazine published and written by a fan and/or a fan club. These amateur magazines can range from just a few pages to well over a hundred pages. Many are extremely well done and are usually dedicated to one specific area of collecting. The dozens of fanzines published in recent years solely on the television show "Beauty and the Beast" are wonderful examples. Today the collector can still find fanzines on such subjects as "Space 1999," "Star Trek," "The Avengers," "Dark Shadows," "Lost in Space," and countless other shows and movies. A fanzine's value is based on its content, whether or not it contains an exclusive interview with a star (one that has not been published elsewhere), and if it includes rare unpublished photos. The quality of stories can also play a role in its value. Most fanzines of the 'sixties, 'seventies, 'eighties, and 'nineties sell for $2 to $5, with the more desirable valued at $7 to $10.

Prozines are basically fanzines put together on a more professional level. Prozines generally have a larger production budget and are often printed by a local print shop. Examples of prozines would be such titles as: *The Japanese Fantasy Film Journal, Top Secret, The Old Dark House, Cinemagic* (pre-*Starlog*), *Little Shop of Horrors, Gore Creatures, Midnight Marque, SPFX, Photon,* and *Bizarre.* In our value section we will be listing some of the more noted titles. Most prozines are valued at $3 to $7.

Finally we come to the monster/horror illustrated magazines. These magazines are just now coming into their own, after many years of "getting no respect." Collectors and investors are appreciating the fine artwork of such magazines as *Eerie, Creepy,* and *Vampirella.* Also appreciated is the macabre artwork of *Eerie Tales, Weird Mysteries, Tales from the Tomb, Weird, Witches' Tales, Tales of Voodoo, Shock,* and others. In the past these illustrated horror magazines were valued and graded by the comic book world. Today, collectors of monster magazines actively include these extremely imaginative horror magazines in their collections. Certain titles of illustrated horror magazines have not been listed in this guide (for example, *Monsters Unleashed, Dracula Lives,* and a few others). These titles are more highly regarded by comic collectors than monster magazine collectors at present. If you wish to research illustrated horror magazines not listed in this guide, refer to *The Confident Collector: The Overstreet Comic Book Price Guide* by Robert M. Overstreet.

BUYING MONSTER MAGAZINES

Today purchasing monster magazines is accomplished in three ways:

1. MAIL ORDER

Dealers specializing in monster magazines can be found in the classified sections of many publications, such as:

The Comic Buyer's Guide, 700 East State Street, Iola, Wisconsin 54990

Toy Shop, 700 East State Street, Iola, Wisconsin 54990

Film Collectors World, 700 East State Street, Iola, Wisconsin 54990

Starlog, 475 Park Avenue South, New York, New York 10016

Fangoria, 475 Park Avenue South, New York, New York 10016

Gorezone, 475 Park Avenue South, New York, New York 10016

Filmfax, Box 1900, Evanston, Illinois 60204

Model Toy Collector, 15354 Seville Road, Seville, Ohio

The Illustrator Collector's News, P.O. Box 19598, Sequim, Washington 98382

PCM (*Paper Collector's Marketplace*), 470 Main Street, P.O. Box 127, Scandinavia, Wisconsin 54977

When selecting a mail-order dealer be certain that the dealer offers return privileges (generally within seven days), as the seller's idea of condition may be different from your own. Usually, the collector is only fully satisfied when he has the magazine in his own hands and can determine for himself the condition of the magazine. Mail-order dealers are the best source, since most keep complete runs of all titles in stock and offer them on a consistant basis. If a mail-order dealer does not have your issues in stock or an issue in the condition you are seeking, more often than not he will be able to locate that copy at a later date. Two companies have been selling monster magazines for more than twenty-five years: The Back Issue, 24 Orchard Street, Ridgefield Park, New Jersey 07660, 201-641-7212; and The Passaic Book Center, 594 Main Avenue, Passaic, New Jersey 07055, 201-778-6646.

A collector should also consider taking out his or her own classified ad. Often this will lead to trading and buying through the mail from fellow enthusiasts at very agreeable terms, and it can lead to mail-order friends.

2. COMIC BOOK AND BACK-ISSUE MAGAZINE SHOPS

Comic shops don't always monitor their inventory carefully, so when entering the comic shop always ask to speak to the owner and ask for the magazine you want. Too often collectors, not seeing monster magazines on display, will turn around and quietly walk out. But if you follow this advice and ask, you may be pleasantly rewarded, as comic dealers have been known to price issues lower than their true value. Back-issue magazine stores are a different story since they are not as plentiful as the comic shops. Issues of monster magazines will be clearly on display. Again The Passaic Book Center is a terrific shop, or check your local phone directory under ''Magazines'' for a store in your own area.

3. MONSTER AND SCIENCE FICTION CONVENTIONS

A convention is where nonstop excitement is found; dozens of dealers at small shows to hundreds of dealers at the big conventions offer thousands of magazines and related memorabilia to the attendees. Conventions offer vintage horror and fantasy flicks, autograph sessions, and lectures by celebrities in the horror field. In addition, they comprise a source for meeting and making new friends. To learn of upcoming conventions check the trade publications. Two excellent sources that list conventions are *Starlog* and *Fangoria* magazines.

SELLING MONSTER MAGAZINES

When selling your magazines, first consider selling them through an inexpensive classified in a trade publication such as *The Comic Buyer's Guide, Toy Shop, PCM,* or others. Ads in these journals can cost pennies per word and usually deliver good results. If you have an extensive collection, which is of high quality and quantity, you may consider advertising in *Starlog, Fangoria, Gorezone,* or *Filmfax.* Ads in these publications can cost several dollars per word but reach a much wider audience. It is not unusual for a collector, while in the process of selling his or her collection, to find himself becoming a part-time dealer and enjoying it. Many of today's most respected dealers started out in this manner.

Selling to dealers is advisable if the seller wishes to sell the collection quickly. Do not expect very high values, because a dealer has overhead costs and must make a profit from the magazine's resale in order to stay in business. Dealers will usually offer anywhere from 10 to 50 percent of an issue's resale value with common magazines bought for 10 to 25 percent of the resale value. Rarer issues (which are most desirable and therefore faster selling) will sell to the dealer at 25 to 50 percent. For example, if you are fortunate enough to offer a dealer vintage copies of *Famous Monsters* (numbers 1 through 22 and 38), *Monster Parade, Shock Tales, World Famous Creatures,* and *Thriller* in extremely fine to mint condition, do not settle for less than 75 percent of the current resale value. These issues are a premium and sell very quickly. Be patient, be flexible, and you will get a decent price from one dealer or another.

Again, conventions are the most exciting way to sell your collection or duplicate issues. Dealers' tables are available for (depending on the show) just a few dollars to several hundred dollars at the larger conventions. Not only do you get to sell your magazines (whether it be a few or your whole inventory), you also share and enjoy the day with fellow fans. When selling at conventions, price your magazines competitively and you should have an experience of a lifetime.

For up-to-date convention information write: Kevin Clement, % Chiller Theater, P.O. Box 2608, Bloomfield, New Jersey 07003; or call the Horror Convention Hotlines at: 201-804-8040 or 201-641-7212.

GRADING

The grading of monster magazines is very important to the collector and should be equally as important to the dealer/seller. Properly grading older issues of monster magazines is an absolute must. Collectors of these earlier and rarer issues want to know each imperfection that may exist on the outside and on the inside of the magazine before they make the purchase. Collectors of other types of magazines (rock and teen magazines, or adult magazines, for example) are much more tolerant of an issue's condition.

Note: For grading conditions, refer to the grading section of this book.

Monster/Science Fiction Magazine Values

YEAR	ISSUE/NUMBER	DESCRIPTION	VALUE

Adventures into Horror (Stanley Publications)

1970	#1		$7–15
	#2		6–12

Alien (Alien: The Movie One Shot published by Warren)

1979		Includes scenes cut from the film, special effects photos	$2–5

Alien Nation Television Special
(illustrated; Malibu Graphics Publishing Group)

1991	One Shot	The Lost Episode	$2–4

All About Star Trek Fan Clubs (Ego Enterprises)

1977	#1–5		$5–10

Amazing Cinema (Cinema Enterprises)
Publishing begins in 1981

	All issues		$5–10

Amazing Forries
(one issue published by Metropolis Publications)

1976		Dedicated to Forrest J. Ackerman . . . this is your life	$20–40

American Cinematographer (ASC Holding Co.)

1980	February	Star Trek the Motion Picture cover and feature . . . A Look Behind the Scenes	$3–6

YEAR	ISSUE/NUMBER	DESCRIPTION	VALUE
1989	October	Lon Chaney cover and feature: Phantom of the Opera . . . The Legend Continues	$3–5

Ancient Astronaut Special Edition/Star Wars versus Alien (Countrywide Publications)

1979	Fall	The Nightmare Worlds of Alien, Behind the Scenes at Alien, Star Wars: Droids Take Over, Meet H. R. Giger: Horror Master	$3–6

Bananas

1979	#33	Star Trek cover and movie preview	$3–5

Battlestar Galactica Official Poster Magazine

	#1–4		$5–10

Black Zoo (Charlton Publications)

1963		One shot of the movie, a picture-by-picture chiller mag	$10–20

Castle of Frankenstein (Gothic Castle Publishing Company)
1962–1975

	#1		$15–30
	#2	The many faces of Christopher Lee, superheroes, etc.	15–30
	#3	The Karloff story, the Frankenstein story, son of Chaney, etc.	15–30
	#4	Special vampire issue, Lon Chaney Jr., etc.	12–25

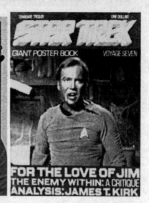

#15, September 1975   #25, 1976

#1, 1979   #2, 1979   Volume 17

#2, 1979   #10, 1979   #22, 1979

YEAR	ISSUE/NUMBER	DESCRIPTION	VALUE
	#5	Edgar Rice Burrough's Frankenstein, The Evil of Frankenstein, the Peter Lorre story, etc.	$ 7–15
	#6	Christopher Lee returns in the Gorgon, radio horrors, Alfred Hitchcock interview, Dracula and the Wolfman, Lon Chaney Jr.'s monsters, another lost Frankenstein, etc.	7–15
	#7	Die, Monster, Die: a visit to the set . . . Boris Karloff's first monster role since 1929, the night Richard Burton turned into a monster, Bela Lugosi versus Christopher Lee, Dracula Prince of Darkness	7–15
	#8	Christopher Lee as Dracula cover, Fu Manchu: behind the scenes, David McCallum: The Man from M.O.N.S.T.E.R., Bela Lugosi's last days, Batman and Robin: from the serial to TV	10–20
	#9	Batman's TV Joker cover, TV villains: Catwoman, Fantomas, Boris Karloff, Victor Buono, and others, a Batman special	15–30+
	#10	TV's Green Hornet cover and feature, King Kong, Bela Lugosi's tragic addiction, Christopher Lee and Lon Chaney exclusive interviews	10–20+

YEAR	ISSUE/NUMBER	DESCRIPTION	VALUE
	#11	Leonard Nimoy/Star Trek cover and feature, a talk with Christopher Lee, the man behind Marvel Comics, The Horror Chamber of Dr. Faustus, UFO: flying saucers and worldwide blackouts	$15–30+
	#12	Raquel Welch/One Million Years B.C. cover and feature, Spock/Leonard Nimoy speaks, interview with Marvel Comics, etc.	7–15
	#13	Planet of the Apes cover and feature, 2001: A Space Odyssey, Ray Bradbury interview, Dark Shadows, etc.	10–20
	#14	Star Trek cover and feature: Star Trek is back, etc.	10–20
	#15	Witches and demons special, Planet of the Apes, etc.	7–15
	#16	Satanism and vampires issue, Dark Shadows cover and feature, the history of horror films, etc.	7–15
	#17	Magic and occult issue, history of fantasy and horror films, Ray Harryhausen's films, etc.	6–12
	#18	Frankenstein, The Night of the Living Dead, etc.	6–12
	#19	Ray Harryhausen special, etc.	6–12
	#20	Frankenstein, The Mummy, Wolfman, First Men on the Moon	6–12

YEAR	ISSUE/NUMBER	DESCRIPTION	VALUE
	#21	Frankenstein, Sinbad	$ 6–12
	#22	The Exorcist, Linda Blair cover and feature, exclusive interview with The Exorcist's director Bill Friedkin, The Exorcist: behind the scenes	10–20
	#23	Return to the Planet of the Apes cover and special feature, Roger Corman interview, George Pal's Doc Savage, etc.	6–12
	#24	Memorial to Boris Karloff special, The Evil of Frankenstein, freaks and mutations, the $25,000 monster, The Exorcist Part II	6–12
	#25	The Time Machine cover and feature, The Night Stalker, Andy Warhol's Frankenstein, Mel Brooks's Frankenstein, Phantom of the Paradise, etc.	6–12
1967	Annual		12–25+

Chilling Monster Tales (MM Publishing, Ltd.)

1966	#1	Them: Giant Ants, Dracula's Lost Chapter, House of Frankenstein, Island of Dr. Moreau	$10–20

Chilling Tales of Horror
(Stanley Publications, Inc.; illustrated horror)

1969	#1 (June, vol. 1, #1)	After Death, Epitaph, The Shadow in the Mirror, The Bloodstone	$10–20

YEAR	ISSUE/NUMBER	DESCRIPTION	VALUE
1969	#2 (August, vol. 1, #2)	The Book of Doom, Contract in Blood, Corpse in the Coffin, Vampire	$10–20
	#3 (October, vol. 1, #3)	Ghostly Revenge, Rotting Flesh of the Dead, Twin of Terror, Curse of the Vampires	10–20
1970	#4 (June, vol. 1, #4)	The Tomb of the Unseen, A Live Corpse for the Zombie, The Specter's Revenge, Payment in Full	5–10
	#5 (August, vol. 1, #5)		15–30+
	#6 (October, vol. 1, #6)	The Demon Master, King of the Vampires, Howl of the Hunter, The Devil on Your Dial	5–10
	#7 (December, vol. 1, #7)	Slave of the Living Hell, The Vampire's Fate, Within the Tomb of Terror, Wings of Darkness	5–10
1971	#8 (February, vol. 2, #2)	The Day the World Died, Spirit of Frankenstein, The Vampire's Prey, The Man Who Tried to Live Forever	5–10
	#9 (April, vol. 2, #2)	Face of the Fiend, Five Found Dead, The Flying Head, The Hands of Darkness	5–10
	#10 (June, vol. 2, #4)	Priestess of the Sphinx, The Creekmore Curse, Deity of Death, Vampire's Bane, Phantom Fountain	5–10
	#11 (August, vol. 2, #4)	Bride of the Beast, Assault from the Unknown, Vampire Cat, The Soul Collectors	5–10

YEAR	ISSUE/NUMBER	DESCRIPTION	VALUE
1971	#12 (October, vol. 2, #5)	The Winged Creatures of Satan, The Ghost Tiger, Subway Spectre, The Witches' Curse	$5–10

Cinefantastique (Frederick S. Clarke Publishing)

#1		**Note:** This title started out as a prozine with the first issue being mimeographed. This mimeographed first edition is extremely rare and if offered would easily be valued at over $100. When offered, it would be advisable to ask for bids. This would help the seller to better determine its present market value.	
#1		Professionally published issue	$15–30
#2		Dark Shadows cover and feature	20–30
#3		Review of horror, fantasy, and science fiction films	10–20
#4		George Pal's The Time Machine cover and special	12–25+
#5		Paul Wendkos interview, Mark Wolfe on Fantasy Film Animation	5–10
#6		Planet of the Apes special	10–20+
#7		Interview with George Romero	5–10
#8		Amicus Films issue special	5–10
#9		Christopher Lee special	5–10
#10		The Golden Voyage of Sinbad	5–10
#11		Zardoz special	5–10
#12		The Exorcist special	6–12+
#13		Christopher Lee: The Man with the Golden Gun	5–10
#14		Phantom of the Paradise	5–10

YEAR	ISSUE/NUMBER	DESCRIPTION	VALUE
	#15	The Films of Terence Fisher	$ 5–10
	#16	The Day the Earth Stood Still special	5–10+
	#17	A Boy and His Dog	4–8
	#18	Logan's Run Special	10–20
	#19	The Omen	6–12
	#20	War of the Worlds special	5–10
	#21	Carrie special	6–12
	#22	Ray Harryhausen special, The Eye of the Tiger	6–12
	#23	The Wicker Man	4–8
	#24	Double issue special	10–20
	#25	Hans Salter cover and feature	3–5
	#26	Close Encounters special, a double issue	5–10
	#27	The Primevals	5–10
	#28	Forbidden Planet Special, a double issue	10–20
	#29	Donner on Superman	3–5
	#30	Alien special	10–20
	#31	Salem's Lot special	5–10
	#32	The Black Hole, a double issue	3–5
	#33	John Carpenter: The Director Who Came in from the Fog	3–5
	#34	Alfred Hitchcock's The Birds	3–5
	#35	Clash of the Titans	3–5
	#36	The Explosive Films of David Cronenberg	3–5
	#37	Dick Smith: Altering States	3–5
	#38	The Filming of Altered States	3–5
	#39	Conan the Barbarian	3–5
	#40	Stop Motion Magician: George Pal	3–5

YEAR	ISSUE/NUMBER	DESCRIPTION	VALUE
	#41	Ghost Story	$ 3–5
	#42	The Filming of Conan the Barbarian	3–5
	#43	Cat People	4–8
	#44	Double issue special with two different covers: Blade Runner and Star Trek II	7–15
	#45	The Scariest Men in America	3–5
	#46	Double issue special with two different covers: Krull and The Thing	3–12
	#47	The Dark Crystal	3–5
	#48	Something Wicked This Way Comes	3–5
	#49	Double issue special . . . 3-D	4–8
	#50	The Dead Zone	3–5
	#51–55		3–5
	#56	The Return of the Living Dead special	7–15
	#57–62		3–5
	#63	Star Trek special	10–20
	#64–Present		3–5

Note: Double issue specials are generally valued at $3 to $6 or $4 to $8. A recent back issue can climb in value quite rapidly if the subject featured in that issue becomes popular with collectors, such as issues with specials on *Star Trek,* cult films, and so on.

Cinefex (Don Shay Publishing)
First issue published in March 1980

	#1	Star Trek	$10–20
	#2–7		5–10
	#8–Present		4–8

Cinemacabre (prozine published by George Strover)

	#1		$10–20
	All other issues		5–10

YEAR	ISSUE/NUMBER	DESCRIPTION	VALUE

Cinemagic (prozine published by Cinema Enterprises)

| | #1–3 | | $10–20 |
| | #4–11 | | 3–6 |

Cinemagic (published by O'Quinn)

| | #1 | Remaking Rocketship X-M | $5–10 |
| | #2–37 | | 2–4 |

Cinema Odyssey (one issue only)

| 1981 | | For Your Eyes Only, Raiders of the Lost Ark, and Superman II Exclusive behind-the-scenes photos, meet the director of Revenge of the Jedi, sexy ladies of the silver screen, the new Rocky Horror flick, interviews with John Carpenter, Susannah York, and Ray Harryhausen | $3–6 |

Cinefan

| 1974 | #1 | King Kong, Max Steiner, 2001: A Space Odyssey, Lesley Ann Warren, the Toho legend | $5–10 |

Close Encounters of the Third Kind
(Official Authorized Edition) Warren

| 1977 | | All about the astonishing film with dazzling photos | $1–3 |

Close Encounters of the Third Kind
(Official Collectors Edition) Warren

| 1978 | | The fully authorized story packed with dozens of color photographs | $1–3 |

YEAR	ISSUE/NUMBER	DESCRIPTION	VALUE

Communicator, The

| 1975 | Fall | Star Trek | $2–4 |

Cracked's Collectors' Edition/Those Cracked Monsters
(Major Magazines, Inc.) one issue only

| 1978 | | | $3–6 |

Cracked's For Monsters Only (Major Magazines, Inc.)
Issued from 1965 through 1972 with one issue being published in 1987

	#1	The Masters of Terror	$6–12
	#2	Bela Lugosi, Boris Karloff, Lon Chaney, The Munsters	10–20
	#3	The Horror Worlds of Boris Karloff	2–10
	#4	Two Kings of Terror: Vincent Price and Christopher Lee	5–10
	#5	Jack Pierce: The Man Behind the Monsters, Peter Lorre	5–10
	#6	John Carradine, Frankenstein '68	4–8
	#7	Karloff and Lugosi, Vampire Hunt '69	4–8
	#8	Fantasy Films of the 'Forties Featuring Lon Chaney, Jr.	5–10
	#9	Trog, Blood Relations	5–10
	#10	Scream and Scream Again, Dark Shadows	6–12
1967	Annual		5–10
1972	Annual		5–10
1987	Single issue		3–5

Creepy (Warren; illustrated horror)

| | #1 | | $10–20 |
| | #2–15 | | 5–10 |

YEAR	ISSUE/NUMBER	DESCRIPTION	VALUE
	#16, #17		$3–6
	#18–23		4–8
	#48	1973 Annual	4–8
	#55	1974 Annual	4–8
	#65	1975 Annual	3–6
	All other issues		3–5

Creepy Annual

1971		$5–10+
1972		5–10+

Creepy Yearbook

1968		$6–12+
1969		6–12+
1970		7–15+

Cue

1975	December	Star Trek cover and feature: Can 1999 Match Trek	$3–5

Curse of Frankenstein/Horror of Dracula
(one shot published by Warren)

1964	Special magazine on the two great horror flicks	$5–10

Dawn of the Dead Official Poster Book
(one shot published by MM Communications)

1979	Exclusive photos from George Romero's movie, behind-the-scenes look, magazine opens to become a giant color wall poster A. with movie title on poster	$10–20

YEAR	ISSUE/NUMBER	DESCRIPTION	VALUE
1979		B. with movie title on poster/signed by Tom Savini	$25–50
		C. without movie title on poster	30–60+

Demonique (The Journal of Obscure Horror Cinema)

	All issues		$5–10

Doctor Who Weekly
(British magazine published by Marvel Comics)
Publishing begins in 1979

	All issues		$2–4

Dracula (Ideal Publishing)

1977		Frank Langella as Dracula cover and feature	$3–5

Dracula Classic
(one issue only published by Eerie Publications, Inc.)

1976		Bela Lugosi: the man who made Dracula famous, a new generation of vampires, a history of vampires, Dracula's Guest by Bram Stoker	$3–6

Dracula Official Movie Magazine (Merit Publications, Inc.)

1979		(one shot featuring Frank Langella)	$4–8

Dracula '79 (one shot published by Warren)

1979		Christopher Lee cover, the film stars who created the Dracula legend: Bela	

YEAR	ISSUE/NUMBER	DESCRIPTION	VALUE
1979		Lugosi, Christopher Lee, Frank Langella, and others, vampires of the movies: a complete photo history	$3–6

Dragonslayer (Marvel Super Special #2)
Official Movie Edition — $2–4

Dynamite

	ISSUE/NUMBER	DESCRIPTION	VALUE
	#65	Star Trek: The Motion Picture	$2–4

Eerie (Warren; illustrated horror)

	ISSUE/NUMBER	DESCRIPTION	VALUE
	#1	First printing	$100–200+
	#1	Second printing	100–200+
	#2		10–20
	#3		10–20
	#4–50		4–8
	All other issues		2–4

Eerie Yearbook

YEAR	VALUE
1970	$5–10
1971	5–10
1972	5–10

Electric Company
(published by Children's Television Network)

YEAR	ISSUE/NUMBER	DESCRIPTION	VALUE
1980	January	Star Trek cover and feature: The Outer Space Creatures of Star Trek	$2–4
1981	January	Flash Gordon	2–3
1982	June	Star Trek Rides Again	2–3

#1, Summer 1992   *1977*   *#18, 1972*

1979   *#1, May 1977*   *#1, 1969*

YEAR	ISSUE/NUMBER	DESCRIPTION	VALUE

Elvira's Mistress of the Dark (illustrated movie adaptation)
#1 $3–6

Enterprise (Star Trek)
#1–13 All issues $2–4

Enterprise Incident (Star Trek)

#1, #2		$10–20
#3, #4, #12		6–12
#5–11		5–10
#13 and up		2–4

Enterprise Incident's Collectors' Edition
All issues $2–4

*Enterprise Incident's Spotlight on Interviews
with Star Trek Personalities* $2–4

Enterprise Incident's Spotlight on Leonard Nimoy $2–4

Enterprise Incident's Spotlight on the Technical Side $2–4

Enterprise Incident's Spotlight on William Shatner $2–4

Enterprise Spotlight 2 (Star Trek) One issue only
#1 $2–4

Famous Films

1978	December	Leonard Nimoy cover and feature: Spock Speaks	$4–8

#1

#2

#10

#14

#15

#16

#17

#30

#63

YEAR	ISSUE/NUMBER	DESCRIPTION	VALUE

Famous Monsters of Filmland (Warren Publishing)

	#1	1958 . . . The behind-the-scenes story of Hollywood's House of Horrors, the 10 most frightening faces ever filmed, Alice in Monsterland: a history of horror films, The Frankenstein Story, out of this world monsters, how Hollywood creates a monster, TV means terrifying vampires, monster quiz	$200–400+
	#1	British edition	175–350+
	#2	Monsters are badder than ever, the monster who made a man: Boris Karloff, Mad Magazine creates a monster, girls will be ghouls: all about girls who have made good being bad little monsters, public vampire #1: Bela Lugosi, terrorvision, monsters of the world unite, message from the monster	75–150+
	#2	British edition	50–100+
	#3	Photos never before seen: boy into monster, Frankenstein from space	125–250+
	#4	Zacherly: how be became king of the ghouls in New York, The Mummy: printed on tanna leaves, Christopher Lee: the handsome horror	175–350+

YEAR	ISSUE/NUMBER	DESCRIPTION	VALUE
	#4	Ghoul's eye sticker cover issue	$175–375+
	#5	The untold illustrated Black Lagoon story, why they had to bring back The Fly, movies you shouldn't see, photo contest: 10 best	150–300+
	#6	King Kong returns, sneak preview of 1960 horror films, Zacherly's shocking revival, exclusive: secrets of The Time Machine	125–250+
	#6	M. T. Graves sticker cover issue	200–375+
	#7	Zacherly: Zach comes out of his cave, cyclops and lollipops, Dr. Cyclops, mad laboratories: exclusive photos from Hollywood, letter from a vampire	75–150+
		With lucky 7 printed inside	100–250+
	#7	Remember Roland? He's back again printed on cover	100–250+
		With lucky 7 printed inside	125–250+
	#7	First pictures—tomorrow's monsters printed on cover	100–200+
		With lucky 7 printed inside	125–250+
	#8	Lon Chaney: Man of a Thousand Faces, what's the new look in monsters, 13 Ghosts photo preview, monster marketplace	75–150
	#9	Vincent Price from The Fall of the House of Usher cover and feature, a strange story about Lugosi, rare photos: Phantom of the	

YEAR	ISSUE/NUMBER	DESCRIPTION	VALUE
		Opera, how you can get monster masks by mail, giant Halloween special issue	$ 50–100
	#10	Claude Rains is back in Phantom Returns, special movie preview special, first time ever: a picture story of Flash Gordon, a terrific article by the man who wrote Psycho	60–120
	#11	Gorgo: MGM's new release, a picture history: Dr. Jekyl and Mr. Hyde, best movies from Edgar Allan Poe	100–200
	#12	Curse of the Werewolf	100–200
	#13	Collector's 13th issue, Frankenstein cover, preview: St. George and the Seven Curses, The Beasts of Tarzan, The Thing from Another World: the monster unmasked, The Incredible Shrinking Man, Claude Rains revealed, Rocket to the Rue Morgue, monsters in review	75–150
	#14	Vincent Price cover and Pit and the Pendulum feature	50–100
	#15	Zacherly cover and feature: He's Back to Judge Our Makeup Contest, more mad robots issue, the return of things to come, return of the burn: Bob Burn, Invasion of the Body Snatchers	75–150+

YEAR	ISSUE/NUMBER	DESCRIPTION	VALUE
	#16	Lon Chaney cover, the man who lost his face: Dick Smith, the clown at midnight: Robert ''Psycho'' Bloch Part I, The Mask, Cristiano's caricatures, Lon Chaney shall not die, free flight to Karloffornia	$50–100
	#17	Elsa Lanchester as the Bride of Frankenstein cover, the clown at midnight: conclusion, Lon Chaney shall not die, Glen Strange interview	40–80
	#18	Sardonicus unmasked, War of the Colossal Beast with photos	45–90+
	#19	Tales of Terror: Peter Lorre, Basil Rathbone, and Vincent Price	40–80+
	#20	Lon Chaney, the man who saw King Kong ninety times	40–80+
	#21	The Bride of Frankenstein cover and photo filmbook, Route 66 Horror Show	75–150+
	#22	The life and times of Dracula: photographs from Bela Lugosi's own scrapbook, eye-popping news on all future horror films, 5th anniversary special	75–150+
	#23	The most unusual Frankenstein photo ever, Son of Kong: Final Chapter, Karloff Speaks exclusive interview	25–50

YEAR	ISSUE/NUMBER	DESCRIPTION	VALUE
	#24	Werewolf of London, a forbidden look inside the house of Ackerman, a return visit to the Phantom	$ 25–50
	#25	King Kong: special photo filmbook . . . a photographic record never before published	40–80
	#26	Outer Limits exclusive: Things to See on TV's New Show, a new Dracula: from the other side of the world, the small and the tall of Hollywood's tiny terrors	50–100+
	#27	New fears: a preview of things and creatures to come, the voice of fiendom, conclusion of the King Kong story, Hall of Fame	25–50
	#28	Lon Chaney's Phantom face unmasked, the most exciting collection of horror photos in seven years, two-faced monsters	25–50
	#29	The Flesh Eaters: exclusive sneak preview, Jerry Lewis attacked by monsters, Christopher Lee talks about monsters, The Mole People, The Seven Faces of Dr. Lao, The Mexicreatures	35–75
	#30	The Powers of Dracula: 25 facts about the most feared vampire of all time, Return of Frankenstein, how they	

YEAR	ISSUE/NUMBER	DESCRIPTION	VALUE
		made Godzilla: a report on all those great Japanese monsters, Menace of the Red Death: a hair-raising visit to the set of a new horror film	$35–75
	#31	The Mummy, secrets you never knew about Lon Chaney Sr., monster eye: a look at things to come, return of the creatures from south of the border, headlines from Horrorville	25–50
	#32	King Kong cover, the incredible Aurora–Famous Monsters Universal Pictures master monster-makers contest issue, Horror of Dracula in comic strip, The Munsters roll out their blood-red carpet, The Horrible Sun Demon	35–70+
	#33	The Hunchback of Notre Dame complete photo story, Castle of Terror	10–20
	#34	Mr. Hyde, Horrors of Spider Island, cheers for Chaney, The Stone Men Strike, Werewolf in a Girl's Dormitory, The Change of the Leech Woman, William Castle, Dr. Jekyl and Mr. Hyde filmbook	10–20
	#35	Bela Lugosi cover, when Dracula invaded England, Night of the Blood Feast, Godzilla: King of the	

YEAR	ISSUE/NUMBER	DESCRIPTION	VALUE
		Creatures, headlines: all about Boris Karloff, Fay Wray, Bert Gordon, John Carradine and Velma the Vampire, fantastic Frankensteins from France, the Gordons will get you: Hollywood's monster-making brothers	$ 7–15
	#36	The Mummy's Ghost, The House of Wax face of fire revealed, second annual amateur makeup contest issue, The Alligator People, St. George and the Seven Curses: Bert Gordon, The Return of the Fly	5–10
	#37	Harryhausen's Horror from Venus, inside Lugosi's haunted house, see The Fiend Without a Face, the story of the terrifying giant monster Ymir, Village of the Giants, The Skull, the Hunch facts of Notre Dame, 20 Million Miles to Earth filmbook, The Black Heart of Dorian Gray, Blood Creature	5–10
	#38	Curse of the Demon, Invasion of the Saucermen	50–100+
	#39	Frankenstein Conquers the World, son of One Million Years B.C.: first pix of three new Harryhausen dinosaurs, the man who killed The Fly: Farewell to	

YEAR	ISSUE/NUMBER	DESCRIPTION	VALUE
		Herbert Marshall, the men behind the monsters: a new department begins, what make Luna tick: Carroll Borland, the 13 faces of Frankenstein: Willis O'Brien exclusive	$5–10
	#40	40th Anniversary issue, Horror Hotel: Meet Its Ghastly Guest . . . Christopher Lee, dinosaurs, the Great Lugosi Mystery solved, Mummy's Hand, Dracula after midnight, The She Creature	6–12
	#41	The Werewolf of London, Munster Go Home, Curse of the Mummy's tomb, the thin monster captured: exclusive interview with John Carradine, The Black Zoo, Vampires 3: Bela Lugosi Bites Again, farewell to Ford, Horror Hall of Fame: favorite fiends and cool scenes	4–8
	#42	Frankenstein Meets the Wolfman special, The Creepers, King Kong Returns, carry on screaming, Christopher Lee talks about The Mummy and more	4–8
	#43	Christopher Lee as Dracula, Dracula flies again: it happened in Horrorwood, Fantastic Voyage, In the Days of the

YEAR	ISSUE/NUMBER	DESCRIPTION	VALUE
		Dinosaurs: lost worlds of O'Brien and Harryhausen, the scream test, Carradine, Rathbone and Buster Crabbe, House of Dracula: Chaney, Atwill, Carradine and Strange, Verne Langdon strikes again	$4–8
#44		Willis O'Brien's King Kong, Karloff without makeup, Chamber of Horrors, Horror Castle: Christopher Lee, The Attack of Mr. Black, Tarantula, The Daleks are coming	4–8
#45		The Projected Man, House of Wax, Vincent Price, Doctor Blood's Coffin, return of the vampire: Lugosi lives again, the human monster: Lugosi	4–8
#46		Vampire of the Opera, Boris Karloff in The Magic Castle, The Mummy's Shroud, The Vampire and the Ballerina, The Mole People	4–8
#47		Phantom of the Opera: Claude Rains Comes Back, photos of the mad fiend in the new James Bond movie You Only Live Twice, Horror of Dracula, The Black Cat strikes again, return of the monster Ghidrah photo exclusive, Karloff: The Magic Castle	4–8

YEAR	ISSUE/NUMBER	DESCRIPTION	VALUE
	#48	Santa Kharis, The Ghost of Frankenstein: complete story in pictures, The Sorcerers, monsterrific movies of tomorrow, The Monster from One Billion B.C.: a new comic strip	$10–20
	#49	Henry Hull as the Werewolf of London, Bram Stoker's Dracula with Bela Lugosi, hidden horrors: The Son of Dr. Jekyl and Mr. Hyde, the ghost of the ghost of Frankenstein, Footsteps of Frankenstein: a comic strip	7–15
	#50	Gorgo: filmbook for prehistoric buffs, Tarantula, Devil Bat: Bela Lugosi, Meet Mr. Nye: The Man Behind the Masks, Horror of Dracula: a comic strip, 50th anniversary issue	7–15
	#51	The Wolfman: Lon Chaney in his greatest role, Curse of Frankenstein: a comic strip, Jane Fonda: Barbarella . . . new pictures of the female Flash Gordon, Boris Karloff interviewed, return of Kong, The Black Heart of Dorian Gray	5–10
	#52	Barnabas: The Vampire of Dark Shadows . . . exclusive photos and story, Planet of the Apes: incredible pictures, death visits Dr. Cyclops . . .	

YEAR	ISSUE/NUMBER	DESCRIPTION	VALUE
		Albert Dekker enters Monster Hall of Fame, Son of Frankenstein filmbook	$10–20+
	#53	Flesh Crawling Monster issue	4–8
	#54	The Invasion of the Saucermen cover, Dear Mr. Lee: the British king of monsters talks about his favorite monster movies, Lon Chaney talks to you, behind the ape-ball: Tarzan to the Rescue, King Kong returns: a special feature, Dracula 2000, Invasion of the Vampires	5–10
	#55	Land of the Giants exclusive, animals, creatures and things special	7–15+
	#56	Frankenstein: rare pictures, all about Boris Karloff: his life in pictures, comments on Karloff's death by Christopher Lee and Peter Lorre and others, Vincent Price	30–60
	#57	The Green Slime, the original Frankenstein picture book, Invasion of the Vampires	5–10
	#58	Karloff as the Mummy, Rowan and Martin as the werewolf in The Maltese Bippy, Lon Chaney in Return of the Vampire, Monster in the House: Karloff, the maddest doctor: Lionel Atwill, Frankenstein 1970	4–8

YEAR	ISSUE/NUMBER	DESCRIPTION	VALUE
	#59	All about Barnabas Collins, Frankenstein Must Be Destroyed movie preview, Christopher Lee in Dracula Has Risen from the Grave, John Carradine exclusive interview, Lugosi's haunted house	$10–20
	#60	Dorian Gray, White Zombie: Lugosi, Roland Bryce, Frankenstein Part 3, man-eating plants photo story	4–8
	#61	Mark of the Vampire: a tale of the undead featuring the great Bela Lugosi	5–10
	#62	Dr. Jekyl and Mr. Hyde, The Thing, Mark of the Vampire	4–8
	#63	The Fiendish Hands of Orlac featuring Peter Lorre, Boris Karloff in rare Frankenstein makeup photos	4–8
	#64	Bela Lugosi: Murders in the Rue Morgue, Boris Karloff's Grandchildren, Destroy All Monsters, Terrors of the Third Dimension: those great eye-popping 3-D movies	4–8
	#65	The Mask of Fu Manchu: Karloff, The Phantom Strikes Again, The Seven Faces of Dr. Lao, the man who made The Mummy is no more: a tribute to the	

YEAR	ISSUE/NUMBER	DESCRIPTION	VALUE
		late Karl Freund, beasts, creatures and things, when Karloff played Chaney, girls and ghouls gallery	$ 4–8
	#66	The Old Dark House: a filmbook on the Karloff classic	4–8
	#67	Witches and warlocks special issue featuring The Black Cat with Boris Karloff and Bela Lugosi	4–8
	#68	Mysterious Island issue	4–8
	#69	London After Midnight filmbook featuring Lon Chaney	4–8
	#70–79	No issues were published with the title *Famous Monsters,* instead numbers 70 to 79 were published under the title *Monster World* and were numbered 1 to 10	
	#80	Beneath the Planet of the Apes, London After Midnight, girls and ghouls gallery: portrait #7 ... Florence Marly, Chasndu the Magician: Lugosi Is Loose Again	10–20+
	#81	Jungle Captive cover, Island of Lost Souls filmbook, The Captive Wild Woman, Fires of Death, He Killed Dorian Gray, The House in the Twilight Zone: First of a Series	5–10

YEAR	ISSUE/NUMBER	DESCRIPTION	VALUE
	#82	House of Dark Shadows special, Mummy's Tomb filmbook, Disneyland's House of Horrors	$12–25+
	#83	The Mummy's Tomb, When Dinosaurs Ruled the Earth, The Hunchback of Notre Dame, The Raven	5–10
	#84	Christopher Lee, The Monster That Challenged the World, The Hunchback of Notre Dame, House of Dracula, The Raven: the conclusion of the great 1935 Universal flick	6–12
	#85	Escape from the Planet of the Apes preview issue, Ghost of Frankenstein: complete story in pictures, faces that launched a thousand shrieks	10–20
	#86	The House That Dripped Blood with Christopher Lee, House of the Damned, Werewolf of London, The Masked Marvel of Monsterville: all about Don Post, Devil Bat: Bela Lugosi, girls and ghouls portrait #13, Fearjerkers	5–10
	#87	The She Creature, Curse of Frankenstein superspecial filmbook, photo-comics, Footsteps of Frankenstein comic strip, The Abominable Dr. Phibes	7–15
	#88	Night of Dark Shadows: First Photos of the New	

YEAR	ISSUE/NUMBER	DESCRIPTION	VALUE
		Movie, The Munsters, Michael Rennie: Farewell to the Master, In the Days of the Dinosaur, Blood of Kryon: monster comics	$ 6–12+
	#89	Dracule versus Frankenstein, The Black Zoo, The Devil Commands, The Black Heart of Dorian Gray, Rip Van Dracula	5–10
	#90	Scream and Scream Again, death of a giant: Tor (Lobo) Johnson, The Black Sleep, Horror Castle, The Vampire Lovers, Attack of the Giant Tarantula, The Call of Dracula: Christopher Lee	5–10
	#91	Frogs, Godzilla versus the Smog Monster, Smile If You Call Him Monster: The Late Basil Rathbone Interviewed, Count Yorga, Vampire, The Return of Count Yorga	10–20
	#92	Lugosi: The Life of Filmland's Dracula special issue, The Dracula Report, Public Vampire #1, The Great Lugosi Mystery, Unholy 13, Count Dracula's Vampire Ring	7–15
	#93	Tales from the Crypt cover, a special fearbook issue, The Mask: A nightmare movie in 3-D, man-eating plants, Son of	

YEAR	ISSUE/NUMBER	DESCRIPTION	VALUE
		Kong, I Was a Tin Age Robot Part II, Lon Chaney shall not die, King Kong is coming back	$7–15
	#94	Frankenstein, Dr. Jekyl and Sister Hyde, Shock-a-Bye Baby, how to make a mummy, In the Days of the Dinosaurs, Murders in the Rue Morgue, Dorian Gray strikes again, fascinating Karloff facts	5–10
	#95	Guess What Happened to Count Dracula, Attack of the Giant Insects, Conquest of the Planet of the Apes, Dr. Phibes rises again, Blackula	7–15
	#96	Special Wolfman issue, letter to an angel: Tribute to Chaney, Twins of Evil, Hands of the Ripper, Frankenstein Meets the Wolfman, Dracula in Flames, Frankenstein and the Vampire, The Wolfman: Larry Talbot	4–8
	#97	Asylum: Attack by a Dead Hand, fright flicks in '73, farewell to James Nicholson, Dracula after Death, Baron Blood	4–8
	#98	Invasion of the Saucermen cover, When Dracula Met the Vampires: Christopher Lee addresses the Count Dracula Society, The Black Sleep takes Tamiroff:	

YEAR	ISSUE/NUMBER	DESCRIPTION	VALUE
		obituary for Akim, Blood from the Mummy's Tomb, The Thing with Two heads, spotlight on Lon Chaney Sr.: Happy Birthday Dear Phantom, cheers for Chaney	$ 2–8
	#99	Karloff, Lon Chaney Jr., Carradine, Glenn Strange, J. Carroll Naish, House of Frankenstein 16-page bonus special, Blobs, Brains and Other Gooey Objects	4–8
	#100	100th great issue special, Alice in Monsterland, farewell to Edward G. Robinson, Humorous History of Famous Monsters, The Return of Lugosi, The Bride of Frankenstein: Mae Clarke Reminisces	20–40
	#101	Captain Marvel versus the Mysterious Scorpion, The Phantom's last fright: that sad day when Claude Rains passed on to the invisible world, Shazam, The Pit and the Pendulum, James Bond meets the Fiend, The Projected Man revisited, Dracula 2000, Flash Gordon attracts the world	3–7
	#102	Lon Chaney Sr.: an incredible 20 pages on the legendary Chaney, the	

YEAR	ISSUE/NUMBER	DESCRIPTION	VALUE
		Diabolic Duo, Master of the Masks: Verne Langdon, Death Takes Horror Director Edgar G. Ulmer	$3–7
	#103	The Creature from the Black Lagoon, Blackula Is Beautiful, the loss of Captain Nemo: Robert Ryan, Beyond the Planet of the Apes, the soul of a gentle man: this was the late George Macready, farewell to Jack Hawkins, Lon is gone	3–7
	#104	The Fly, Robert Bloch, Frankenstein 1973, Son of Psycho: Bloch, The Vault of Horror	3–5
	#105	Christopher Lee invades Los Angeles special issue, memorial to Glenn Strange, Abbott and Costello Meet Frankenstein, tears for Chaney, Joe E. Brown: The Mouth That Roared	3–7
	#106	The Sun Demon cover, The Curse of the Katz-Man People: a famous producer dies, The Living Ghost: John Agar, Dracula TV, The Golden Voyage of Sinbad, Vampire Circus, Witches and Demons Are Among Us	3–7

YEAR	ISSUE/NUMBER	DESCRIPTION	VALUE
	#107	Westworld: the frightening amusement park of the future, the new Canadian Dracula, Kane Richmond dies, Westmore brothers gone	$ 3–5
	#108	King Kong special photo filmbook issue, The Battle for the Planet of the Apes	10–20
	#109	Vincent Price in Madhouse, Son of Kong, TV's Monster Hall of Fame, Night of the Living Dead, Karloff revisited	2–8
	#110	Karloff in The Ghoul, Vincent Price in The Pit and the Pendulum, The Trail of Dracula, Lon Chaney as Frankenstein, Japan's giants: Godzilla, Gigantis and Gorath, The Time Machine, Willis O'Brien farewell repeated from 1962	5–10
	#111	The Exorcist, Zardoz: It's Wilder Than Oz, Young Frankenstein, Nosferatu: The Silent Vampire, Devils of Darkness	5–10
	#112	Bride of Frankenstein cover, a unique Lugosi feature: such men are dangerous, Warhol's Frankenstein, Fantastic Planet, end of Endora: the death of Agnes Moorehead, Horror Express: Christopher Lee	5–10

YEAR	ISSUE/NUMBER	DESCRIPTION	VALUE
	#113	The Mystery of the Wax Museum, Frankenstein and the Monster from Hell, beauty escapes the beast: Fay Wray, Evelyn Ankers, and Barbara Steele, Otto Kruger: Time Stops, The Hunchback of Notre Dame revealed, Return of the Ghoul, Sidney Blackmer farewell	$ 4–8
	#114	All of Japan monsters 100-page special issue, Godzilla: The King Kong of Kung Fu Goes Gung-ho, The Manster: half man and half monster, Frankenstein Conquers the World, Blue Kong, King Kong versus Godzilla, Mothra, The Return of Ghidrah, Boris Karloff, Lon Chaney Sr., Christopher Lee, Peter Cushing and Dwight Frye	40–80+
	#115	A history of Jekyl and Hyde, Lugosi book Part I by his son, Famous Monster Convention report, Phantom of the Paradise	3–5
	#116	The Land That Time Forgot, Humphrey Bogart returns as Mr. X?, Japanese monsters, Lon Chaney's tribute to his father	3–6
	#117	Tribute to Ray Harryhausen 20-page special, Peter Cushing and	

YEAR	ISSUE/NUMBER	DESCRIPTION	VALUE
		Christopher Lee, Forrest Ackerman's five favorite fright films, Ray Harryhausen's birthday, 20 Million Miles: Part I	$ 3–6
	#118	Ray Harryhausen's Cyclops cover, 20 Million Miles to Earth, the Peter Cushing story, 1974 Famous Monsters Convention	10–20
	#119	100-page superspectacular issue, Karloff, Lugosi, Christopher Lee, dinosaurs, Night of the Blood Beast, Horror Hotel	4–8
	#120	The Creature from the Black Lagoon cover, never seen before Exorcist pictures: The Return of Regan, Fantasy Filmcon 1975, The Devil's Rain, Fredric March tribute, Larry Vincent	5–10
	#121	Boris Karloff as the Mummy cover, those weird monsters from Mexico, Cher is Frankenstein's new bride, Rod Serling farewell	4–8
	#122	Ingrid Pitt cover and feature, Famous Monsters Convention, The Man-made Monster filmbook, Beyond the Door, monsters from Mexico	4–8
	#123	Special holiday issue, Plague of the Zombies cover, the Phantom lives:	

YEAR	ISSUE/NUMBER	DESCRIPTION	VALUE
		Lon Chaney honored, Bela Lugosi at the deli, Go to the Devil photo feature, a sound of thunder, monsters versus Stooges: The Three Stooges, Carreras and Hammer Films	$3–5
	#124	Mexico vampire cover, Terror of Transylvania: Lugosi Still Lives, Frankenstein's director James Whale, The Daleks are coming, The Hindenburg, monsters from Mexico	3–5
	#125	All about the new King Kong, Dark Shadows, monsters from Mexico	3–5
	#126	Mr. Sardonicus grins again, King Kong's colorful crash, Lugosi's Transylvania trip, Renfield revisited at last, Dr. Who	3–6
	#127	New Bride of Frankenstein cover, Baby Frankenstein, The Golem's Gonna Getcha, Hammer's horrific monsters, The Unholy 2: Karloff and Lugosi, Exorcist actor dies: Lee J. Cobb, Marcel Delgado interview	3–6
	#128	Food of the Gods, happy birthday John Carradine, Revenge of the Zombies, The Art of Lugosi, Farewell to Freda Inescort	3–6

YEAR	ISSUE/NUMBER	DESCRIPTION	VALUE
	#129	Futureworld cover and feature, Drac Invades England: Lugosi, At the Earth's Core, Witches and Demons, Daleks Invade England, Prehistoric Story, The Green Slime	$3–5
	#130	Peter Cushing as Van Helsing cover, Space 1999, The Mad Ghoul Part II, Squirm, The Time Travelers, Richard Arlen obituary	3–6
	#131	Christopher Lee in Horror of Dracula cover, Creatures of the Deep, Vultura: Last Chapter . . . Gene Roth has died, Lugosi's hidden films, Bride of the Monster, Bedlam: Boris Karloff	4–8
	#132	King Kong special, King Kong in New York, The Q Experiments, The Great Lugosi, Old Kong Lives, Fritz Land: The Great Man Is Gone, Death Takes David Bruce, Here There Be Dragons	4–8
	#133	Forbidden Planet cover, Dracula After Midnight, 100 horror preview, Lugosi's last years, King Kong's creator dies: Marcel Delgado, The Outer Limits	4–8

YEAR	ISSUE/NUMBER	DESCRIPTION	VALUE
	#134	Dr. Jekyl and Mr. Hyde cover, Outer Limits monsters, King Kong clashes, The Black Cat, Twin Titans of Terror, the death of a phantom: Jack Cassidy, Mysterious Lon Chaney	$ 4–8
	#135	Godzilla versus Bionic Monster, Terror Times Two, Lee Danforth, The Kentucky Fried Movie, The Black Cat Part II, Caligula and Dracula	4–8
	#136	Sinbad and the Eye of the Tiger, Close Encounters, Farewell Frankenstein, Dale Van Sickel, The Empire of the Ants, A Star is Re-Born: Robert Clarke, The Werewolf Dies: Henry Hull	3–6
	#137	Star Wars special issue, 1977 yearbook, Horror in the Lighthouse: Poe and Bloch, The Call of Dracula: Christopher Lee, 6 monsters for the price of one, Black Heart of Dorian, The Mysterious Island, Devil Bat, The Unholy 13, Horror Hall of Fame, Brontosaurus Battle	5–10
	#138	Star Wars: what science fiction experts say about it, special giant summer issue, all about the amazing new Dr. Moreau, A Look at the	

YEAR	ISSUE/NUMBER	DESCRIPTION	VALUE
		Golden Years of Terrorvision, Stephen Boyd: His Last Voyage, Tales of Frankenstein, Reunited with Chaney, The Vampire Killers	$5–10
	#139	Star Wars special: More about it, The Vampire Killers Part II, Ricardo Cortez: He Walked with Death, werewolves, Invaders from Space, The Tribe, 50-Foot Woman Dies: Allison Hayes	5–10
	#140	The Mosy Hellish Frankenstein, the incredible films to come, War of the Worlds refought, When Worlds Collide again, Star Wars rare pix, Tim Barr is gone	3–6
	#141	Close Encounters of the Third Kind, Godzilla, Sinbad, Alien	2–5
	#142	Star Wars cover and feature ... Star Wars Revisited, The Aliens are coming, Twilight Zone House, Starship Invasions, Star Trek, Horror Hall of Fame, Richard Carlson: Gone to the Other Side	3–7
	#143	The Mummy, some Close Encounters, The Alien Factor, R is for Revenge, Starcrash Flash, Twilight Zone House II	3–5

YEAR	ISSUE/NUMBER	DESCRIPTION	VALUE
	#144	The Mummy Part II, a lark with Quark, special effects, Dr. Paul Bearer	$2–5
	#145	The Incredible Melting Man cover, Star Wars II, Monster Maker's Queen, Fire, Felines and Demons, Blood Banquet, Star Trek: 23rd Century, Carroll Luna ill, Gertrude Astor gone	2–5
	#146	Jaws versus Ape, Star Wars: Christopher Lee talks about the movie, Star Wars 2, Peter Cushing interview, Lost Continent	4–8
	#147	Star Wars special, Pinnacle of Terror, Carrie Fisher: Starry-Eyed Warrior, Benign King Boris, Vampire Death: Barry Atwater, Mr. Special Effects Arnold Gillespie	3–6
	#148	Darth Vader special	3–6
	#149	Battlestar Gallactica special: All about Galactica, Mars Invades the Earth, Luna Lives: Carroll Borland, Black Cat Strikes Again, Under Planet of Apes, House of Wax	3–6
	#150	Battlestar Galactica or Star Wars? . . . Which One Is the Best?, Mighty Joe Young breaks loose, Dracula Quartet, Joe Bonomo Dies, Return of Frankenstein, Dear Dracula: Christopher Lee	2–5

YEAR	ISSUE/NUMBER	DESCRIPTION	VALUE
	#151	Star Wars contest winners issue, Lord of the Rings, John Dykstra, Superman movie, Body Snatchers, Fantasy Film Festival, Warlords of Atlantis, Might Joe Young	$ 2–5
	#152	Superman special issue, Valerie Perrine Talks, Wide World of Monsters, Among the Vamps, Florence Marley Dies, John Carradine, Boris Karloff Lives	2–5
	#153	Nosferatu: The Terror of Transylvania, David Prowse interview, Creatures from the 7 Seas	2–5
	#154	Love at First Bite, Moonraker, Alien, Amityville Horror, Meteor, all the new vampire films	2–5
	#155	Doctor Who, Starcrash, Alien movie preview	2–5
	#156	Alien: terrifying photos from the movie, Star Wars II feature with giant color foldout, Moonraker: James Bond Blasts Off	5–10+
	#157	The New Dracula: Frank Langella, Moonraker's Jaws	2–5
	#158	Alien issue, exclusive interview with H. R. Giger, The 3-D Horrors, Star Wars, Golem, House that Bled, Godzilla versus the Badair, John Chambers:	

YEAR	ISSUE/NUMBER	DESCRIPTION	VALUE
		Men Behind Monsters, fascinating facts about the first film Frankenstein	$ 5–10+
	#159	More on the Alien movie, all about Time After Time	5–10+
	#160	Meteor, exclusive Buck Rogers interview, The Martian Chronicles: Science Fiction TV, The Brood, Nosferatu	2–5
	#161	Star Trek the Motion Picture, Disney's Super Space Thriller: The Black Hole, Buck Rogers, Christopher Lee's new film: Arabian Adventure	3–6
	#162	The Black Hole: a closer look at this sensational film, Star Trek The Motion Picture special	2–5
	#163	Friday the 13th exclusive, The Fog, new fright films photos	15–30
	#164	Saturn 3, The Humanoids, The Crimson Cult, Manikins of Menace	2–5
	#165	The Empire Strikes Back special, Darth Vader interview	3–6
	#166	The Empire Strikes Back special	3–6
	#167	The Empire Strikes Back special, the inside story on Godzilla, all about The Shining	3–6
	#168	Close Encounters of the Third Kind special and 1981 yearbook	2–5

YEAR	ISSUE/NUMBER	DESCRIPTION	VALUE
	#169	Ray Harryhausen, Alien on Earth, fantasy film forecast	$2–5
	#170	Battle beyond the Stars, meet Ming the Merciless in Flash Gordon, The Awakening	2–5
	#171	Fabulous photos of the legendary Lon Chaney Sr., Flash Gordon, TV's Alien Invasion, why Sammy Davis Jr. loves monster movies	3–5
	#172	The Incredible Shrinking Woman, The Omen III, Fiend, Scanners	2–5
	#173	The Devil and Max Devlin, The Funhouse, meet Famous Film Monsters in the flesh	2–5
	#174	Star Wars special: The Empire Strikes Back	3–6
	#175	Superman II: first photos and story, Clash of the Titans, Raiders of the Lost Ark	2–5
	#176	The Mutations cover, monster maker Terence Fisher dead, Mindwarp, Dragonslayer, Rodan, Excalibur	3–6
	#177	Superman II, The Empire Strikes Back featuring an exclusive interview with Boba Fett, Outland revisited, Raiders of the Lost Ark, James Bond's new flick: For Your Eyes Only	3–6

YEAR	ISSUE/NUMBER	DESCRIPTION	VALUE
	#178	Raiders of the Lost Ark revisited, American Werewolf in London exclusive, Superman II: Terence Stamp talks, Dracula: The Filmbook of the Bela Lugosi Classic, Frankenstein I, II, and III	$3–6
	#179	Superman II, Raiders of the Lost Ark Revisited, a special interview with Zod the Villain Leader from Superman II	3–5
	#180	Frankenstein cover, The Grim Reaper, American Werewolf in London interviews, Linda Blair's Hell Night, The Mad Ghoul	3–6
	#181	Heartbeeps, The Origin of the Lost Ark, Inside the Mausoleum, Ghost Story	2–5
	#182	Mausoleum: exclusive photos, Ray Harryhausen's views on Clash of the Titans, Caroline Munroe interview: story and photos, special feature: The Bloodiest Films of 1981	4–8
	#183	Swamp Thing, The Lost World	3–6
	#184	Dragonslayer, Conan, Hercules, Samson, Goliath and Atlas: Famous Barbarians of Filmland	3–6
	#185	The Mummy cover, Star Trek: The Wrath of Khan, Blade Runner, The Thing, Poltergeist, Conan, Mutant	3–6

YEAR	ISSUE/NUMBER	DESCRIPTION	VALUE
	#186	Poltergeist, Tron, The Road Warrior, Beastmaster, Star Trek: The Wrath of Khan	$4–8
	#187	Star Trek: The Wrath of Khan special	4–8
	#188	Fearbook special, Frankenstein, Mummy's Ghost, Dr. Jekyl and Mr. Hyde, The Phantom Strikes: Lon Chaney, Monster Marathon	3–6
	#189	Close Encounters of the Third Kind: Steven Spielberg the Dream-Maker, the magic of 3-D revealed, The Incubus, Halloween III, The Legendary John Carradine	3–6
	#190	The Empire Strikes Back, Superman III: an exclusive preview, Moldy Mummy Movies, Future Fantasy Films, Wells's Time Machine, The Beast Within	5–10
	#191	The Dark Crystal: an enlightening look, great moments reviews	4–8

Famous Monsters of Filmland Convention Magazine

1974	$25–50
1975	50–100+

Famous Monsters of Filmland Do-It-Yourself Monster Makeup Handbook (Dick Smith's)

1965	One issue only	$10–20

YEAR	ISSUE/NUMBER	DESCRIPTION	VALUE

Famous Monsters of Filmland Paperbacks

1964	#1	The Best from Famous Monsters of Filmland	$50–100+
	#2	Son of Famous Monsters of Filmland	60–100+
1965	#3	Famous Monsters of Filmland Strike Back	25–50+

Famous Monsters of Filmland Yearbook

1962			$75–150+
1964			30–60
1965			25–50
1966			15–30
1967			10–20
1968			5–10
1969			6–12
1970			10–20
1971			10–20
1972			20–40+

Famous Monsters Game Book (Warren)

1982	One issue only		$3–6

Famous Monsters Star Wars Spectacular (Warren)

1977		How they did the special effects and other Star Wars features	$5–10

Fangoria (published by O'Quinn Studios)
1979–Present

Note: *Fangoria* back-issue values are greatly influenced by *Fangoria's* back-issue department. Many back issues are available directly through *Fangoria* at very reasonable prices; however, when an issue is no longer offered by *Fangoria* the value on that particular

YEAR	ISSUE/NUMBER	DESCRIPTION	VALUE

issue can increase considerably. In some cases, if a collector shops around or attends conventions, copies can be purchased for *less* than the *Fangoria* back-issue price.

YEAR	ISSUE/NUMBER	DESCRIPTION	VALUE
	#1	25 years with Godzilla, Alien photo preview, Christopher Lee interview, The making of The Creature from the Black Lagoon, Battlestar Galactica's Lost Aliens, Dr. Who	$12–25
	#2	Prophecy, Robert Bloch and Richard Matheson Interviewed, Carl Lundgren, The making of Phantasm, War of the Worlds, Dracula, issue includes a Dr. Who poster	2–4
	#3	Christopher Lee: Arabian Adventure, Night Stalker episode guide, The Brood, the art of Mike Sullivan, Jack Arnold: Tales of the Unexpected, issue includes a giant Alien poster	2–4
	#4	Star Trek: Spock and the New Aliens, Salem's Lot TV special, a talk with Caroline Munroe, The Robots of Disney's The Black Hole, issue includes giant robot poster	10–20
	#5	Saturn 3, The Coming, The Fog, Monsters of Star Command, The Art of Dennis Anderson, issue includes a 16-page posterbook	5–10

YEAR	ISSUE/NUMBER	DESCRIPTION	VALUE
	#6	Anthony Daniels in The Empire Strikes Back, Vincent Price Remembers, Count Fangor introduction, Friday the 13th: A Day for Terror, Stephen King, George Romero, Quartermass, issue includes a giant poster . . . A Tribute to Hammer Films	$ 5–10
	#7	Jack Nicholson in The Shining, The Terror Factor, alien creatures from Galaxina, Savini Strikes Back: Maniac, The Hitchcock Legacy, Vincent Price, Hammer Films	2–4
	#8	Zombie, from the producers of Halloween and Fade to Black, George Pal, Escape from New York: a talk with John Carpenter, Force Five, Horror of Dracula	3–6
	#9	Motel Hell, The Howling, Terror Train, The Elephant Man, Conan	50–100
	#10	Scanners, Mother's Day, Outer Limits, Altered States, Mighty Joe Young, Hammer and Sangster	10–20
	#11	Funhouse, The Howling, My Bloody Valentine, Excalibur	10–20
	#12	Friday the 13th Part II, Hammer on TV, The Hand, Clash of the Titans, Romero's Knightriders, Tobe Hooper	10–20

YEAR	ISSUE/NUMBER	DESCRIPTION	VALUE
	#13	Dragonslayer, The Beast Within, An American Werewolf in London, the George Romero interview	$10–20
	#14	An American Werewolf in London, The Power, Dead and Buried, Caveman, John Carpenter on Halloween II and The Thing, Shock FX special	10–20
	#15	Halloween II, on the set of Swamp Thing, Alfred Hitchcock's Television Legacy, Siskel and Ebert Talk Back, The Beast, Jamie Lee Curtis: An End to Terror, Incredible Creatures of Ray Harryhausen, Beyond Rocky Horror . . . Shock Treatment	10–20+
	#16	Ghost Story, Basket Case, creations of Chris Tucker, The Legendary Dick Smith, Rick Baker's EFX	2–4
	#17	The Grisley Independents . . . Pranks, The Deadly Spawn and Bloody Pulp, Ghost Story, Cat People's screenwriter Alan Ormsby, White Doc, Dark Shadows: The Gothic Soap	3–6
	#18	Cat People: FX by Burman, Rest in Peace, John Carpenter's The Thing, The Beast Within, on the set of George Romero's Creepshow	3–6

YEAR	ISSUE/NUMBER	DESCRIPTION	VALUE
	#19	Poltergeist, Road Warrior: Mad Max Returns, Parasite, The Thing	$ 2–4
	#20	Creepshow's E. G. Marshall, Stephen King and George Romero, Joe Dante: After The Howling, The Scaly Star of Death Bite, The Undiscovered Joe Blasco, Fear on Film: Carpenter, Landis and Cronenberg	5–10
	#21	Rob Botton and the FX of The Thing, Friday the 13th Part III, The Sword and the Sorcerer, The Great Zacherly, monsters versus wrestlers	3–6
	#22	Halloween III/Season of the Witch, George Romero on Creepshow, Friday the 13th Part III: The FX, Pink Floyd's The Wall, Elvira, Ingrid Pitt	3–6
	#23	Evil Dead, Poltergeist, Halloween III: The Effects, The Dreaded Incubus, Texas Chainsaw Massacre	5–10
	#24	XTRO, The Grisly FX of Steve Neilli, Larry Cohen's Q, The Sender, Poltergeist's FX, Klaus Kinski	2–4
	#25	Videodrome: TV with Guts, Tom Savin, Scalps, Gordon on Wood, the editorial Famous Monsters wouldn't print	2–4

YEAR	ISSUE/NUMBER	DESCRIPTION	VALUE
	#26	The Hunger's Dick Smith's FX, Ed French, Amityville II FX, issue includes Scream Greats poster #1	$2–4
	#27	Grande Illusions: Gore and Me by Tom Savini, The Timewalker, Evil Dead, Psycho II, Forrest J. Ackerman on Lon Chaney	2–4
	#28	Spasms, on the set of The Dead Zone and Psycho II, The Deadly Spawn, Veronica Carlson, Fullerton and Buechler, Scream Greats poster #3 . . . Friday the 13th Part 2	2–4
	#29	Gates of Hell, Jaws 3-D, Brain of Blood, Rotted Flesh, Twilight Zone: Behind the Scenes, Dead Zone, An American Werewolf in London, Dead of Night, Scream Greats poster #4 . . . American Werewolf in London	2–4
	#30	The Nightmare Effects of Twilight Zone, John Carpenter on Halloween, Cujo: Behind the Scenes, Joe Dante Speaks, Freda Francis, James Herbert, Vincent Price, Scream Greats poster #5 . . . The Beast Within	2–4
	#31	Amityville 3-D, Dead Zone, Exorcist FX, The Keep, Matheson, Scream Greats poster #6 . . . The Funhouse	2–4

YEAR	ISSUE/NUMBER	DESCRIPTION	VALUE
	#32	Christine, Scorsese on Cronenberg, Cujo FX, C.H.U.D., Stan Wilson, Friday the 13th poster	$ 3–6
	#33	The SFX of The Keep, Christine, Splatter, Futurekill, Strange Invaders FX, Ed French, Italian Zombies, The Shining poster	3–6
	#34	The Terror of Mutant, Stephen King's Firestarter: On the Set, Chainsaw's Ed Neal, The Hills Have Eyes, Reardon and Dreamscope, Videodrome poster	2–4
	#35	Ozzy Osbourne's Bark at the Moon, Stephen King's Children of the Corn, Firestarter, Baker, Twilight Zone: The Movie poster	2–4
	#36	Friday the 13th: The Final Chapter, Stephen King's Firestarter, The Brood poster	2–4
	#37	Gremlins: interview with Joe Dante, Dick Miller, The Hills Have Eyes, Mark Shostrom FX, Creepshow poster	5–10
	#38	The Fantastic Gremlins FX, Friday the 13th, The Mutilator, Jonathan Haze, Salem's Lot poster	2–4
	#39	The Makeup FX of V, Ghostbusters FX, Jason versus Michael Meyers,	

YEAR	ISSUE/NUMBER	DESCRIPTION	VALUE
		Attack of the 50-Foot Woman, Gremlins FX, Dreamscape, Amityville 3-D poster	$ 2–4
	#40	Return of the Living Dead, Ghostbusters FX, Nightmare on Elm Street, Night of the Comet, Arnold Schwarzenegger on The Terminator, Michael McDowell, Hammer's Vamps, Ghostbusters poster	5–10
	#41	Ghoulish FX of The Jacksons' Torture, Christopher Lee Speaks, The Terminator, C.H.U.D., Darkside, Larry Buchanan, Motel Hell poster	2–4
	#42	The Nightmare World of Company of Wolves, Stephen King and Peter Straub on The Talisman, Body Double, Blood Simple Christopher Lee, Silent Night, Deadly Night	2–4
	#43	Day of the Dead: On the Set, Cat's Eye, House on Haunted Hill, Silver Bullet, John Ashley Rambaldi FX, Creepshow poster	2–4
	#44	Friday the 13th: A New Beginning, After the Fall of New York, Return of the Living Dead, Nightmare on Elm Street, Jonathan Frid, Company of	

YEAR	ISSUE/NUMBER	DESCRIPTION	VALUE
		Wolves, Friday the 13th poster	$2–4
	#45	Friday the 13th: A New Beginning, Elm Street's Scream Queen: Heather Langenkamp, Elvira, Creepshow poster	2–4
	#46	Lifeforce: interview with Tobe Hooper, The Re-Animator, Day of the Dead, Night of the Living Dead, Zombies, Caroline Munroe Nightmare on Elm Street poster	2–4
	#47	Day of the Dead: Tom Savini's FX, Mad Max Beyond Thunderdome, Lifeforce FX, Fright Night, Terminator poster	2–4
	#48	Return of the Living Dead, Tales from the Darkside, Fright Night, Silver Bullet, Stephen King revisited, Day of the Dead poster	2–4
	#49	Nightmare on Elm Street: Freddy's Revenge, Fright Night: Makeup FX, Creepers, Silver Bullet, The Howling II, Fright Night poster	2–4
	#50	Nightmare on Elm Street II, The Re-Animator, Hammer Monster Secrets, Tom Savini, The Twilight Zone, Angelo Rossitto	2–4
	#51–Present		2–4

YEAR	ISSUE/NUMBER	DESCRIPTION	VALUE

Fangoria: Bloody Best of

	#1–4		$5–10
	#5		3–7
	#6		5–10
	#7		3–7
	#8 up		3–5

Fangoria/Freddy:
The Official Magazine of a Nightmare on Elm Street $2–4

Fangoria Postcards Magazines

| | #1 | | $2–4 |

Fangoria Poster Magazine
Each issue contains 10 color wall posters

| | All issues | | $2–4 |
| | Volume I up | | 2–4 |

Fantastic Films (Blake Publishing Corporation,
Fantastic Films Magazine, Inc.)
1978–1985

	#1	Close Encounters of the Third Kind, Star Wars, The Day the Earth Stood Still	$5–10
	#2	Superman, Close Encounters of the Third Kind	3–6
	#3	Special Effects issue	5–10
	#4	Metamorphoses, The Lord of the Rings, Greg Jein interview	2–5
	#5	Battlestar Galactica, Star Trek, The Outer Limits	3–6
	#6	Battlestar Galactica, The Lord of the Rings	3–6

YEAR	ISSUE/NUMBER	DESCRIPTION	VALUE
	#7	The Selling of Superman, Star Wars, The Lord of the Rings	$ 2–5
	#8	Superman, Star Wars	2–5
	#9	First Alien issue	5–10
	#10	First all-Alien cover	10–20
	#11	Second all-Alien cover	10–20
	#12	Alien feature	3–5
	#13	Godzilla and His Creators, Meteor	3–6
	#14	Star Trek, The Black Hole	3–5
	#15	The Black Hole, Star Trek	2–4
	#16	Saturn III, The Fog	2–4
	#17	The Empire Strikes Back	2–5
	#18	The Empire Strikes Back	2–5
	#19	The Empire Strikes Back	2–4
	#20	Special Collectors Edition . . . Clone Wars Explained	2–4
	#21	Special Collectors Edition . . . Asteroid Worm Captured/Forbidden Planet	2–4
	#22	The Very Best of Fantastic Films, Star Wars, Empire Strikes Back	3–5
	#23	Special . . . From Star Wars to The Empire Strikes Back	3–6
	#24	Star Wars, Excalibur	3–6
	#35	Return of the Jedi	4–8+
	#25–46		2–5

Fantastic Monsters of the Films (Black Shield Publications)
1962–1963

	#1	$25–50
	#2, #3	30–60+
	#4–7	20–40

YEAR	ISSUE/NUMBER	DESCRIPTION	VALUE

Fantastic Worlds
    All issues $5–10

Fantasy Empire (dedicated to Dr. Who and published by New Media Publishing, Inc.)
    All issues $4–8

Fantasy Enterprises (one issue only)
1985   Star Trek $2–4

Fantasy Film Guide Book: 1967
(zine published by The Sci-Fi Club)
1968   #1 $5–15

Fantasy Film Journal
(published by Quarterly Nostalgia Graphics)
1977   #1   Special Star Wars issue including an interview with John Dykstra $3–7

Fantasy Image
1985   March #2   Star Trek $3–6

Fantasy Magazine Index
1976 $10–20
    All other issues   3–6

Fear of Darkness (bizarre and unusual cinema)
    All issues $5–10

Femme Fatale
1992   #1, #2, #3 $5–10

#18

#20

#21

#22

#23

#24

#26

#29

#32

YEAR	ISSUE/NUMBER	DESCRIPTION	VALUE

Film Fantasy Yearbook (Warren Publishing)

1982	#1	Raiders of the Lost Ark, Dragonslayer, Superman II, An American Werewolf in London, The Howling, Outland, Clash of the Titans, Wolfen, Friday the 13th Part II	$4–8
1983	#2	E.T., Star Trek II, Tron, The Thing, Halloween III, The Road Warrior, Conan, Creepshow, Poltergeist	3–7

Filmfax (Michael Stein Publishing)

1986	#1	Space Patrol: Behind the Scenes with the Original Cast and Crew, actor Dick Miller: His Early Years with Roger Corman, The Bowery Boys: The Director Tells It, Cult Films . . . Plan 9 from Outer Space and Tobor the Great	$75–150+
	#2	Invaders from Mars: The 1953 Classic versus the 1986 Remake, Space Patrol Part II, Abbott and Costello, Gumby Animator	50–100+
	#3	All Horror issue special, Bela Lugosi: The Final Years, Gloria Stuart on The Old Dark House, Dark Shadows' Vampire Jonathan Frid, Classic Scare Comedies, Reginald Leborg, Shock and Schlock of William Castle	10–20+

YEAR	ISSUE/NUMBER	DESCRIPTION	VALUE
1986	#4	The Men in The Grey Rubber Suit special edition, Space Patrol, Plan 9 from Outer Space, The Adventures of Captain Midnight, Forrest J. Ackerman, Dick Miller, Candid Horror Photo Album, Films of Ed D. Wood Jr., Tobor the Great	$10–20+
	#5	Little Shop of Horrors, The Big Bug Films of the 1950s	25–50+
	#6	Beverly Garland: Her Early Years, Forrest J. Ackerman on Elsa Lanchester, Gimmick Films, Friends of Ed D. Wood Jr.	25–50+
	#7	Four decades of Horror Noir film classics	30–60+
	#8	Special flying saucer anniversary edition, first UFO film, The Flying Saucer, Earth versus the Flying Saucers, The Three Stooges in Orbit, Battle in Outer Space, Flying Disc Man from Mars	20–40+
	#9	The Best of Filmfax 100-page special, Space Patrol TV, Adventures of Captain Marvel, Plan 9 from Outer Space, Tobor the Great, Candid Horror Photo Album, Films of Ed D. Wood Jr.	10–20+

YEAR	ISSUE/NUMBER	DESCRIPTION	VALUE
1986	#10	Special 100-page anniversary issue, Bob Hope interview on his early career, The Films of Allison Hayes and Ed D. Wood, Night of the Ghouls, Robert Stack on Colorization, Cat and the Canary, Space Patrol	$10–20+
	#11	Detour retrospective, Films of Edgar Ulmer: Part 1, Moe's Daughter Remembers the Three Stooges, Tom Neal Jr., Lost City of the Jungle, The Death of TV Superman George Reeves	10–20+
	#12	The Man from Planet X, The Bat Whispers, Douglas Fairbanks Jr. interview, The Films of Edgar Ulmer: Part 2, Ted Browning's freaks, Jungle Girl serial, Virginia Karns and Lois Laurel interviews on Laurel and Hardy	15–30+
	#13	Boris Karloff, A History of TV Horror Hosts, Superman overview and interviews with cast, The Ritz Brothers and the Gorilla, Ben Welden interview, One Step Beyond and the John Newland interview, Curt Siodmak interview	15–30+

YEAR	ISSUE/NUMBER	DESCRIPTION	VALUE
1986	#14	Zacherly interview, John Carradine tribute, the Marx Brothers' lost sitcom, Stanley Kramer interview, Veronica Carlson interview, Jungle Jim, Mad Love, Curt Siodmak interview	$15–30+
	#15	Mel Blanc interview, Robinson Crusoe on Mars, Monogram Pictures, Ken Tobey interview, The Making of The Attack of the B Movie Monster, Perils of Nyoka, Ingrid Pitt interview, Return to Robin Hood's Sherwood Forest	7–15+
	#16	The complete history of Batman . . . serials and TV, Adam West, Yvonne Craig, Gorilla Stuntman Steve Calvert, Carnival of Souls, The Lost Worlds of Willis O'Brien, Sabu, Colossus of New York	7–15+
	#17	Science Fiction Theatre, Richard Webb interview, Captain Midnight, The Day the Earth Stood Still, Michael Rennie, The Angry Red Planet, Glamor Girls from Outer Space, The Queen of Outer Space	7–15+
	#18	The Monster of Piedras Blancas, Bela Lugosi's Last Screen Rites, Brain Movies, The Brain That Wouldn't Die, Great Horror Detectives	7–15+

YEAR	ISSUE/NUMBER	DESCRIPTION	VALUE
1986	#19	Rocky Jones, Space Ranger, Arthur Dagwood Lake, Barbara Steele, The Monster That Challenged the World, William Bakewell on Douglas Fairbanks Sr., Thief of Baghdad	$7–15+
	#20	Lon Chaney Jr.'s last interview, TV's Rocky Jones, Space Ranger: Part 2, serial king Henry Macrae, Hazel Court, Robert Campbell on working with Roger Corman, Jock Mahoney	7–15+
	#21	Men into Space TV Science Fiction Docudrama, SPFX makeup artist Harry Thomas, Lon Chaney Jr. Remembered: Part 2, The History of Dick Tracy, Virginia Christine interview, Forrest J. Ackerman on his late wife Wendayne	5–10+
	#22	I Was a Teenage Werewolf exclusive, Abbott and Costello Meet—movies, director Gene Fowler and actor Whit Bissel interviewed, Laurette Luez star of Prehistoric Women interviewed, Dick Tracy Part 2, B Movies' Hidden Heroines	5–10+

YEAR	ISSUE/NUMBER	DESCRIPTION	VALUE
1986	#23	Mamie Van Doren, Bwana Devil: A 3-D Classic, Huntz Hall, Sylvia Sydney interview, Turgid Teen Films, Ackerman's Hellvision, Prehistoric Women, Sam Abarbanel	$5–10+
	#24 up		5–10

Note: Prices for *Filmfax* are greatly influenced by the publisher who offers many issues through its back-issue department. Most of these publisher-offered issues are priced at $10 to 15 each for mint copies only one month after they are off the newsstands or have been sent out via subscription. When a back issue is no longer offered by *Filmfax* that particular issue can easily double or even triple in value.

Films Fortnightly
(British magazine published by London Publications)

1971	April 3	Godzilla cover and feature, Science Fiction Film special	$10–20

Frankenstein Classic (Modern Day Periodicals)

1977	One issue only		$3–5

Free Paper, The (tabloid, Boston's weekly newspaper)

1974	February 6	King Kong cover and feature: The Life and Hard Times of King Kong	$3–5

Future/Future Life (O'Quinn Studios)
1978–1981

	#1	Close Encounters of the Third Kind Special Effects	$2–4
	#2–31		2–3

YEAR	ISSUE/NUMBER	DESCRIPTION	VALUE

Future Fantasy (Cousins Publications, Inc.)

1978   (published in February, April, and June)

      #1   Beautiful Space Heroines, Close Encounters of the Third Kind, Captain Cosmos, William Shatner: Spider Fighter, Futuristic Sounds of the Rock Group Kiss, Pink Floyd, Todd Rundgren, Robot Takeover, Science Fiction Art $5–10

Note: Issue #1's value is based more on its popularity with collectors of the rock group Kiss than with collectors of monster magazines

      #2   Close Encounters of the Third Kind, Flying Saucer in Fact and Fantasy, Authentic UFO Photos, Booung the Space Villain, Peter Frampton Meets R2D2, Godzilla, Captain Cosmos, Damnation Alley   3–6

      #3   Close Encounters versus Star Wars, The Resurrection of Star Trek   3–5

Galactic Journal (one issue only)

1987   Director Paul Verhoeven on Robocop, Star Trek: The Next Generation preview, James Doohan and Robin Curtis on the old generation $5–10

Ghoul Tales (Stanley Publications, Inc.; illustrated horror)

1970   #1 (November, vol. 1, #1)   The Bogeyman, The Voice of Doom, Terror on TV, Destiny's Double Deal $7–15

YEAR	ISSUE/NUMBER	DESCRIPTION	VALUE
1971	#2 (January, vol. 1, #2)	You Look Good Enough to Eat, The Curse of the Pirate's Gold, Bloody Spawn of the Cat, The Evil Eye	$6–12
	#3 (March, vol. 1, #3)	Corpse in the Coffin, Voodoo Dolls, The Witches' Curse, Eternal Death	6–12
	#4 (May, vol. 1, #4)	Terror of the Deep, Bloodstone, Medusa's Head, Death Takes a Holiday	6–12
	#5 (July, vol. 1, #5)	The Buried Curse, Werewolves of the Rockies, The Evil Secret of Black Hollow, Undying Brain	5–10

Gore Creatures (prozine)

#1, #2	$15–30
#2–9	15–30
#10 up	5–10

Gorezone (O'Quinn Studios)

Note: Back issues of *Gorezone* can be purchased directly through the publisher

#1	$3–6
All other issues	2–5

Gothism (prozine)

All issues	$5–10

Gremlins Souvenir Magazine (Official Collector's Edition)

1984	All about Gremlins with exclusive interviews	$2–4

YEAR	ISSUE/NUMBER	DESCRIPTION	VALUE

Halls of Horror
(formerly House of Horror/House of Hammer)

Note: British monster magazine with American distribution

	#21	Christopher Lee, Boris Karloff, The Werewolf, Warlords of the Deep	$5–10
	#22	Christopher Lee/The Mummy	4–8
	#23	Enemy from Space, Frankenstein	4–8
	#24	Seven Shock-Filled Creature Classics special . . . Aliens, Vampires, Dragons, and Monsters	4–8
	#25	The Spawn of Psycho: The Robert Bloch Interview, Hammer's Psycho Screamers, The History of Slash Movies	4–8
	#26	Masters of the Macabre special . . . Karloff, Lugosi, Pleasence, Carradine, and Lorre, Barbara Steel interview, The House of the Long Shadows	4–8
	#27	Special Blood Hunters edition featuring Jaws 3-D and The Night Stalker, Brides of Dracula	4–8+
	#28	Vincent Price on Film and Video, Close-Up on Ingrid Pitt, Brides of Dracula, H. G. Lewis	4–8+
	#29	Mad Max: The Day After, The Poetry of Evil: Vincent Price, Mutant	5–10

YEAR	ISSUE/NUMBER	DESCRIPTION	VALUE
	#30	Horror Fantasy and Science Fiction: An A-to-Z Guide	$4–8

Heidi Saha (an illustrated history of, published by Warren)

	One shot		$15–30

Horror Monsters (Charleton Publications)
1961–1965

	#1	How to Build Your Own Monster	$15–30
	#2	The Pit and the Pendulum	15–30+
	#3	The Mask, The Devil's Hand, Bloodlust, The Stein of Frankenbride	12–25
	#4	Shock Theater, Mummy's Curse, Bob Burns: Man of Horror	10–20
	#5	The Head: Peter Lorre . . . The Little Giant of Monsterland, Burn Witch Burn	10–20
	#6	Frankenstein 1970, Dracula	7–15
	#7	Werewolf in a Girls' Dorm	7–15
	#8	The Brain That Wouldn't Die, Where Monsters Walk, The Fly	10–20
	#9	The House on Haunted Hill, The Black Sleep, George Zucco	7–15
	#10	The Curse of Frankenstein, The Black Sleep, Vincent Price special	7–15

YEAR	ISSUE/NUMBER	DESCRIPTION	VALUE

Horror Movie Yearbook (Warren Publishing)

1981		Friday the 13th, Fade to Black, The Fog, The Changeling, The Shining, Without Warning, The Alien, Silent Scream, etc.	$4–8

Horror of Party Beach (Warren Publishing)

1964			$5–10

Horror Tales (Eerie Publications; illustrated horror)

YEAR	ISSUE/NUMBER	DESCRIPTION	VALUE
1969	#1 (June, vol. 1, #7)	Satan's Plaything, Screams in the Night	$7–15
	#2 (August, vol. 1, #8)	Wall of Blood, This Head is Mine	7–15
	#3 (November, vol. 1, #9)	The Slime Creatures, Werewolf, Bury Her Deep	7–15
1970	#4 (January, vol. 2, #1)	House of Monsters, The Witch and the Werewolf	5–10
	#5 (March, vol. 2, #2)	Witches' Nightmare, Ghoul Without Pockets, The Slimy Gargoyle	4–8
	#6 (May, vol. 2, #3)	Tombstone for a Ghoul, Monsters Nightmare	3–7
	#7 (July, vol. 2, #4)	Vampires from Beyond, The Doom Witch	3–7
	#8 (September, vol. 2, #5)	Into the Land of Ghoulish Monsters, Vampires and Things from Beyond	3–7
	#9 (November, vol. 2, #6)	Spine-Chilling Horror from the Edge of Darkness	3–7

#7, December 1970   *July 1970*   *January 1971*

March 1971   *April 1974*   *October 1974*

March 1970   *November 1970*   *March 1971*

YEAR	ISSUE/NUMBER	DESCRIPTION	VALUE
1971	#10 (January, vol. 3, #1)	The Terror of the Mummy, The Shocking Death of the Witch, The Terrifying Satan the Demon	$3–7
	#11 (March, vol. 3, #2)	Body Snatcher, Sawdust Banshee	3–7
	#12 (May, vol. 3, #3)	The Bloody Thing, Zombie Magic	3–7
	#13 (July, vol. 3, #4)	The Witches' Coven, Curse of the Vampire	3–7
	#14 (September, vol. 3, #5)	The Vampire Lives, The Curse of the Dead Witch, The Nightmare	3–7
	#15 (November, vol. 3, #6)	The Blood Demon, The Weird and Beastly Monster, The Wild One	3–7
1972	#16 (January, vol. 4, #1)	The House of Blood, The Monster, Satan's Corpse	3–7
	#17 (March, vol. 4, #2)	The Hairy Beast, Walls of Fear	3–7
	#18 (April, vol. 4, #3)	Special Total Shock Issue, The Terrifying Bloody Corpse, The Mad Ones	3–7
	#19 (June, vol. 4, #4)	The Ghastly Terror of the Skeleton, The Rhyme of Shock	3–7
	#20 (August, vol. 4, #5)	The Demon, Grotesque	3–7
	#21 (October, vol. 4, #6)	The Ghoul, Bloody Nightmare	3–7
	#22 (December, vol. 4, #7)	The Devil's Witch, The Corpse That Lives	3–7
1973	#23 (February, vol. 5, #1)	The Blood-Chilling Flesh-Eaters, Terror Below	3–7
	#24 (April, vol. 5, #2)	The Bloody Wolfman, Ghoul's Mansion	3–7
	#25 (June, vol. 5, #5)	Blood-Sucking Vampires, Strange Monsters and Evil Beings	4–8

YEAR	ISSUE/NUMBER	DESCRIPTION	VALUE
1973	#26 (August, vol. 5, #4)	The Manbeast, The Evil One	$ 3–7
	#27 (October, vol. 5, #5)	The Monster in Cloth, The Mad Witch	4–8
	#28 (December, vol. 5, #6)	Circle of Terror, Deadman's Tomb, The Devil You Say?	3–7
1974	#29 (February, vol. 6, #1)	The Grotesque Checkmate, The Spooks, The Tomb of Hate	3–7
	#30 (April, vol. 6, #2)	The Awesome Demons and Skeletons, Satan's Toys, Fang of Revenge	3–7
	#31 (June, vol. 6, #3)	The Blood-Chilling Living Dead, Head-Chopper, The Fighting Vampire	3–7
	#32 (August, vol. 6, #4)	The Vampires, The Spirit of Evil, The Broomstick Witch	3–7
	#33 (October, vol. 6, #5)	Skin Crawlers, Evil Idol	3–7
	#34 (December, vol. 6, #6)		3–7
1975	#35 (February, vol. 7, #1)	The Screaming Hell, Signed in Blood, The Creatures' Crypt	5–10
1976	#36 (May, vol. 7, #2)	Jumbo-size giant issue Never Kill a Corpse, Vampire Bride, Cats of Doom, Satan's Revenge, Horror with Fangs	5–10
	#37 (August, vol. 7, #3)	Jumbo-size giant issue	5–10
	#38 (November, vol. 7, #4)	Jumbo-size giant issue House of Blood, The Vampire Flies, The Thing, The Supernatural, Satan's Demon, The Dead Demons	5–10

YEAR	ISSUE/NUMBER	DESCRIPTION	VALUE
1977	#39 (May, vol. 8, #2)	Jumbo-size giant issue Curse of the Vampire, Nightmare in Blood, Spirit of the Witch, Pool of Evil	$5–10
	#40 (August, vol. 8, #4)	The Head-Chopper, The Skeletons, The Fanged Freak	4–8
	#41 (November, vol 8, #5)		4–8
1978	#42 (February, vol. 9, #1)	The Demon, Tear 'Em Apart, Bloodsucker, The Skull	4–8
	#43 (May, vol. 9, #2)	The House of the Vampire, Head Full of Snakes, Black Light Terror	4–8
	#44 (August, vol. 9, #3)	Swamp Monster, The Vampire, Voodoo Terror, Satan's Pit of Evil, Nightmare in Blood	4–8
1978	#45 (November, vol. 9, #4)		4–8

House of Hammer
(British horror magazine dedicated to Hammer Films, published by Top Sellers, Ltd./Quality Communications)

	#1	Dracula: An Illustrated Adaptation	$4–12
	#2	The Curse of Frankenstein, The Texas Chainsaw Massacre	5–10
	#3	All Monster special	5–10
	#4	Legend of the Seven Golden Vampires	5–10
	#5	Death in Space, Peter Cushing	5–10
	#6	Dracula: Prince of Darkness	6–12

YEAR	ISSUE/NUMBER	DESCRIPTION	VALUE
	#7	Burn Witch Burn, Twins of Evil	$5–10
	#8	Shandor, The Quatermass Experiment, King Kong, Christopher Lee's New Dracula Film, Jekyl and Hyde, Hammer's Science Fiction	4–8
	#9	Carrie, King Kong, Squirm, Seizure	4–8
	#10	Curse of the Werewolf, Sentinel, Satan's Slave	4–8
	#11	Peter Cushing is Tender Dracula, Ray Harryhausen on Horror, Zoltan, The Gorgon	5–10
	#12	Witchfinder General, The Exorcist II: The Heretic, The Gorgon	5–10
	#13	Plague of the Zombies, Star Wars, Mansion of the Doomed, Victor Frankenstein, Blood City	5–10+
	#14	Raquel Welch: One Million Years B.C., John Carradine interview	6–12+
	#15–18		4–8

House of Horror (formerly *House of Hammer*)

YEAR	ISSUE/NUMBER	DESCRIPTION	VALUE
	#19	Revenge of the Blood Beast, The Yeti, Frankenstein, Dracula, The Reptile: The Full Film in Comic Form	$5–10
	#20	Kronos, The Incredible Melting Man, The Mummy Savage Bees	3–6

YEAR	ISSUE/NUMBER	DESCRIPTION	VALUE

House of Horror (American edition)
Top Sellers, Ltd/Quality Communications

| | #1 | Curse of the Werewolf, Boris Karloff, Vincent Price, George Romero | $7–15 |

House of Horror (Warren Publishing)

| | #1 | Frankenstein cover | $300–400+ |

Note: Only 400 copies of this issue were printed and prices of over $600 have been paid in the past. It is advisable to offer this issue as a bid item: this way the seller will attain the fairest current market value.

Incredible Science Fiction
(Science Fantasy Film Classics, Inc.)

| 1978 | #1 | The Creature from the Black Lagoon, Five Million Years to Earth, Aliens and Monsters special | $3–7 |

Journal of Frankenstein
(published by New World Enterprises, Syndicated, Inc.)

| 1959 | #1 | The Boris Karloff Story: Master of Horror, The History of Horror Movies: All Manner of Fantasies, House on Haunted Hill, John Zacherly | $50–100 |

Journal of Popular Film and Television

| 1984 | Summer | Star Trek | $2–4 |

YEAR	ISSUE/NUMBER	DESCRIPTION	VALUE

King Kong (Sportscene Publications)

| 1977 | | The Monster That Made History, issue contains an amazing King Kong poster | $5–10 |

King of the Monsters (Cousins Publications)

| 1977 | | The New Kong Movie, Konga and the Monster Menagerie, Kogar the Ape, Kong on Stage | $5–10 |

Kong (Countrywide Communications, Inc.)

| 1976 | | The Most Famous Monster of all Time special, includes a poster | $5–10 |

Larry Ives' Monster and Heroes (M & H Publications)

1967–1968

	#1	A History of Frankenstein, Johnny Shefield Filmland's Son of Tarzan, TV's Costume Heroes, Heroes of Radio, Bat-Men of Darkest Africa	$10–20
	#2	The Monster Men of ERB, The Origin of Altron Boy, The Four Faces of Captain America, The Creators and Actors of Superman	7–15
	#3	The Creation of King Kong, Heroes of TV, Captain Video, The Burroughs Library	6–12
	#4	Movie Serials, Captain Marvel, Werewolves in the Movies	5–10

YEAR	ISSUE/NUMBER	DESCRIPTION	VALUE
	#5	The Creation of Frankenstein, Radio's Captain Midnight, Boris Karloff	$5–10
	#6	Flash Gordon, The World of John Carter, Buster Crabbe	4–8
	#7	The Green Hornet, The Mummy	

Legend Horror Classics (British monster magazine)

All issues		$4–8

Mad Monsters (Charlton Publications)
1961–1965

#1	Konga: A Picture Preview, Saint George and the 7 Curses, Reptilicus: The Evil Creature from a Time Long Dead, Black Sunday, The Truth about Monsters	$10–20
#2	Creature from the Black Lagoon cover, Bela Lugosi: Horror Master, House of Horrors, The Brides of Dracula, Werewolf Album	10–20
#3	Boris Karloff: The Master Monster Talks, She-Beasts on the Prowl, The Immortal Monster Caltoki, Mystery of Black Magic, Attack of the Mad Monsters: Beings from Outer Space	10–20

YEAR	ISSUE/NUMBER	DESCRIPTION	VALUE
	#4	The Beast of Yucca Flats, The House of Frankenstein, Invasion of the Body Snatchers	$10–20
	#5	Frankenstein Meets the Wolfman: Lugosi and Chaney, Abbott and Costello Meet the Monsters, The Three Stooges in Orbit, Journey to the Seventh Planet	10–20
	#6	Boris Karloff: Man of a Million Horrors, Anthony Quinn in The Hunchback of Notre Dame, The Day of the Triffids full-length feature, The Black Zoo Party, Monster on the Campus	10–20
	#7	I Married a Monster from Outer Space, Corridors of Blood, King Kong versus Godzilla	10–20
	#8	Lon Chaney, Jr.: Champion of Chills, The Strangler: Mad Monster on the Loose, The Giant Behemoth, Devil Bat: A Chilling Classic	10–20
	#9	Vincent Price: The Masque of the Red Death, witness the creation of The Devil Wolf of Shadow Mountain, chill to Goliath and the Vampires, The Bat	10–20
	#10	Zombies: The Incredibly Strange Creatures, Cult of Horror special, Basil Rathbone: Demon of Distinction, The Mummy	25–50+

YEAR	ISSUE/NUMBER	DESCRIPTION	VALUE
1981		Christopher Lee cover and feature, Altered States, The Howling's Success, Raiders of the Lost Ark	$15–30+

Magus (RGM Publications)

1981	One issue only		$20–50+

Media Spotlight (IRJAX Enterprises, Inc.)

Publishing begins in 1976

	#1	Star Trek Lives Again, Gene Roddenberry and the Star Trek movie	$5–10
	All other issues		3–6

Midnight Marque (prozine)

#1		$15–30
#2–4		12–25
#5, #6		10–20
#7–15		7–15
#16 up		5–10

Modern Monsters (Prestige Publications)

1966	#1		$12–25
	#2	Count Dracula, Blood, Bullets and Bond, Nick Adams interview	10–20
	#3	The Mummy, The Cosmic Cliffhangers	10–20
	#4	The Invisible Man, King Kong: A Double Take, Spy Smasher, The Green Hornet Strikes	10–20

Mole People, The (Warren Publishing)

1964		A Terrifying story told in 500 photos from the film	$4–8

YEAR	ISSUE/NUMBER	DESCRIPTION	VALUE

Monsterama (Forrest J. Ackerman's)

YEAR	ISSUE/NUMBER	DESCRIPTION	VALUE
1991	#1	Karloff, Lugosi, Chaney, the Wolfman	$4–8+
	#2		3–6+

Monster Attack
(illustrated horror and movie photos and stories)

			VALUE
	All issues		$2–4

Monster Fantasy (Mayfair Publications)

YEAR	ISSUE/NUMBER	DESCRIPTION	VALUE
1975	#1	The Vampire Book: The Legends, The Movies and Terrifying Reality, My Father Peter Lorre: An Exclusive Interview, Sea Creatures and Space Ghouls, Frankenstein's Latest Monster, Horror Headquarters: London Report	$4–7
	#2	The Book of the Mummy: A Full-length Bonus, The Strange Death of Lon Chaney, Satan and Salem: The Witchcraft Movies, Horror's First Lady: Elsa Lanchester, The Hindenburg, The Thing That Was Killing The Girls (fiction)	2–4
	#3	The Space Monster Book featuring Forbidden Planet, etc., The Phantom of the Opera, Monsters from TV's Star Trek and The Outer Limits, The Tragic Life of Laird Cregar, Alfred Hitchcock	3–6

YEAR	ISSUE/NUMBER	DESCRIPTION	VALUE
1975	#4	Lon Chaney Jr.: book-length bonus feature, Zombie: Movies of the Living Dead, The Horror Films of Jack Nicholson, Abbott and Costello Meet the Monsters	$2–4

Monster Howls (Humor Vision, Inc.)

1966	#1	Monster movie photos and illustrations presented in a humorous horror vein . . . one issue only	$10–20

Monster Madness

(monster movie humor with original photos, published by Marvel)

1972–1973

	#1	Frankenstein cover	$2–4
	#2	Frankenstein, Igor, and Basil Rathbone cover	2–4
	#3	The Bride of Frankenstein cover	2–4

Monster Mag

(British monster poster magazine published by Top Sellers Ltd.)

Publishing begins 1973

	#1	Christopher Lee	$5–10
	#2, #3		5–10
	#16	Christopher Lee, Vampire Circus, Death Line, Blood and Bullets	4–8
	All other issues		3–6

YEAR	ISSUE/NUMBER	DESCRIPTION	VALUE

Monster Mania (Renaissance Productions)

1967	#1	Christopher Lee cover, Dracula: Powers of Darkness, The Reptile, Rasputin: The Mad Monk, The Peter Cushing Story, interview with Jack Pierce	$12–25
	#2	Tribute to Hammer Films special	10–20
	#3	Peter Cushing Returns in Frankenstein Created Woman, The Wolfman, Revenge of Frankenstein	15–30

Monster Monthly (Marvel)

1982	#1	Saturn III cover, Robot Monsters	$5–10
	All other issues		4–8

Monster Parade (Magnum Publications)

1958	#1	Issue is marked volume 2, #6	$150–300+
	#2	Issue is marked volume 1, #2	100–200+
	#3	Issue is marked volume 1, #3	75–150
1959	#4	Issue is marked volume 1, #4	50–100

Monsters and Things (Magnum Publications)

1959	#1	The Vampire Legend, Rodan, Frankenstein 1970	$ 85–175
	#2	The Story of Frankenstein, movie monster pinups	100–200+

YEAR	ISSUE/NUMBER	DESCRIPTION	VALUE

Monsters of the Movies (Marvel)
1974–1975

	#1	King Kong special, The Night Stalker, Christopher Lee, Boris Karloff, Bela Lugosi, Lon Chaney	$5–10
	#2	The Frankenstein Monster, Count Yorga, King (Boris) Karloff	3–5
	#3	Special Vampire issue, Inside Hammer Films, Barnabas Collins, Blackula, Count Yorga, Bela Lugosi	3–5

Monster Times: The
(tabloid published by Monster Times Publishing)
1972–1976

	#1	The Man Who Saved King Kong, mushroom monsters, the end of the world	$5–10
	#2	Special Star Trek issue . . . the William Shatner interview, Star Trek production secrets, the Star Trek photo story	7–15
		Bug issue special, King Kong, man-eating plants	4–8
	#4	The Bride of Frankenstein, Tales from the Crypt, Green Lantern and Green Arrow, Dracula Goes to Court	4–8
	#5	Creature from the Black Lagoon, Star Trek special, The Return of Dr. X, mushroom monsters, DC's Tarzan of the Apes	4–8

YEAR	ISSUE/NUMBER	DESCRIPTION	VALUE
	#6	Special all-zombie issue, Tales of the Living Dead	$ 2–4
	#7	Godzilla: King of the Monsters issue, King Kong Meets the Giant Bug, Batman for President	7–15+
	#8	Hammer Horror Films special, Horror of Dracula, Curse of the Werewolf, Christopher Lee exclusive interview, Aurora's Dr. Deadly toys: Terror Toys Invade London	4–8
	#9	This Island Earth, Buck Rogers, Flash Gordon	2–4
	#10	EC comic special	2–4
	#11	The Planet of the Apes special, exclusive Dracula interview	5–10
	#12	Gorgo Speaks, behind the Planet of the Apes, Steranko's history of the comics	6–12
	#13	Meet Marvel's Marvelous Spiderman, Colossal Monsterous Movie Mistakes, Good Vibes from Dr. Phibes, Shazam	4–8
	#14	The Wolfman, exclusive interview with Peter Cushing	3–7
	#15	The Valley of Gwangi, How to Make a Monster, Dracula in Comix, Godzilla	3–7

YEAR	ISSUE/NUMBER	DESCRIPTION	VALUE
	#16	Attack of the Plant Monsters, Godzilla, memoirs of Mighty Joe Young, the return of Dr. Phibes and Count Yorga	$ 3–7
	#17	Super science fiction issue, Forbidden Planet filmbook, Rod Serling Speaks, Meet the Mysterious Mysterians, Asylum, King Kong's Komeback	5–10
	#18	Christopher Lee: Dracula A.D. 1972, King Kong Komix, The Monster of Piedras Blancas	3–7
	#19	Tarantula, The Return of EC, Movies That Don't Die, Monsterous Movie Ads	2–4
	#20	20 Million Miles to Earth, Fu Manchu, Star Trek: A Super Salute, A Warped Neal Adams	5–10
	#21	The Total Frankenstein, includes a Frankenstein filmbook, Frankenstein's castle and a Frankenstein film list	5–10
	#22	Inside The Vault of Horror, The Green Slime, Godzilla versus Ghidrah	3–6
	#23	Godzilla: The King of the Monsters, meet The Rat	7–15+
	#24	Theatre of Blood, Rodan: The Flying Monster, Last of The Planet of the Apes, Mad Basil Wolverton, Return of the History of Comics	5–10

YEAR	ISSUE/NUMBER	DESCRIPTION	VALUE
	#25	Horror Heroines special, The Trouble with Star Trek, King Kung Fu, Werewolves on Wheels, Captain Marvel's Maker, Batman and Superman, The Fly	$5–10
	#26	Destroy All Monsters special, The Return of Star Trek exclusive, Superman Slept Here	3–6
	#27	Bela Lugosi: The Decline and Fall, The Screeb's Strangest Vampires, Blackula Bites Back, Dreaming of Dracula, The World's Best Vampire Story	5–10
	#28	Hammer's House of Horror issue, Great Movie Death Scenes, The Legendary Lon Chaney, Plastic Man	3–6
	#29	The Truth About the Abominable Snowman, EC Lives, Sinbad Sales Again, Japanese Monsters, The House of Frankenstein	3–5
	#30	Special Werewolves and Monsters issue	3–5
	#31	Special All-Martian issue, War of the Worlds, Invaders from Mars, Making Martian Monsters	5–10
	#32	The Beast from 20,000 Fathoms, Marvel's Mightiest Monsters, Werewolf of Washington,	

YEAR	ISSUE/NUMBER	DESCRIPTION	VALUE
		Mexican Monsters, Questor, Bruce Lee Lives, Godzilla	$ 3–5
	#33	The Planet of the Apes, All-Ape issue special, The Complete Saga of The Planet of the Apes, History of Celluloid Simians	5–10+
	#34	Female Fiends, Star Trek's Captain Kirk Speaks, Zardoz, Underground Horrors, The Time Machine, Swamp Thing	4–8
	#35	The Return of Godzilla, Female Fiends Revisited, Makeup Masters, Supernatural Superheroes, Toho's Titans of Terror	4–8
	#36	Curse of the Werewolf, Star Trek's Mr. Spock Speaks, Robot Monsters, Martians Attack	3–6
	#37	Gammera, The Apes (Planet of the Apes) Invade TV	4–8
	#38	A Giant History of Giant Film Giants, Sinbad's Golden Voyage, Conan, Beware the Blob Maker	3–5
	#39	Who Is King . . . Godzilla or King Kong, Dracula, Frankenstein, Planet of the Apes, Ghidrah, Gammera, The Wolfman, The Creature from the Black Lagoon, Rodan, The Mummy, Destroy All Monsters	3–6

YEAR	ISSUE/NUMBER	DESCRIPTION	VALUE
	#40	The Phantom of the Opera, Son of Kong, Fay Wray Remembers, Bela Lugosi Lives	$ 3–6
	#41	The Six Frankensteins of Filmdom, The Terror from Beyond Space, Andy Warhol's Dracula, How to Make a Mummy	3–6
	#42	Godzilla versus The Thing, Star Trek Returns, The Unsinkable Shrinking Man, Horror Movie Comics, Werewolves	3–6
	#43	All-Demon issue, Star Trek's Captain Kirk, The Exorcist	5–10
	#44	One Million Years B.C., Raquel Welch cover, Dinosaur issue special, Cave Girls	4–8
	#45	Jane Fonda as Barbarella cover and feature, A Talk with Long John Carradine, Star Trek's Bill Shatner, The King Kong Disaster, The Worst Fright Film Ever Made, Shriek of the Mutilated, Bugs	4–8
	#46	All-Dracula issue, The Real Dracula, A Conversation with Christopher Lee, Star Trek: The Final Frontier	3–6
	#47	Star Trek versus Space 1999 special, Flash Gordon, Science Fiction Comics	4–8

YEAR	ISSUE/NUMBER	DESCRIPTION	VALUE
	#47	Special Bionic issue, Six Million Dollar Man, The Bionic Woman, Meet Jamie the Bionic Woman	$3–6

Monster Times Collector's Issue

	#3	Godzilla and King Kong: Who is the King?, issue includes 10 wall posters	$7–15

Monster Times/Star Trek Lives

	#1	Star Trek, UFO, Lost in Space, The Outer Limits, etc.	$7–15
	#2	Inside profiles on all the people who made Star Trek, exclusive stories and photos	7–15

Monsterland, Forrest J. Ackerman's (New Media Publishing)
1985–1987

	#1	Forrest Ackerman talks to Steven Spielberg, The Complete Godzilla, Night of the Living Dead, The Hills Have Eyes II, The Company of Wolves	$25–50+
	#2	Elvira, Sybil Danning and Jane Badler cover and feature, a talk with Stephen King, Sting Meets the Bride, Vincent Price, the new Godzilla	15–30+
	#3	Godzilla, the creatures of George Pal, Nightmare on Elm Street, Lifeforce	7–15

YEAR	ISSUE/NUMBER	DESCRIPTION	VALUE
	#4	Fright Night: The Director's Story, Day of the Dead, The Tragic Life of Bela Lugosi, Makeup Master John Carl Buechler, Filmfests	$10–20
	#5	Roddy McDowall, Sting and Jennifer Beals, Day of the Dead, Japan's Frankenstein versus Gammera, Boris Karloff: Titan of Terror, on the set of The Re-Animator, Christopher Lee exclusive interview	5–10
	#6	Werewolves, Vampires and Nightmares, The Return of Freddy Krueger, Caroline Munroe exclusive interview, The Dead Girls, Building Godzilla '85	5–10
	#7	Elvira cover and feature, Psycho III, The Last Day of Lon Chaney, Trolls, Twilight Zone: Behind the Scenes, The Time Machine	10–20
	#8	Psycho III, the Amazing Stories story, Twilight Zone	3–6
	#9	Creature Invasion issue, Invaders from Mars, the Godzilla book, The Fly Flies Again, Peter Lorre, Creating the Killbots, Enemy Mine	3–6

YEAR	ISSUE/NUMBER	DESCRIPTION	VALUE
	#10	Poltergeist II, Tobe Hooper: Director from Mars, Big Trouble in Little China, The House That Dripped Blood, Labyrinth, Curse of Frankenstein	$ 3–6
	#11	Aliens, The Dark Shadows of Barnabas Collins, The Boy Who Could Fly, The Beast from 20,000 Fathoms, John Carpenter	5–10
	#12	Critters, The Outer Limits, Invaders from Mars, The Secrets of Freddy Krueger, Aliens' Sigourney Weaver	4–8
	#13	Poltergeist II, The Creature from the Black Lagoon, On the Set of Aliens, The Hunt for Cherry 2000, Vincent Price: Meet the Grand Master, The Original King Kong	4–8
	#14	King Kong: Censored Scenes, The Flight of the Navigator, Master of Fright: Peter Cushing, The Seventh Voyage of Sinbad, The Boy Who Could Fly, Greg Cannon	3–6
	#15	Elvira cover and feature with poster, Stephen King, Make Your Own Star Trek Costume	10–20
	All other issues		4–8

YEAR	ISSUE/NUMBER	DESCRIPTION	VALUE

Monster Scene Journal
Publishing begins in 1992

	All issues		$3–6

Monsters to Laugh With (Non-Pereil Publications)
1964–1965

	#1–3		$5–10

Monsters Unlimited (formerly Monsters to Laugh With, Magazine Management, Inc.)
1965–1966

	#1	Marked #4	$4–8
	#2	Marked #5	4–8
	#3	Marked #6	4–8
	#4	Marked #7	4–8

Monster World (Mayfair Publishing)
1975

	#1	Vampires of the Screen, Dracula Lives, Monsters Gone Ape, Darren McGavin: The Night Stalker	$5–10
	#2	The Many Faces of Lon Chaney, Vincent Price Unmasked, The Making of King Kong, Nightmare Theatre	3–6

Monster World (Warren)
1964–1966

Note: Numbers 1 through 10 are considered issues 70 through 79 of *Famous Monsters of Filmland*

	#1	The Wolfman cover, Battle of the Frankensteins, monster comics, etc.	$5–10

YEAR	ISSUE/NUMBER	DESCRIPTION	VALUE
	#2	TV's The Munsters cover and feature with exclusive photos, monster comics	$ 7–15
	#3	The She Creature, Battle of the Giant Beetle, Curse of Frankenstein	20–40
	#4	Frankenstein 1970, Horror in the Lighthouse, The Munsters and Their Car, a letter to Christopher Lee, the faces of 7 great fiends	5–10
	#5	Boris Karloff's newest horror film, the monsters of Hammer Films, Bela Lugosi in the Bride of the Monster	5–10
	#6	Horrific Holiday issue, The Revenge of the Zombies, Return of the Vampires	5–10
	#7	Son of Frankenstein special . . . complete with rare photos	5–10
	#8	Dr. X, Jesse James Meets Frankenstein's Daughter, Billy the Kid versus Dracula	5–10
	#9	Meet the Addams Family: cover and special feature	6–12
	#10	Reptiles, Batman and the superheroes, The Ghost in the Invisible Bikini	3–6

Movie Aliens Illustrated (Warren)

1979	#1	Darth Vader and others including Alien the movie	$2–5

YEAR	ISSUE/NUMBER	DESCRIPTION	VALUE

Movie Maker (Fountain Press)

1971	December	Christopher Lee in I Monster cover and feature, Horror Movies: Methods and Mystique	$5–10

Movie Monster Poster Book (published by Watermill Press)

1979		Crammed with information and facts about all kinds of movie monsters; Frankenstein, The Mummy, Gorgo, The Lost Continent, King Kong, This Island Earth, The Creature from the Black Lagoon, Godzilla on Monster Island; magazine opens to become a full-color giant-size wall poster of the first King Kong	$5–10

Movie Monsters (S.J. Publications)

1981	#1	Star Wars, Vampires: The Walking Dead, Dracula: The King of the Vampires, The Female Vampire, Darth Vader Turns Vampire	$5–10
	#2	Star Wars, Boris Karloff: The Man Who Made Frankenstein's Monster Famous, The Bride of Frankenstein, King Kong, Bela Lugosi	3–7
	#3	The Legend of Darth Vader: Fact and Fiction,	

YEAR	ISSUE/NUMBER	DESCRIPTION	VALUE
1981		Superman: The Movie That Made 'Em Forget the Comic, Fantastic Animation: Making Monsters Come to Life, Bugs on the Munch	3–7

$

Movie Monsters (Seaboard Periodicals)

	ISSUE/NUMBER	DESCRIPTION	VALUE
	#1	Planet of the Apes, Dracula, The Exorcist, Gorgo	$5–10
	#2	Planet of the Apes, 2001: A Space Odyssey, Doc Savage, Frankenstein, Rodan, One Million Years B.C.	5–10
	#3	Phantom of the Opera, The Wolfman, Godzilla, Boris Karloff, Batman, Forbidden Planet, Jack the Giant Killer	5–8
	#4	The Thing, Flash Gordon, Lon Chaney Jr., Lost Worlds, The Loch Ness Monster, The Walt Disney Monsters, The Day the Earth Stood Still, The Star Trek Phenomenon, 20 Million Miles to Earth	5–8

Munsters: The Official Magazine (Twin Hits, Inc.)

		DESCRIPTION	VALUE
1965		One shot magazine dedicated to TV's The Munsters, issue includes a Munster calendar and an episode not seen on TV	$45–90+

YEAR	ISSUE/NUMBER	DESCRIPTION	VALUE

Original Monsters (prozine)

	All issues		$10–20+

Newsweek (Newsweek, Inc.)

YEAR	ISSUE/NUMBER	DESCRIPTION	VALUE
1977	June 24	Star Wars cover and feature . . . Why America Loves the Star Wars Heroes	$4–8
1978	September 11	TV's Battlestar Galactica cover and feature, Son of Star Wars	4–8
1986	December 22	Spock cover and Star Trek feature	3–5

Nightmare

(illustrated horror, published by Skywald Publishing Co.)
1970–1975

	#1		$5–10
	#2–7		2–5
	#8	Tales from the Crypt reprint stories	5–10
	All other issues, including annual, yearbook, and special		2–4

Omni (Omni Publications International, Ltd.)

Note: A high-quality science fact and fiction magazine often collected by collectors of monster, science fiction and horror magazines

#1 October 1978		$10–20
#2–12		5–10
All other issues		1–3

Original Monsters (prozine)

	All issues	$10–20

Photon (prozine)

	All issues	$5–10+

YEAR	ISSUE/NUMBER	DESCRIPTION	VALUE

Prevue (formerly Mediascene, Supergraphics)
1980–Present

	#42	First Preview issue, The Empire Strikes Back	$10–20
	#46	Morgan Fairchild cover and feature	5–10
	#52	Debbie Harry cover and feature (**Note:** popular issue with rock fans)	10–20
	#57	Harrison Ford cover and feature . . . The Temple of Doom	4–8
	All other issues		3–5

Psycho (Skywald Publishing)
1971–1975

| | #1 | | $5–10 |
| | All other issues, including annual, yearbook, and special | | 2–4 |

Quasimodo's Monster Magazine (Mayfair Publications)
Note: Issues 1 and 2 are titled *Monster World*
1975–1976

| | #3 | First Quasimodo issue, Christopher Lee exclusive interview, Lugosi: The Man and the Vampire, Earthquake, Nightmare Theatre, A Look at Phase IV | $4–8 |
| | #4 | Son of Chaney: The Story of Lon Chaney Jr., The Making of the Exorcist, The Land That Time Forgot: exclusive interview with Doug McClure, Space 1999: Part 1, The Films of Roger Corman | 4–8 |

YEAR	ISSUE/NUMBER	DESCRIPTION	VALUE
	#5	Jekyl and Hyde: Through the Years, Heroes of Horror, Space 1999: Part 2, The Master of Radio Horror . . . Himan Brown and Mystery Theatre, The Lorre [Peter] Story	$4–8
	#6	Introducing Esmeralda, William Shatner on Star Trek, Karloff: King of Monsters, John Carradine, Life and Death in Death Race 2000	4–8
	#7	The Wolfman, Leonard Nimoy: Star of Star Trek, Bug, Splat Films, Monsters Gone Ape	4–8
	#8	The Invisible Man, Star Trek biographies, All About the Mummy	3–7

Questar (W.G. Wilson/MW Communications)
1978–1981

YEAR	ISSUE/NUMBER	DESCRIPTION	VALUE
	#1	Star Wars cover and feature	$25–50+
	#2	Capricorn I, Phoenix, What's Right with Space 1999, science fiction cinema	7–15
	#3	Superman the Movie, Battlestar Galactica, Invasion of the Body Snatchers, Dawn of the Dead, Lord of the Rings	5–10
	#4	Forrest J. Ackerman's Just Imagine . . . Jeannie, George Romero interview, Buck Rogers	6–12

YEAR	ISSUE/NUMBER	DESCRIPTION	VALUE
	#5	Alien: A Detailed Look at the Most Devastating Thriller, Moonraker: Bond in Space, Star Trek the Movie preview, Kiss up close	$10–20
	#6	The Black Hole, Star Trek, Don Post exclusive interview, The Rocky Horror Picture Show	5–10
	#7	A. E. Vonvoght interview, Conan movie preview, Caroline Munroe portrait album featuring a full-color wall poster	6–12
	#8	Star Wars: Mark Hamill on The Empire Strikes Back, Bigfoot Lives, Robert Bloch, What's Keeping the Space Shuttle	5–10
	#9	Ray Bradbury, Night of the Living Dead retrospective, Battle Beyond the Stars	3–6
	#10	Somewhere in Time, Scared to Death, Battle Beyond the Stars	2–5
	#11	The Art of Boris, Robby the Robot	2–5
	#12	Logan's Run creator interviewed, Star Blasters, Time Machines	2–5
	#13	Isaac Asimov interview, Eroticism in the Fantasy Cinema . . . Barbarella and others	5–10

YEAR	ISSUE/NUMBER	DESCRIPTION	VALUE

Reel Fantasy (Reel Fantasy, Inc.)

1978	#1	Star Wars cover and feature, The Spy Who Loved Me, Lynda Carter: Wonder Woman	$4–8

Revenge of Dracula (Eerie Publications)

1977	One shot		$5–10

Ripley's Believe It or Not . . . True Weird

	All issues		$5–15

Rocky Horror Official Poster Magazine

	#1	Tim Curry: Not Just a Pretty Transvestite	$5–10
	#2	Another Serving of Curry Please, Brien Talks to O'Brien About Rocky Sequel	5–10

Rocky Horror Picture Show Official Magazine

1979	One shot	Exclusive interviews with Richard O'Brien and Richard Hartley, Brian Thompson on the set design, Sue Blaine on the costume design, news of the sequel, on the road with Rocky Horror	$7–15

Scarlet Street (R.H. Enterprises)

1990	#1	Dark Shadows: From The Winds Of War to the Wings of Bats, The Flash: Barry Allen is Alive and	

YEAR	ISSUE/NUMBER	DESCRIPTION	VALUE
1990		Well on CBS, Frankenstein: Unreleased?, Hounded By Holmes: Hounds Abound in Many Versions, Robin Takes Wing, Universal Horrors, Sherlock Holmes Meets Jack the Ripper, Superboy Plays Hooky	$75–150
1990	#2	Hound of The Baskervilles, Dark Shadows, DC Comics TV Gallery of Villains, Atlantis: The Lost Continent, Horror Italian Style, The Black Museum, The Silence of the Lambs, The Golden Years of Sherlock Holmes	20–40+
1991	#3	Barbara Steele: Black Sunday, Tarzan Returns, Collinwood Revisited, SCTV Meets the Addams Family, The Mad Doctor, Night of The Hunter, The Women Who Played The Woman, All About Batman, The 90 Year History of The Hound of The Baskervilles, Rococo: Horror Redefined	15–30+
	Reprint Issue		3–5
	#4	Superboy Speaks Up, The Return of Dracula, By Lovecraft Possessed, The Crucifer of Blood, Zack and Ach Are Back, Interview with Ex-Vampire	15–30

YEAR	ISSUE/NUMBER	DESCRIPTION	VALUE
1992	#5	Barbara Hale, Patrick Macnee, Jack Larson, The House That Screamed Blood, Universal Vs. Hammer Films, Batman Returns, Jeremy Brett, Christopher Lee, The Solitary Cyclist, Star Trek, The Addams Family, Mr. & Mrs. North	$5–10+
	#6	Circus of Horror, Noel Neill, David Nelson, Black Sabbath, The Big Circus, Vampire Circus, The Crooked Man, Batman, Gorgo, Freaks, Berserk, Nightmare Alley, Strangers On A Train	3–6+
	#7	Vincent Price, John Moulder-Brown, Yvette Vickers, Tomb Of Ligeia, The Sussex Vampire, Bluebeard, Batman Returns, House Of Wax, The Raven, They Do It With Mirrors, The Invisible Man Returns, Laura, Innocent Blood, Joan Hickson	3–6+
	#8	Dracula, Dracula's Daughter, Son of Dracula, Sherlock Holmes Confesses: An Exclusive Interview with Peter Cushing, Vampires Over Hollywood: Bram Stoker's Dracula, Vampires Over Pittsburgh: John Landis on Innocent Blood, Sherlock	

YEAR	ISSUE/NUMBER	DESCRIPTION	VALUE
1992		Holmes As Dracula: Jeremy Brett, Rebecca Eaton, Fangs For The Memories: 20 Vampire Classics and Not-So-Classics, Dark Shadows on Videotape	$3–6+
1993	#9	Danny DeVitto: Fine Feathered Fiend, Thomas Beck, The Black Scorpion: Richard Denning and Carlos Rivas, Mornings With Peter Cushing, Veronica Carlson, The Cushing Collection, Joan Bennett	3–6+
	#10	Animated Bat Talk, Kevin Conroy, Loren Lester, Karloff and Lugosi's Lost Film, Beverly Garland, Sherlock Holmes Meets The Twilight Zone, Richard Dempsey: I Was A Teenage Vampyre, The Alligator People, The Hardy Boys	3–6

Scary Monsters

	All issues		$3–6

Science and Fantasy Film Classics (Science and Fantasy Film Classics Inc.)
1977–1978

	#1	Star Wars cover and feaure including a 22-by-32 inch full-color Star Wars wall poster, 2001: A Space Odyssey, Forbidden Planet	$5–10

YEAR	ISSUE/NUMBER	DESCRIPTION	VALUE
	#2	Close Encounters of the Third Kind special issue, Silent Running, War of the Worlds	$2–4
	#3	Star Trek special issue, Laserblast, This Island Earth	3–5
	#4	Battlestar Galactica special issue, Journey to the Far Side of the Sun, When Worlds Collide	3–5

Science Fiction, Horror and Fantasy (DW Enterprises)
1977–1978

	#1	The Making of Star Wars, a Star Wars special issue, Christopher Lee, Ray Harryhausen	$5–10
	#2	Star Wars: Creators Reveal Production Secrets, Mark Hamill Reveals the Problems in Making Star Wars, Douglas Trumball: Film Genius, Leonard Nimoy: Invasion of the Body Snatchers, Christopher Lee, Superman, Meteor, Ray Bradbury, The Swarm, Witch Mountain	$3–6

Science Fiction Illustrated (LC Print Publications)

1977	#1	King Kong: The Ninth Wonder of the World, Sinbad and the Eye of the Tiger: Ray Harryhausen's Newest Creation, The Making of Star Trek, The Future of Logan's Run	$4–8

YEAR	ISSUE/NUMBER	DESCRIPTION	VALUE

Scream (illustrated horror, Skywald Publishing Corp.)
1973–1975

| | #1 | | $3–6 |
| | #2–11 | | 3–5 |

Screen Chills (Pep Publishing)
One issue only

| 1957 | | I Was a Teenage Werewolf, Dead That Walk | $200–400+ |

Screen Monsters (S.J. Publications)

| 1981 | #1 | Frankenstein special issue | $3–6 |

Screen Thrills Illustrated (Warren Publishing)

	#1–4		$10–20
	#5	Batman's Boy Wonder Robin, The Beverly Hillbillies, James Cagney	6–12
	#6	The Phantom, Charlie Chan, Robert Taylor	6–12
	#7	Captain America, Humphrey Bogart, Kings of Comedy	5–10
	#8	Sinister Spider, The Marx Brothers, Sabu	4–8
	#9	Zorro, Alan Ladd, Superheroes	5–10
	#10	James Bond, The Lone Ranger, The Beatles, The Three Stooges	10–25

Screen Superstar/Star Wars Special

| | #8 | The full story, a special expanded edition packed with full-color photographs from the film | $5–12 |

YEAR	ISSUE/NUMBER	DESCRIPTION	VALUE

SF Movieland
1985
| | All issues | | $2–4 |

SFTV (HJS Publications)
1984–1985
| | All issues | | $5–10 |

Shock (Stanley Publications, Inc., illustrated horror)

1969	#1 (May, vol. 1, #1)	Voodoo Dolls, Eternal Death, Witch's Curse, Cremation	$12–25
	#2 (July, vol. 1, #2)	Curse of the Zamboori, Swamp Monster, The Other World, More Deadly Than the Male	12–25
	#3 (September, vol. 1, #3)	The Hidden Horror, Artist of Evil, Within the Tomb, Snake Goddess, Million Year Monster	10–20
	#4 (November, vol. 1, #4)	The Flapping Head, Claws of the Hungry Demon, The Destroyer Fiend of Midnight	6–12
1970	#5 (January, vol. 1, #5)	The Grave Robber, The Ghost's Revenge, Only the Evil Need Fear the Bogeyman, A Hex on My Brother	5–10
	#6 (March, vol. 1, #6)	Evil Returns, Ghostly Destroyer, The Land of Living Myths, Fangs of the Fiend	5–10
	#7 (May, vol. 2, #2)	Terror House, The Evil Secret of Black Hollow, The Undying Brain	5–10

YEAR	ISSUE/NUMBER	DESCRIPTION	VALUE
1970	#8 (July, vol. 1, #8)	Vampire's Castle, The Howling Head, The Noose of Pearls, Hypnotist of Death	$5–10
	#9 (September, vol. 2, #4)	The Mark of the Monster, The Spectral Sister, Vampire Master, Sleep of Death	5–10
	#10 (November, vol. 2, #5)	Tomb of the Cursed Corpse, Vision of Death, The Vampire Swoops, Killers from Hell	5–10
1971	#11 (January, vol. 2, #6)	The Vampire's Bones, Were-Fiends of Finland, The Girl Who Died Twice, Haunt of the Hyena, The Bat and the Brain	5–10
	#12 (March, vol. 3, #1)	Vigil of the Vampires, Three Hours to Doom, Fiend of the Undead, The Floating Coffin	3–6
	#13 (May, vol. 3, #2)	Queen for the Voodoo Chief, The Ghost in the Show Window, Lady of Death, The Faceless Legion	3–6
	#14 (July, vol. 3, #3)	Grave of Doom, The Spectral Bride, Vampire Castle, Madman's Manor	5–10
	#15 (September, vol. 3, #4)	A Living Corpse for the Zombie, the Pulverizing Peril, Murder Stalks New York, An Unknown Universe, The Vanishing Submarine	5–10

Shock Tales (MF Enterprises)

1959	#1	Funeral for a Vampire, The Most Perfect Monster	$150–300+

YEAR	ISSUE/NUMBER	DESCRIPTION	VALUE

Shriek (Acme News)
1965–1967

	#1	Vincent Price: Sovereign of the Sinister, The Flesheaters, Girl Vampire, Secret of Blood Island, Horror Hags: Joan Crawford and Bette Davis, History of the Horror Movie, Die Die My Darling	$25–50
	#2	My Life of Terror: An Interview with Boris Karloff, Devils of Darkness, Vincent Price in Wargods of the Deep, Dr. Terror's House of Horror, Devil Doll	25–50
	#3	Dracula: Prince of Darkness, The Face of Fu Manchu, Rasputin the Mad Monk, The Reptile, The Zombies, The Psychopath	20–40
	#4	Frankenstein Conquers the World, The Brides of Fu Manchu, The Mask, Daleks Invade the Earth, Carrying on Screaming, Munsters Go Home	20–40

Silver Screen Horror, Vincent Price Presents
(Globe Communications Corp.)

| 1977 | May #1 One issue only | | $5–12 |

Slaughter House Magazine

| | All issues | | $3–6 |

YEAR	ISSUE/NUMBER	DESCRIPTION	VALUE

Spaceballs: The Magazine $2–4

Spacemen (Warren Publishing)

	#1	When Worlds Collide, Voyage of the Space Eagle, space ships, monsters	$100–175
	#2	H. G. Wells's Things to Come, space movie previews	50–100
	#3	Girl in the Moon	75–150
	#4	Flash Gordon	25–50
	#5	Yesterday's Spacemen, The First Buck Rogers on Film, Radar Men from the Moon	15–30
	#6	Rocketman, Metropolis	15–30
	#7	Hollywood's Astronauts, King of the Lost Planet, Rocketmen, Twins from other Worlds	15–30
	#8	Boris Karloff: Out of this World, The Farenheit Chronicles, 20 Million Miles to Earth	10–25

1965 Yearbook $25–50

Space: 1999 Magazine (Charlton Publications)

| | #1–8 | | $5–10 |

Space Trek (Stories and Layouts Press)
1978–1979

| | #1 | Battlestar Galactica special, Superman, Star Trek, Earth versus the Flying Saucers, Japanese Weirdos | $2–5 |

YEAR	ISSUE/NUMBER	DESCRIPTION	VALUE
	#2	The Incredible Hulk, Battlestar Galactica, Superman, Flash Gordon, Strange Demonic Children in the Monster Movies, Clones: A Look at Futuristic Flicks	$2–5
	#3	Battlestar Galactica versus Star Wars special, Flying Saucer Attack, Superman, The First Men in the Moon, Star Trek	4–8

Space Wars (Stories and Layouts Press)
1977–1979

	ISSUE/NUMBER	DESCRIPTION	VALUE
	#1	Star Wars special: The Science Fiction Movie of the Decade, 2001: A Space Odyssey, Flash Gordon, The Return of Star Trek, Famous Movie Robots	$5–10
	#2	Silent Running, The Greatest Collection of Spaced-Out Movie Posters Ever Spawned, Star Wars	3–6
	#3	Mars Attacks, Robots: The Metal Horde in Film, Sexy Space Ladies, Bizarre Monsters: The History of the Pulps	3–7
	#4	Close Encounters versus Star Wars, Mars Attacks Revisited	2–6
	#5	H. G. Wells's Things to Come	2–6
	#6–11		2–5

YEAR	ISSUE/NUMBER	DESCRIPTION	VALUE
	#12	Star Wars special, Invasion of the Body Snatchers, Superman II, Build Your Own Daggit	$5–10

Spectre (horror filmzine)

	All issues		$5–10

SPFX (SPFX Publications)

1977	#1	The War of the Worlds special	$10–20
	#2	The Day the Earth Stood Still special	5–10

Splatter Times, The (tabloid)

	All issues		$15–30

Star Battles (Stories and Layouts)
1978–1979

	#1	Superman extra, Battlestar Galactica versus Buck Rogers	$3–5
	#2	Star Wars: How to Meet Luke Skywalker and R2D2, Battlestar Galactica, Superman II	2–6

Star Blaster

	All issues		$4–6

Starblazer (Liberty Communications, Inc.)

1984	All issues		$3–6

YEAR	ISSUE/NUMBER	DESCRIPTION	VALUE

Starburst (Starburst Magazine, Ltd.)
1977–Present

	#1	Star Wars special	$10–20
	#2	Space Cruiser, The Prisoner, Star Wars, Close Encounters	5–10
	#3	Close Encounters of the Third Kind, Logan's Run, Star Trek, Star Wars	4–8
	#4	The Hulk, War of the Worlds, Star Trek, Tolkien, Merlin	3–6
	#5	The Filming of Superman the Movie, Battlestar Galactica, Dark Star	2–4
	#6	Close Encounters of the Third Kind, Message from Space, Silent Running, Superman, Dalek index	2–4
	#7	Battlestar Galactica Special, Superman the Movie, Invasion of the Body Snatchers	5–10
	#8	Space 1999 special, Superman II, Alien, Leonard Nimoy, Star Wars II	5–10
	#9	The Making of the Lord of the Rings, Invasion of the Body Snatchers, Forbidden Planet, Tales of the Unexpected	2–4
	#10	Dr. Who, Star Trek: The Motion Picture, Aliens in the Cinema, The Shapes of Things to Come, Lost in Space	2–3

YEAR	ISSUE/NUMBER	DESCRIPTION	VALUE
	#11	Star Wars, Inside Star Trek the Motion Picture, Lord of the Rings, James Bond special effects exclusive, The Humanoid: Behind the Scenes	$ 3–5
	#12	Bond in Space: Special Effects, The China Syndrome, The Spaceman and King Arthur, 007's Jaws Interviewed, Screen Robots portfolio	3–6
	#13	Buck Rogers in the 25th Century, The Art of Space 1999, The Omega Man, Alien, Moonraker, The Avengers	3–6
	#14	Alien special, Dr. Who special effects, The Avengers, The Time Machine	10–15
	#15	Alien effects, Gandahar, Quatermass, Dr. Who, Sapphire and Steel, Serial Superheroes	2–3
	#16	The Black Hole, Alien Art, Planet of the Apes, Kronos	2–3
	#17	Star Trek the Movie special	5–10
	#18	Meteor, Blake 7, Movie Aliens, George Pal, Project UFO	2–3
	#19	Science Fiction Movie Bonanza, Star Trek, Saturn 3, The Black Hole, Meteor, Tom Baker	3–6
	#20	Fantasy Females special, Blake 7, Star Trek versus The Black Hole, 20,000	

YEAR	ISSUE/NUMBER	DESCRIPTION	VALUE
		Leagues Under the Sea, The Thing, The Outer Limits	$10–20
	#21	Special Effects spectacular, Jules Verne, Battlestar Galactica	3–7
	#22	The Empire Strikes Back special	5–10
	#23	The Empire Strikes Back special	5–10
	#24–33		2–5
	#34	Special Werewolf issue, The Howling, Movie Werewolves, Outland Special Effects, For Your Eyes Only	3–6
	#35–42		2–5
	#43	Star Wars special	4–8
	#56	Fantasy Females special issue	5–10
	#59	Return of the Jedi special	5–10
	#71	Indiana Jones and the Temple of Doom special	3–6
	#86	The Emerald Forest	3–6
	#87	Mad Max III, Tina Turner cover	3–5
	#100	Michael Jackson: Captain Eo cover and feature	3–6
	All other issues		2–4

Star Encounters (Stories and Layouts)
1978–1979

YEAR	ISSUE/NUMBER	DESCRIPTION	VALUE
	#1	Star Wars	$3–6
	#2	Star Wars, Close Encounters of the Third Kind, The Rocky Horror Picture Show, Meat Loaf, Capricorn I	3–6

YEAR	ISSUE/NUMBER	DESCRIPTION	VALUE
	#3	Beyond Star Trek, Star Wars, First Cloning of Apes, Ray Bradbury, Swarm: Killer Bees	$1–2

Star Force (Reliance Publications)

1978	#1	Lynda Carter: Wonder Woman cover and feature, The Incredible Melting Man, Close Encounters of the Third Kind, Star Trek the Movie, Star Wars Conquers All at the Awards	$4–8
	#2	The Empire Strikes Back Special Edition	4–8
	All other issues		3–6

Star Invaders (Liberty Communications)

Publishing begins in 1984

	All issues	$2–4

Starlog (O'Quinn Studios)

1976–Present

Note: *Starlog* back-issue prices are greatly influenced by *Starlog's* back-issue department. Before buying or selling issues of *Starlog* it is wise to purchase the most current issue and refer to its back-issue department ad for prices, because prices on issues offered by the publisher can increase quite dramatically. Although the publisher's price can be quite high on back issues of *Starlog,* copies can be purchased, not through the publisher (for example, at conventions, in comic shops, and from mail-order dealers), for as much as 50 percent less. This fact does not take away the reality that many collectors are willing to pay a higher price for certain issues. When an issue is no longer offered through *Starlog's* back-issue department, that issue will, in most cases, retain a higher value than all listed issues. It is not unusual to find issues of *Starlog* in a comic shop, flea market, or back-issue magazine store for

YEAR	ISSUE/NUMBER	DESCRIPTION	VALUE

as little as $1 each. This is generally due to the seller's ignorance and/ or the seller's acceptance that he does not have the steady clientele to realize high market prices. *Starlog's* popularity has well circulated its issues; however, with collecting interest growing every day, the occasional $1-an-issue find will soon become extinct.

	#1	Star Trek, Space 1999, The Bionic Woman, David Bowie	$10–25+
	#2	Space 1999, Star Trek, H. G. Wells	10–20
	#3	Star Trek, The Six Million Dollar Man, Space 1999	10–20
	#4	The Six Million Dollar Man, Nick Tate interview, The Bionic Woman	10–20
	#5	UFO episode guide, Star Trek, Space 1999	10–20
	#6	The Making of Destination Moon, Star Wars, Special Effects Part I, Fantastic Journey Interviews, Star Trek the Movie, Space 1999	10–20
	#7	Star Wars, Robby the Robot, Rocketship XM, Star Trek	7–15
	#8	Model Animation special, Star Wars, Saturday Morning TV, The Fly	5–10
	#9	TV's Logan's Run, Patrick Duffy, Lynda Carter, Jared Martin, William Shatner, a special all-TV issue	15–25+
	#10	George Pal exclusive interview, Isaac Asimov, Close Encounters of the Third Kind, Space 1999 set designs	10–20

YEAR	ISSUE/NUMBER	DESCRIPTION	VALUE
	#11	The Makeup Men special, The Prisoner, Close Encounters of the Third Kind, The Superman Movie, Science Fiction Comics, The Incredible Shrinking Man	$5–10
	#12	The Making of Close Encounters of the Third Kind, Star Trek's Enterprise	5–10
	#13	Exploring the Planets special, David Darth Vader Prowse interview, Close Encounters of the Third Kind	5–10
	#14	Special Effects . . . Star War's Matte Painter, Star Trek's Final Voyage	5–8
	#15	This Island Earth, Blood Beast, Rod Serling's Twilight Zone	5–8
	#16	Buck Rogers, Leonard Nimoy in Invasion of the Body Snatchers, The Invaders	5–8
	#17	Battlestar Galactica, The Incredible Hulk, Dr. Strange	5–8
	#18	Hollywood Halloween issue special . . . Special Effects, Wizards, Tricks and Treats, The Star Wars Sequel, Star Trek, Vampire Movies	5–8
	#19	Star Wars TV special, Backstage with Galactica's Athena, Leonard Nimoy: Body Snatchers Return,	

YEAR	ISSUE/NUMBER	DESCRIPTION	VALUE
		TV's Buck Rogers, The Lord of the Rings, Superman, Roger Corman: Master of the B Movies	$5–10
	#20	Superman the Movie Arrives, Mindy Talks About Mork, Buck Roger's 50th Anniversary, Jason of Star Command	4–5
	#21	Buck Rogers the Movie, Mark Hamill, Venus Movies, Lost in Space episode guide, Stop-Motion Animation	3–6
	#22	Moonraker, Science Fiction Films in '79, Lorne Greene, The Shape of Things to Come	5–10
	#23	Alien, Darth Vader, Dr. Who	10–20+
	#24	Starlog Through the Years, Science Fiction Spectacular	5–10
	#25	Star Trek, Alien, The Thing, Ray Bradbury interview	5–10
	#26	The Making of Alien	10–20
	#27	Battlestar Galactica, Alien: The Special Effects, Star Trek: The Special Effects, The Black Hole: A Day on the Set, Time After Time	5–10
	#28	Buck Rogers, TV's Wonder Woman, Battlestar Galactica, The Hulk	5–7
	#29	Meteor, Space 1999, TV's Buck Rogers, The Incredible Shrinking Man	3–6

YEAR	ISSUE/NUMBER	DESCRIPTION	VALUE
	#30	Star Trek Movie Preview, The Incredible Science Fiction Stuntwomen	$ 7–15
	#31	The Black Hole, The Empire Strikes Back, Star Trek, 20,000 Leagues Under the Sea	3–6
	#32	Star Trek exclusive, Meteor, Buck Rogers, Robots on Film	4–8
	#33	Saturn 3, Harlan Ellison on Star Trek, Voyage to the Bottom of the Sea	3–5
	#34	Battlestar Galactica 1980, The Alien Returns exclusive, interview with the director of The Empire Strikes Back, Twikki: Buck Roger's Robot, The Martian Chronicles, Dr. Who	3–5
	#35	Darth Vader Returns: The Empire Strikes Back, Star Blazers, The Black Hole, Battle Beyond the Stars	5–10
	#36	Science Fiction spectacular	3–6
	#37	Harrison Ford exclusive interview, Star Trek, Dr. Who	5–10
	#38	Close Encounters of the Third Kind: Inside the Mothership, The Empire Strikes Back, Buck Rogers, Star Trek	3–5
	#39	Buck Rogers: Exciting Changes, Battlestar Galactica, Mork & Mindy,	

YEAR	ISSUE/NUMBER	DESCRIPTION	VALUE
		The Hulk, Battle Beyond the Stars, Star Trek, Tom Corbett	$ 3–5
	#40	The Empire Strikes Back, Mark Hamill, Gene Roddenberry on Star Trek, Buck Rogers, Space 1999	5–10
	#41	The New Flash Gordon Movie, 3-D SFX, Escape from New York, The History of Science Fiction Comics Part I, The UFO Chronicles	3–6
	#42	Star Trek's Other Alien: An Exclusive Interview with Mark Leonard, Dr. Who, The Wild Wild West Revisited	4–8
	#43	Scanners, Farewell to the Empire: Gary Kurtz, Altered States, Popeye	3–5
	#44	Altered States, Flash Gordon, The Incredible Shrinking Woman	3–5
	#45	Buck Rogers's New Alien Hero, Outland, Apes on TV	3–5
	#46	Clash of the Titans, Superman II, Altered States	4–8
	#47	Superman II, Dr. Who, Outland, Sarah Douglas interview	3–5
	#48	5th Anniversary special, exclusive George Lucas interview	3–6
	#49	For Your Eyes Only: James Bond Is Back, Escape from New York	3–6

YEAR	ISSUE/NUMBER	DESCRIPTION	VALUE
	#50	The Empire Returns: Boba Fett Unmasked, Outland, Heavy Metal: Sound and Vision, The Six Dr. Whos	$5–15
	#51	Lawrence Kasdan, William Shatner on the New Star Trek Project	3–5
	#52	Blade Runner, Heart Beeps, H. R. Giger art	3–6
	#53	Heart Beeps, The Greatest American Hero Returns, Patrick Macnee: The Avengers, Ray Bradbury on His Science Fiction Films of the Past and Present	3–5
	#54	3-D issue special, The Greatest American Hero, Special Effects of Raiders of the Lost Ark, Star Trek	3–5
	#55	Time Bandits, Quest for Fire, Star Trek	3–5
	#56	The Empire Strikes Back Special Effects Secrets, The Time Machine, Forbidden Planet, Things to Come, 20,000 Leagues Under the Sea, The Thing, The Invisible Man, The Black Hole, This Island Earth	5–10
	#57	The Empire Strikes Back, The Return of the Lost in Space Robot	5–10
	#58	Blade Runner, Should Spock Die?, John Carpenter's The Thing, Battlestar Galactica, Star Trek bloopers	5–10

YEAR	ISSUE/NUMBER	DESCRIPTION	VALUE
	#59	Conan, Tron, Star Trek, Krull, Filming the Thing	$5–10
	#60	Science Fiction Spectacular special issue, Star Trek, Tron, E.T., Star Trek, The Thing, Blade Runner, Poltergeist	3–5
	#61	Star Trek special: On the Set and behind the Scenes, Revenge of the Jedi, Megaforce, The Thing, Road Warrior	6–12
	#62	Star Trek II: An Interview with Kirk, Tron, Conan, Star Wars Revisited	3–6
	#63	E.T., Beastmaster, Android, Kirk Russell interview	3–5
	#64	E.T., Poltergeist, Star Trek, The Thing	3–5
	#65	Mark Hamill, E.T. SFX, 2010: Odyssey Two	5–10+
	#66	The Dark Crystal, Dune, The Time Tunnel, Raiders of the Lost Ark	3–6
	#67	Superman III, Exclusive Interview with the Man Who Killed Spock, Airplane II: William Shatner, Star Trek II	3–6
	#68	007 Is Back . . . a special double Bond issue: Sean Connery and Roger Moore, Star Trek III and Beyond	4–8
	#69	Return of the Jedi	5–10+
	#70	Blue Thunder, Space Hunter, Something Wicked This Way Comes	3–6

YEAR	ISSUE/NUMBER	DESCRIPTION	VALUE
	#71	Return of the Jedi special issue	$7–15+
	#72	Science Fiction spectacular special	3–5
	#73	Superman III, Octopussy's Maud Adams	3–5
	#74	Return of the Jedi, Jaws 3-D, Never Say Never Again, War Games	5–10
	#75	Never Say Never Again, The Art of Return of the Jedi	4–8
	#76	Summer Films special	3–6
	#77	The Right Stuff, Brainstorm, Dr. Who Turns 20	3–5
	#78	Brainstorm, The Right Stuff, Arthur C. Clarke Meets Indiana Jones	3–5
	#79	Knight Rider interview, The Right Stuff, Fiona Lewis, Never Say Never	3–5
	#80	Return of the Jedi Special Effects special, Star Trek III, The Last Starfighter	4–8
	#81	Greystoke: The Ultimate Tarzan, Indiana Jones and the Temple of Doom	3–6
	#82	Star Trek III, Conan, Return of the Jedi Special Effects	4–8
	#89	V: The Visitors, Starman, Return of the Jedi	5–10
	#99	Star Wars and the Droids, Amazing Stories, Mad Max, Twilight Zone	3–6
	#109	Sigourney Weaver/Aliens, Star Trek IV, Space Camp	5–10+

YEAR	ISSUE/NUMBER	DESCRIPTION	VALUE
	#115	Aliens's Viva Vasquez exclusive interview, Superman IV, Tom Baker	$4–8
	#120	Star Wars, 100-page science fiction special issue	4–8
	#124	TV's New Star Trek: The Next Generation, 100-page science fiction spectacular	4–8
	All other issues		3–5

Starlog, The Best of

All issues		$2–5

Starlog Photo Guidebooks

All issues		$5–10

Starlog Specials
(including poster magazines, Addams Family special, etc.)

All issues		$2–5

Starscene (tabloid published by Ptolemy Publications)
Publishing begins in 1981

All issues		$3–5

Star Trek Official Poster Monthly

#1		$10–20
#2–10		6–12
All other issues		5–10

Star Trek: The Next Generation (O'Quinn Studios)

All issues		$3–6

YEAR	ISSUE/NUMBER	DESCRIPTION	VALUE

Star Warp (Stories, Layout and Press, Inc.)

YEAR	ISSUE/NUMBER	DESCRIPTION	VALUE
1978	#1	Fantastic Animation issue	$2–4
	#2	Star Wars, The Girls of Star Trek, The Day the Earth Stood Still, Japanese Science Fiction Monsters, Close Encounters of the Third Kind	3–6
	#3, #4		2–4

Star Wars Official Poster Monthly

	All issues		$5–10

Star Wars Return of the Jedi Official Collectors Edition

1983			$5–10

Star Wars Spectacular (Warren)

1977	One shot		$5–10

Star Wars The Empire Strikes Back Official Collectors Edition Magazine

1980			$5–10

State of Shock (adult horror/fantasy journal)

	All issues		$5–10

Stark Terror (Stanley Publications; illustrated horror)

YEAR	ISSUE/NUMBER	DESCRIPTION	VALUE
1970	December #1	The Executioner, In the Snake Pit, Hallucinations, The Gorilla	$10–20
1971	February #2	Black Cat from Hell, The Devil Walks on Halloween, The Wizard Wiped Out Time, Death Was the Witness	7–15

YEAR	ISSUE/NUMBER	DESCRIPTION	VALUE
1971	April #3	Voodoo Magic, Swamp Monster, More Deadly Than the Male, Final Choice, Vampire	$7–15
	June #4	Contract on Blood, Book of Doom, I Killed Mary, Life Insurance	7–15
	August #5	The Zombie's Revenge, Fangs of the Fiend, The Weird Wager, Mirror of Doom, Grave Robber	7–15

Strange Galaxy (Eerie Publications, Inc.; illustrated horror)

1971	#1 (February, vol. 1, #8)	The Unknown, Space Monsters, The Moon Is Red	$15–30
	#2 (April, vol. 1, #9)	Dimension X, Human Monster	15–30
	#3 (June, vol. 1, #10)	The Space Demons, The Planetoid Monsters, Metal Terror	15–30
	#4 (August, vol. 1, #11)	The Black Void Beyond	15–30

Strange Unknown (Tempest Publications)

Note: This is an occult magazine that has been included in many collections of monster, horror, and science fiction magazines.

1969	May #1		$10–20
	July #2		7–15

Superheroes (Warren)

1966	#1		$10–20

Supernatural (Dorset Publishing)

1969	#1, #2		$10–25+

YEAR	ISSUE/NUMBER	DESCRIPTION	VALUE

Superstar Heroes (Ideal Publishing)
1978–1979
        All issues $4–6

Suspense (Suspense Publications)
1959   #1–4 $50–100+

Take One (Canadian film magazine)
1971   September/October Godzilla cover and feature: Godzilla . . . the Monster Behind the Myth $2–5

Tales from the Crypt
(Eerie Publications, Inc.; illustrated horror)
1968   #1 (July) $12–25

Tales from the Tomb
(Eerie Publications, Inc.; illustrated horror)

YEAR	ISSUE/NUMBER	DESCRIPTION	VALUE
1969	#1 (July, vol. 1, #6)	He Rose from the Grave and Became a Terror Among Us, The Hell Below, Werewolf	$9–18
	#2 (September, vol. 1, #7)	Three Times Dead, The Corpse Came Home	5–10
1970	#3 (January, vol. 2, #1)	Gruesome Shock, The Bloody Thing, The Corpse Macabre	5–10
	#4 (April, vol. 2, #2)	Ghouls' Graveyard, The Swamp Monsters	5–10
	#5 (June, vol. 2, #3)	The Thing from the Grave, Fire Monster	3–6
	#6 (August, vol. 2, #4)	Zombies, Ghouls, and Creatures from Another World	3–6

YEAR	ISSUE/NUMBER	DESCRIPTION	VALUE
1970	#7 (October, vol. 2, #5)	The Creatures, The Call of the Monsters, The Slimy Corpse	$ 4–8
	#8 (December, vol. 2, #6)	Killer Creatures, Food for Ghouls	5–10
1971	#9 (February, vol. 3, #1)	Zombie, Werewolf, The Blood Totem	5–10
	#10 (April, vol. 3, #2)	Vampire, The Deadly Demon	5–10
	#11 (June, vol. 3, #3)	The Night of the Vampire, The Strange Secret of Torture Castle	3–6
	#12 (August, vol. 3, #4)	The Living Horror of Worlds Unknown	5–10
	#13 (October, vol. 3, #5)	Blood Goddess, The Weird House, The Ghosts	5–10
	#14 (December, vol. 3, #6)	The Spine-Chilling Zombies, The Gruesome Cannibal, The Hair-Raising Deadman, Ghouls and Werewolves	3–6
1972	#15 (February, vol. 4, #1)	The Ghoul, Satan's Blood Bath	4–8
	#16 (March, vol. 4, #2)	A Horrorama of Terrifying Vampires, Ghouls and Demons	4–8
	#17 (July, vol. 4, #3)	The Corpse, The Cat Is Evil, The Blood-Sucking Vampires	4–8
	#18 (September, vol. 4, #4)	The Weird Corpse, Naked Horror, The Strange Friend	4–8
	#19 (November, vol. 4, #5)	The Demon Strikes, Cup of Death	6–12
1973	#20 (January, vol. 5, #1)	The Monster of Darkness, A Coffin for Two	5–10
	#21 (March, vol. 5, #2)	A Chillerama of Blood-Draining Horror: Blood-Sucker, The Open Grave	3–6

YEAR	ISSUE/NUMBER	DESCRIPTION	VALUE
1973	#22 (May, vol. 5, #3)	The Bloody Thing, Seat of Doom	$ 3–6
	#23 (July, vol. 5, #4)	The Fiendish Savagery of the Blood Cult, The Monster	3–6
	#24 (September, vol. 5, #5)	The Fleshless Corpse, Fingers of Doom	3–6
	#25 (November, vol. 5, #6)	The Dead Can't Sleep, The Monster Is Hungry, A Thing of Flesh and Wire	4–8
1974	#26 (January, vol. 6, #1)	The Spider, The Mummy's Evil Eyes, Chop Their Heads Off	4–8
	#27 (March, vol. 6, #2)	Where the Flesh-Eaters Dwell, The Hanged, The Bloody Vampire	4–8
	#28 (May, vol. 6, #3)	The Curious Coffin, A Tomb of Ice, Burn Witch Burn	4–8
	#29 (July, vol. 6, #4)	Heads of Horror, The Demon, The Skin-Rippers	5–10
	#30 (September, vol. 6, #5)	A Living Corpse, The Skull, Horror Doll	5–10
	#31 (November, vol. 6, #6)	A Dead Thing Among Us, Monster, Terror in Black	5–10
1975	#32 (February, vol. 7, #1)	Head-Chopper, The Skeletons, The Fanged Freak	6–12

Tales of Terror (Eerie Publications; illustrated horror)

1964	#1 (summer)		$15–35

Tales of Voodoo (Eerie Publications; illustrted horror)

1968	#1 (November, vol.1, #11)	Eerie Bones, Bloody Mary, Crack-Up	$10–20
1969	#2 (February, vol. 2, #1)	Death Strikes Four, Hairee, Dragon Egg	6–12

October 1970   June 1971   November 1972

January 1973   February 1973   November 1973

March 1974   May 1974   July 1974

March 1971   *May 1971*   *July 1971*

November 1969   *May 1971*   *August 1973*

October 1974   *July 1977*   *October 1970*

YEAR	ISSUE/NUMBER	DESCRIPTION	VALUE
1969	#3 (May, vol. 2, #2)	Chant of the Dead, Skeletons Have No Secrets, Drums of Doom	$5–10
	#4 (July, vol. 2, #3)	The Bloody Ax, Witches' Curse	5–10
	#5 (September, vol. 2, #4)	Corpses of the Jury, The Dead Went Marching By, Murder on the Floor	5–10
1970	#6 (January, vol. 3, #1)	Signed in Blood, Voodoo Terror, House of Shock	5–10
	#7(March, vol. 3, #2)	The Slimy Snake Man, The Old Crones' Voodoo	5–10
	#8 (May, vol. 3, #3)	The Devil's Zombie, Demons and Vampires	4–8
	#9 (July, vol. 3, #4)	Blood-Hungry Vampires, Terrifying Creatures, Flesh-Eating Ghouls	4–8
	#10 (September, vol. 3, #5)	The Witch's Pit, Bloody Head, Horrible Thing	4–8
	#11 (November, vol. 3, #6)	The Demon Is a Hangman, The Shocking Gutless Thing	4–8
1971	#12 (January, vol. 4, #1)	The Spider, Voodoo Witch, Deadman's Duel	4–8
	#13 (March, vol. 4, #2)	Blacklight Monsters, Terror of the Dead	4–8
	#14 (May, vol. 4, #3)	The Shocking Horror of the Twisted Brain, There Is a Blood-Sucker Among Us	4–8
	#15 (July, vol. 4, #4)	The Incredible Terror of the Mummies, Witch of Doom, A Thing of Horror	4–8
	#16 (September, vol. 4, #5)	An Inferno of Shocking—Weird and Bizarre Tales of the Supernatural	4–8
	#17 (November, vol. 4, #6)	Step into the Scarifying World of Bizarre Monsters, Vampires and Ghouls	4–8

YEAR	ISSUE/NUMBER	DESCRIPTION	VALUE
1972	#18 (January, vol. 5, #1)	Zombie Maker, The Bloody Creature	$4–8
	#19 (March, vol. 5, #2)	Demons and Things from the Chilling Pit of Voodoo Horror	4–8
	#20 (April, vol. 5, #3)		4–8
	#21 (June, vol. 5, #4)	The Cave of Vampires, The Transparent Ones	4–8
	#22 (August, vol. 5, #5)	The Pit of the Monsters, Horror Bells	4–8
	#23 (October, vol. 5, #6)	The Blood-Dripping Head, The Cat of Horror	4–8
	#24 (December, vol. 5, #7)	Satan's Dead Demons, The Bloody Horror	4–8
1973	#25 (January, vol. 6, #1)	The Blood-Dripping Scarecrow, Horror Face	4–8
	#26 (March, vol. 6, #2)	The Monster Cloud, Force of Horror	4–8
	#27 (May, vol. 6, #3)	A Horror Spectacular of Blood-Dripping Terror	4–8
	#28 (July, vol. 6, #4)	From out of the Coffin, Pit of Horror, The Ice Monsters	4–8
	#29 (September, vol. 6, #5)	Tear Him Apart, Man-Rat	4–8
	#30 (November, vol. 6, #6)	A Garden of Corpses, Satan's Bloody Pearls, Claws of Horror	4–8
1974	#31 (January, vol. 7, #1)	Pool of Evil, Midnight Hag, The Blood Slave	4–8
	#32 (March, vol. 7, #2)	Vampire, Satan's Demon, Horror with Four Legs, The Unknown Nightmare	4–8
	#33 (May, vol. 7, #3)		4–8
	#34 (July, vol. 7, #4)		4–8

YEAR	ISSUE/NUMBER	DESCRIPTION	VALUE
1974	#35 (September, vol. 7, #5)	The Rats Are Coming, Horror in Jade, The Weird Corpse	$5–10
	#36 (November, vol. 7, #6)	Its Fangs Cried for Blood, Lighthouse Terror, The Monsters	5–10

Talking Pictures Magazine

1965	#2	The Addams Family and The Munsters: A Special Issue	$10–20

Terratoid Guide, The (The International Guide of Science Fiction/Fantasy/Horror Films)

	All issues		$5–10

Terrors of Dracula
(Modern Day Periodicals; illustrated horror)

1979	#1 (May, vol. 1, #3)	The Blood-sucking Vampire, The Flies, The Bride with Fangs, Cat of Doom, The Flesh-Ripper, Horror Pool	$5–10
	#2 (August, vol. 1, #4)	The Strange Vampire Rises Thirsty, Horror Without a Head, Bloodbath, The Skin-Rippers, Satan's Warlock, A Head Full of Snakes	3–6
	#3 (November, vol. 1, #5)	Vampire, Evil Black Cats, The Spider, The Alien Monsters, The Fangs	3–6
1980	#4 (February, vol. 2, #1)	Fangs of Horror, The Strange Vampire Plague, The Flesh-Eaters, The Vampire Ghouls, Demons and Skeletons	3–5

YEAR	ISSUE/NUMBER	DESCRIPTION	VALUE
1980	#5 (May, vol. 2, #2)	The Vampire, Eat the Flesh and Drink the Blood, The Ghoul, Blood Goddess, Satan's Demons, Voodoo Terror	$3–5
	#6 (August, vol. 2, #3)	The Evil Trip, Tomb of Ice, Satan's Demons, Claws of Horror, The Bloody Witch	3–5
	#7 (November, vol. 2, #4)		3–5

Terror Tales (Eerie Publications; illustrated horror)

1969	#1 (March, vol. 1, #7)	Skulls of Doom, Sales of Death	$12–25
	#2 (May, vol. 1, #8)	Meet Me in the Tomb, The Shelf of Skulls, Death Claws	10–20
	#3 (July, vol. 1, #9)	The Deadly Ghouls, Satan's Vault of Horror, The Unseen Terror	7–15
	#4 (November, vol. 1, #10)	Vampires, Dig Me a Grave	7–15
1970	#5 (January, vol. 2, #1)	The Hanging Ghoul, The Vampire Flies	5–10
	#6 (March, vol. 2, #2)	The Vampire Monster Trap, The Dead Demons	5–10
	#7 (May, vol. 2, #3)	The Zombie's Vault, Witch's Ghost	5–10
	#8 (July, vol. 2, #4)	The Evil Monsters, The Isle of Demons	5–10
	#9 (September, vol. 2, #5)	Unearthly Creature Features and Monsters from Worlds Beyond	5–10
	#10 (November, vol. 2, #6)	The Bloody Ax, The Shrunken Glass Corpse	5–10

YEAR	ISSUE/NUMBER	DESCRIPTION	VALUE
1971	#11 (January, vol. 3, #1)	The Zombie's Cave, The Jungle Ghost	$5–10
	#12 (March, vol. 3, #2)	Creature of Evil, The Corpse They Couldn't Bury	5–10
	#13 (May, vol. 3, #3)	The Strange Horror of the Wooden Menace, The Evil Ones	5–10
	#14 (July, vol. 3, #4)	The Tomb, The Unknown, House of Worm	5–10
	#15 (September, vol. 3, #5)	Uncanny, Spine-Shattering Weird Tales from Beyond the Dark Shadows	5–10
	#16 (November, vol. 3, #6)	The Blood-Chilling Werewolf, Ghostly Gardener	5–10
1972	#17 (January, vol. 4, #1)	The Demon's Night, The Swamp Devils	5–10
	#18 (March, vol. 4, #2)	Shrieking Vampires, Monsters and Strange Tales from the Unknown	5–10
	#19 (April, vol. 4, #3)	Creatures, Strange Monsters, Servants of Satan	4–8
	#20 (June, vol. 4, #4)	The Bloody Vampires, Things of Horror	4–8
	#21 (August, vol. 4, #5)	The Graveyard, A Feast for Rats	4–8
	#22 (October, vol. 4, #6)	The Gruesome Creatures, Chamber of Horrors	4–8
	#23 (December, vol. 4, #7)	The Monster, A Thing of Horror	4–8
1973	#24 (February, vol. 5, #1)	Stage of Horror, Torture, The Shape of Evil	4–8
	#25 (April, vol. 5, #2)	Curse of the Mummies, The Monster	4–8

YEAR	ISSUE/NUMBER	DESCRIPTION	VALUE
1973	#26 (June, vol. 5, #3)	A Shocking Explosion of Horror Where Demons, Evil Fiends, and Dead Things Live	$ 4–8
	#27 (August, vol. 5, #4)	The Werewolves, Pool of Horror	4–8
	#28 (October, vol. 5, #5)	Lighthouse of Horror, The Hungry Slime	4–8
	#29 (December, vol. 5, #6)	The Hungry Corpsemakers, The Horror Bugs, Madman's Knife	4–8
1974	#30 (February, vol. 6, #1)	The Undead, The Demon Ghost, A Jury of Skeletons	4–8
	#31 (April, vol. 6, #2)	The Buried, The Skeletons, Fangs of Terror	4–8
	#32 (June, vol. 6, #3)	Zombies Coast to Coast, The Tomb of Terror, Rat Feast	4–8
	#33 (August, vol. 6, #4)	Satan's Revenge, Give Me Back My Brain, The House of Blood	4–8
	#34 (October, vol. 6, #5)	The Spider, The Seven Skulls, Creature of Evil	4–8
	#35 (December, vol. 6, #6)	The Flesh-Ripper, Never Kill a Corpse, The House Is Haunted	4–8
1976	#36 (April, vol. 7, #1)	Beyond the Grave, The Flesh-Eaters, A Tomb of Horror, Vampires' Plague	5–10
	#37 (July, vol. 7, #3)	Blood Bath, Voodoo Terror, Skin-Rippers, The Hungry Slime, A Head Full of Snakes, The Strange Vampire	5–10
	#38 (October, vol. 7, #4)		5–10

YEAR	ISSUE/NUMBER	DESCRIPTION	VALUE
1977	#39 (April, vol. 8, #1)	House of Blood, The Vampire Lives, The Bloody Monster	$5–10
	#40 (July, vol. 8, #2)	Ghoul's Mansion, Invitation from a Vampire, Satan's Demons, A Ring of Corpses, Witch's Horror	5–10
	#41 (October, vol. 8, #3)	The House That Dripped Blood, The Dead Live, The Rack, Devil's Monster	5–10
1978	#42 (January, vol. 9, #1)		5–10
	#43 (April, vol. 9, #2)	Fangs of Horror, The Spider, The Seven Skulls, Things of Evil, The Corpse	5–10
	#44 (July, vol. 9, #3)		5–10
	#45 (October, vol. 9, #4)		5–10

Transylvanian, The (The Rocky Horror Picture Show News)

1978	#1		$10–20

3-D Monsters (Fair Publications)

1964	#1		$20–50

Thriller (Tempest Publishing)

1962	#1	The Vampire Was a Sucker, Her Blood Ran Hot	$75–200+
	#2	The Monster That Ate Candy, The Mummy Who Wanted a Daddy	75–200+
	#3	Necking with a Vampire, Werewolves Are Funny, Monsters for Hire	75–200+

YEAR	ISSUE/NUMBER	DESCRIPTION	VALUE

Tron Official Giant Collectors' Edition Poster Magazine
1982 $2–4

True Twilight Tales
1964   One issue only $5–10

True Weird
1955–1956

Note: Collected by some monster magazine collectors for its strange and fantastic true stories

        All issues $10–20

TV Chariot
        All issues $5–10+

TV Greats' Space Stars
1978   Superman versus Wonder Woman, Battlestar Galactica special 12-page section, The Incredible Hulk, The Scoop on the New Star Trek, Mork & Mindy, The Who's Who in Space, Star Wars $4–8

TV Science Fiction Monthly
(British poster magazine published by Sportscene Ltd.)
Publishing begins in 1976
        All issues $3–7

Twilight Zone Magazine (TZ Publications)
Publishing begins in 1980
           #1 $5–10
        All other issues   2–4

YEAR	ISSUE/NUMBER	DESCRIPTION	VALUE

2010 (The Official Movie Magazine)

1984	#1		$1–2

UFO Universe Presents Space Monsters (Condor Books, Inc.)

1990	#1	A horror-filled collection of the scariest space creatures, a brief history of space monster films, The Hidden, Strange Invaders, The Abyss, The Thing (1982), This Island Earth, Aliens, Karloff and the Alien Invasion, The Outer Limits	$3–5

Vampirella (Warren)
1969–1988

	ISSUE/NUMBER	DESCRIPTION	VALUE
	#1		$50–100+
	#2		25–50+
	#3		50–100+
	#4		35–50
	#5		20–40
	#6		20–40
	#7		20–40
	#8		20–40
	#9		20–40
	#10		15–30
	#11		15–30
	#12		12–25
	#13		12–25
	#14		12–25
	#15		12–25
	#16		10–20
	#17		9–18
	#18		7–15
	#19	1973 annual	9–18
	#20		9–18

YEAR	ISSUE/NUMBER	DESCRIPTION	VALUE
	#21		$9–18
	#22		9–18
	#23		7–15
	#24		7–15
	#25		6–12
	#26		5–10
	#27	1974 annual	5–10
	#28		5–10
	#29		5–10
	#30		7–15
	#31		7–15
	#32		5–10
	#33		4–8
	#34		4–8
	#35		4–8
	#36		4–8
	#37	1975 annual	5–10
	#38		4–8
	#39		4–8
	#40		4–8
	#41		3–6
	#42		3–6
	#43		3–6
	#44		3–6
	#45		3–6
	#46		5–10
	#47		3–5
	#48		3–5
	#49		3–5
	#50		3–6
	#51–113		3–5

Vampirella Annual
1972 $50–100+

Vampirella Special
1977   #1 $7–15

YEAR	ISSUE/NUMBER	DESCRIPTION	VALUE

Vampire Tales, Stan Lee Presents (illustrated horror, Marvel)
1973–1975

	#1		$5–10
	#2–11		2–5
	#1	1975 annual	2–5

Vampir (German monster magazine popular with American collectors)

	All issues		$5–10+

Web of Horror (Major Magazine; illustrated horror)
1969–1970

	#1		$10–20
	#2, #3		7–15

Weird (Eerie Publications; illustrated horror)

1966	#1 (January, vol. 1, #10)		$10–20
	#2 (April, vol. 1, #11)	Vampires, Werewolves, and Monsters special	5–10
	#3 (October, vol. 1, #12)	Black Death, Blood Blossom, Fanged Terror	5–10
	#4 (December, vol. 2, #1)	Tiger-Tiger, Fatal Scalpel, They Couldn't Die	5–10
1967	#5 (April, vol. 2, #2)	Fiends from the Crypt, Doom at the Wheel, Dying Is So Contagious	5–10
	#6 (June, vol. 2, #3)	Ghoul for a Day, Horror in the Mine, Gruesome Garden	5–10
	#7 (October, vol. 2, #4)	The Ghostly Guillotine, Madness of Terror	6–12
1968	#8 (January, vol. 3, #1)	Secret Coffin, Carnival of Terror, Demon in the Dungeon	5–10

YEAR	ISSUE/NUMBER	DESCRIPTION	VALUE
1968	#9 (April, vol. 2, #6)	Careless Corpse, Death's Shoes, Hands of Terror	$5–10
	#10 (July, vol. 2, #8)	Werewolf Castle, The Ghoul and the Guest, Corpses Coast-to-Coast	6–12
	#11 (October, vol. 2, #9)	Death Makes Three, Skull Scavenger, House of Chills	5–10
	#12 (December, vol. 2, #10)	Torture Garden, Idol of Evil, Death on Ice	5–10
1969	#13 (February, vol. 3, #1)	Nightmare Mansion, Hissing Horror	5–10
	#14 (May, vol. 3, #2)	Monster Mill, The Empty Coffin	5–10
	#15 (July, vol. 3, #3)	Ghoul's Castle, Horror Hour	5–10
	#16 (September, vol. 3, #4)	Fanged Horror, Now I Lay Me Down to Die	5–10
	#17 (December, vol. 3, #5)	Blackness of Evil, Blood Bath	5–10
1970	#18 (February, vol. 4, #1)	The Sewer Werewolves, The Vampire Witch, Devil Ghouls	5–10
	#19 (April, vol. 4, #2)	Zombie for a Day, Witches' Revenge	5–10
	#20 (June, vol. 4, #3)	The Shrunken Monster, The Evil Black Art Called Witchcraft	5–10
	#21 (August, vol. 4, #4)	Vampire Ghouls, Werewolf	5–10
	#22 (October, vol. 4, #5)	Feast for Vampires, Zombie Army, Dead Man's Train	5–10
	#23 (December, vol. 4, #6)	The Angry Vampire, Terror of Black Magic	5–10
1971	#24 (February, vol. 5, #1)	The Terror of the Swamp Monster, Feast for Rats	4–8
	#25 (April, vol. 5, #2)	Devil Statues, The Wax Witch	5–10

YEAR	ISSUE/NUMBER	DESCRIPTION	VALUE
1971	#26 (June, vol. 5, #3)	The Beast from Below, The Evil Ones	$ 4–8
	#27 (August, vol. 5, #4)	Vampire Flies, The Beast	4–8
	#28 (October, vol. 5, #5)	Satan's Warlock, The Bloody House, The Premiere	4–8
	#29 (December, vol. 5, #6)	The Weird World of Zombies, Vampires and Monsters	5–10
1972	#30 (February, vol. 6, #1)	Beyond Evil, Thing in the Box, Death Demon	4–8
	#31 (March, vol. 6, #2)	Demons and Vampires special	4–8
	#32 (April, vol. 6, #3)		4–7
	#33 (June, vol. 6, #4)	The Stone Monsters, The Beast	4–7
	#34 (August, vol. 6, #5)	The Bloody Corpse, The Mummies	4–7
	#35 (October, vol. 6, #6)	Mask of Horror, Dead Man's Rope	4–8
	#36 (December, vol. 6, #7)	The Skin-Crawlers, The Evil Idol	4–8
1973	#37 (February, vol. 7, #1)	From the Grave Below, Sorceress	4–8
	#38 (April, vol. 7, #3)	Poison of Evil, The Geek	3–7
	#39 (June, vol. 7, #4)	The Rotting Ghouls, Jaws of Terror	3–7
	#40 (August, vol. 7, #5)	A Head Full of Snakes, The Blind Terror	4–8
	#41 (October, vol. 7, #6)	The Flesh-Rippers, Drowned in Sand	4–8
	#42 (December, vol. 7, #7)	The Swamp Creature, Satan's Mad Dog	4–8

YEAR	ISSUE/NUMBER	DESCRIPTION	VALUE
1974	#43 (February, vol. 8, #1)	A Storm of Blood, A Shadow of Evil, The Thing with the Empty Skull	$ 4–8
	#44 (April, vol. 8, #2)	Scream in Terror, Eye of Evil, The Rotting Coffin	3–7
	#45 (June, vol. 8, #3)	The Shape of Evil, The Fanged Monster, Supernatural	3–7
	#46 (August, vol. 8, #4)	Tomb of Horror, Monster Maker, The Dead Live	3–7
	#47 (October, vol. 8, #5)	The Evil Black Cats, Blood Bath	4–8
	#48 (December, vol. 8, #6)		4–8
1975	#49 (January, vol. 9, #1)	A Thing with Fangs, Coils of Terror, Blind Monsters	6–12
1976	#50 (June, vol. 9, #2)	The Fleshless Corpse, The Living Dead, I Chopped Her Head Off, Seat of Doom, The Open Grave	5–10
	#51 (September, vol. 9, #3)	Mask of Horror, The Blood-Dripping Head, The Deadly Corpse, The Hungry Ghoul, House of Monsters	5–10
	#52 (December, vol. 9, #4)	The Vampire Lives, Ghoul's Mansion, The Spirit of Evil, The Witch Doctor, Swamp Creature	5–10
1977	#53 (June, vol. 10, #2)	Vampire, The Coffin, Horror Without a Head, Monster Maker	5–10
	#54 (September, vol. 10)		5–10
	#55 (December, vol. 10, #3)	Cave of Vampires, Open Grave, House of Monsters, The Evil Cat, The Awesome Thing	5–10

YEAR	ISSUE/NUMBER	DESCRIPTION	VALUE
1978	#56 (March, vol. 11, #1)	Werewolf, Cat of Evil, The Dead Witch, The Ghoul	$ 3–7
	#57 (June, vol. 11, #2)	The Monster from Saturn, The Man in the Heavy Metal Suit, Terror Asteroid, The Invaders, The Thing from Out There	3–7
	#58 (September, vol. 11, #3)	Stay out of My Grave, Vampire Flower, The Sewer of Werewolves, Deathtrap	3–7
	#59 (December, vol. 11, #4)	Vampire, Give Me Back My Brain, Tear Him Apart, Never Kill a Corpse	5–10
1979	#60 (June, vol. 12, #1)		4–8
	#61 (September, vol. 12, #2)		4–8
	#62 (December, vol. 12, #3)		4–8
1980	#63 (March, vol. 13, #2)	Bloody Thing, Chop Their Heads Off, The Ghoul, Horror in Wood, The Monster, Mud Creatures, Seat of Doom	5–10
	#64 (June, vol. 13, #3)	The Hairy Beast, Bagpipes from Hell, Tomb of Terror, Headless Horror, Monster Maker	5–10
	#65 (September, vol. 13, #3)	Claws of Horror, Beyond Evil, The Bloody Head	5–10
	#66 (December, vol. 13, #4)		5–10
1981	#67 (vol. 14, #1)		5–10
	#68 (vol. 14, #2)		5–10
	#69 (November, vol. 14, #3)	The Bloody House, Ghouls, The Corpse, Devil's Plaque, The Blind Monsters, Tunnel Crawlers	6–12

YEAR	ISSUE/NUMBER	DESCRIPTION	VALUE

Weird Vampire Talks
(Modern Day Periodicals; illustrated horror)

YEAR	ISSUE/NUMBER	DESCRIPTION	VALUE
1979	#1 (April, vol. 3, #1)	It Cried for Blood, The River Is Red, The Skin-Rippers, Deadman's Dance, Open Grave	$4–8
	#2 (July, vol. 3, #2)		4–8
	#3 (October, vol. 3, #3)		4–8
1980	#4 (January, vol. 3, #4)	Bloodsucker, Fanged Freak, The Demon, Fangs of Revenge, Invitation from a Vampire	4–8
	#5 (April, vol. 4, #2)		4–8
	#6 (July, vol. 4, #3)	The Fanged Flies, The Corpse, Man in the Heavy Metal Suit, Horror Stage, Wax Witch, Skeleton, Monster	4–8
	#7 (October, vol. 4, #4)		4–8
1981	#8 (January, vol. 5, #1)	Fangs and Claws, The Flesh-Rippers, Werewolf, Fangs of Terror, Space Invaders, Vampires	3–5
	#9 (August, vol. 5, #2)	The Bloodsucking Vampire Strikes, Satan's Warlock, Give Me Back My Brain, Vampire's Bride, Fanged Terror	3–5
	#10 (vol. 5, #3)		3–5
1982	#11 (March, vol. 6, #1)		5–10

YEAR	ISSUE/NUMBER	DESCRIPTION	VALUE

Weird Worlds (Eerie Publications, Inc.; illustrated horror)

YEAR	ISSUE/NUMBER	DESCRIPTION	VALUE
1970	#1 (December, vol. 1, #10)	The Space Vampires, Tomorrow's Atomic Monsters, The Green Horror	$12–25
1971	#2 (February, vol. 2, #1)	The Hungry Brain, The Eerie Space Spirits, The Unusual Weird Robots	10–20
	#3 (April, vol. 2, #2)	The Demon Star, Ogre from Space	6–12
	#4 (June, vol. 2, #3)	The Metal Replacements, The Evil Trap, Chain Reaction, Space Rot	6–12
	#5 (August, vol. 2, #4)	Gut-Clutching Tale of Shocking Terror, Eerie Suspense, Weird Horror in Outer Space	7–15

Weird Worlds (Scholastic Inc.)

Publishing begins in 1980

		VALUE
All issues		$4–8

Werewolves and Vampires (Charlton Publishing)

1962	One shot	$10–30

Witchcraft and Sorcery (illustrated horror)

All issues		$5–10

Witches' Tales (Eerie Publications, Inc.; illustrated horror)

YEAR	ISSUE/NUMBER	DESCRIPTION	VALUE
1969	#1 (July, vol. 1, #7)	Ghost-Bait, Broom for a Witch, Green Horror	$10–20
	#2 (September, vol. 1, #8)	A Taste of Blood, Witches' Haunt, From Beyond the Grave	7–15
	#3 (December, vol. 1, #9)	Devil's Monster, Doom Creatures, Nightmare	7–15

February 1971   August 1971   July 1973

September 1974   February 1971   August 1974

October 1974   April 1970   December 1970

YEAR	ISSUE/NUMBER	DESCRIPTION	VALUE
1970	#4 (February, vol. 2, #1)	The Mummies, Witch's Claws, The Demon from Beyond	$6–12
	#5 (April, vol. 2, #2)	Claws of Horror, Monster in White	6–12
	#6 (June, vol. 2, #3)	House of Vampires, Spirits of the Witch	5–10
	#7 (August, vol. 2, #4)	Special Bewitching Issue Loaded with Horror, Monsters and Vampires	6–12
	#8 (October, vol. 2, #5)	The Skeleton, Vampire	5–10
	#9 (December, vol. 2, #6)	Winged Monsters, The Hungry Vampire	5–10
1971	#10 (February, vol. 3, #1)	The Weird Terror of the Zombie Manikins, A Flesh-Rotting Thing Called the Strange Corpse, Voodoo Terror	5–10
	#11 (April, vol. 3, #2)	The Evil Black Cats, Morgan's Ghost	5–10
	#12 (June, vol. 3, #3)	Mask of Horror, The Weird and Unusual Silver Demon	5–10
	#13 (August, vol. 3, #4)	The Bloody Blob, Dark Horror, Tales from the Witches' Cauldron	5–10
	#14 (October, vol. 3, #5)	One Step Beyond, Bloody Tales, Terror from the Sky	5–10
	#15 (December, vol. 3, #6)	The Conjurer, Jeb's Bloody Ghost	5–10
1972	#16 (February, vol. 4, #1)	House of the Vampire, Spirits of Doom	6–12
	#17 (March, vol. 4, #2)	Shocking Horror Tales of Strange Monsters 'n' Evil Things	5–10
	#18 (May, vol. 4, #3)	The Witch's Horror, The Ghouls	4–8

YEAR	ISSUE/NUMBER	DESCRIPTION	VALUE
1972	#19 (July, vol. 4, #4)	Monsters of Evil, The Terrifying and Gruesome Zombies	$ 4–8
	#20 (September, vol. 4, #5)	Evil Is the Witch, The Slimy Thing	4–8
	#21 (November, vol. 4, #6)	Stay out of My Grave, Bloody Ten Fingers	6–12
1973	#22 (January, vol. 5, #1)	The Monster That Burns, A Scream of Horror	4–8
	#23 (March, vol. 5, #2)	Web of Horror, A Thing of Evil	4–8
	#24 (May, vol. 5, #3)	The Cave Monsters, River of Blood	4–8
	#25 (July, vol. 5, #4)	The Fiend from the Outside, The Mud Creatures	4–8
	#26 (September, vol. 5, #5)	A Horror in Wood, The Vampire	6–12
	#27 (November, vol. 5, #6)	Eat the Flesh, Drink the Blood, Deadman's Tree, A Tomb of Ice	6–12
1974	#28 (January, vol. 6, #1)	The Vampire, The Headless Ones	4–8
	#29 (March, vol. 6, #2)	The Screaming Things, Fangs of Horror, The Creatures	7–15
	#30 (May, vol. 6, #3)		5–10
	#31 (July, vol. 6, #4)		4–8
	#32 (September, vol. 6, #5)	Horror Without a Head, Swamp Terror, The Doll Witch	4–8
	#33 (November, vol. 6, #6)	The Thing That Screamed, The Coffin, Satan's Demons	7–15
1975	#34 (February, vol. 7, #1)	Gruesome Nightmare, Night Monsters, The Slimy Haunt	7–15

YEAR	ISSUE/NUMBER	DESCRIPTION	VALUE

World Famous Creatures (Magsyn Publications)
1958–1959

	#1	The World's Most Frightening Horror	$100–150+
	#2	The She Demon	75–150+
	#3	Bela Lugosi's Life Story	95–150+
	#4	How to Buy Hollywood Monster Equipment	75–125+

World of Horror (Dallruth Publishing)

| 1972 | #1–6 | | $10–20 |
| | #7–9 | | 5–10 |

Rock-and-Roll
and Teen Magazines

Rock magazine collecting is more than just a hobby, it is an important part of the collector's life-style. For each rock star there are thousands, if not millions, of fans who enjoy the music and style of their fave performer. Collectors actively seek out magazines that feature these stars. Such rock greats as the Rolling Stones and the Grateful Dead have been around for more than twenty-five years. Today, such groups are more popular than ever. With this continued growth in popularity, each new generation of fans adds to the number of active collectors. These collectors want any magazine that features their particular fave. With the longevity of many of today's rock performers, magazines that feature them can be twenty, twenty-five, or even thirty years old. By nature, the rock and teen magazine was not designed to last beyond the first few hours with the magazine purchaser. In the past, as well as today, fans who buy a rock/teen magazine will take it home and start clipping all the photos and pulling out the posters. These clipped photos and posters generally end up in scrapbooks or on a fan's wall. Regrettably, this procedure renders the rock/teen magazine totally worthless. Few teen magazines from the 'fifties and 'sixties survived this practice, making complete copies from these two decades very much sought after and very expensive to purchase when found. However, it does not always take decades for a rock magazine's value to rise beyond its cover price. Current issues, issues perhaps just a few months old, can appreciate by as much as 50 percent. This is most times due to the quality of photos, posters, and story on a particular star and the overall distribution of the magazine. A recent magazine with a cover and special on Jim Morrison, KISS, or Jimi Hendrix, just to mention a few, is all but guaranteed to quickly rise in value. In this section of the guide we have listed individual values for many of the most popular rock and teen magazine titles. We have also listed the value range for average issues and for issues that

657

feature specific performers for each decade. For a complete guide, listing over 10,000 rock and teen magazines from 1957 to 1992, with detailed information on each issue's contents, we suggest House of Collectibles' *Official Price Guide to Rock and Roll . . . Magazines, Posters, and Memorabilia.* This book can be ordered by calling our twenty-four-hour Collectors' Hotline 201-641-7212. Our Collectors' Hotline is also available to answer any questions the reader may have pertaining to collecting magazines.

BUYING AND SELLING ROCK/TEEN MAGAZINES

Back issues of music magazines are not commonly found at the same sources as are other magazine types. The collector will have to be a bit more aggressive if he or she wishes to acquire such magazines at a low price. Mail-order dealers, such as The Back Issue (24 Orchard Street, Ridgefield Park, New Jersey 07660), offer a single source where the collector can find almost any issue, be it this month's most recent copy or a copy from 1956. Prices asked by mail-order dealers will reflect the current market value, but you will be able to find what you want at the time you want it. In a collecting field where many vintage issues are quickly disappearing off dealers' shelves and heading into collectors' hands, this availability is a luxury that is soon to be no more. To the adventurous collector, I recommend taking out an inexpensive classified ad in a local music or entertainment paper. The following is a list of the larger music tabloids; all feature low-cost advertising.

The Record Finder, P.O. Box 1047, Glen Allen, Virginia 23060, (804) 266-1154

Discoveries, P.O. Box 255, Port Townsend, Washington 98368, (206) 385-1200

IE (Illinois Entertainer), 2250 East Devon, Suite 150, Des Plaines, Illinois 60018, (708) 298-7970

The Music Paper, P.O. Box 304, Manhasset, New York 11030, (516) 883-6707

East Coast Rocker, Box 137, Montclair, New Jersey 07042

When placing your ad to buy or sell magazines, clearly state what magazines and pop performers you are looking for or what you are offering for sale.

Back-issue magazine stores, record shops, flea markets, garage sales, and music conventions are also sources for buying and selling rock and teen magazines.

AVERAGE ROCK/TEEN MAGAZINE VALUES
(NOT FEATURING THE MOST-COLLECTIBLE STARS)

ISSUES	VALUE
1957	$10–25
1958	10–20
1959	10–20
1960–1962	8–20
1963–1966	7–20
1967–1969	5–10
1970, 1971	3–7
1972–1975	3–6
1976–1980	2–4
1981–1989	1–4
1990–Present	1–3

MOST-COLLECTIBLE ROCK-AND-ROLL STARS/GROUPS
OF THE 'FIFTIES

| SUBJECT | VALUE | | | |
	COVER & FEATURE	COVER ONLY	FEATURE ONLY	CAMEO
Chuck Berry	$20–40	$20–40	$20–40	$10–20
Dick Clark/ American Bandstand	25–65	25–50	20–40	10–20
Bobby Darin	25–50	20–40	20–40	10–20

	VALUE			
SUBJECT	COVER & FEATURE	COVER ONLY	FEATURE ONLY	CAMEO
Dion and the Belmonts	$25–75	$20–50	$20–45	$10–20
James Dean (teen idol)	25–50	20–40	15–35	10–20
Fats Domino	20–40	20–40	15–30	10–20
Connie Francis	25–45	20–35	20–30	10–20
Annette Funicello	25–50	20–40	20–40	10–20
Clarence "Frogman" Henry	25–50	25–50	20–40	10–20
Buddy Holly	25–100	25–100	25–60	20–30
Brenda Lee	25–40	20–30	20–30	10–20
Roy Orbison	30–60	25–50	20–35	10–20
Elvis Presley	25–75	20–40	20–35	10–20
Conway Twitty	20–40	20–35	20–35	10–20

Most-Collectible Rock-and-Roll Stars/Groups

of the 'Sixties

	VALUE			
SUBJECT	COVER & FEATURE	COVER ONLY	FEATURE ONLY	CAMEO
Beach Boys	$20–40	$20–35	$15–30	$10–20
Beatles	20–40	20–40	20–40	10–20
Bobby Darin	20–40	15–30	12–25	10–20
Dick Clark/ American Bandstand	15–30	15–30	15–30	10–20
Dion	25–50	25–50	20–40	10–20

SUBJECT	VALUE			
	COVER & FEATURE	COVER ONLY	FEATURE ONLY	CAMEO
Doors/Jim Morrison	$25–100	$15–50	$20–40	$10–20
Grateful Dead	25–50	20–40	20–40	12–20
Bob Dylan	20–40	20–40	20–40	12–20
Shelley Fabares	15–30	15–30	10–25	10–20
Fleetwood Mac	15–30	15–30	15–30	10–20
Connie Francis	15–30	15–30	15–30	10–20
Bobby Fuller	25–50	25–50	20–40	12–25
Annette Funicello	15–30	15–30	10–30	10–20
Jimi Hendrix	25–100	20–60	25–75	15–30
Jan and Dean	25–50	25–50	25–50	20–30
Jefferson Airplane	20–30	20–30	10–25	10–20
Janis Joplin	25–75	20–40	20–40	10–20
Led Zeppelin	15–30	10–20	15–30	10–20
Brenda Lee	15–25	15–20	10–20	10–20
Hayley Mills (teen idol)	15–30	15–30	15–30	10–20
Monkees	20–40	20–30	10–20	10–20
Ricky Nelson	25–50	20–40	15–30	12–25
Roy Orbison	20–30	15–20	10–20	10–20
Elvis Presley	10–30	10–30	10–30	10–20
Rolling Stones	25–50	20–40	15–35	10–20
Rolling Stones/ Brian Jones	25–75	25–75	25–50	10–20
Sonny and Cher	15–30	15–30	10–25	12–20
Supremes/Diana Ross	20–40	15–30	10–25	10–20
The Who	20–30	20–30	10–20	10–20

Most-Collectible Rock-and-Roll Stars/Groups

OF THE 'SEVENTIES

| SUBJECT | VALUE | | | |
	COVER & FEATURE	COVER ONLY	FEATURE ONLY	CAMEO
Beach Boys	$ 8–20	$ 8–20	$ 8–15	$ 5–10
Beatles	5–20	5–10	5–12	5–10
Blondie/Debbie Harry	10–30	10–30	5–25	5–10
David Bowie	5–20	5–20	5–20	4–8
Brady Bunch (teen idols)	15–30	15–30	10–20	10–20
David Cassidy/ Partridge Family	15–30	15–30	10–20	10–20
Cher	5–15	5–15	5–15	4–8
Alice Cooper	5–30	5–25	5–20	4–8
Doors/Jim Morrison	10–100	10–100	5–40	5–10
Grateful Dead	5–30	5–30	5–25	5–10
Bob Dylan	5–25	5–25	5–20	3–7
Fleetwood Mac	5–20	5–20	5–20	5–10
Fleetwood Mac/ Stevie Nicks	5–25	5–25	5–25	5–10
Heart	5–15	5–15	5–15	5–10
Jackson Five	5–25	5–25	5–25	5–10
Jimi Hendrix	5–100	5–100	5–50	5–20
Jefferson Airplane	5–20	5–20	5–20	5–10
Joan Jett/Runaways	5–20	5–20	5–20	4–8
Janis Joplin	5–75	5–50	5–60	5–10
KISS	5–30	5–20	5–25	5–10
Led Zeppelin	5–20	5–15	5–15	4–8
Osmonds/ Donny and Marie	10–25	10–25	10–25	5–10
Suzi Quatro	10–20	10–20	10–20	5–10

SUBJECT	VALUE			
	COVER & FEATURE	COVER ONLY	FEATURE ONLY	CAMEO
Ramones	$10–20	$10–15	$10–20	$5–10
Rolling Stones	5–40	5–40	5–25	5–10
Diana Ross	5–20	5–20	5–20	4–8
Sex Pistols	10–20	10–20	10–20	5–10

MOST-COLLECTIBLE ROCK-AND-ROLL STARS/GROUPS

OF THE 'EIGHTIES

SUBJECT	VALUE			
	COVER & FEATURE	COVER ONLY	FEATURE ONLY	CAMEO
Lee Aaron	$ 5–15	$ 5–15	$ 5–12	$ 4–8
Pat Benatar	5–15	5–10	5–10	4–8
Blondie/Debbie Harry	10–20	10–20	10–20	5–10
David Bowie	3–7	3–7	3–7	3–5
Belinda Carlisle	4–8	4–8	4–8	2–4
Cher	5–10	5–10	5–10	3–5
Alice Cooper	3–7	3–6	3–6	3–5
Doors/Jim Morrison	5–20	5–10	5–15	3–5
Grateful Dead	4–8	4–7	4–8	2–4
Fleetwood Mac	4–10	4–8	4–8	2–4
Fleetwood Mac/ Stevie Nicks	5–20	5–20	5–20	5–10
Nina Hagen	5–15	5–15	5–10	4–8
Heart	5–10	5–10	5–10	2–4
Jimi Hendrix	5–10	5–10	5–10	2–4
Joan Jett	5–20	5–15	5–20	2–4
KISS	5–15	5–10	5–12	2–4
Madonna	5–15	5–10	5–10	2–4

| SUBJECT | VALUE | | | |
	COVER & FEATURE	COVER ONLY	FEATURE ONLY	CAMEO
Marie Osmond	$5–10	$5–10	$5–10	$2–4
Rolling Stones	4–10	4–10	4–10	2–4
Diana Ross	4–7	3–6	3–5	2–4

ROCK/TEEN MAGAZINE VALUES

YEAR	ISSUE/NUMBER	DESCRIPTION	VALUE

Circus Magazine (formerly Hullabaloo)

1969	March	Jimi Hendrix	$40–80
	May	Janis Joplin	40–80
	June	Frank Zappa	20–40
	July	Rock and Revolution	20–40
	August	Johnny Cash/Bob Dylan/ The Byrds	20–40
	September	The MC5	30–60
	October	The Beatles	25–50
	November	Bob Dylan	20–40
	December	John Lennon and Yoko Ono	25–50
1970	January	The Doors	20–40
	March	The Grateful Dead	20–40
	April	John Lennon and Yoko Ono	25–50
	May	Ten Years After	20–40
	June	Grace Slick	20–40
	July	Steve Winwood	20–40
	August	Joe Cocker	20–40
	September	The Band	20–40
	October	Janis Joplin	40–80
	December	Jimi Hendrix memorial	45–90
1971	January	Grand Funk Railroad	30–60
	February	Leon Russell	30–60
	March	Jerry Garcia	20–40

YEAR	ISSUE/NUMBER	DESCRIPTION	VALUE
1971	April	Crosby, Stills, Nash, and Young	$20–40
	May	James Taylor	20–40
	June	Alice Cooper	20–40
	July	Cat Stevens	20–40
	August	Paul McCartney	20–40
	September	Jim Morrison death issue	45–90
	October	George Harrison	20–40
	November	Ringo Starr	20–40
	December	John Lennon	20–40
1972	January	The Doors	30–60
	February	Ray Davies	30–60
	March	Emerson, Lake and Palmer	20–40
	April	Ian Anderson	20–40
	May	Humble Pie	20–40
	June	Graham Nash	20–40
	July	Stephen Stills	20–40
	August	Alice Cooper	20–40
	September	Leon Russell	45–90
	October	Marc Bolin	20–40
	November	Cat Stevens	20–40
	December	Moody Blues	20–40
1973	January	Carole King	20–40
	February	Edgar Winter	20–40
	March	Carly Simon	15–30
	April	Elton John	15–30
	May	Steve Marriot	15–30
	June	Rod Stewart	15–30
	July	David Bowie	20–40
	August	Rick Wakeman	15–30
	September	Ian Anderson	15–30
	October	Robert Plant	15–30
	November	Uriah Heep	15–30
	December	Elton John	15–30
1974	January	Alice Cooper	10–20
	February	The Band	10–20
	March	Johnny Winter	10–20
	April	Jeff Beck	10–20

YEAR	ISSUE/NUMBER	DESCRIPTION	VALUE
1974	May	Mark Farner	$10–20
	June	Ian Hunter	10–20
	July	Edgar Winter	10–20
	August	David Byron	10–20
	September	Jim Dandy	10–20
	October	Gregg Allman	10–20
	November	Peter Wolf	10–20
	December	The State of Future Rock	10–20
1975	#102	Elton John	8–15
	#104	Jimmy Page	8–16
	#106	Peter Gabriel	8–16
	#108	David Bowie	8–16
	#110	Alice Cooper	10–20
	#112	Rick Derringer	8–16
	#114	Todd Rundgren	10–20
	#116	Mick Jagger	10–20
	#118	Ron Wood	8–16
	#120	Gregg Allman	8–16
	#122	Rod Stewart	8–16
	#124	Ian Anderson	8–16
	#125	Linda Ronstadt	5–10
1976	#126	Ray and Dave Davies	5–10
	#127	Bob Dylan	5–10
	#128	Bruce Springsteen	5–10
	#129	Lou Reed	5–10
	#130	KISS	10–20
	#131	David Bowie	5–10
	#132	Robert Plant	5–10
	#133	Mick Jagger and Keith Richards	5–10
	#134	Steven Tyler	5–10
	#135	Emerson, Lake and Palmer	5–10
	#136	Jeff Beck	5–10
	#137	King Kong	5–10
	#138	Alice Cooper	5–10
	#139	Caroline Kennedy	5–10
	#140	Saturday Night Live cast	5–10
	#141	Lindsay Wagner	5–10

YEAR	ISSUE/NUMBER	DESCRIPTION	VALUE
1976	#142	Clint Eastwood	$ 5–10
	#143	The Captain and Tennille	5–10
	#144	Cherrie Currie	5–10
	#145	John Travolta	5–10
	#146	ZZ Top	5–10
1977	#147	Breakouts	10–20
	#148	Kris Kristofferson	5–10
	#149	Lindsay Wagner	5–10
	#150	David Bowie	5–10
	#151	Paul Rogers	5–10
	#152	Christine McVie	5–10
	#153	Ian Anderson	5–10
	#154	Keith Emerson	5–10
	#155	Alice Cooper	5–10
	#156	Sex and Today's Teenager	5–10
	#157	Jimmy Page	5–10
	#158	Ted Nugent	5–10
	#159	Linda Blair	6–12
	#160	Sissy Spacek	5–10
	#161	KISS	10–20
	#162	Peter Frampton	5–10
	#163	Rick Wakeman	5–10
	#164	The Fonz	5–10
	#165	Keith Richards	5–10
	#166	Hall and Oates	5–10
	#167	Linda Ronstadt	5–10
	#168	TV's Logan's Run	5–10
	#169	Nancy Wilson	6–12
	#170	Cindy Williams	5–10
	#171	Gene Simmons	10–20
1978	#172	Dolly Parton	5–10
	#173	Freddie Mercury	5–10
	#174	The Bee Gees	5–10
	#175	Linda Ronstadt	5–10
	#176	Jackson Browne	5–10
	#177	Ted Nugent	5–10
	#178	Barry Gibb	6–12
	#179	Peter Criss	10–20

YEAR	ISSUE/NUMBER	DESCRIPTION	VALUE
1978	#180	Grace Slick	$ 6–12
	#181	Paul Stanley	10–20
	#182	Paul McCartney	8–16
	#183	Carly Simon	10–20
	#184	Robbie Robertson of The Band	5–10
	#185	John Travolta	5–10
	#186	Foghat	6–12
	#187	Bob Seger	5–10
	#188	Andy Gibb	5–10
	#189	Texas Jam	5–10
	#190	Peter Frampton	5–10
	#191	Barry Gibb	5–10
	#192	The Beatles	5–10
	#193	Shaun Cassidy	5–10
	#194	KISS	10–20
	#195	25 Years of Rock	6–12
	#196	Linda Ronstadt	5–10
	#197	Ian Anderson	4–8
	#198	Billy Joel	4–8
	#199	Elton John	4–8
	#200	Ted Nugent	4–8
	#201	Steve Tyler	4–8
	#202	Freddie Mercury	4–8
	#203	Alice Cooper	4–8
1979	#204	Steve Martin	4–8
	#205	David Lee Roth	4–8
	#206	Marijuana	4–8
	#207	Rod Stewart	4–8
	#208	Mork & Mindy	3–6
	#209	Robert Plant	4–8
	#210	Sex in America	3–6
	#211	Dan Aykroyd and John Belushi	4–8
	#212	Animal House	3–6
	#213	Eddie Money	3–6
	#214	The Bee Gees	3–6

YEAR	ISSUE/NUMBER	DESCRIPTION	VALUE
1979	#215	Cheryl Ladd and Miss Piggy	$ 3–6
	#216	Elvis Presley	3–6
	#217	Debbie Harry	3–6
	#218	Bucky Dent	3–6
	#219	Jane Fonda	3–6
	#220	Stockard Channing	3–6
	#221	Hair's Donnie Dacus	3–6
	#222	Patti Hansen	3–6
	#223	Ron Wood and Keith Richards	3–6
	#224	Cher	3–6
	#225	Summer Movie Magic	3–6
	#226	Most Influential People	3–6
	#227	The Best of Circus	3–6
	#228	Woodstock	3–6
	#229	Gilda Radner	3–6
	#230	Robert Plant	3–6
	#231	Ric Ocasek	4–8
	#232	Stevie Nicks	6–12+
	#233	Steve Martin	2–5
	#234	Cheap Trick	3–6
	#235	Styx	3–6
	#236	Foreigner	3–6
1980	#237	Debbie Harry	6–10
	#238	Debbie Harry and Robert Plant	6–10
	#239	Steve Tyler	4–8
	#240	Rush	4–8
	#241	Pink Floyd	4–8
	#242	David Lee Roth	4–8
	#243	Bob Seger	4–8
	#244	Summer Rock special	3–6
	#245	Journey	4–8
	#246	Black Sabbath	3–6
	#247	Freddie Mercury	4–8
	#248	KISS	8–16
	#249	Ric Ocasek	4–8

YEAR	ISSUE/NUMBER	DESCRIPTION	VALUE
1980	#250	Year-end special	$5–10
1981	#251	Jim Morrison	5–10
	#252	Awards issue	4–8
	#253	Rush	4–8
	#254	Ritchie Blackmore	4–8
	#255	The New British Invasion	4–8
	#256	Ozzy Osbourne	4–8
	#257	AC/DC	4–8
	#258	Tom Petty	4–8
	#259	The Moody Blues	4–8
	#260	12th anniversary special	4–8
	#261	The Rolling Stones	4–8
	#262	Stevie Nicks	5–10+
1982	#263	Phil Collins	3–6
	#264	Pat Benatar	3–6
	#265	Angus Young	3–6
	#266	Ozzy Osbourne	3–6
	#267	Ritchie Blackmore	3–6
	#268	Rock and tour issue special	3–6
	#269	Debbie Harry	3–6
	#270	REO Speedwagon	4–8
	#271	David Lee Roth	3–6
	#272	Ozzy Osbourne	3–6
	#273	Rush	3–6
	#274	The Year in Review	3–6
1983	#275	Led Zeppelin	3–6
	#276	David Lee Roth	3–6
	#277	Ozzy Osbourne	3–6
	#278	Steve Perry	3–6
	#279	David Lee Roth	3–6
	#280	Rock on the Road	3–6
	#281	Def Leppard	4–8
	#282	Def Leppard	3–6
	#283	Def Leppard	3–6
	#284	14th anniversary special	3–6
	#285	Quiet Riot	3–6
	#286	The Year in Rock	3–6

YEAR	ISSUE/NUMBER	DESCRIPTION	VALUE
1984	#287	Quiet Riot	$3–6
	#288	Joe Elliot	3–6
	#289	Vince Neil	4–8
	#290	Heavy Metal special	3–6
	#291	David Lee Roth	3–6
	#292	Rock on the Road special	3–6
	#293	Klaus Meine	3–6
	#294	Motley Crue	3–6
	#295	Stephen Percy	3–6
	#296	Ratt	3–6
	#297	Dee Snider	3–6
	#298	Stephen Percy	3–6
1985	#299	Bruce Dickinson	3–6
	#300	Paul Stanley	4–8
	#301	Vince Neil	4–8
	#302	Gene Simmons	4–8
	#303	Paul Stanley	4–8
	#304	KISS	4–8
	#305	Queensryche	3–6
	#306	Dokken	3–6
	#307	Motley Crue	3–6
	#308	Motley Crue	3–6
	#309	Jon Bon Jovi	3–6
	#310	Nikki Sixx	3–6
1986	#311	Paul Stanley	4–8
	#312	Vince Neil	3–6
	#313	Ratt	3–6
	#314	Motley Crue	3–6
	#315	Ozzy Osbourne	3–6
	#316	Eddie Van Halen	3–6
	#317	Judas Priest	3–6
	#318	Bon Jovi	3–6
	#319	David Lee Roth	3–6
	#320	Motley Crue	3–6
	#321	Motley Crue	3–6
	#322	Cinderella	3–6
	#323	Motley Crue	3–6
	#324	Bon Jovi	3–6

YEAR	ISSUE/NUMBER	DESCRIPTION	VALUE
1986	#325	Bon Jovi	$3–6
	#326	Bon Jovi	3–6
	#327	Bon Jovi	3–6
	#328	Bon Jovi	3–6
	#329	Motley Crue	2–4
	#330	Bon Jovi	2–4
	#331	Bon Jovi	2–4
	#332	Bon Jovi	2–4
	#333	Def Leppard	2–4
	#334	The Year in Rock	2–4
1988–Present			2–4

Circus Magazine Pinups

YEAR	ISSUE/NUMBER	DESCRIPTION	VALUE
1975	#1	Mick Jagger	$15–35
	#2	The Rolling Stones	15–35
	#3	Elvis Presley	15–30

Circus Raves

YEAR	ISSUE/NUMBER	DESCRIPTION	VALUE
1974	#1 February	Johnny Winter	$15–30
	#2 March	Roger Daltry	15–30
	#3 April	Paul McCartney	15–30
	#4 June	Noddy Holder	15–30
	#6 August	Keith Emerson	10–20
	#7 September	Bill Wyman	15–25
	#8 October	Eric Clapton	12–25
	#9 November	Ian Anderson	12–25
	#10 December	Rod Stewart	12–25
1975	#101	Ritchie Blackmore	10–20
	#103	Mark Farner	12–25
	#105	Freddie Mercury	15–30
	#107	Robin Trower	10–20
	#109	Steve Marriot	10–20
	#111	David Bowie	10–20
	#113	Paul Rogers	8–15
	#115	Elton John	8–15
	#117	David Byron	8–15
	#119	Ozzy Osbourne	8–15

YEAR	ISSUE/NUMBER	DESCRIPTION	VALUE
1975	#121	Edgar Winter	$8–15
	#123	Pete Townshend	8–15

Circus Rock Immortals Magazine
1980	#1	Jim Morrison	$15–25

Creem
1967	Vol. 1, #1		$50–100
	All other issues		25–50
1968	Vol. 2, #1–7		25–50
	#8	Adolf Hitler	15–30
	#9	Ted Nugent	30–60
	#10	Scot Richardson	20–40
	#11 (issue marked vol. 2, #10) The Rationals		15–30
1970	All issues		20–40
1971	January–July		20–40
	August, September, October		15–30
	November	Grand Funk Railroad	12–25
	December	Pete Townshend	12–25
1972	January	Alice Cooper	15–30
	February	Bob Dylan	15–30
	March	John Lennon	15–35
	April	Smokey Robinson	15–30
	May	T. Rex	15–30
	June	Black Sabbath	15–30
	July	The Beach Boys	15–30
	August	Rod Stewart	15–30
	September	The Rolling Stones	15–30
	October	Humble Pie	15–30
	November	Allman Brothers	10–20
	December	Leon Russell	12–25
1973	January	The Rolling Stones	10–20
	February	Chuck Berry	10–20
	March	Edgar Winter	10–20
	April	Amazing Spiderman	10–20

YEAR	ISSUE/NUMBER	DESCRIPTION	VALUE
1973	May	Jethro Tull	$10–20
	June	Alice Cooper	10–20
	July	Johnny Winter	10–20
	August	David Bowie	10–20
	September	Led Zeppelin	10–20
	October	Guitar special	10–20
	November	Jimi Hendrix	15–30
	December	The Rolling Stones	15–30
1974	January	Pete Townshend	10–20
	February	Elton John	10–20
	March	Emerson, Lake and Palmer	10–20
	April	Iggy Pop	10–20+
	May	Alice Cooper	10–20
	June	David Bowie	10–20
	July	The Rolling Stones	10–20
	August	Alice Cooper	10–20
	September	Rick Wakeman	10–20
	October	Rod Stewart	10–20
	November	The Allman Brothers	10–20
	December	Frank Zappa	10–20
1975	January	David Bowie	10–20
	February	Jimmy Page	10–20
	March	Lou Reed	10–20
	April	Gregg Allman	10–20
	May	Elton John	10–20
	June	Gallery of Rock Graves	15–30
	July	Alice Cooper	10–20
	August	Mick Jagger	10–20
	September	Pete Townshend	7–15
	October	The Rolling Stones	7–15
	November	Rod Stewart	6–12
	December	David Bowie	6–12
1976	January	John Denver	6–12
	February	Bob Dylan	6–12
	March	KISS	10–20
	April	The Beatles	7–15
	May	Led Zeppelin	6–12
	June	The Rolling Stones	6–12

YEAR	ISSUE/NUMBER	DESCRIPTION	VALUE
1976	July	KISS	$7–15
	August	Paul McCartney	7–15
	September	Rod Stewart	5–10
	October	The Rolling Stones	5–10
	November	Sex and Rock and Roll	5–10
	December	Steve Tyler	5–10
1977	January	KISS	7–15
	February	Peter Frampton	5–10
	March	Jefferson Airplane	5–10
	April	Jimmy Page	5–10
	May	Queen	5–10
	June	Keith Richards	5–10
	July	Robert Plant	5–10
	August	KISS	7–15
	September	Ted Nugent	5–10
	October	Peter Frampton	5–10
	November	Rod Stewart	4–8
	December	Grace Slick	4–8
1978	January	Mick Jagger	4–8
	February	Jimmy Page	4–8
	March	Johnny and Edgar Winter	3–6
	April	Johnny Rotten	3–6
	May	Ted Nugent	3–6
	June	Jethro Tull	3–6
	July	Mick Jagger	4–8
	August	Bob Seger	3–6
	September	David Bowie	4–8
	October	Bruce Springsteen	4–8
	November	The Who	4–8
	December	Mick Jagger and Keith Richards	4–8
1979	January	Ted Nugent	4–8
	February	Led Zeppelin	4–8
	March	Debbie Harry	4–8
	April	The Blues Brothers	4–8
	May	Elvis Costello	4–8
	June	Debbie Harry	4–8
	July	Cheap Trick	4–8

YEAR	ISSUE/NUMBER	DESCRIPTION	VALUE
1979	August	The Rolling Stones	$4–8
	September	The Who	4–8
	October	Aerosmith	4–8
	November	Jimmy Page	4–8
	December	Cheap Trick	4–8
1980	January	Joe Jackson	4–8
	February	Debbie Harry	4–8
	March	Debbie Harry	4–8
	April	The Knack	4–8
	May	Debbie Harry	4–8
	June	The Clash	4–8
	July	David Lee Roth	4–8
	August	The Pretenders	4–8
	September	Bob Seger	4–8
	October	Judas Priest	4–8
	November	Pete Townshend	4–8
	December	Cheap Trick	4–8
1981	January	Bruce Springsteen	4–8
	February	Rockpile	4–8
	March	Bruce Springsteen	4–8
	April	The Police	4–8
	May	Eddie Van Halen	4–8
	June	Debbie Harry	4–8
	July	Angus Young	4–8
	August	Judas Priest	3–6
	September	Journey	3–6
	October	Van Halen	3–6
	November	Pat Benatar	4–8
	December	Ray Davies	4–8
1982	January	Mick Jagger	4–8
	February	Keith Richards	4–8
	March	Pat Benatar	3–6
	April	The Police	3–6
	May	The Cars	3–6
	June	Joan Jett	4–8
	July	The B-52's	3–6
	August	Debbie Harry	4–8
	September	David Lee Roth	4–8

YEAR	ISSUE/NUMBER	DESCRIPTION	VALUE
1982	October	Robert Plant	$3–6
	November	John Cougar	3–6
	December	The Who	3–6
1983	January	Mick Jagger	3–6
	February	Keith Richards	3–6
	March	Pat Benatar	3–6
	April	Tom Petty	3–6
	May	Prince	3–6
	June	Michael Jackson	3–6
	July	Joan Jett	3–6
	August	Ray Davies	3–6
	September	David Lee Roth	2–6
	October	Robert Plant	2–6
	November	The Police	2–6
	December	Brian Setzer	3–6
1984	All issues		3–6
1985	All issues		3–6
1986	All issues		3–6
1987	All issues		3–6
1988	All issues		3–6

Hit Parader

1957	All issues		$10–20
1958	All issues		10–20
1959	All issues		10–20
1960	All issues		10–20
1961	All issues		10–15
1962	All issues		10–15
1963	All issues		10–20
1964	All issues		15–30
1965	All issues		15–30
1966	All issues		15–30
1967	All issues		15–30
1968	All issues		15–30

YEAR	ISSUE/NUMBER	DESCRIPTION	VALUE
1969	All issues		$15–30
1970	January	Jimi Hendrix	25–50
	February	Mick Jagger and Keith Richards	10–20
	March	Joe Cocker	10–20
	April	Grace Slick	10–20
	May	The Beatles	10–20
	June	Harry Nilsson	10–20
	July	Alvin Lee	10–20
	August	John Lennon and Yoko Ono	10–20
	September	Janis Joplin	10–20
	October	Paul McCartney	10–20
	November	The Who	10–20
	December	Blood, Sweat and Tears	10–20
1971	January	Mick Jagger	10–20
	February	Neil Diamond	10–20
	March	Eric Burdon and War	8–20
	April	Melanie	10–20
	May	Jethro Tull	10–20
	June	The Kinks	8–20
	July	Grand Funk Railroad	10–20
	August	John Lennon and Yoko Ono	10–20
	September	James Taylor	10–20
	October	Janis Joplin	15–25
	November	Paul McCartney	10–20
	December	Blood, Sweat and Clayton	10–20
1972	January	Mick Jagger	10–20
	February	John Lennon and Yoko Ono	8–20
	March	The Beach Boys	8–20
	April	Carole King	8–20
	May	Mick Jagger	8–20
	June	Melanie	8–20
	July	Rod Stewart and Faces	8–20
	August	Marc Bolan	10–20
	September	Bangladesh	10–20

YEAR	ISSUE/NUMBER	DESCRIPTION	VALUE
1972	October	Elton John	$10–20
	November	David Cassidy	8–15
	December	Elvis Presley	10–20
1973	January	Alice Cooper	10–20
	February	David Bowie	7–15
	March	Blood, Sweat and Tears	7–15
	April	David Cassidy	7–15
	May	Alice Cooper	7–15
	June–December		5–10
1974	All issues		5–10
1975	January	Jimmy Page	5–10
	February	Bad Co.	5–10
	March	John Lennon	5–10
	April	Keith Richards	5–10
	May	Paul and Linda McCartney	5–8
	July	Ian Anderson	5–10
	August	Mick Jagger	5–10
	September	Ian Anderson	5–10
	October	Edgar Winter	5–10
	November	Elton John	5–10
	December	Freddie Mercury	7–15
1976	January	Eric Clapton	5–10
	February	Roger Daltry	5–10
	March	The Who	7–15
	April	Bryan Ferry	5–10
	May	Aerosmith	5–10
	August	Bad Co.	6–12
	September	Mick Jagger	5–10
	October	Led Zeppelin	5–10
	November	Elton John	5–10
	December	Peter Frampton	4–8
1977	January	Lynyrd Skynyrd	6–12
	February	Led Zeppelin	6–12
	March	KISS	10–20
	April	Rod Stewart	5–10
	May	Fleetwood Mac	5–10
	June	Queen	5–10

May 1988

May 17, 1991

August 1990

August 1988

May 1991

May 1989

1990

December 1990

December 1991

YEAR	ISSUE/NUMBER	DESCRIPTION	VALUE
1977	July	Led Zeppelin	$5–10
	August	Boston	5–10
	September	Peter Frampton	5–10
	October	The Beatles	4–8
	November	Led Zeppelin	5–10
	December	The Rolling Stones	8–15
1978	January	Elvis Presley	4–8
	February	Yes	4–8
	March	Linda Ronstadt	4–8
	April	Steely Dan	3–6
	May	Gene Simmons	5–10
	June	Rod Stewart	5–10
	July	The Bee Gees	4–8
	August	Fleetwood Mac	4–8
	September	Hall and Oates	4–8
	October	The Rolling Stones	4–8
	November	Elvis Costello	4–8
	December	Andy Gibb	4–8
1979	January	Led Zeppelin	4–8
	February	Gene Simmons	5–10
	March	Boston	4–8
	April	Aerosmith	4–8
	May	Neil Young	4–8
	June	Paul Stanley	4–8
	July	Foreigner	5–10
	August	Cheap Trick	4–8
	September	Ted Nugent	4–8
	October	Pete Townshend	4–8
	November	Paul Stanley	4–8
	December	Aerosmith	4–8
1980	January	Robert Plant	5–10
	February	Freddie Mercury	5–10
	March	Jimmy Page	4–8
	April	Cheap Trick	4–8
	May	Led Zeppelin	4–8
	June	Tom Petty	4–8
	July	Debbie Harry	4–8
	August	Aerosmith	4–8

YEAR	ISSUE/NUMBER	DESCRIPTION	VALUE
1980	October	Mick Jagger and Keith Richards	$4–8
	November	Heart	4–8
1981	January	The Cars	4–8
	February	Cheap Trick	3–6
	March	David Lee Roth	3–6
	April	Fleetwood Mac	4–8
	June	Debbie Harry	3–6
	September	Van Halen	3–6
	October	Queen	3–6
	December	Debbie Harry	3–6
1982	All months		3–6
1983	January	Ozzy Osbourne	3–6
	February	Pat Benatar	3–6
	March	Robert Plant	3–6
	April	Tom Petty	3–6
	May–August		3–6
	September	Def Leppard and Iron Maiden	2–4
	October	Robert Plant	2–4
	November	AC/DC	2–4
	December	Judas Priest	3–6
1984–1989			2–4
1990–Present			2–3

Rock Scene

1973	March #1	David Bowie	$20–30
	May #2	Ray Davies	12–20
	July #4	Slade	10–20
1974	August #8	David Bowie	8–15
	October #9	Mick Jagger	7–15
1975	January #10	Roxy Music	7–15
	March #11	Lou Reed	7–15
	May #12	Peter Gabriel	7–15
	July #13	Elton John	5–12
	September #14	KISS	10–20

YEAR	ISSUE/NUMBER	DESCRIPTION	VALUE
1975	November #15	Aerosmith	$ 7–15
1976	January	Mick Jagger	10–20
	March	David Bowie	10–20
	May	Patti Smith	6–12
	July	KISS	7–15
	September	Keith Richards	5–10
	November	The Rolling Stones	5–10
1977	January	Robert Plant	4–8
	March	The Ramones	4–8
	May	Ted Nugent	3–6
	June	Bryan Ferry	3–6
	July	Iggy Pop	4–8
	September	Television	4–8
	October	Joe Perry	3–6
	December	Johnny Rotten	4–8
1978	January	Keith Richards	4–8
	March	The Ramones	4–8
	May	Queen	4–8
	June	Patti Smith	4–8
	July	David Johansen	3–6
	September	KISS	10–20
	October	Bruce Springsteen	7–15
	December	KISS	10–20
1979	February	Queen	4–8
	March	Meat Loaf	4–8
	May	Aerosmith	5–15
	July	Steve Tyler	5–15
	September	Debbie Harry	10–20
	November	The Clash	4–8
1980	January	KISS	7–15
	March	Queen	4–8
	May	Led Zeppelin	4–8
	July	Dr. Hook	5–10
	September	Christie Hynde	4–8
1981	January	The Rolling Stones	5–10
	March	Talking Heads	4–8
	May	The Rolling Stones	5–10

YEAR	ISSUE/NUMBER	DESCRIPTION	VALUE
1982	January	Debbie Harry	$7–15

Rolling Stone Magazine

YEAR	ISSUE/NUMBER	DESCRIPTION	VALUE
1967	#1	John Lennon	$150–300+
	#2	Tina Turner	100–200
	#3	The Beatles	100–200
	#4	Jimi Hendrix	100–200
1968	#5	The Beatles	50–100
	#6	Janis Joplin	75–150
	#7	Jimi Hendrix	90–180
	#8	Lou Adler and John Phillips	50–100
	#9	The Beatles	50–100
	#10	Eric Clapton	40–80
	#11	Baron Wolfman	40–80
	#12	Bob Dylan	40–80
	#13	Tiny Tim	40–80
	#14	Frank Zappa	40–80
	#15	Mick Jagger	50–100
	#16	The Band	50–100
	#17	Pete Townshend	45–90
	#18	Pete Townshend	45–90
	#19	Mick Jagger	45–90
	#20	The Beatles	45–80
	#21	The Beatles	45–80
	#22	John Lennon and Yoko Ono	75–150
	#23	The Beatles	30–60
	#24	The Beatles	35–70
1969	#25	MC5	40–80
	#26	Jimi Hendrix	50–100
	#27	Groupies	25–50
	#28	Japanese Rock	25–50
	#29	Janis Joplin	50–100
	#30	American Revolution 1969	40–75
	#31	Sun Ra	40–75
	#32	Traffic	35–70

YEAR	ISSUE/NUMBER	DESCRIPTION	VALUE
1969	#33	Joni Mitchell	$ 25–50
	#34	Jimi Hendrix	75–100
	#35	Chuck Berry	25–40
	#36	John Lennon and	
		Yoko Ono	35–60
	#37	Elvis Presley	25–40
	#38	Jim Morrison	75–125+
	#39	Brian Jones	75–125+
	#40	Jerry Garcia	30–50
	#41	Joe Cocker	20–40
	#42	Woodstock	20–40
	#43	Bob Dylan	20–40
	#44	David Crosby	20–40
	#45	Tina Turner	20–40
	#46	The Beatles	20–40
	#47	Bob Dylan	20–40
	#48	Miles Davis	20–40
	#49	Mick Jagger	20–40
	#50	The Rolling Stones	30–60
1970	#51	John Lennon	30–50
	#52	John Fogarty	25–40
	#53	The Grateful Dead	30–50
	#54	Sly and the Family Stone	20–40
	#55	Abbie Hoffman	20–40
	#56	John Lennon	25–40
	#57	Paul McCartney	20–40
	#58	Captain Beefheart	20–40
	#59	Little Richard	25–50
	#60	George Harrison	20–40
	#61	Charles Manson	20–40
	#62	The Beatles	20–40
	#63	David Crosby	20–30
	#64	Janis Joplin	50–100
	#65	Mick Jagger	30–50
	#66	The Grateful Dead	25–40
	#67	The Rascals	20–40
	#68	Jimi Hendrix	60–100+
	#69	Janis Joplin	55–100+

YEAR	ISSUE/NUMBER	DESCRIPTION	VALUE
1970	#70	Grace Slick	$20–40
	#71	The Beatles	20–40
	#72	Leon Russell	15–30
	#73	Rod Stewart	15–30
1971	#74	John Lennon	25–40
	#75	John Lennon	15–35
	#76	James Taylor	15–30
	#77	Bob Dylan	20–30
	#78	Muhammad Ali	10–30
	#79	Captain Beefheart	15–30
	#80	Joe Dellesandro	10–30
	#81	Michael Jackson	25–45
	#82	Peter Fonda	10–30
	#83	Country Joe McDonald	15–30
	#84	Elton John	15–30
	#85	White House	10–25
	#86	John Lennon and Yoko Ono	25–40
	#87	Jethro Tull	15–20
	#88	Jim Morrison	65–100+
	#89	Keith Richards	30–50
	#90	George Harrison	25–50
	#91	The Incredible Hulk	10–25
	#92	Abbie Hoffman	10–25
	#93	Sly and the Family Stone	20–30
	#94	The Beach Boys	20–30
	#95	The Beach Boys	20–30
	#96	Duane Allman	15–30
	#97	Pete Townshend	20–30
	#98	Elvis Presley	15–30
1972	#99	Cat Stevens	15–20
	#100	Jerry Garcia	10–25
	#101	The Grateful Dead	10–22
	#102	Janis Joplin	30–55
	#103	Bob Dylan	10–25
	#104	Bob Dylan	10–25
	#105	Alice Cooper	10–25
	#106	Pete Seger	10–18

May 1979

November 1985

May 1979

1980

1964

January 1990

#382

Summer 1981

Fall 1964

YEAR	ISSUE/NUMBER	DESCRIPTION	VALUE
1972	#107	Marvin Gaye	$10–22
	#108	David Cassidy	25–50
	#109	Jane Fonda	8–20
	#110	Rod Stewart	10–20
	#111	Van Morrison	10–18
	#112	Mick Jagger	12–25
	#113	Paul Simon	10–20
	#114	Huey Newton	10–20
	#115	The Eagles	12–20
	#116	Randy Newman	10–20
	#117	Three Dog Night	10–20
	#118	The Grateful Dead	10–20
	#119	Sally Struthers	10–20
	#120	Jeff Beck	10–20
	#121	David Bowie	10–20
	#122	Chuck Berry	10–20
	#123	Carlos Santana	4–8
	#124	Keith Moon	20–30
1973	#125	James Taylor and Carly Simon	10–20
	#126	Genesis	10–20
	#127	Diana Ross	20–30
	#128	Bette Midler	5–10
	#129	The Rolling Stones	10–20
	#130	Robert Mitchum	5–10
	#131	Dr. Hook	5–10
	#132	Truman Capote	5–10
	#133	Mark Spitz	5–10
	#134	Alice Cooper	10–25
	#135	Sonny and Cher	5–12
	#136	Yes	5–10
	#137	Rod Stewart	5–10
	#138	Paul Newman	5–10
	#139	Tatum O'Neal	5–10
	#140	Leon Russell	5–10
	#141	Elton John	5–10
	#142	Dan Hicks	4–10
	#143	Stevie Wonder	4–10

YEAR	ISSUE/NUMBER	DESCRIPTION	VALUE
1973	#144	Stephen Stills	$ 4–10
	#145	Art Garfunkel	5–10
	#146	Gene Autry	5–10
	#147	Liza Minnelli and Ronnie Spector	4–8
	#148	The Grateful Dead	6–15
	#149	The Allman Brothers	5–12
	#150	Hugh Hefner	4–8
1974	#151	The Who	5–10
	#152	Ringo Starr	5–10
	#153	Paul McCartney	5–10
	#154	Bob Dylan	5–10
	#155	David Bowie	5–10
	#156	Bob Dylan	5–10
	#157	World's Sexiest Calendar issue	5–10
	#158	Marvin Gaye	5–10
	#159	Kris Kristofferson	5–10
	#160	Paul Getty	5–10
	#161	Jackson Browne	4–8
	#162	Gladys Knight and the Pips	12–20
	#163	James Dean	5–10
	#164	The Carpenters	5–12
	#165	Eric Clapton	5–10
	#166	Maria Mauldaur	5–10
	#167	Steely Dan	5–10
	#168	Crosby, Stills, Nash and Young	5–10
	#169	Jan and Dean	5–10
	#170	Tanya Tucker	5–10
	#171	Lily Tomlin and Richard Pryor	5–10
	#172	Lily Tomlin	5–10
	#173	Evel Knievel	5–10
	#174	Elton John	5–10
	#175	Dustin Hoffman	5–10
	#176	George Harrison	5–10

YEAR	ISSUE/NUMBER	DESCRIPTION	VALUE
1975	#177	Suzi Quatro	$ 5–10
	#178	Gregg Allman	5–10
	#179	Freddie Prinze	4–8
	#180	Les Paul	4–8
	#181	Loggins and Messina	4–7
	#182	Led Zeppelin	12–20+
	#183	Linda Ronstadt	5–10
	#184	Roger Daltry	5–10
	#185	Peter Falk	4–8
	#186	John Denver	4–8
	#187	Carly Simon	10–20
	#188	Phoebe Snow	5–10
	#189	Stevie Wonder	4–8
	#190	LaBelle	4–8
	#191	The Rolling Stones	5–10
	#192	Richard Dreyfuss	4–8
	#193	Neil Young	4–8
	#194	Doonesbury	4–8
	#195	Mick Jagger	5–10
	#196	The Eagles	5–10
	#197	Muhammed Ali	4–8
	#198	Bob Dylan	4–10
	#199	Rod Stewart and	
		Britt Ekland	4–8
	#200	The Who	4–8
	#201	Jack Nicholson	4–8
	#202	Bonnie Raitt	4–8
	#203	Jefferson Starship	4–8
1976	#204	Bob Dylan	4–8
	#205	Pat Boone	4–8
	#206	David Bowie	4–8
	#207	Howlin' Wolf	4–8
	#208	The Osmonds	4–8
	#209	Mary Hartman	4–8
	#210	Robert Redford and	
		Dustin Hoffman	4–8
	#211	Peter Frampton	4–8
	#212	Santana	4–8

YEAR	ISSUE/NUMBER	DESCRIPTION	VALUE
1976	#213	Marlon Brando	$ 4–8
	#214	Freddy Fender	3–5
	#215	Paul McCartney	4–8
	#216	Paul Simon	4–8
	#217	The Beatles	4–8
	#218	Loggins and Messina	4–8
	#219	Bob Marley	4–8
	#220	Aerosmith	4–8
	#221	Stephen Stills and Neil Young	4–8
	#222	Neil Diamond	5–10
	#223	Elton John	4–8
	#224	Electric Light Orchestra	3–5
	#225	Brian Wilson and the Beach Boys	3–5
	#226	Janis Joplin	6–10
	#227	Linda Ronstadt	5–10
	#228	Jackson Browne	5–18
	#229	The Band	3–6
	#230	Rod Stewart	4–8
1977	#231	Jeff Bridges	3–6
	#232	Peter Frampton	3–5
	#233	Boz Scaggs	3–5
	#234	Princess Caroline	3–5
	#235	Fleetwood Mac	5–12+
	#236	Lily Tomlin	4–8
	#237	Hall and Oates	3–5
	#238	Keith Richards	3–5
	#239	Van Morrison	3–6
	#240	Crosby, Stills and Nash	3–6
	#241	Robert De Niro	3–6
	#242	Diane Keaton	3–6
	#243	The Bee Gees	3–6
	#244	Heart	5–10
	#245	Diana Ross	4–8
	#246	Star Wars	4–8
	#247	O. J. Simpson	3–5
	#248	Elvis Presley	5–12

YEAR	ISSUE/NUMBER	DESCRIPTION	VALUE
1977	#249	Paul McCartney and Wings	$ 3–6
	#250	The Sex Pistols	4–8
	#251	The Rolling Stones	4–8
	#252	The Who	4–8
	#253	Steve Martin	3–5
	#254	10th anniversary issue	3–6
	#255	James Taylor	3–6
	#256	Fleetwood Mac	8–15+
1978	#257	Bob Dylan	3–7
	#258	Jimmy Thudpucker	3–6
	#259	Rita Coolidge and Kris Kristofferson	3–6
	#260	Jane Fonda	3–6
	#261	Donna Summer	4–8
	#262	Brooke Shields	3–6
	#263	The Bee Gees	3–6
	#264	Muhammad Ali	3–6
	#265	Jefferson Starship	3–6
	#266	Carly Simon	3–6
	#267	John Travolta	3–6
	#268	Mick Jagger	3–6
	#269	Willie Nelson	3–5
	#270	Patti Smith	3–6
	#271	John Belushi	3–6
	#272	Bruce Springsteen	3–6
	#273	The Rolling Stones	3–6
	#274	Buddy Holly	3–6
	#275	Steve Martin	3–6
	#276	Linda Ronstadt	3–6
	#277	Gilda Radner	3–6
	#278	Bob Dylan	3–6
	#279	The Who	3–6
	#280	Cheech and Chong	3–5
1979	#281/282	Richard Dreyfuss	3–5
	#283	The Cars	3–6
	#284	Neil Young	3–6
	#285	Dan Aykroyd	3–6
	#286	Ted Nugent	3–6

YEAR	ISSUE/NUMBER	DESCRIPTION	VALUE
1979	#287	Johnny Carson	$ 3–6
	#288	Michael Douglas	3–6
	#289	The Village People	3–6
	#290	Richard Pryor	3–6
	#291	The Bee Gees	3–6
	#292	Jon Voight	3–6
	#293	Cheap Trick	3–6
	#294	Debbie Harry/Blondie	5–10
	#295	Paul McCartney	3–6
	#296	Joni Mitchell	3–6
	#297	Rickie Lee Jones	3–6
	#298	Robin Williams	3–6
	#299	James Taylor	3–6
	#300	The Doobie Brothers	3–6
	#301	Jimmy Buffet	3–6
	#302	Sissy Spacek	3–6
	#303	Martin Sheen	3–6
	#304	Bruce Springsteen	3–6
	#305	The Eagles	3–6
	#306	Bette Midler	3–6
1980	#307/308	The Year in Music special	3–6
	#309	Pink Floyd	6–15
	#310	Fleetwood Mac	3–6
	#311	Tom Petty	3–6
	#312	Richard Gere	3–6
	#313	Bob Hope	3–6
	#314	Linda Ronstadt	3–6
	#315	The Clash	3–6
	#316	Bob Seger	3–6
	#317	Heart	4–8
	#318	The Pretenders	3–6
	#319	Hard Rock	3–6
	#320	Pete Townshend	3–6
	#321	John Travolta	3–6
	#322	The Empire Strikes Back	5–12
	#323	Jackson Browne	3–6
	#324	The Rolling Stones	3–6
	#325	Billy Joel	3–6

YEAR	ISSUE/NUMBER	DESCRIPTION	VALUE
1980	#326	The Commodores	$ 3–6
	#327	Robert Redford	3–6
	#328	Pat Benatar	3–6
	#329	The Cars	3–6
	#330	Mary Tyler Moore	3–6
	#331	Jill Clayburgh	3–6
	#332	Dolly Parton	3–6
	#333/334	The Beatles	3–6
	#335	John Lennon and Yoko Ono	5–10
	#336	Bruce Springsteen	4–8
	#337	The Police	3–6
	#338	Goldie Hawn	3–6
1981	#339	Warren Zevon	3–6
	#340	Roman Polanski	3–5
	#341	Jack Nicholson	3–5
	#342	Gary U.S. Bonds	3–5
	#343	John Lennon	3–5
	#344	Susan Sarandon	3–5
	#345	James Taylor	3–5
	#346	Harrison Ford	3–6
	#347	Margot Kidder	3–5
	#348	Tom Petty	3–5
	#349	Rickie Lee Jones	3–6
	#350	Bill Murray	3–5
	#351	Stevie Nicks	10–25+
	#352	Jim Morrison	4–7
	#353	Yoko Ono	3–6
	#354	Meryl Streep	3–6
	#355	Elvis Presley	3–6
	#356	Keith Richards	3–6
	#357	Bill Hurt	3–6
	#358	Carly Simon	3–6
	#359/360	1981 Yearbook	3–6
1982	#361	John Belushi	3–6
	#362	Timothy Hutton	3–6
	#363	Steve Martin	3–6
	#364	Peter Wolfe	3–6

YEAR	ISSUE/NUMBER	DESCRIPTION	VALUE
1982	#365	Simon and Garfunkel	$ 3–6
	#366	Warren Beatty	3–6
	#367	Mariel Hemingway	3–6
	#368	John Belushi	3–6
	#369	Sissy Spacek	3–6
	#370	Natassja Kinski	3–6
	#371	David Letterman	3–6
	#372	Pete Townshend	3–6
	#373	Sylvester Stallone	3–6
	#374	E.T.	3–5
	#375	The Go-Go's	5–10
	#376	Tron	3–6
	#377	Elvis Costello	3–6
	#378	Pink Floyd	3–6
	#379	Richard Gere	3–6
	#380	John Lennon and Yoko Ono	3–6
	#381	Billy Joel	3–6
	#382	The Who	3–6
	#383	Matt Dillon	3–6
	#384	Bette Midler	3–5
	#385/386	The Year in Music special	3–6
	#387	Paul Newman	3–6
	#388	Dustin Hoffman	3–6
	#389	Michael Jackson	3–6
	#390	Stray Cats	3–6
	#391	Jessica Lange	3–5
	#392	Dudley Moore	3–6
	#393	Joan Baez	3–6
	#394	Prince and Vanity	3–6
1983	#395	David Bowie	3–6
	#396	Sean Penn	2–6
	#397	Health Clubs	2–6
	#398	Men at Work	2–6
	#399	Eddie Murphy	2–6
	#400/401	Star Wars	2–6
	#402	John Travolta	3–6
	#403	The Police	2–6

YEAR	ISSUE/NUMBER	DESCRIPTION	VALUE
1983	#404	Jackson Browne	$2–6
	#405	Eurythmics	2–6
	#406	Chevy Chase	2–6
	#407	Sean Connery	3–6
	#408	Culture Club	3–6
	#409	Mick Jagger	3–6
	#410	Michael Jackson and Paul McCartney	3–6
	#411/412	Great Faces of '83	3–6
1984	#413	Eric Clapton	3–6
	#414	Duran Duran	3–6
	#415	The Beatles	2–6
	#416	The Police	2–6
	#417	Michael Jackson	2–6
	#418	Jack Nicholson	2–6
	#419	Eddie Murphy	2–6
	#420	Daryl Hannah	2–6
	#421	Marvin Gaye	4–8
	#422	Cyndi Lauper	3–6
	#423	Culture Club	3–6
	#424	Bob Dylan	3–6
	#425	The Go-Go's	3–6
	#426/427	The Thompson Twins	3–6
	#428	Bill Murray	3–6
	#429	Prince	3–6
	#430	Huey Lewis	3–6
	#431	John Belushi	3–6
	#432	Tina Turner	3–6
	#433	David Bowie	3–6
	#434	Steve Martin	3–6
	#435	Madonna	3–6
	#436	Bruce Springsteen	3–6
1985	#437/438	Great Faces of '84	3–5
	#439	Hall and Oates	3–6
	#440	Billy Idol	3–6
	#441	Mick Jagger	3–6
	#442	Bruce Springsteen	3–6
	#443	U2	3–6

YEAR	ISSUE/NUMBER	DESCRIPTION	VALUE
1985	#444	Miami Vice	$3–6
	#445	David Lee Roth	3–6
	#446	Richard Gere	3–6
	#447	Madonna and Rosanna Arquette	3–6
	#448	Phil Collins	3–6
	#449	Julian Lennon	3–6
	#450	David Letterman	3–5
	#451	Clint Eastwood	3–5
	#452/453	John Travolta and Jamie Lee Curtis	3–6
	#454	Live Aid	3–5
	#455	Mel Gibson and Tina Turner	3–5
	#456	Prince	3–6
	#457	Sting	3–6
	#458	Bruce Springsteen	3–6
	#459	Steven Spielberg	3–5
	#460	Don Johnson	2–4
	#461	Dire Straits	3–6
	#462	Bob Geldorf	3–5
1986	#463/464	1985 Rock Yearbook	3–6
	#465	Michael Douglas	2–5
	#466	John Cougar Mellencamp	4–8
	#467	Ricky Nelson	3–6
	#468	Bruce Springsteen	3–5
	#469	Jim McMahon	3–5
	#470	Bruce Willis	3–5
	#471	Stevie Wonder	3–5
	#472	Wendy and Lisa of Prince	3–6
	#473	Whoopi Goldberg	2–4
	#474	Michael J. Fox	2–4
	#475	Madonna	3–7
	#476	Tom Cruise	2–4
	#477	Van Halen	3–6
	#478/479	Bob Dylan and Tom Petty	3–6
	#480	Jack Nicholson	2–4
	#481	Boy George	3–6

YEAR	ISSUE/NUMBER	DESCRIPTION	VALUE
1986	#482	Paul McCartney	$3–5
	#483	Don Johnson	2–4
	#484	Cybill Shepherd	2–4
	#485	Tina Turner	3–6
	#486	Billy Joel	3–6
	#487	Huey Lewis	3–6
	#488	Run DMC	2–4
	#489/490	1986 Yearbook special	3–5
1987	#491–500		3–6
	#501	Jimi Hendrix	4–8
	#502–514		3–6
	#515/516	1987 Yearbook special	4–8
1988	#517–540		3–6
	#541/542	Bruce Springsteen	3–6
1989	#543–566		3–6
	#567/568		3–6
1990	All issues		3–6
1991	All issues		2–5
1992	All issues		2–4
1993–1994	All issues		1–3

16 Magazine

YEAR	ISSUE/NUMBER	DESCRIPTION	VALUE
1958	#1		$25–75
	#2		20–40
1959	January–April		20–40
	May	Elvis Presley	40–60
	All other issues		20–40
1960	All issues		20–30
1961	All issues		20–40
1962	January	Bobby Rydell	25–50
	All other issues		15–30
1963	All issues		15–30
1964	All issues		15–30
1965	All issues		15–35

#3, January 1984

Volume 2, #8

Volume 4, #1

Volume 4, #3

Volume 4, #8

March 1983

February 1989

July 1989

January 1990

YEAR	ISSUE/NUMBER	DESCRIPTION	VALUE
1966	All issues		$15–35
1967	All issues		20–40
1968	All issues		15–30
1969	All issues		10–30
1970	All issues		10–30
1971	All issues		10–30
1972	All issues		10–25
1973	January–October		10–20
	November, December		5–10
1974	All issues		5–10
1975	All issues		5–10
1976	All issues		4–8
1977	All issues		3–7
1978	July, October		5–10
	All other issues		3–7
1979	All issues		5–10
1980	All issues		5–10
1981	January–August		5–10
	September–December		4–8
1982	January–August		4–8
	September–December		3–6
1983	All issues		3–6
1984	All issues		3–6
1985	All issues		2–6
1986	All issues		2–6
1987	All issues		2–4
1988	All issues		2–4
1989	All issues		2–4
1990	All issues		2–4
1991	All issues		1–3
1992–Present	All issues		1–2

YEAR	ISSUE/NUMBER	DESCRIPTION	VALUE
Song Hits			
1964	All issues		$10–20
1965	All issues		10–20
1966	All issues		10–30
1967	All issues		15–30
1968	March	Jim Morrison	20–40
	All other issues		10–30
1969	May	The Doors	15–30
	All other issues		10–20
1970	All issues		8–16
1971	July		15–30
	All other issues		4–8
1972	All issues		4–8
1973	February	The Who	5–10
	July	Carly Simon	5–10
	December	The Carpenters	5–10
	All other issues		4–8
1974	May	Todd Rundgren	5–10
	August	Three Dog Night	4–8
	All other issues		3–6
1975	July	Olivia Newton-John	5–10
	December	Jefferson Starship	5–10
	All other issues		3–6
1976	November	America	4–8
	All other issues		3–6
1977	September	Fleetwood Mac	10–20
	December	KISS	10–20
	All other issues		3–6
1978	All issues		3–6
1979	March	Linda Ronstadt	3–6+
	April	Jethro Tull	3–6
	May	Queen	4–8
	July	The Bee Gees	3–6
	All other issues		2–4

YEAR	ISSUE/NUMBER	DESCRIPTION	VALUE
1980	January	KISS	$6–12+
	February	The Eagles	3–8
	April	Jefferson Starship	3–6
	August	Van Halen	3–6
	All other issues		3–5
1981	July, September		2–4
	All other issues		3–6
1982	April	KISS	5–12+
	All other issues		3–6
1983	April	Jefferson Airplane	3–6
	All other issues		2–4
1984	August	Christine McVie	4–8
	All other issues		2–4
1985–1988			2–4
1989–Present			1–3

Spin

YEAR	ISSUE/NUMBER	DESCRIPTION	VALUE
1985	May #1	Madonna	$8–15+
	June #2	Talking Heads	5–10
	July #3	Sting	4–8
	August #4	Annie Lennox	4–8
	September #5	Pat Benatar	4–8
	October #6	Keith Richards	4–8
	November #7	Bruce Springsteen	4–8
	December #8	Bob Dylan	4–8
1986	January	Debbie Harry	5–10+
	February	ZZ Top	3–6
	March	Mick Jones	3–6
	April	David Lee Roth	3–6
	May	Charlie Sexton	3–6
	June	Billy Idol	3–6
	July	Prince	3–6
	August	Mick Jagger	3–6
	September	Ozzy Osbourne	3–6
	October	R.E.M.	3–6
	November	Iggy Pop	3–6

February 1985

November 1980

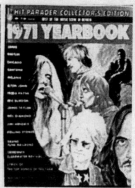

1971

May 1967

April 1970

January 1992

July 1991

October 1960

March 1957

YEAR	ISSUE/NUMBER	DESCRIPTION	VALUE
1986	December	Chrissie Hynde	$ 4–7
1988	January	Janet Jackson	4–7
	February	Duran Duran	3–6
	March	The Beastie Boys	3–5
	April	Madonna	5–10+
	May	Joan Jett	5–10+
	June	Michael Jackson	3–6
	July	Susanna Hoffs	4–7
	August	Simple Minds	3–6
	September	John Cougar Mellencamp	3–5
	(no issues published for October or November)		
	December	Sting	3–6
1989	January	Steven Tyler	3–6
	February	Inxs	3–5
	March	The Cure	3–5
	April	Sa-fire	3–5
	May	Run DMC	2–4
	June	Morrissey	2–4
	July	Belinda Carlisle	3–6+
	August	Comics	2–4
	September	Tracy Chapman	1–3
	October	Jazzy Jeff and Fresh Prince	2–4
	November	Bon Jovi	2–4
	December	The Bangles	4–6
1989	January	U2	3–6
	February	Nick Cave	2–4
	March	Edie Brickell and the New Bohemians	2–4
	April	Madonna	4–8
	May	Elvis Costello	2–4
	June	John Cougar Mellencamp	2–4
	July	Elvis Presley	3–5
	August	Tom Petty	2–4
	September	10,000 Maniacs	2–4
	October	Terence Trent D'Arby	1–3
1980–1982	All issues		1–3
1983–Present			1–2

July 1988

December 1990

October 17, 1988

#2, July 1982

February 3, 1990

July 1984

January 1992

#1, 1965

April 1989

October 1984

October 1991

July 1965

November 1965

December 1966

June 1967

August 1961

November 1963

July 1972

YEAR	ISSUE/NUMBER	DESCRIPTION	VALUE
Tiger Beat			
1965	September #1	Annette Funicello	$25–60
	October #2	Annette Funicello	25–50
	November #3	Sonny and Cher	20–50
	December #4	Leslie Gore	20–40
1966	January–September		15–30
	October–December		10–25
1967	All issues		10–25
1968	All issues		12–25
1969	All issues		10–20
1970	All issues		10–20
1971	All issues		10–20
1972	All issues		8–15
1973	January–March		10–20
	April–December		7–15
1974	All issues		5–10
1975	All issues		3–8
1976–1981	All issues		3–6
1982–1986	All issues		2–4
1987–Present			1–3

Sports Magazines

With the tremendous increase in sport card collecting (baseball, in particular) has come an interest in magazines that feature sport figures on the cover or that feature them as the subjects of articles. Values of sports magazines are determined primarily by three factors—besides condition—(1) historical importance, (2) greatness of subject, and/or (3) regional interest. An example of the first factor would be Bobby Thomson's "shot heard 'round the world" in the 1951 National League baseball playoffs—he was an average player at the center of a very dramatic, historic moment in sports history. The second factor would not be confined only to great athletes of the past and present but would also include, say, great race horses of the past, such as Man O' War, Secretariat, and others. As an example of the third factor, the value of a magazine focusing on the Boston Red Sox would be higher in the Massachusetts area than in California. Sometimes two—or all three—of these factors might be present. Take, for example, Willie Mays's great over-the-shoulder catch in the 1954 World Series. A magazine from 1954 featuring this great star at this great moment would indeed have great value in the collectors marketplace, particularly in the New York area.

The following values are for sports magazines (defined as *any* magazine that features a sports figure or theme on its cover and includes at least one sports article within) that are average issues (issues with common players or athletes). For issues that are exceptional (such as an issue featuring the Mays catch cited above), add 100 to 500 percent to the value, depending upon how many of the aforementioned factors are present.

SPORTS MAGAZINE VALUES
(BY DECADE)

DECADE	VALUE
Baseball	
1900–1910	$20–30
1911–1920	20–30
1921–1930	15–25
1931–1940	10–20
1941–1950	10–15
1951–1960	5–10
1961–1970	3–4
1971–1980	2–3
1981–Present	1–2
Football	
Pre-1930	$10–20
1931–1940	7–12
1941–1950	5–10
1951–1960	3–5
1961–1970	2–4
1971–1980	2–3
1980–Present	1–2
Wrestling	
Pre-1960	$3–5
1961–1970	2–4
1971–1980	2–3
1981–1990	1–2
1991–Present	1–3

DECADE	VALUE

Boxing

Pre-1900	$20–35
1901–1910	20–30
1911–1920	10–20
1921–1930	7–15
1931–1940	5–10
1941–1950	4–8
1951–1960	3–5
1961–1970	2–4
1971–Present	1–2

Auto and Car Racing Magazines

Pre-1910	$25–50
1911–1920	20–40
1921–1930	10–20
1931–1940	5–10
1941–1950	3–8
1951–1960	3–6
1961–1970	2–4
1970–Present	1–2

Other Sports/Athletic Events

Pre-1910	$10–25
1911–1920	10–20
1921–1930	10–15

Magazine Index

Most-Collectible
Personalities Index